Foundation PHP
for Dreamweaver 8

David Powers

friendsof

DESIGNER TO DESIGNER™

an Apress• company

Foundation PHP for Dreamweaver 8

Credits

Lead Editor
Chris Mills

Technical Reviewer
Jason Nadon

Editorial Board
Steve Anglin, Dan Appleman,
Ewan Buckingham, Gary Cornell,
Tony Davis, Jason Gilmore,
Jonathan Hassell, Chris Mills,
Dominic Shakeshaft, Jim Sumser

Project Manager
Richard Dal Porto

Copy Edit Manager
Nicole LeClerc

Copy Editor
Andy Carroll

Assistant Production Director
Kari Brooks-Copony

Production Editor
Kelly Winquist

Compositor
Katy Freer

Proofreader
Nancy Sixsmith

Indexer
Diane Brenner

Cover Artist
Corné van Dooren

Interior and Cover Designer
Kurt Krames

Manufacturing Director
Tom Debolski

CONTENTS

Chapter 2: Dreamweaver and PHP—A Productive Partnership . . 13

Chapter 3: Getting the Work Environment Ready 43

Chapter 6: Getting Feedback from an Online Form 161

Chapter 7: Putting the Power of a Database
Behind Your Pages 211

Chapter 10: Using Sessions to Track Visitors and Restrict Access 331

Chapter 11: Displaying a Blog and Photo Gallery 377

ABOUT THE AUTHOR

David Powers is a professional writer who has been involved in electronic media for more than 30 years, first with BBC radio and television, and more recently with the Internet. He's now written or coauthored five books on PHP, including the highly successful *Foundation PHP 5 for Flash* (friends of ED, ISBN 1-59059-466-5) and *PHP Web Development with Dreamweaver MX 2004* (Apress, ISBN 1-59059-350-2), as well as acting as technical reviewer on some of friends of ED's best-selling titles.

What started as a mild interest in computing was transformed almost overnight into a passion, when David was posted to Japan in 1987 as a BBC correspondent in Tokyo. With no corporate IT department just down the corridor, he was forced to learn how to fix everything himself. When not tinkering with the innards of his computer, he was reporting for BBC TV and radio on the rise and collapse of the Japanese bubble economy.

It was back in 1995 that David began experimenting with web design, creating and maintaining an 80-page bilingual website for BBC Japanese TV, of which he was Editor for five years. He began the hard way, coding by hand, and then trying all variety of HTML editors, good and bad, before settling on Dreamweaver, which he has used since version 3. The constant demands of updating a large static website prompted the search for a server-side solution, and after experimenting with classic ASP and ColdFusion, David settled on PHP. Since leaving the BBC to work independently, he has built up an online bilingual database of economic and political analysis for Japanese clients of an international consultancy.

When not pounding the keyboard writing books or dreaming of new ways of using PHP and other programming languages, David enjoys nothing better than visiting his favorite sushi restaurant. He has also translated several plays from Japanese.

ABOUT THE TECHNICAL REVIEWER

Jason Nadon started using Dreamweaver around the release of version 2.0. He manages the Ann Arbor Area Macromedia User Group and is an active member of the Macromedia Community. Jason has been in the Information Technology field for the past nine years, and has been building web applications and solutions with Macromedia tools for the past six. He holds several industry certifications and is currently employed by Thomson Creative Solutions as a Web Services Administrator.

ABOUT THE COVER IMAGE

Corné van Dooren designed the front cover image for this book. Having been given a brief by friends of ED to create a new design for the Foundation series, he was inspired to create this new setup combining technology and organic forms.

With a colorful background as an avid cartoonist, Corné discovered the infinite world of multimedia at the age of 17—a journey of discovery that hasn't stopped since. His mantra has always been "The only limit to multimedia is the imagination," a mantra that is keeping him moving forward constantly.

After enjoying success after success over the past years—working for many international clients, as well as being featured in multimedia magazines, testing software, and working on many other friends of ED books—Corné decided it was time to take another step in his career by launching his own company, *Project 79*, in March 2005.

You can see more of his work and contact him through www.cornevandooren.com or www.project79.com.

If you like his work, be sure to check out his chapter in *New Masters of Photoshop: Volume 2*, also by friends of ED (ISBN: 1-59059-315-4).

ACKNOWLEDGMENTS

Although I'm the only one to get my name on the front cover, like all books, this one would never have seen the light of day without the help and cooperation of many others. First and foremost, my editor, Chris Mills, who endured my interminable phone calls and pointed me in the right direction when I couldn't see the wood for the trees. Chris, a recent Mac convert, also reminded me whenever I'd overlooked the needs of the Mac community. Then there's Richard Dal Porto, who kept things on track while wondering if I'd ever get the final chapter written. (I often wondered myself.) I should also mention Andy Carroll, the copy editor. No author likes to have his carefully crafted prose scrutinized by another, but Andy's vigilance helped remove many ambiguities.

I also received invaluable help from several members of the Dreamweaver development team, who provided many insights into the way Dreamweaver works, and even incorporated some of my suggestions into the final version of Dreamweaver 8. Special thanks must go to one member of the team, Josh Margulis, who helped me unravel the mysteries of the new XSL Transformation server behavior and XPath Expression Builder.

Thanks, too, to Alexandru Costin of InterAKT, who gave me a sneak preview of the updated MX Kollection tools that take working with Dreamweaver 8 to a new level.

Finally, a big thank you to Jason Nadon for his expert technical review. He even tore himself away from the beach on the weekend to work on the book. Now, there's dedication for you . . . or perhaps it was raining. (I'd better not ask.)

INTRODUCTION

Confession time. When I first started developing dynamic websites with Dreamweaver UltraDev 4, I made a complete mess of things. I believed rather naively that Dreamweaver would "do it all" for me, and that all I needed to do was point and click. The first couple of projects actually went well, giving me a false sense of security. As soon as I attempted anything that didn't fit into the same pattern as the basic tutorials, things began to go horribly wrong. Even though I've always been happy working with code, one look inside Code view sent shivers up my spine.

Part of the problem was that I didn't have a clear grasp of database structure or of what server-side technology really involved. The other part of the problem was that I was treating Dreamweaver as a WYSIWYG (What You See Is What You Get) program. If I saw something wasn't in the right place, I just highlighted it in Design view and hit *Delete*. What I didn't realize was that this left behind messy code that caused even the simplest of applications to break. The more I deleted, the worse it got.

I don't want that to happen to you. That's why I wrote this book.

Who this book is for

To be able to develop dynamic websites with a server-side language like PHP, you need to have a good grasp of the principles of web design. You should be familiar with the basics of HTML (Hypertext Markup Language) or XHTML (Extensible Hypertext Markup Language), and preferably have some knowledge of CSS (Cascading Style Sheets). You don't need to know how to hand-code a web page, but this book involves switching frequently into Dreamweaver's Code view and making adjustments to the code. Unless you are familiar with the basic structure of a web page, you are likely to find it difficult to follow all the steps.

I assume no prior knowledge of PHP or working with a database. There are detailed instructions on how to set everything up, and I will teach you the basic principles of both PHP and SQL, the language used to interact with databases. The purpose is not to turn you into a "programmer," but to give you sufficient understanding of what is happening—and why—to help you avoid the mistakes I first made.

I hope this book will also be of value to readers who already have some knowledge of PHP, the MySQL database, or both. Even the chapters that deal with PHP basics are designed to help you work more efficiently in the Dreamweaver 8 environment. And by the end of the book, you will be working on relatively advanced topics. I have included a number of custom functions that the more code-minded reader will probably enjoy deconstructing and adapting. If coding isn't your idea of fun, you can just use the functions and not worry about how they work.

Do I need to have Dreamweaver 8?

This is a book written specifically for Dreamweaver 8, and you're unlikely to get the best value out of it if you're using an earlier version of Dreamweaver. At a pinch, you could probably use Dreamweaver MX 2004, because most of the server behaviors are identical, although bugs in the MX 2004 versions of the User Authentication server behaviors will prevent some parts of Chapter 10 working as described, and you will not be able to do any of Chapter 12, which covers the new—and fascinating—XSL Transformation server behavior. However, you'll also miss out on the important enhancements that have been made to CSS rendering and Code view.

If you don't have Dreamweaver 8—or any version of Dreamweaver, for that matter—all is not lost. You can download a 30-day trial version from www.macromedia.com/cfusion/tdrc/ index.cfm?product=dreamweaver.

All the other software required is either available as part of the Windows or Mac OS X operating systems, or free for download from the Internet. Download locations are given when needed, throughout the course of the book.

Windows- and Mac-friendly

Everything in this book has been tested on both Windows and Mac OS X 10.3 and 10.4. Most of the screenshots have been taken on the Windows version, but I have included separate screenshots or descriptions when referring to features that are either exclusive to Mac OS X or that are substantially different from the Windows version. Fortunately, there are very few differences between the Windows and Mac versions of Dreamweaver 8, so Mac users should have no difficulties in following the instructions.

All keyboard shortcut references are given in the order *WINDOWS/MAC*. If you're a newcomer to Mac OS X and don't have a U.S. keyboard, you might be confused by keyboard shortcut references to the *OPT* key. On the U.K. Mac keyboard, at least, this is labeled *ALT*. Whichever Mac keyboard you're using, you can recognize it by the symbol shown alongside.

What if I'm new to Dreamweaver?

This is a Foundation book, so detailed instructions are given for each step. However, I recommend that you familiarize yourself first with the Dreamweaver workspace. Open Dreamweaver Help by pressing *F1*, and take a look at Getting Started with Dreamweaver and Dreamweaver Basics.

The following screenshot shows the Dreamweaver workspace in Windows, using the Designer layout. (The position of each element is identical in the Mac version.) The screenshot shows a PHP document open in Split view, which enables you to view part of the underlying code while seeing a reasonably accurate representation of the final design. As long as you familiarize yourself with the parts of the workspace labeled here, and have a good understanding of web page layout, you should have no difficulty following the instructions in this book. Of the panel groups shown on the right, the two most important ones for building dynamic sites—Applications and Files—are shown expanded.

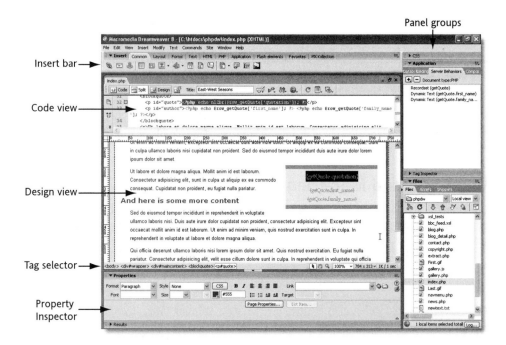

What this book covers

The book's title really says it all: It's about using PHP with Dreamweaver 8. If you're new to expressions like PHP and server-side programming, Chapter 1 gives you both an overview of what's involved and a brief explanation of what the server behaviors in Dreamweaver 8 are for. Chapter 2 looks at the new features of Dreamweaver 8, with particular emphasis on PHP. Chapters 3 and 7 provide detailed installation instructions for PHP, MySQL, and the phpMyAdmin graphical interface to MySQL.

Chapter 4 sets up the East-West Seasons case study that runs throughout the book, covering the basics of PHP (Chapters 5 and 6) and all the PHP-related server behaviors in Dreamweaver 8 (Chapters 8 through 12). The book also covers building your own server behaviors (in Chapters 10 and 11).

The book focuses exclusively on PHP, so no time is wasted on how something is done differently in ASP, JSP, or ColdFusion. If it's ASP that you're interested in, take a look at *Foundation ASP for Dreamweaver 8* by Omar Elbaga and Rob Turnbull (friends of ED, ISBN 1-59059-568-8), which is equally focused. Take a look, but buy my book first.

Support for this book

All the necessary files for this book can be downloaded from `www.friendsofed.com/downloads.php` If you run into a problem with any of the instructions, compare your code with the download files using the new File Compare feature in Dreamweaver 8 (as described in Chapter 2). If that doesn't work, check the errata page for this book at `www.friendsofed.com/books/1590595696`. I try not to make any mistakes, but they occasionally slip through. The errata page is also where you'll find information that came to light after this book went to print.

If you still don't find the answer, post a question in the friends of ED forum at `www.friendsofed.com/` forums, and I'll try to help you as quickly as possible. Please be as precise as you can about the nature of the problem. It's much easier to answer a question along the lines of "I did this in step 7 on page so and so of *Foundation PHP for Dreamweaver 8*, and this happened" than "Chapter 2 (of unnamed book) doesn't work."

Layout conventions

Important words or concepts are normally highlighted on the first appearance in **bold type**.

Code is presented in fixed-width font.

New or changed code is normally presented in **bold fixed-width font**.

Pseudocode and variable input are written in *italic fixed-width font*.

Menu commands are written in the form Menu ➤ Submenu ➤ Submenu.

Where I want to draw your attention to something, I've highlighted it like this:

> *Ahem, don't say I didn't warn you.*

Sometimes code won't fit on a single line in a book. Where this happens, I use an arrow like this ➡

```
This is a very, very long section of code that should be written all on
➡ the same line without a break.
```

Chapter 1

SO, YOU WANT TO BUILD DYNAMIC SITES?

What this chapter covers:

- Understanding what makes a site dynamic
- Introducing PHP and MySQL—the dynamic duo
- Understanding the interaction between a database and a website
- Learning how Dreamweaver automates communication with a database

Dreamweaver, like the Internet itself, has come a long way in the past few years. It's not only the premier design tool for creating **static** websites (ones in which all the information is hard-coded into each page); since 2002 when it incorporated support for PHP, ASP, ASP.NET, ColdFusion, and JSP, it's also become the tool of choice for many developers of **dynamic** websites. As the title of this book indicates, I'm going to concentrate on using PHP with Dreamweaver 8. So, if you've already made up your mind that PHP is for you, welcome aboard. If you're unsure, I hope to have whetted your appetite sufficiently by the end of this chapter to entice you to stay along for the rest of the ride.

Over the next few pages, I'll explain how dynamic websites work, what's so special about PHP and the MySQL database that integrates so closely with it, and how Dreamweaver 8 can make development of a database-driven website both easy and enjoyable. In subsequent chapters, I'll show you how to use some of the brilliant new features in Dreamweaver 8 and how to set up your computer with the right development environment for dynamic sites, and I'll teach you the basics of working with PHP. Then, it's on to the core theme of the book—creating dynamic web pages that interact with a database. By the time you finish, you should have a solid understanding not only of the tools provided by Dreamweaver, but also of the basic technology involved. The aim is not to turn you into a hardened code warrior, but to give you the knowledge and confidence to dive under the hood when necessary to troubleshoot problems or customize things to your own liking.

First of all, what does the term "dynamic" really mean when applied to a website?

What makes a site dynamic?

Several years ago, **DHTML** (Dynamic HTML) was regarded as *the* next big thing on the Web. Yet you may be surprised to discover that DHTML has never been an official standard. As far as the World Wide Web Consortium (W3C) is concerned, DHTML simply describes "the combination of HTML, style sheets and scripts that allows documents to be animated" (www.w3.org/DOM/faq.html#DHTML-DOM).

In other words, DHTML is what Dreamweaver has always been so good at: automating rollovers and other onscreen effects through JavaScript-based behaviors. Combined with CSS (Cascading Style Sheets), this has become standard on the Web, which may explain why DHTML is no longer the buzzword it once was. Most web developers now just refer to JavaScript and CSS directly by name.

Confusingly, even when a website uses DHTML effects, it's often referred to as "static." That's because the underlying code is always the same each time it's downloaded from the web server; the dynamic effects are controlled entirely on the user's computer, normally in response to mouse movements or clicking form elements. In formal terms, this is **client-side** technology (see Figure 1-1).

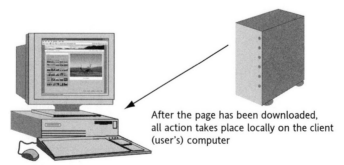

After the page has been downloaded, all action takes place locally on the client (user's) computer

Figure 1-1. Dynamic effects created with JavaScript and CSS involve no direct interaction with the server.

Increasing response to the user with server-side technology

These days, "dynamic"—when applied to a website—usually refers to the ability to change the content or look of a web page *before* it's downloaded to the user's computer. In other words, the changes are implemented on the web server. This is known as **server-side** technology, and the languages used to build such sites—like PHP, ASP.NET, ColdFusion, and so on—are called **server-side languages**. Perhaps the best-known example is Amazon.com. Although most pages look very similar, the content has an amazing variety, and it changes in response to user action. Do a search for your favorite author (well, my favorite author), and you'll be presented with something like Figure 1-2.

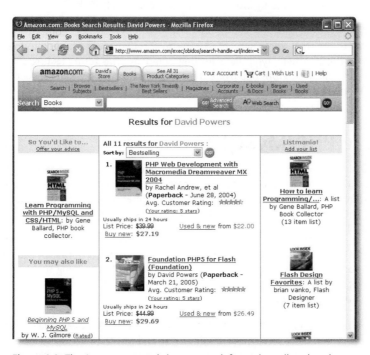

Figure 1-2. The Amazon.com website presents information tailored to the user's requirements through the use of server-side technology.

If you have ever used the Show/Hide Layer behavior in Dreamweaver, you'll know that it's possible to put some of your page content in a hidden layer, and reveal it only when the user hovers over an image or clicks on a particular link. Just imagine, though, if Amazon tried to do that! With literally tens, maybe hundreds of thousands of items in the Amazon catalog, it would be impossible to download all that information to your computer and use client-side technology to display just the parts you're interested in. It makes much more sense to use server-side technology to select the appropriate content and send you no more than necessary. It's fast, efficient, and very effective.

Amazon.com stores most of its content in a database, and it uses a server-side language to extract and display the relevant information. The system is based on a scripting language known as Perl, but similar functionality is available by choosing any of the popular server-side languages supported by Dreamweaver: ASP (Active Server Pages), ASP.NET, ColdFusion, JSP (JavaServer Pages), and PHP. The initials PHP originally stood for Personal Home Page, but that was considered inappropriate when it developed into the sophisticated language it has become today, so it's now one of those curious recursive names—PHP Hypertext Processor.

The word **server** will crop up frequently in this book, and it's important to understand that it has two separate, but closely related, meanings. Primarily, it refers to a computer that stores files, such as web pages, and "serves" them to other computers on request. This is known as a file server. A computer that makes a request to a file server is known as a **client**—hence the expression "client-side," which refers to anything that happens on a user's computer without further intervention by the file server.

The second meaning of server refers to the various types of software that process the requests from visitors to a website. So, in addition to the physical file server, a web server, such as Apache, is needed; and, if a site uses a database, you also need a database server, such as MySQL. Apache and MySQL are software programs that are commonly installed on the same physical computer. I'll show you how they all fit together in the "How dynamic sites work" section later in this chapter.

Dreamweaver uses the term "remote server" to refer to the file server where you upload your web files for display on the Internet—typically a hosting company. The term "testing server" identifies where you test your PHP files before deploying them live on the Internet. Full instructions for setting up a testing server are in Chapter 3.

Why choose PHP/MySQL?

Arguments of an almost religious nature often break out when discussing which is the "best" server-side technology. All the languages supported by Dreamweaver are good, but it's a good idea to pick one and get to know it well. Once you have become proficient at one server-side language, you'll find the transition to another a lot easier, because they share many elements in common.

Strictly speaking, it *is* possible to mix different server-side technologies in the same website, as long as the server supports them. I ran a hybrid ASP-PHP site for several months because I had an existing site that I wanted to convert from ASP to PHP. Instead of waiting until everything had been converted, I did the changeover in two stages. But this is an unusual scenario. It worked because I kept the two parts of the site completely separate from each other.

So, why choose PHP/MySQL in preference to the others? Well, I wouldn't have slaved over a hot keyboard night and day to write this book if I didn't think PHP and MySQL were pretty special. And I'm not alone: PHP is the Web's most widely available server-side language. As of September 2005, it was in use on more than 22.1 million domains (www.php.net/usage.php). MySQL is also reputed to be the most popular open source database, with more than 6 million active installations (www.mysql.com). Because PHP is a server-side language, it needs to work in connection with a web server. More often than not, you'll find it in combination with Apache, the software that runs more than two out of every three web servers in the world today (http://news.netcraft.com/archives/web_server_survey.html).

Apache, PHP, and MySQL run on just about every operating system, including Windows, Mac OS X, and Linux. This flexibility is one of the great advantages of developing with PHP/MySQL. Let's quickly review the others:

- **Cost**: They're free. Don't be fooled into thinking this means they're just for hobbyists. PHP 5 has full object-oriented capability. It can also work with all leading database systems (Dreamweaver's automatically generated PHP code, however, supports PHP only in combination with MySQL). MySQL is used by many leading organizations, including NASA, the U.S. Census Bureau, Yahoo!, and the New York Stock Exchange. The fact that more than two out of every three web servers run on Apache speaks for itself.

- **Open source**: As open source technologies, all three benefit from a rapid upgrade policy based on need rather than commercial pressures. If a bug or security risk is identified, the input of many volunteers helps the core development teams solve problems rapidly. Future versions are available for beta testing by anybody who wants to take part, and they aren't declared stable until they really are. The same thriving community offers assistance and advice to newcomers and experienced programmers alike.

- **Cross-platform capability**: You can develop on your personal computer and deploy exactly the same code on the production server, even if it's running on a different operating system.

- **Security**: Although it's impossible to predict future developments, Apache servers are less vulnerable to virus attacks. Access to sensitive content can be restricted through PHP session control (this is the subject of Chapter 10).

One thing missing from that list is "ease of learning." That's not because they're difficult—far from it. All are relatively easy to pick up, but they do require a bit of effort on your part. If you have experience with other programming languages, your progress is likely to be much faster than if you are a complete beginner. This book is designed to ease your progress, whatever your level of expertise.

> *Although Apache is the web server that I recommend for developing with PHP, you can also use Microsoft IIS on some Windows systems. Instructions for setting up both will be given in Chapter 3.*

How dynamic sites work

Although I refer specifically to Apache, PHP, and MySQL, exactly the same principles lie behind all server-side languages and database-driven websites. The web server and the databases may be different, but the component parts all fit together in the same way.

With an ordinary web page, the information is fixed at the time of design. All text, links, and images are hard-coded into the underlying XHTML (Extensible Hypertext Markup Language). Although dynamic effects, such as rollovers, can be achieved with JavaScript or CSS, the basic content remains unchanged until the designer alters it in an editor like Dreamweaver and uploads it again to the server. As was shown in Figure 1-1, there's no direct interaction with the server once the page has been loaded; everything takes place on the client computer.

Using code that acts as a template

Dynamic web pages built with a server-side language like PHP work in a very different way. Instead of all content being embedded in the underlying code, much of it is automatically generated by the server-side language or drawn from a database. A simple way of thinking about it in Dreamweaver terms is that a dynamic page is rather like a template. Those parts of the page that you want to remain constant are created in standard XHTML, while dynamic elements are scripted in a server-side language.

That *doesn't* mean you need to use Dreamweaver templates to work with a server-side language, and I won't be covering their use in this book. You *can* use templates with PHP if you want, but often a single PHP document is all you need to create in order to display hundreds, even thousands, of different pages on your website. (Think how many books must be in the Amazon catalog, yet every page has the same basic structure.) You build the basic structure in XHTML, and you rely on PHP to generate the actual content dynamically, usually—but not always—drawing the content from a database.

To show you a simple example of how this works, consider a copyright notice at the bottom of a web page. In a static website, the code would probably look something like this:

```
<div id="footer">&copy; 1999-2005 David Powers</div>
```

The problem is that you need to change the second date on January 1 every year. Of course, you could use a client-side solution, such as JavaScript, but there are two problems with this approach:

- Date functions in JavaScript rely on the user's computer clock being set correctly.
- If the user has disabled JavaScript, the function will fail, almost certainly making a mess of your design, unless you build in preventive measures.

A server-side solution eliminates both problems: The server makes sure the date is right, and it inserts the necessary code before sending it to the client. If your server clock isn't set correctly, the date will still be wrong, but you have much more control over the clock on your own server than those on the computers of your visitors.

So, how does the server-side approach work? You create a web page as normal, but instead of giving it an .html extension (the default for static web pages on both Windows and Mac in Dreamweaver 8), you give the filename a special extension that instructs the web server to process any dynamic code before sending the page to the browser. Inside the page itself, you insert the necessary code where you want the dynamic data to be displayed. In the case of PHP, you would give the filename a .php extension and rewrite the previous copyright code like this:

```
<div id="footer">&copy; 1999-<?php echo date('Y'); ?> David
➥ Powers</div>
```

> You won't be able to run this code on your local computer until you have installed PHP and a web server as described in Chapter 3.

Figure 1-3 shows how the web server handles the code. Anything between opening and closing PHP tags (<?php and ?>) is sent to the PHP engine, converted into XHTML output, and sent to the browser with the rest of the content. If you open the source view in a browser, the PHP code is nowhere to be seen. It always remains on the server (hence the name ww "server-side technologies"). In this particular example, what lies between the PHP tags is an instruction to get the current year and display it.

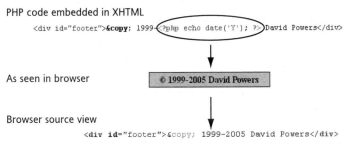

PHP code embedded in XHTML

As seen in browser

Browser source view

Figure 1-3. The server-side code remains exclusively on the server, and ordinary XHTML output is sent to the browser.

Consequently, as soon as the New Year is rung in—even at the stroke of midnight—the correct year will be displayed without any need to update the underlying code. In fact, as I'll show you in Chapter 5, you can instruct the server to add the same block of code to every page on a site. So, you can make the changes to just one page that contains the common code, rather than needing to update every single one. In this respect, it's similar to the principle of CSS, where a single stylesheet can control an entire website, no matter how many pages it contains.

This example involves no user interaction; it simply displays the year. But server-side technology really comes into its own when responding to user input. In Chapter 6, I'll show you how you can use PHP to email the contents of an online feedback form to your own mailbox; and in the second half of the book, you'll work with a database to create a random quotation generator (Chapters 8 and 9), a blog (Chapter 11), and an image gallery (Chapter 11), as well as looking at how to password-protect selected parts of your site (Chapter 10) and display input from a live news feed (Chapter 12).

Pretty powerful stuff, this server-side technology—and Dreamweaver takes much of the hard work out of it, particularly when it comes to working with a database.

Taking a peek behind the scenes

Without getting too technical, let's take a quick look behind the scenes to see how a dynamic page is served up when a request comes from a user. Figure 1-4 shows the sequence of events.

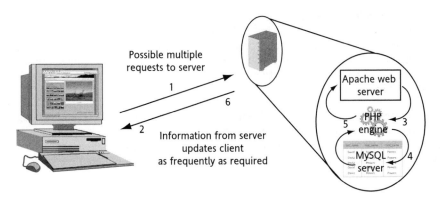

Figure 1-4. A diagrammatic representation of what happens when a client computer makes a request to PHP

1. The client computer sends a request to the web server (normally Apache).

2. If the requested page contains no PHP script, the XHTML, CSS, images, and any other page assets are sent to the client.

3. If the requested page contains any PHP, the web server passes the script to the PHP engine for processing.

4. If the PHP script initiates a database query, a request is sent to the MySQL server.

5. The results of the database query are sent back to the PHP engine for processing and insertion into the page.

6. The web server assembles the entire page as XHTML and sends it to the client, together with any images or other assets.

Once the client receives the data from the server, the page is displayed in the browser, which is ready to receive any input from the user.

There's a lot going on here, and this process can be repeated many times as the user interacts with the page. Sometimes all six stages are required, and, at other times, PHP may simply do all the processing itself without having to query the database. Although it sounds complicated, PHP, MySQL, and Apache can search through many thousands of records in a fraction of a second, so the user may be totally unaware of anything going on in the background. The biggest delay is often caused by a slow Internet connection or network bottlenecks.

Apache, PHP, and MySQL are frequently located on the same computer (although in large operations they may be distributed across several). Apache and MySQL run unobtrusively in the background, consuming very few resources, and are ready to spring into action whenever a request comes in.

> *Programs like Apache and MySQL that run in the background are normally referred to as* **daemons** *on Unix, Linux, and Mac OS X. Windows calls them* **services***.*

Building dynamic sites with Dreamweaver

Dreamweaver 8 has a lot of new features to improve your productivity when working with PHP. I'll cover these in detail in the next chapter, but while I'm talking about databases, I'd like to take a look ahead to what lies in store for you in the second half of the book. Dreamweaver makes connecting to a database a breeze. It creates the code that displays the results of a database query in seconds, and it automatically sets up navigation systems to page through a long set of results. (You'll learn how to do both of these in Chapter 8.)

PHP is the language you'll be using to communicate with your MySQL database, and although I'll also be showing you how to write your own PHP, Dreamweaver takes care of much of the complex coding on your behalf by offering an extensive suite of server behaviors. You use server behaviors in a very similar way to the JavaScript-driven behaviors that you might have used in Dreamweaver for validating a form or creating rollover effects.

An overview of Dreamweaver server behaviors

You can access Dreamweaver's server behaviors in three different ways:

- By clicking the plus (+) button in the Server Behaviors panel, located in the Application panel group
- By selecting the Insert ➤ Application Objects menu option
- By clicking the appropriate icon in the Application category of the Insert bar

You won't be able to use either of the first two methods until you have defined a PHP site in Dreamweaver (covered in Chapter 3), but the Insert bar is always visible, and it's where you find a lot of the most commonly used features in Dreamweaver. If you're new to Dreamweaver, you can learn all about the Insert bar by selecting Help ➤ Getting Started with Dreamweaver. When the help window opens, select Dreamweaver Basics ➤ Getting to know the Dreamweaver 8 workspace ➤ The Insert bar. Let's take a quick look at the Application category, so you have an idea of what Dreamweaver can do when working with a dynamic data.

The Insert bar is displayed by default at the top of the workspace. If you can't see it, select Window ➤ Insert or press *CTRL+F2/⌘ +F2*. Normally, the Insert bar displays only the last category you were working in, as shown here:

The other categories are accessed from the drop-down menu at the left end of the Insert bar. I find it a nuisance to open the menu every time I want to select another category, and prefer to have the categories shown as tabs that can be seen at all times. To select this option, choose Show as Tabs at the bottom of the drop-down menu (as shown alongside). With the Application tab selected, the Insert bar will then look like this:

If you prefer to revert to the default display, right-click/*CTRL*-click the title bar of the Insert bar, and select Show as Menu. Throughout the book, I'll use the tabbed interface, so if you're using the default layout, just select the appropriate category from the drop-down menu. There's no difference in functionality, but the tabbed interface takes up an extra 20 pixels of vertical space on your monitor; so if you have a small monitor, the menu interface will give you a precious bit of extra real estate.

As you can see, the Application tab of the Insert bar has a lot of icons, some of which activate drop-down menus. I don't intend to go into minute detail about what each one does—it's easier to understand their functions by actually using them—but the following quick rundown will give you an insight into what you can expect to have learned by the end of this book.

Recordset and Stored Procedure One of the most fundamental operations when working with a database is retrieving records that match your search criteria. This may be a list of products in an online catalog, a staff list, or even the latest entries in a blog. Dreamweaver gathers the results of your search into a **recordset** (in other words, a set of records), ready for you to display in your web page. Clicking the Recordset icon opens the dialog box where you define which records you want a recordset to contain. Dreamweaver then creates all the necessary PHP code, as well as a query written in SQL (Structured Query Language), the language used to interact with all major relational databases. Most of the process is automatic, although you will need some knowledge of SQL to build more complex queries. I'll be covering the main SQL commands as you progress through the second half of the book.

 Stored procedures are very similar to recordsets, except they use preset queries stored inside your database. Stored procedures aren't available in MySQL prior to version 5.0, so Dreamweaver doesn't yet support them for PHP/MySQL, although it is hoped that an update will eventually add this feature. Until then, the Stored Procedure icon serves no purpose when developing a PHP site.

 Dynamic Data This icon activates a drop-down menu with six options that enable you to populate a variety of web page elements, such as tables, drop-down menus, and text fields with data from your database. Normally, the data will be taken from a recordset. Although this option appears on the Insert bar, it's normally much quicker to access the same lightning bolt icon in the Property inspector or in a dialog box. You will become very familiar with this icon in a variety of contexts by the time you reach the end of this book.

 Repeated Region and Show Region When displaying a list of products in a static web page, you normally need to create a table and insert every item individually. That's not necessary with PHP. You just create a single row, insert the appropriate dynamic data, and then apply Dreamweaver's Repeated Region server behavior, which loops through all the results and creates the code automatically. You can also choose whether to display all results, or limit the page to just a specific number. (Recordset Paging, described in the next section, automates the creation of a navigation system to move back and forth through a long set of results.) Repeated Regions don't apply only to tables; you can also use them with <div>s, paragraphs, or any other integral page element.

Sometimes, your recordset may not contain any relevant results. The Show Region server behavior creates the "smart" code that decides whether to display certain parts of the page when that happens. You'll learn how to use the Repeated Region server behavior in Chapter 8 and Show Region in Chapter 11.

 **Recordset Paging, Go to Detail Page, and Display Record Count** These server behaviors enable you to help visitors find their way around your website. The most useful of these is Recordset Paging, which automates the construction of a navigation system that lets users move backwards and forwards through a long set of database results by spreading them over several pages. Recordset Paging is covered in Chapter 8.

Master Detail Page Set, Insert Record, Update Record, and Delete Record The Master Detail Page Set is probably my least favorite server behavior. It's a good idea, but it's complicated to set up, and very inflexible. I'll show you a better solution using other server behaviors in Chapter 11. The three other server behaviors—Insert Record, Update Record, and Delete Record—are the bread and butter of working with a database. The names are self-explanatory. They're very efficient and easy to use. You'll learn how to use them in Chapters 8 and 9.

User Authentication This set of server behaviors makes light work of password-protecting sections of your site, such as a members-only area or the administrative back-end of a database. You'll use this suite of server behaviors in Chapter 10.

XSL Transformation This is a major new feature in Dreamweaver 8 that makes working with XML very easy. You can either convert entire existing XHTML pages to incorporate XML data, or you can create what Dreamweaver 8 calls an XSLT Fragment for incorporation into a PHP page. Suitable XML sources can be files that you create yourself or a remote source, such as an RSS feed. I'll show you how to incorporate a live news feed into your website using an XSLT Fragment and PHP in Chapter 12. (And if you're confused by all this alphabet soup, everything will be explained at the same time.) Although the code created by Dreamweaver 8 is compatible with both PHP 4 and PHP 5, you will need access to PHP 5 to make full use of this feature, as XSLT support is not enabled by default in PHP 4.

Looking ahead

As you can see, Dreamweaver puts at your disposal an impressive arsenal of tools that automate a large part of building a database-driven website with PHP and MySQL. It's important to realize, though, that automatic code generation is only part of the story. No computer program, however sophisticated, can completely automate everything for you.

Although working with a database is what puts real power behind dynamic websites, PHP is used for much more. One of its most practical uses is gathering information from an online form and emailing it. Sadly, this isn't one of the functions that Dreamweaver automates for you.

So, rather than diving straight into working with databases and server behaviors, I intend to show you first how to understand the basics of PHP, and use that knowledge to build an online contact form. As well as being of immediate practical use, this knowledge will ease the transition to working with databases and customizing Dreamweaver's automatically generated code.

Dreamweaver 8 has some excellent new features that make diving under the hood into the underlying code an experience to be enjoyed—and not something to fear. We'll take an in-depth look at them in the next chapter. Then, in Chapter 3, I'll show you how to set up the development environment for working with PHP in Dreamweaver. The rest of the book will be centered on a case study called East-West Seasons that will be used to demonstrate the transition from a static website to a dynamic one—setting that up is the subject of Chapter 4. Chapters 5 and 6 will be devoted to the basics of PHP and getting that contact form online. Then, from Chapter 7 onward, you'll be working with databases. There's a lot to cover, so let's get on with it!

Chapter 2

DREAMWEAVER AND PHP
—A PRODUCTIVE PARTNERSHIP

What this chapter covers:

- Visualizing dynamic pages with CSS and Live Data view
- Creating and sharing customized workspace layouts
- Introducing tabbed documents for Mac OS X
- Getting the best out of Code view with the Coding toolbar and the Code Collapse feature
- Using PHP code completion and code hints
- Comparing files with a code comparison utility
- Deciding which is right for you—HTML or XHTML?
- Setting the right DOCTYPE for your pages

If you're already using Dreamweaver, there's a strong likelihood that you're a designer, rather than a programmer, or that you're a developer who wants to combine web design with programming. Although I plan to concentrate mainly on the PHP side of things in this book, I intend to combine both the design and coding aspects of building a dynamic website. Dreamweaver 8 is ideal for this, because it's a visual design tool and a highly sophisticated programming environment all rolled into one.

At first glance, Dreamweaver 8 looks no different from the previous two versions of Dreamweaver—unless you're a Mac user, that is (more about that in a moment); however, huge changes have been made to many of the program's features. For designers, the biggest wow factors are likely to be the improved CSS rendering, and what's known as CSS Layout Visualization, which allows you to see where padding and margins have been applied to many block elements. When working with PHP, you'll spend a fair bit of time in Code view, which also benefits from great productivity features. To describe all the enhancements in this new version of Dreamweaver would take up several chapters, so I'll concentrate on the most important, particularly from the perspective of working with PHP.

Working with dynamic code also means you need to pay greater attention to what's happening behind Design view. Modern browsers are often very forgiving of even quite serious mistakes in HTML markup, but with server-side languages, a single comma out of place can bring your site crashing down around your ears. So I'll round off this chapter with advice on good coding practice and choosing the right DOCTYPE for your web pages.

Taking a quick first look at Dreamweaver 8's new features

Windows and Mac users are likely to have opposite reactions when they first open Dreamweaver 8. Windows users will see the same orderly framework of workspace and panels occupying the full screen—beloved by many, but hated by those who long for the return of floating windows last seen in Dreamweaver 4. Mac users, on the other hand, will discover that *their* floating windows are no longer quite the way they used to be. I first opened the Mac version in a monitor set to a resolution of 1024 × 768 (the minimum required size), and it looked as though everything had been locked into the same rigid framework as the Windows version. But first impressions can be misleading—both the Windows and the Mac versions are now infinitely configurable.

You can either use the built-in layouts or design your own. Can't make up your mind, or need to work on a different type of project? Simply switch between layouts on the fly, save them, and even transfer them to other computers—very handy when upgrading, or if you work on more than one machine. I'll describe how to do that a little later in the chapter.

Improved CSS support

The biggest leap forward in Dreamweaver 8 is the way it handles CSS. The new unified CSS panel makes the creation and control of style rules much easier than before. Design view has vastly improved CSS rendering. This, in turn, makes Live Data view a more effective tool for visualizing the eventual look of a PHP site. As Figure 2-1 shows, real data replaces the placeholders for dynamically generated content in Live Data view, giving you a realistic preview of what the page will look like in a browser. It's not a perfect rendition, but it's very close, and there are many new visual aids that enable you to tweak settings without the need to swap back and forth between Dreamweaver and a browser. (The use of Live Data view is covered in Chapter 5.)

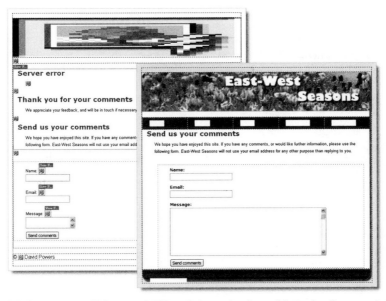

Figure 2-1. Dreamweaver 8's improved CSS rendering makes it possible to visualize accurately how dynamic code will be rendered without the need to leave the authoring environment.

A more productive coding environment

Code view also gets a significant makeover. As shown in Figure 2-2, you can collapse sections of code, enabling you to work simultaneously with parts of a script that may be hundreds of lines apart; and if you ever need a quick reminder of what's in the collapsed section, just hovering your mouse pointer over it displays the first dozen lines. There's also a new Coding toolbar down the left side of Code view that puts all the most frequently used operations within easy reach.

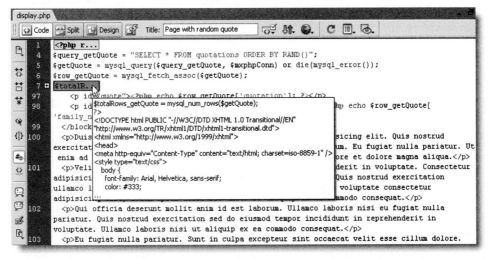

Figure 2-2. The new Code Collapse feature not only allows you to hide sections of your code temporarily but you can also check what's hidden by hovering your mouse pointer over the collapsed section.

Another important improvement for working on code is the ability to integrate a third-party file comparison application, such as Beyond Compare or WinMerge for Windows, or FileMerge or BBEdit for Mac OS X. This enables you to select two versions of a file—even if one of them is on your remote server—and compare them for differences without leaving the Dreamweaver environment. I'll describe these improvements in more detail later in the chapter.

Support for PHP 5

Changes specifically related to PHP include the addition of code hints for nearly 300 more PHP functions, bringing Dreamweaver up to date with the new features of PHP 5.0. This means that if you're willing to do some hand-coding, you can use the MySQL Improved (mysqli) PHP extension to work with MySQL 4.1 or above, as well as SQLite, a lightweight, but powerful database system that is bundled with PHP 5.

However, Dreamweaver 8 still uses the original MySQL extension in its server behaviors. This, I think, is a wise decision. Even though many hosting companies have adopted MySQL 4.1, they have been much slower migrating to PHP 5. The original MySQL extension is a solid workhorse that's still available in PHP 5, and it means that you don't have to worry about selecting different options depending on what your hosting company happens to offer. PHP websites built with Dreamweaver 8 work with any version of PHP 4.3.0 or later, and any version of MySQL 3.23.31 or later.

One disappointment, perhaps, is that there's only one new server behavior for the server-side languages supported by Dreamweaver—XSL Transformation, which is covered in Chapter 12. I would have liked to see support added for commonly used features such as mail or creating a horizontal looper. You can buy commercial extensions to do this, and I'll show you how to use some of the very impressive extensions created by InterAKT (www.interaktonline.com) in Chapters 10 and 11. But don't worry if you can't afford to buy commercial extensions. Trial versions of the InterAKT extensions are available. Above all, the main emphasis in this book is on using the standard features of Dreamweaver 8, and Chapters 5 and 6 guide you through the process of hand-coding the dynamic side of an online form that emails user comments directly to your mailbox.

With so many other improvements, Dreamweaver 8 has plenty to offer, making it an indispensable tool for any serious web designer or application developer. Let's take a more detailed look now at the most important features for developing sites with PHP.

> *By the time this book is published, or shortly thereafter, PHP 5.1 will have been released. Dreamweaver 8 is based on PHP 5.0, so does not support PDO (PHP Data Objects), an advanced—and at the time of this writing, still experimental—interface for accessing databases (www.php.net/manual/en/ref.pdo.php).*

Organizing your workspace

Although the Windows and Mac layouts now look almost identical, there are some important differences between the two. First, I'll take a look at what's new in each of them, and then describe how you can save your personal configurations. The ability to save personal layouts is common to both versions—better still, you can transfer layouts from Windows to Mac and vice versa.

Preset workspace layouts in Windows

One of the biggest complaints from Windows users has been that the integrated workspace introduced in Dreamweaver MX makes it nigh on impossible to work with multiple monitors. No more. The development team has listened, and the Windows version of Dreamweaver 8 comes with three preset layouts, which you can switch between by selecting Workspace Layouts on the Window menu:

- **Coder:** This puts the main panel groups on the left of the monitor and collapses the Property inspector, as shown on the left of Figure 2-3. It's based on the layout of HomeSite, popular with many hand-coders.

- **Designer:** This puts the main panel groups on the right and displays the Property inspector fully expanded at the bottom of the screen, as shown on the right of Figure 2-3.

- **Dual Screen:** This detaches the panel groups and Property inspector, and opens the Code Inspector, and positions them in front of the main workspace, ready to be moved onto a secondary monitor. You must, of course, have the capability to expand your display across multiple monitors to use this option.

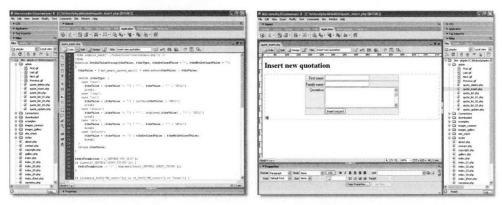

Figure 2-3. The two main workspace layouts in Windows—Coder (left) and Designer (right)

The preset layouts are just a start. You can undock any panel group by hovering your mouse pointer over the left side of a panel's title bar until it turns into a four-headed arrow, as shown alongside. Hold down your mouse button and drag the panel to wherever you want.

Tabbed documents in Mac OS X

If you're a Mac user, this is something that you're either going to love or hate. Depending on the size of your monitor, when you open your first document, Dreamweaver 8 will either fill the entire screen like the Windows Designer layout in Figure 2-3, or it will look like Figure 2-4. At first glance, Figure 2-4 looks identical to the layout in MX 2004, except that the panel groups on the right of the screen now stretch all the way down to the Dock, or to the bottom of the screen if your Dock is on either side or set to hide automatically. It's when you open a second document that you notice the real change—the Mac version of Dreamweaver 8 now has the same tabbed interface as Windows.

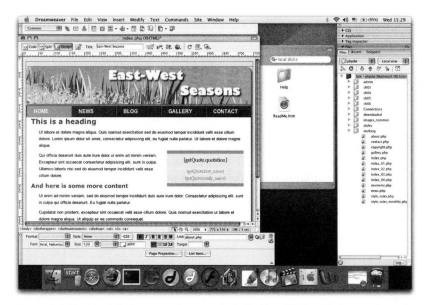

Figure 2-4. The Mac interface now shares many similarities with the Windows version of Dreamweaver.

Each document is identified by a separate tab at the top of the main workspace, as shown below. It makes switching between documents much easier—just click the appropriate tab—and you can close any document quickly by clicking the X in a circle on the left side of each tab. If you want to close all open documents, *Ctrl*-click any one of the tabs, and select Close All. Alternatively, just press *Shift*+⌘+*W*. As you can see from the screenshot, the Mac close, minimize, and zoom buttons are still there at the top left of the workspace, as is the resizing handle at the bottom right. This means that you lose none of the Mac flexibility.

Still, if you don't like being boxed in by the tabbed documents, all you have to do is *Ctrl*-click the tab of any document and select Move to New Window from the context menu. That works only with individual documents, so if you want to get rid of tabbed documents altogether, select Preferences from the Dreamweaver menu, and then choose the General category. Deselect the Open documents in tabs option.

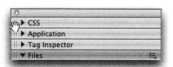

By default, all panel groups that give you access to some of the most important features of Dreamweaver, such as the Tag Inspector and the unified CSS panel, are docked together on the right side of your monitor. If you don't like the rigidity (I call it tidiness), you're free to reorganize things as you want. Just hover your mouse pointer over the left side of a panel's title bar until it turns into a hand, as shown alongside. Hold down your mouse button, and drag the panel to wherever you want.

As Figure 2-5 shows, you can position any panel wherever you like, expanding and collapsing it by clicking the disclosure triangle at the top left of the panel title bar. When you exit Dreamweaver, it will remember where you left all the panels and will open them in the same place next time. If you prefer to organize your workspace in a different way depending on the task in hand, you can save any number of customized layouts. The method of doing this is the same for Windows, so it is explained in the next section.

Figure 2-5. Dreamweaver gives you the freedom to move panels around the workspace, so they're exactly where you want them to be.

If, on the other hand, you get tired of the chaos onscreen, just choose Window ➤ Workspace Layout ➤ Default. Everything will disappear for a few moments and then snap back into the original layout you saw when first running the program. If you're lucky enough to have two monitors, you can also select Dual Screen from the Workspace Layout submenu. This resizes and separates some of the panels so they're ready for moving across to your second monitor.

If, like me, you fall in love with tabbed documents, you can get Dreamweaver to use tabbed display even with only one document onscreen. Open Dreamweaver ➤ Preferences, choose the General category, and select the Always show tabs option.

The one thing I don't like about the new Mac interface is something that will affect anyone working on a 1024×768 resolution monitor. Figure 2-4 shows the default layout in a 15-inch PowerBook (1280×854), and you can see that the Property inspector is about 55 pixels wider than the document. I understand it was originally designed to be the same width, so that everything would fit perfectly in the minimum size monitor. However, at a very late stage in the development process, it needed to be made bigger. As a result, on a small monitor the Property inspector flops in front of and behind the Files panel group, depending on whether it has focus. This is untidy, but doesn't affect performance.

Saving and sharing customized workspace layouts

In addition to being able to undock panel groups in both Windows and Mac OS X, you can reorganize the various panels into completely different groups to suit your own work style or to reflect different priorities for various projects. To move a panel, open its parent panel group and select the panel you want to move. Then right-click/_CTRL_-click the icon on the right of the panel group's title bar to display the option menu, as shown in the screenshot below. You can choose to move the panel to an existing group or to create a new panel group. The menu offers other options, including renaming the panel group. (The same options are available from a larger menu if you use your main mouse button.)

Once everything is the way you want it, you can save the new workspace layout by choosing Window ➤ Workspace Layout ➤ Save Current. The name you give your customized workspace will appear at the top of the Workspace Layout submenu. There is no limit to the number of preset layouts that you can create, and you can switch freely between layouts without having to restart the program. To rename or remove customized layouts, use the Manage option at the bottom of the Workspace Layout submenu.

You can easily transfer your customized layouts to another computer by copying the XML files that store the details; you can even share them between Windows and Mac users. On Windows, the files are stored in C:\Documents and Settings\<username>\Application Data\Macromedia\Dreamweaver 8\ Configuration\Workspace, where <username> is the Windows account to which you are currently logged in. On a Mac, they are in Macintosh HD:Users:<username>:Library:Application Support: Macromedia:Dreamweaver 8:Configuration:Workspace. The XML files have the same name that you used to save the layout. Simply copy them to the other computer and restart Dreamweaver. The new layouts will be immediately available.

> The Application Data *folder is normally hidden on Windows. If you can't see it, open the* Tools *menu in Windows Explorer, select* Folder Options, *and then click the* View *tab. In* Advanced Settings, *select* Show hidden files and folders, *and click* OK.

Getting the best out of Code view

Many web designers are terrified of working with the code that lies under Dreamweaver's Design view. There's nothing to be worried about. Each version of Dreamweaver has improved the quality of the code that it produces, so most of the time you can leave it alone, and Dreamweaver will create efficient, standards-compliant code. But when you start mixing server-side code with your web pages, you need to have a solid understanding of (X)HTML. That doesn't mean you need to learn every tag and attribute, and code all your pages by hand. But you do have to know when something is in the wrong place, and where to locate your cursor for Dreamweaver to insert dynamic code. New features in Dreamweaver 8 have made Code view a much easier place to work.

Using the Coding toolbar

The Coding toolbar is a very useful new feature, and it is displayed by default on the left side of Code view. It's also available in the Code Inspector (*F10/OPT+F10*), which allows you to view the underlying code of a page in a separate window. The Coding toolbar can't be undocked, but in the unlikely event that you want to get it out of the way in Code view, you can hide it by deselecting it from the View ➤ Toolbars menu (or from the context menu of any toolbar). In the Code Inspector, it's controlled independently by the View Options menu at the top of the inspector.

Open documents

Collapse full tag
Collapse section
Expand all

Select parent tag
Balance braces

Line numbers
Highlight invalid code

Apply comment tags
Remove comment tags
Wrap tag
Recent snippets

Indent code
Outdent code
Format source code

The illustration alongside shows you what each button is for, and the same information is displayed as a tooltip whenever you hover your mouse pointer over one of them. Most are self-explanatory.

When you click the top button, it displays a list of currently open documents together with the full pathname of each file. This is very useful if you have several pages open, all with the same name (such as index.php from different folders or different sites). Click the name of the file you want to view or edit, and it comes to the front. No more guessing whether you have the correct file open.

From the PHP point of view, the most useful tools in the Coding toolbar are Balance braces, Apply comment tags, and Remove comment tags. Rather than go into the details now, I'll show you them in action in Chapters 5 and 6.

A really cool aspect of the Coding toolbar is what happens when there's not enough room to display all the buttons. As shown in Figure 2-6, a double chevron appears after the last button that can fit into the available space. If you click it, the rest of the toolbar sits neatly at the bottom of Code view.

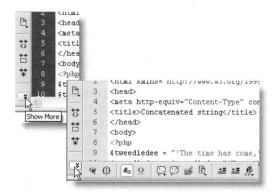

Figure 2-6. The Coding toolbar can be expanded along the bottom of the code area when there's not enough room for it on the left.

Collapsing code sections

This is a real productivity booster. If you have used HomeSite before, you will know just how useful it can be to hide sections of code temporarily, to enable you to work on related lines of code that may be many lines apart. No more scrolling up and down the screen, or needing to display the related sections in separate windows.

There are several ways to collapse code while working in Code view:

- To collapse any section of code, first highlight the code—it can be as short as a few characters within a line, or many hundreds, even thousands of lines. A minus character (the Mac version uses a disclosure triangle) will appear in the left margin on the first and last line (or on the line itself, if you have selected just one line or part of a line). Click one of the minus characters (disclosure triangles) or the Collapse Selection button (illustrated alongside) on the Coding toolbar to collapse the highlighted code. If you're a keyboard-shortcut specialist, use *CTRL+SHIFT+C/SHIFT+⌘+C*.

- To collapse all code *outside* a selection, hold down *ALT/OPT* while clicking the minus character (disclosure triangle) or the Collapse Selection button. The value of doing this is that it leaves just your selection onscreen, removing temporarily the distraction of the surrounding code. The keyboard shortcut is *CTRL+ALT+C/OPT+⌘+C*.

- To collapse a specific code block—such as a <div>, paragraph, or list—place your cursor anywhere inside that element, and click the Collapse Full Tag button (illustrated alongside) on the Coding toolbar. The keyboard shortcut is *CTRL+SHIFT+J/SHIFT+⌘+J*.

This can be very useful, because you don't have to bother highlighting anything—Dreamweaver selects the nearest relevant tag and collapses everything inside, including both the opening and closing tags. One minor drawback is that Collapse Full Tag doesn't treat a pair of PHP tags as a target for selection—it takes the nearest HTML tags instead. As you can see from the following screenshots, placing the cursor in the middle of line 12 and clicking Collapse Full Tag doesn't collapse the PHP code block on lines 8 through 16; instead it collapses lines 7 through 17 by selecting the opening and closing <body> tags. The tag chosen for collapse is always the outermost tag closest to the cursor. So, if you have a <div> with lots of paragraphs, placing your cursor inside one of the paragraphs will collapse that single paragraph. If your cursor is inside either the opening or closing <div> tag, the entire <div> with all nested paragraphs inside will be collapsed.

```
 5   <title>Combined assignment - strings</title>
 6   </head>
 7   <body>
 8   <?php
 9   $tweedledee = "'The time has come,' the Walrus said,\n";
10   $tweedledee .= "'To talk of many things:\n";
11   $tweedledee .= "Of shoes, and ships, and sealing wax,\n";
12   $tweedledee .= "Of cabbages, and kings,\n";
13   $tweedledee .= "And why the sea is boiling hot,\n";
14   $tweedledee .= "And whether pigs have wings.'";
15   echo $tweedledee;
16   ?>
17   </body>
18   </html>
```

```
 5   <title>Combined assignment - strings</title>
 6   </head>
 7 ⊞ <body> ...
18   </html>
```

- If you find you have collapsed too much, just double-click the collapsed section, or click the plus character (disclosure triangle) in the left margin, and it will snap open again.

- To collapse the code *outside* a full tag, hold down the *ALT/OPT* key while clicking the Collapse Full Tag button. Again, this is useful for isolating a block of code and hiding the rest of the page. The keyboard shortcut is *CTRL+ALT+J/OPT+⌘ +J.*

- To expand all collapsed sections, click the Expand All button (shown alongside) on the Coding toolbar, or press *CTRL+ALT+E/OPT+⌘ +E.*

Even when you collapse a section of code, it affects only what you see in Code view; the contents remain fully expanded in Design view. Dreamweaver remembers which sections of code are collapsed when a page is saved, so the same layout is visible in Code view the next time you open a document.

If you expand a collapsed section by double-clicking it or using Expand All, you cannot reverse the process by selecting Undo from the Edit menu, or using the History panel. If you want to inspect the content of a collapsed section and then collapse the same section again, either highlight it and use the plus button (disclosure triangle) to expand it (as shown alongside), or hover your mouse pointer over it and view the content as a tooltip (see Figure 2-2 at the beginning of the chapter).

Formatting code with context menus

One of the main features of Dreamweaver is that it has always been context-sensitive—it tries to offer you only those tools that are relevant to the task at hand. Sometimes this can be frustrating, because an option that you want to select is grayed out, but actually, it's very helpful—Dreamweaver is telling you that you're trying to do something that won't work on the Web. It's also very reassuring to know that Dreamweaver won't suddenly insert ColdFusion or ASP.NET code in the middle of your PHP pages. This contextual sensitivity also applies to menus activated by using right-click/*CTRL*-click.

One menu that has been considerably enhanced in this release of Dreamweaver is the menu that appears in Code view, as shown alongside. If you have any code selected when launching the menu, you will be offered an amazing set of options. Many of the options are the same as on the Coding toolbar, but if you're a context menu fan, it's certainly worth exploring, and there are some extra options there, too.

Using PHP code hints and auto completion

Like all programming languages, PHP makes use of variables and functions (how they're used will be explained in Chapter 5). All variables in PHP begin with a dollar sign ($), and a particularly important set of variables called superglobals (explained in Chapter 6) all begin with $_. If you type $_ inside a block of PHP code, Dreamweaver is smart enough to realize that you probably want to use a superglobal, so it pops up a context menu, as shown alongside, with all the available options. You can continue typing, use your keyboard arrow keys, or click with your mouse pointer to select the one you want, and then just press *ENTER/RETURN*. $_SERVER has a large number of options, so selecting that one brings up another context menu. This can be a great time-saver: It not only saves typing; it ensures you get the spelling right.

> *You won't be able to see PHP code hints or automatic completion until you have defined a PHP site in Dreamweaver. You'll do that in the next chapter.*
>
> *Not everyone likes this type of intervention by software, so you can switch off code hints in Dreamweaver by choosing* Preferences *from the* Edit *menu (or the* Dreamweaver *menu in the Mac version), and then selecting the* Code Hints *category. The settings allow you to delay the appearance of code hints by up to five seconds, or to disable them completely.*

Wouldn't it be a wonderful idea, I thought, if Dreamweaver could do the same with more PHP code? PHP has more than 2,600 functions, and even though most developers only ever use a tiny handful, it can still be difficult to remember the correct spelling or syntax of those you do use on a regular basis. So I put the idea to the Dreamweaver development team. Like a shot, the answer came back: "Oh, you can already do that. It's been available since Dreamweaver MX, back in 2002. Just press *CTRL+SPACE*."

Now, this must be Dreamweaver's best-kept secret. I asked several experienced Dreamweaver users if they knew about it. None of them did, and they all said it blew their socks off when they saw how it worked. Again, you won't be able to test this until you have defined a PHP site, as described in the next chapter, but all you need to do is place your cursor anywhere in a PHP block in Code view, and then press *CTRL+SPACE* (the shortcut is the same on Windows and Mac OS X). You'll be presented with a pop-up menu like the one shown here.

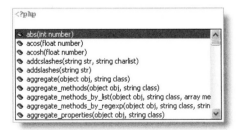

The pop-up menu contains more than 2,600 items—just about every PHP function imaginable, together with the correct syntax. For beginners, this may seem overwhelmingly complex, but it's a real gem that you'll come to appreciate once you become more familiar with PHP. Let's say that you want to split apart a comma-separated list and store each item in a separate variable; the PHP function for doing that is called explode. If you start typing, the menu will start scrolling. By the time you have typed the first four letters, it will have reached explode, and you can just press *TAB* or *ENTER/RETURN*. Dreamweaver not only completes the code; it then displays code hints like this:

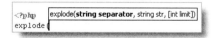

The code hints tell you what arguments the function expects, as well as the format it expects them to be in. As you can see in the screenshot, the first section is in bold type. This tells you what you're expected to insert at this point. The first word (string) indicates the datatype, and the second word (separator) indicates the type of content expected. In the example I've given, you want to split a comma-separated list, so the comma is the separator. The function expects it as a string, so it must be enclosed in quotes. In other words, you begin like this:

```
explode(','
```

Don't worry if all this sounds like incomprehensible geekspeak to you at the moment. I promise that by the end of the book, you will be delighted with this feature in Dreamweaver. The various datatypes and the uses of functions will be explained once you start working with PHP proper in Chapter 5.

Comparing different versions of files

If you've ever run into problems with the code in a friends of ED book (yes, it sometimes happens!), one of the first suggestions you'll be given in the online forum is to compare your code with the download files. The prospect of checking hundreds of lines of code for the missing tag or misplaced element is enough to make grown men cry—unless, of course, they already know the secret of file comparison utilities.

Dreamweaver 8 doesn't incorporate file comparison features of its own, but it does allow you to specify a third-party application, which can be used to compare two local files, two remote files, or the local and remote versions of a file—all from within the Dreamweaver interface.

Setting up the File Compare feature

If you already have a file comparison utility installed on your computer, all that's necessary is to register the location of the program inside the Dreamweaver Preferences panel. If you don't yet have one, here are some suggestions (with their prices at the time of this writing):

- Windows
  - **WinMerge:** A good open source file comparison utility, free from http://winmerge. sourceforge.net
  - **Beyond Compare:** An excellent tool, which you can try free for 30 days; thereafter, it costs $30 for an individual license from www.scootersoftware.com

- Mac OS X
  - **FileMerge:** This is part of the Xcode Tools package on the OS X installation disk, but it doesn't handle complex files very well, so is best avoided
  - **TextWrangler:** Not just a file comparison utility; it's an excellent script editor, free from www.barebones.com
  - **BBEdit:** Again, does much more than file comparison—BBEdit is the granddaddy of Mac script editors ($199 from www.barebones.com, or $129 for registered users of TextWrangler—www.barebones.com/products/textwrangler/crossupgrade.shtml)

Once you have installed a file comparison utility, open Edit ➤ Preferences (or Dreamweaver ➤ Preferences on a Mac), and select File Compare. Click the Browse button and navigate to the executable file for the program. Windows users should have little difficulty recognizing the correct file to select; it will normally be in a subfolder of Program Files. On a Mac, the location for each of the three programs suggested is somewhere you may never even have known existed:

- **FileMerge:** Macintosh HD:usr:bin:opendiff
- **TextWrangler:** Macintosh HD:usr:bin:twdiff
- **BBEdit:** Macintosh HD:usr:bin:bbdiff (this is the BBEdit file comparison utility—make sure you choose bbdiff, and not bbedit, which is listed just below it)

Even though the usr:bin directory is normally hidden on a Mac, the Dreamweaver Select External Editor dialog box will display it by default. All you need to do is select the correct filename and click Open.

Using File Compare

As the name suggests, File Compare allows you to compare the contents of two files. I don't intend to go into the details of how to use the individual comparison utilities, because they offer different ranges of features. However, they all work according to the same principle, and the way you launch them from Dreamweaver is the same for all of them. For the benefit of anyone who has never used a file comparison program, however, it's worth showing the type of thing such programs can be useful for.

The following screenshot shows the result of comparing two sample files from Chapter 5, using the Beyond Compare program:

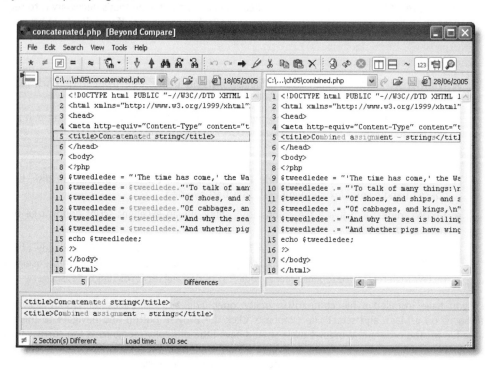

As you can see, the files are set alongside each other in separate panes. Since this book is printed in black and white, you may not be able to see the differences as easily as in a computer monitor, so I've reproduced line 5 from each page. The differences highlighted in red onscreen are shown here in bold type:

```
<title>Concatenated string</title>
<title>Combined assignment - strings</title>
```

The differences between the currently highlighted lines are also shown at the bottom of the screenshot, and right at the very bottom, it reports that two sections of the entire file are different. The second section with differences is highlighted on lines 10 through 14.

BBEdit and TextWrangler on a Mac display the differences in a slightly different format, but the principle is the same. As the following screenshot shows, the two pages being compared are in separate windows, with a third window at the bottom listing all the differences.

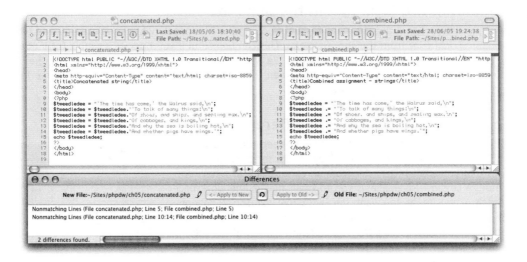

The differences in the previous example are pretty easy to spot, but just imagine you're searching for a needle in a haystack (as might happen when trying to compare your own file with the download files from friends of ED). The next screenshot shows how Beyond Compare handles two versions of a file that's nearly 600 lines long:

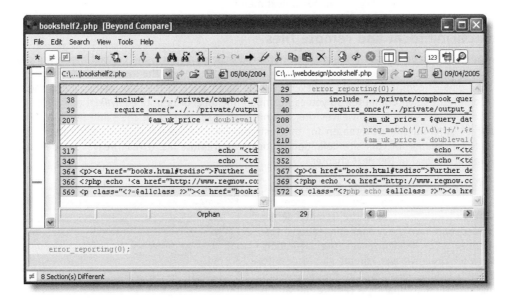

You can hide all matching lines and concentrate solely on the differences, which are highlighted in a way that's easy to comprehend. No more searching in vain for that missing comma or closing quote.

You don't even have to do any typing yourself to resolve the differences between the files. All file comparison programs have features that allow you to synchronize the content of two files, line by line, section by section, or in their entirety.

Comparing two local files in the same site

To compare two files in the same site, highlight both in the Files panel, right-click/*CTRL*-click, and select Compare Local Files from the context menu. This can be useful if you operate a simple form of version control, such as saving each version of a file with an incremental number. By comparing the two, you can see what differences there are between them, and use the comparison utility's merge function to update one file from another.

Comparing two local files in different sites

You may make different versions of sites to keep a record of how the site changes over time, or you may have a set of standard features that you want to transfer from an existing site to a new one. Although Dreamweaver allows you to open files in the workspace from as many sites as you want, the Files panel will display only one site at a time. However, as long as both files are on the same disk in your local file system, you can still compare them without leaving Dreamweaver.

Open the drop-down menu at the top of the Files panel, as shown in the screenshot alongside, and select the disk on your local file system where both files are located. You can then select files from different sites. In fact, you can select files that aren't even in Dreamweaver sites. Once both target files have been selected, right-click/*CTRL*-click, and select Compare Local Files from the context menu.

Comparing local and remote files

If you select just one file in the Files panel, and right-click/*CTRL*-click, the context menu will display either Compare with Remote or Compare with Local, depending on the location of the selected file. For this type of comparison, Dreamweaver will only select a file of the same name, and in the same location on the other computer. So you can compare the local or remote equivalent of `myfile.php` in `myfolder` in the same Dreamweaver site, but not `myotherfile.php`, or the same file in a different folder or different site. The reason for this restriction is that Dreamweaver uses the details in the Remote Info section of your site definition to locate the remote file. (Dreamweaver site definition is covered at the end of the next chapter.)

To compare local and remote files, you must, of course, be connected to the Internet or to the network on which the remote server is located, and have the proper connection information in your Dreamweaver site definition. Otherwise, Dreamweaver cannot gain access to the remote file. As shown in the screenshot alongside, when comparing a remote file with a local one, the comparison is not made with the actual remote file, but with a copy that is created in a temporary folder on your computer called `_compareTemp`.

Although Dreamweaver automatically cleans up the temporary files, their use does cause a problem for anyone working with Beyond Compare. Fortunately, the remedy is simple, as described in the next section.

> *You cannot use the merge or copy feature of your file comparison program to make changes to a remote file, as they will be discarded once the temporary file is deleted from your system. Local files can be changed, because you always work with the original.*

Problems with File Compare

Because File Compare relies on third-party software, it's not always possible to predict how it will perform. So far, I've come across three issues that may cause confusion.

False negatives in Beyond Compare The use of a temporary file causes the default setup of Beyond Compare to produce a false negative when comparing the remote and local versions of a file. This is easily remedied by changing the default options. Open the main Beyond Compare window, and select Tools ➤ Options ➤ Startup. Set Show dialog with quick comparison results to Rules-based quick compare, as shown here.

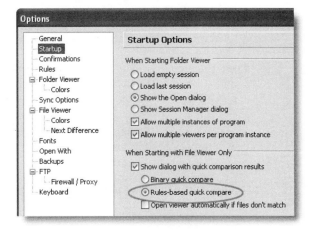

Failure of BBEdit to display results BBEdit responds in a rather disconcerting way when both pages being compared are identical—or to be more precise, it frequently fails to respond at all. If BBEdit isn't running, Dreamweaver will launch it and simply display a blank page. If BBEdit is already running, nothing happens at all—the focus doesn't even switch to the file comparison program. This is simply the way BBEdit has of saying there is nothing to compare. If you add or delete a single character in one of the files, and compare them again, the differences will be displayed immediately.

TextWrangler keeps focus on first use If you have designated TextWrangler as your file comparison program, you may see the Dreamweaver icon bouncing furiously in the Dock while a blank TextWrangler page hogs the screen. This happens *only* if both files are identical *and* TextWrangler wasn't running when you compared them. Switch back to Dreamweaver, and you should see a Dreamweaver alert box reporting No differences found between these files.

Creating standards-compliant code

Back in 2001, a pressure group known as the Web Standards Project (WaSP) persuaded the Dreamweaver development team to improve the quality of HTML and CSS markup generated by Dreamweaver (www.webstandards.org/act/campaign/dwtf). The result was Dreamweaver MX, released in May 2002, which—for the first time—produced code in line with the World Wide Web Consortium (W3C) recommendations (www.w3.org/MarkUp).

This latest version of Dreamweaver is the most standards-compliant version yet, allowing you to choose from six different **document type definitions** (DTDs). A DTD is a short section of code—known as the DOCTYPE declaration—that should appear at the top of every web page. The DTD for XHTML 1.0 Transitional looks like this:

```
<!DOCTYPE html PUBLIC "-//W3C//DTD XHTML 1.0 Transitional//EN"
"http://www.w3.org/TR/xhtml1/DTD/xhtml1-transitional.dtd">
```

The purpose of the DTD is to tell the browser how you want your web page to be treated. For a lot of pages, however, the presence or absence of a DTD makes little or no difference when viewed in a computer browser. So what's the point? There are two important ones:

- More and more devices are being used to display web pages, particularly mobile or handheld ones. Using a DTD tells the device what sort of content to expect, speeding up loading and display. As the Web becomes more sophisticated, the importance of a DTD is likely to grow.

- The absence of a DTD, or the use of an incomplete one, forces most browsers to display CSS in "quirks" mode. The implications of this are explained in the "Treat the DOCTYPE declaration with respect" section later in this chapter.

> *The original Dreamweaver MX (versions 6 and 6.1) inserted an incomplete* DOCTYPE *declaration, without a URL, so you should update any pages created in MX or any earlier version of Dreamweaver.*

Choosing the right DTD

A great deal of hype, myth, and misinformation surround XHTML. It won't supercharge your websites; it won't send you spinning out of telephone boxes with your underwear on top of your tights; nor will it make all your toes fall off.

XHTML 1.0 is exactly the same as HTML 4.01, except that it has been reformulated to follow the stricter rules of XML. By default, Dreamweaver 8 creates new pages with an XHTML 1.0 Transitional DTD. Whether this is the right choice for you is something you need to spend a few moments thinking about. You can find full details of the differences between XHTML 1.0 and HTML 4 at www.w3.org/TR/xhtml1/#diffs, but the main ones are as follows:

- All tags are written in lowercase—<a></a>, not <A></A>

- All tags must be properly nested—<p><strong>This is bold.</strong></p>, not <p><strong>This is bold.</p></strong>

- Certain elements cannot be nested inside others—for instance, you cannot have one form inside another

- All event handlers are written in lowercase—onmouseover, not onMouseOver
- All elements require the correct closing tag—no more leaving off the optional </p> or </td> tags
- Elements without a closing tag end with />—
 becomes <br />, and <hr> becomes <hr />
- Certain attributes (such as selected in <option> lists) need qualifying—for example: selected="selected"
- All attributes must be enclosed in quotes—height="100", not height=100
- Special characters (such as &) must be represented by their character entities (&)
- Embedded JavaScript and styles must not be surrounded by HTML comment tags; otherwise they are likely to be ignored

If you already have a sound knowledge of HTML, adapting to these slightly stricter rules takes very little effort. But what, if anything, will it do for your websites? The honest answer is *nothing*. In today's browsers, properly written, valid HTML will display just as well as the equivalent page written in XHTML 1.0. XHTML 1.0 is merely a transitional language on the way to a proposed standard called XHTML 2.0, which is still in the process of formulation, and which is likely to contain major changes.

My personal view is that even though using XHTML 1.0 won't make a difference to your websites at the moment, it does have the advantage of teaching you to adapt to the stricter demands of XML. When the time comes to move to XHTML 2.0 (which, admittedly, may be many years away), it will be a lot easier to convert pages of well-formed XHTML 1.0 than pages written to the looser standards of HTML. By making the move to XHTML 1.0 now—if you've not already done so—you will be preparing yourself better for future changes to the Web. But it's not a decision you should take lightly.

Be aware of potential pitfalls in XHTML

Don't fool yourself that simply putting an XHTML DTD at the top of your page is like some magic charm that "future-proofs" your site. It won't. One of the most potent arguments against moving to XHTML 1.0 is that the MIME type most web servers use to serve XHTML pages is text/html, instead of application/xhtml+xml. As a result, what the browser sees is HTML, not XHTML.

Figure 2-7 demonstrates the difference. The larger screenshot shows the same page served as application/xhtml+xml. The background image has shifted down because the relevant style rule was applied to the document <body>, which uses a deep top and left margin to position the main text, like this:

```
body {
  margin: 180px 10% 20px 230px;
  padding: 0;
  background: #FFF url(../images/topbg.jpg) repeat-x;
}
```

To get the page to display correctly when served as application/xhtml+xml, the style rules need to be changed, like this:

```
html {
 background: #FFF url(../images/topbg.jpg) repeat-x;
}
body {
  margin: 180px 10% 20px 230px;
  padding: 0;
}
```

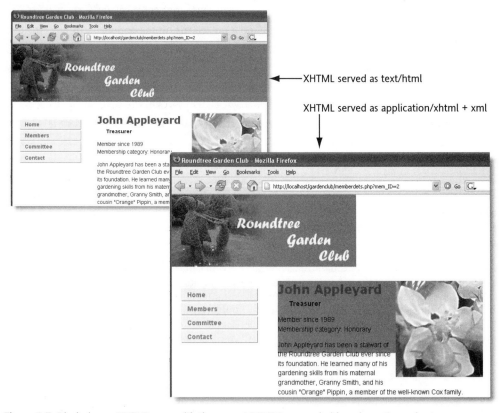

XHTML served as text/html

XHTML served as application/xhtml + xml

Figure 2-7. Displaying an XHTML page with the correct MIME type can hold unpleasant surprises.

The problem with the CSS is easily solved, but serving XHTML as application/xhtml+xml holds an even greater surprise for the unaware. Figure 2-8 shows what happens to the same page if you make just a single coding mistake.

Figure 2-8. A single improperly closed tag can bring an entire page to a grinding halt.

If you look back to the list of differences between HTML and XHTML, you'll see that you have to insert a forward slash before the closing bracket of tags that don't have a corresponding closing tag. What I did to create the error in Figure 2-8 was remove the final forward slash (highlighted in bold) from this line:

```
<link href="externals/main.css" rel="stylesheet" type="text/css" />
```

Of course, this is not normally an issue—a server has to be specially configured to serve XHTML pages as application/xhtml+xml. If you forget the forward slash before the closing bracket, your pages will still display correctly—for the time being, at least. Time and time again, I see pages that mix HTML and XHTML styles with wanton abandon. Current browsers will let you do it, but future ones may not.

The point of this discussion is to alert you to the fact that XHTML is not just a "cool" new feature; it has much stricter rules than HTML. You should learn to use it properly. Fortunately, Dreamweaver 8 has a lot of built-in features to help you do that, but if you don't feel ready for the transition to XHTML, you would be well advised to switch the default DTD back to HTML. On the other hand, you may already be fully at home with XHTML and want to use an even stricter DOCTYPE. Or you may have already weighed up the odds and decided to stick with HTML. Whatever you decide, the next section shows you how to set the DTD of your choice.

> For two different, but well argued, viewpoints on the merits or otherwise of adopting XHTML 1.0, visit the W3C's XHTML FAQ at www.w3.org/MarkUp/2004/xhtml-faq and read the interview with Tommy Olsson at http://webstandardsgroup.org/features/tommy-olsson.cfm.

Changing the DTD in Dreamweaver 8

Developers have different ways of working, so Dreamweaver offers a number of ways to set the document type.

When creating a new document from the File menu Whenever you create a new web page by selecting File ➤ New, there is a drop-down menu in the lower-right corner marked Document Type (DTD). As Figure 2-9 shows, it offers the following choices:

- **None**: You should not normally select this option—all pages should have a DOCTYPE declaration
- **HTML 4.01 Transitional**: This is the least strict option—choose it if you don't feel ready to make the move to XHTML
- **HTML 4.01 Strict**: This DTD excludes the use of deprecated elements (those destined for eventual elimination)—use this only if you have a good knowledge of HTML and have made a conscious decision not to use XHTML
- **XHTML 1.0 Transitional**: This is the default setting in Dreamweaver 8, and it will be used throughout this book—it offers the same flexibility as HTML 4.01 Transitional by permitting the use of deprecated elements, but applies the stricter rules of XML
- **XHTML 1.0 Strict**: This excludes all deprecated elements—use this only if you are competent with HTML
- **XHTML 1.1**: This is an even stricter level—use it only if you are an expert and have a server that uses the correct MIME type (you should also be aware that your pages will not display in Internet Explorer 6 or earlier)

- **XHTML Mobile 1.0**: This is a subset of XHTML Basic for mobile devices—you can find the full specification at www.openmobilealliance.org/tech/affiliates/wap/wap-277-xhtmlmp-20011029-a.pdf

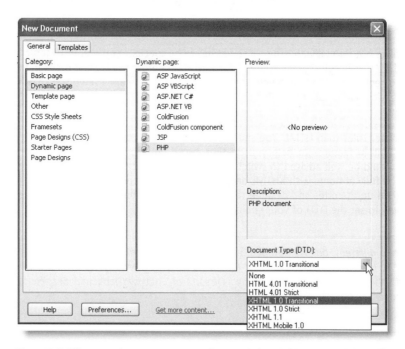

Figure 2-9. When creating a new page, you have a choice of six DTDs or of not using one at all.

By setting the Dreamweaver preferences If you are a fan of the Dreamweaver start screen (see Figure 2-10), you get no choice of DTD. Dreamweaver simply uses the program default. Although the default settings are designed to meet the needs of most users, it's a good idea to check them yourself and make sure they're what you want.

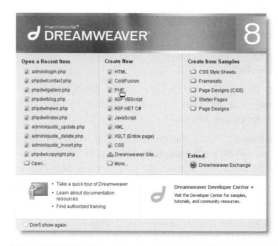

Figure 2-10. The Dreamweaver start screen doesn't give you a choice of DTD.

To check or make changes to the default settings, select Preferences from the Edit menu (or from the Dreamweaver menu on a Mac). In the dialog box that opens, select New Document from the Category list on the left side, and you should see the options shown in Figure 2-11.

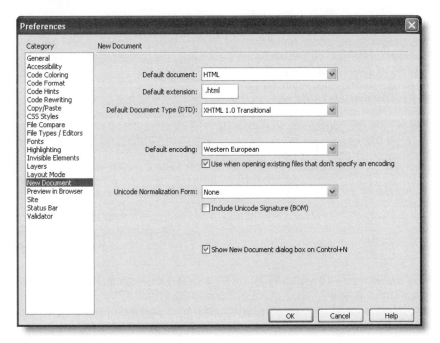

Figure 2-11. You can set the default document type, filename extension, DTD, and encoding for new documents in the Preferences dialog box.

- Default document lets you choose the type of document that will be created by default when you use the keyboard shortcut for a new document (*CTRL+N*/⌘ *+N*). For this to work, you must deselect the option at the bottom labeled Show New Document dialog box on Control+N/Cmd+N. Otherwise the dialog box shown in Figure 2-9 will appear.

- Default extension lets you set the default filename extension for (X)HTML files. This is a lot easier than having to edit an XML file, as in previous versions of Dreamweaver. By default, Windows now uses .html instead of .htm.

- Default Document Type (DTD) lets you choose the default DOCTYPE declaration. This applies to all new documents regardless of the Default document setting.

- Default encoding lets you choose the default character set to be used in all web pages. The check box below this option tells Dreamweaver to use the same character set to display existing pages that don't specify a particular encoding. It doesn't insert any extra coding in such pages.

- Unicode Normalization Form is a specialist setting for working with UTF-8 documents. It should normally be set to None, and the Include Unicode Signature (BOM) check box should be deselected.

By using Dreamweaver's Convert feature

Normally, you should choose the appropriate DTD for your pages at the outset, and leave it at that. However, Dreamweaver will also convert existing documents. In addition to changing the DOCTYPE declaration, Dreamweaver sweeps through your code, either converting it to conform to the stricter rules of XHTML, or removing XHTML-only features. In previous versions of Dreamweaver, conversion was a one-way process (from HTML to XHTML).

To get Dreamweaver to convert an existing page to a different DTD, choose File ➤ Convert, and select the required document type from the submenu, as shown in Figure 2-12.

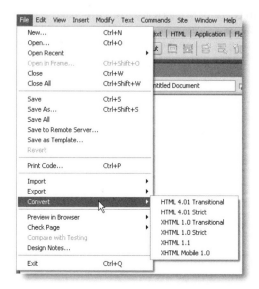

Figure 2-12. Dreamweaver 8 automatically converts HTML to XHTML and vice-versa.

> *If you choose HTML 4.01 Strict as your DTD, do not rely on Dreamweaver's Validator (File ➤ Check Page ➤ Validate Markup or SHIFT+F6), as it will fail to detect deprecated attributes. Use the W3C Validator at* http://validator.w3.org *instead. Other DTDs are not affected.*

Treat the DOCTYPE declaration with respect

Giving a page a DTD is particularly important in making sure that your CSS is rendered properly. However, *nothing* should be sent to the browser before the DOCTYPE declaration—not even white space. Most browsers will still display your page correctly if you break this rule, but Internet Explorer 6—currently the most widely used browser—will switch into quirks mode. The "quirks" refer to the incorrect interpretation of the CSS box model applied by earlier versions of Internet Explorer.

Explaining quirks mode used to be difficult, but Dreamweaver 8 makes it easy, because it emulates the behavior of IE6 in this regard, and switches Design view into quirks mode when any output precedes the DOCTYPE declaration. With the help of Dreamweaver 8's new visual aids in Design view, you can see exactly what happens.

Figure 2-13 shows the impact of placing an HTML comment above the DOCTYPE declaration. The <div> in the top screenshot is rendered in standards-compliant mode, while the same <div> is displayed much narrower in the lower screenshot because the HTML comment above the DTD forces Design view into quirks mode. The figure also demonstrates a superb feature new to Dreamweaver 8—the ability to inspect the main CSS rules for a highlighted block element by hovering your mouse pointer over it. As you can see, the 300px width in the top screenshot is applied correctly to the <div> content only, whereas in the bottom screenshot the content is rendered only 142 pixels wide, the remaining 158 pixels being taken up by the padding and border.

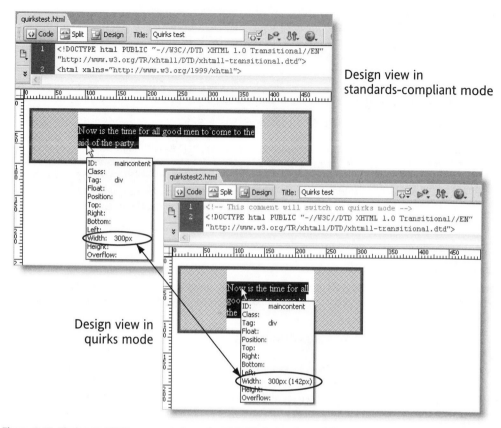

Figure 2-13. Placing an HTML comment above the DOCTYPE declaration switches Dreamweaver 8 into quirks mode.

As you will discover in the second half of the book, when you start working with a database, Dreamweaver puts a lot of PHP code above the DOCTYPE declaration. But, as Figure 2-14 shows, this does *not* switch Dreamweaver 8 into quirks mode—the full 300-pixel width is applied to the content, with the padding and border treated separately. This is because the only scripts that Dreamweaver puts above the DTD interact directly with a database or check variables that control access to a page. None of the code sends direct output to the browser ahead of the DOCTYPE declaration.

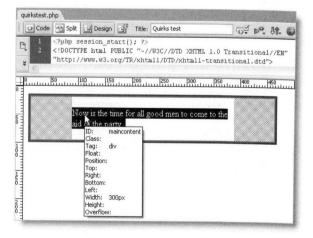

Figure 2-14. Placing PHP code above the DOCTYPE declaration doesn't trigger quirks mode, as long as no output is sent to the browser.

39

> As long as nothing is output ahead of the DOCTYPE declaration, you can process hundreds of lines of server-side code stored above the DTD. Although Internet Explorer 6 is the only major browser that switches to quirks mode if it detects anything ahead of the DTD, this is not just an IE6 issue. You should never send any output to the browser ahead of the DOCTYPE declaration—not even any white space or new line characters—as this could invalidate the DTD. The only exception is the XML declaration:
>
> ```
> <?xml version="1.0" encoding="ISO-8859-1" ?>
> ```
>
> However, the XML declaration is optional when using XHTML. Although Dreamweaver MX inserted the XML declaration in XHTML pages, it stopped doing so in MX 2004 because of the problem of triggering quirks mode. If you have any XHTML pages created in Dreamweaver MX, you should remove the XML declaration to make sure that your pages are rendered correctly both in Dreamweaver 8 and in all modern browsers.

Meet Mark of the Web

There's a new item at the bottom of the Commands menu that may have many of you scratching your heads: Insert Mark of the Web. Click it, and it inserts the following code immediately after the DOCTYPE declaration:

```
<!- saved from url=(0014)about:internet ->
```

This cryptic little piece of code prevents Internet Explorer on Windows XP SP2 from popping up that annoying message that blocks JavaScript and other active content from running when you preview a web page locally. Very simple, very effective, and very useful. You can find out more at the following site: http://msdn.microsoft.com/library/default.asp?url=/workshop/author/dhtml/overview/motw.asp.

Even though this is a Windows issue, Commands ➤ Insert Mark of the Web is also on the Mac version of Dreamweaver 8. After all, Mac developers need to test their pages on what's currently still the world's most popular browser.

Removing unwanted code cleanly

It's important to make correct use of the tools Dreamweaver gives you. For instance, you probably know how to add a behavior to a page by clicking the plus (+) button. But can you put your hand on your heart and say that you always use the minus (–) button to remove a behavior—as shown in Figure 2-15—when you no longer want it?

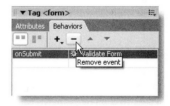

Figure 2-15. It's important to remove unwanted behaviors cleanly through the Behaviors panel.

If you're up against a tight deadline, it's tempting to take shortcuts, but they often end up being more time consuming because of unforeseen problems with code that hasn't been cleanly removed. At best, you may end up with code-bloat; at worst, the rogue code leads to pages that fail to display properly. Once you start building PHP pages, you will make extensive use of Dreamweaver's server behaviors, which are added and removed in the same way from a dedicated panel. Failure to remove a server behavior properly is a sure recipe for disaster.

Watch that cursor!

You should always be aware of where your cursor is before adding new code or applying a Dreamweaver behavior or server behavior. Dreamweaver won't always warn you if you're putting dynamic code in the wrong place. One of the PHP server behaviors in Dreamweaver—Repeated Region—does what it says: It repeats a region of code automatically. If there's a mistake in that code, instead of it being displayed just once, it may end up being displayed 10, 20, 30 times, or more. A tiny glitch becomes a major disaster. Even if your code is clean, you also need to be aware of such rules as using an ID only once on a page. If code inside a repeated region contains an ID, you will end up with multiple instances of the same ID, and then you'll wonder why your CSS or dynamic effect doesn't work correctly.

> Code that's clean and lean loads more quickly and is easier to maintain. If your XHTML is awash with font tags and other presentational markup, it's probably already pretty hard to understand. Once you start adding in dynamic code, it will become even more difficult to handle. If you haven't yet made the switch to styling your pages with CSS, now is the time to start.

The next step

Now that you have a good idea of the coding and development environment Dreamweaver 8 provides for PHP website development, it's time to get your computer ready to work with PHP. Although it's not absolutely essential to install PHP and a web server on your local computer, it speeds up the development process considerably. The next chapter describes in detail how to do this, both for Windows and Mac OS X. The setup process is not difficult, but it's important to get it right. Follow the steps carefully, and you should be up and running in no time at all. If you already have a fully operational PHP setup on your computer, you can skip to the final section of Chapter 3 to see how to define a PHP site in Dreamweaver. I'll also tell you how you can use your remote server for testing if you don't want to install PHP and MySQL on your own computer.

Chapter 3

GETTING THE WORK ENVIRONMENT READY

What this chapter covers:

- Deciding whether to build a local testing server
- Installing the Apache web server and PHP on Windows
- Configuring PHP to work with Apache or IIS on Windows
- Setting up Apache and PHP on Mac OS X
- Learning to read the PHP configuration page
- Creating virtual hosts on Windows and Mac OS X
- Defining a PHP site in Dreamweaver
- Points to watch when using a remote testing server

Now that you've got a good idea of what dynamic sites are all about, and how Dreamweaver can help you build them, you're no doubt raring to go. But hold your horses. As I explained in Chapter 1, PHP pages need to be parsed by a web server. This means you need a testing environment.

Although Dreamweaver lets you use a remote server—such as a hosting company—to test dynamic pages, it's usually more efficient to set up a testing environment on your local computer. All the necessary software can be downloaded free of charge from the Internet, and it's not difficult to set up. This chapter leads you through the installation process step by step for both Windows and Mac OS X, and it discusses various strategies for organizing your web files.

Whether you decide to use a remote server or your own computer as the testing environment, you need to tell Dreamweaver where to find the testing server before you can use any of Dreamweaver's PHP features. I'll show you how to do that at the end of the chapter.

If you already have a functional web server configured to run PHP, there is probably no need to reinstall, but you should take a look at the section titled "Checking your PHP configuration (Windows and Mac)" towards the end of the chapter, and make sure that your setup meets the minimum requirements. But first, a few words about the pros and cons of using remote and local testing environments.

Deciding where to test your pages

Building dynamic pages involves a lot of testing—much more than you might normally do with a static website. It's not only a question of what your pages look like; you also have to check that the dynamic code is working as expected. This becomes particularly important when you add a database into the mix. You need to check that the pages are making contact successfully with the database, and that the results being displayed are what you really intended.

Dreamweaver doesn't mind where your testing server is, as long as it knows where to find it, there's an available connection, and, of course, the server is capable of handling PHP pages. This means that you can test on your local machine, on another computer on a local network, or on a remote host.

These are the advantages of creating a local test environment:

- **Speed:** There's no waiting for a remote server each time you test anything.
- **Cost:** There are no connection charges if you're on a dial-up connection.
- **Convenience:** You can continue development even if there is a disruption to your Internet service.
- **Knowledge:** By working directly with the technologies involved, you expand your skill set and get a better understanding of how they work.

There are also disadvantages to creating a local test environment:

- **Setup time:** Each piece of software requires a multi-megabyte download, which then has to be set up and configured.
- **Complexity:** Some people find configuring the software daunting.

If the prospect of making a few minor changes to configuration files (which are only text files, anyway) sends shivers down your spine, you are also likely to find working with PHP and MySQL difficult. However, no rocket science is involved, and the instructions in this chapter explain not only what to do, but also why you're being asked to do it.

The main rationale for *not* setting up a local testing server is likely to be that you have a fast, permanently-on connection to the Internet. Even so, connection to a remote server is always likely to be slower, and even the most stable connections suffer disruption from time to time. Also, your fast connection means that you can download the necessary software in next to no time. The decision is yours.

Checking the suitability of your remote server for testing

If you want to use your remote server for testing, check first that it's capable of parsing PHP. Open Dreamweaver and create a new PHP page. Switch to Code view, remove everything from the page, and replace it with the following code:

```
<?php phpinfo(); ?>
```

Save the file as test.php, upload it to your remote server, and view it in a browser. If it displays a page full of information about PHP (like that shown in Figure 3-5 later in this chapter), you can skip right to the end of the chapter and the section titled "Defining a PHP site in Dreamweaver." If all you see is the raw code, you will need to find a different hosting company or make arrangements to be moved to a server that supports PHP. In the meantime, why not join everyone else and start testing locally?

Creating a local testing server

To create a local test environment, you need to reproduce on your own computer the setup shown in Figure 1-4. The only difference is that, instead of communicating with another computer, you process everything on your hard disk. For this, you require three things:

- PHP—preferably version 5.0.5 or later
- A web server—Apache 2.0 (1.3 is fine if it's already installed and working) or IIS
- MySQL—preferably version 4.1.14 or later

The versions listed above were used to test everything in this book. Earlier versions will probably work exactly the same, but if you find yourself getting different results, I recommend you upgrade to at least the versions suggested here. I also tested everything on the beta of PHP 5.1.0 (Windows version), so you should be safe to install PHP 5.1 once it emerges as a stable version. This chapter concentrates on getting your web server and PHP running. MySQL setup will be covered in Chapter 7.

Some people worry about creating a local setup that uses later versions of PHP and MySQL than those on their remote server. With a few exceptions (all clearly marked), the code in this book will work as long as your remote server uses at least PHP 4.3.0 and MySQL 3.23.31.

By installing the most recent versions on your testing computer, you can have greater confidence that your code will still be valid when your remote server is upgraded. You can also experiment with new features and put pressure on your hosting company to upgrade. Hosts have been very slow to adopt PHP 5, because they say there has been "little or no demand from users."

Why not use an all-in-one package?

Some people are so terrified of installing programs not originally designed for Windows or Mac OS X that they desperately seek a precompiled package that bundles Apache, PHP, and MySQL together. One that has become very popular recently is XAMMP (www.apachefriends.org/en), which is available for both Windows and Mac OS X. XAMMP has a good reputation, but I still recommend installing each program separately. The problem with an all-in-one package is that it frequently robs you of a great amount of control. You may not get the most up-to-date version of each program, and some packages are reputed to be difficult to uninstall completely.

Perhaps the biggest danger with precompiled packages is that they are often created by individuals or small groups of enthusiasts. There is no guarantee that they will still be around to support you when you need them. PHP, Apache, and MySQL all have the backing of large development teams and an even larger user base. Help for these individual applications is always much more likely to be at hand—and if you run into difficulty with the instructions in this book, I'll be happy to help you out in the Back End Blight section of the friends of ED forum at www.friendsofed.com/forums.

Take your time over installation and you'll save yourself a lot of heartache and problems. This is a long chapter, but large sections of it are specific to one particular type of setup, so you can skip anything that's not relevant to your situation.

If you have already installed an all-in-one package, and want to replace it with the individual programs, make sure you follow any instructions specific to that package regarding uninstalling. A common problem arises with phpdev423 if you uninstall it before removing Apache as a Windows service. I have never used phpdev423, but I understand it includes a file called C:\phpdev\uninstall_apache_service.bat. *I suggest you close down Apache, and then double-click that file's icon before proceeding with the rest of the uninstall process.*

Before getting down to the details of installing PHP, you need to understand the importance of where you store all the web files on your local computer.

Deciding where to locate your sites

If you've been developing static sites with Dreamweaver for some time, you will know all about site definition. As far as Dreamweaver is concerned, it doesn't matter where the files for a particular site are located, as long as each site is in a single parent folder. The parent folders can be scattered all over your computer, because each site definition is treated separately. PHP, however, is a server-side language, which needs to be **parsed** (or processed) by the web server before any output can be sent to the browser. So, in addition to letting Dreamweaver know where each site is located, you also need to tell the web server where to find them.

Two strategies: centralized or distributed

There are two ways you can organize your web files—in a centralized location known as the **server root**, or in separate locations using **virtual hosts** or virtual directories. Both have merits, and your choice is likely to be dictated by your work habits.

Keeping everything together in the server root The server root is a directory or folder where the web server expects to find all public files. The normal practice in a development environment is to create a subfolder for each site inside the server root. You can then test the site in a browser by adding the subfolder's name after http://localhost/. So, if you have a site in a subfolder called phpdw, you can access it by using the address http://localhost/phpdw/.

Whenever I set up a new Windows development computer, I create a folder called htdocs at the top level of my C drive, and put all new sites inside. Figure 3-1 shows the type of structure this creates.

Figure 3-1. The simplest way of setting up a development web server is to keep each site in a subfolder of the server root.

On a Mac computer, the server root is automatically created for each user. It's in your home folder, named, appropriately enough, Sites, as shown in Figure 3-2. Any site within this folder can be viewed in a browser using the address http://localhost/~*username*/ followed by the name of the site's subfolder, where *username* is the long version of your Mac username. So, on my system, a site called phpdw is accessed by using the address http://localhost/~davidpowers/phpdw/.

Figure 3-2. The default location for dynamic sites on a Mac computer is in each user's Sites folder.

> *If you are the only user of a Mac computer, and you normally log on with administrative privileges, you can avoid the need to use your username in the URL for your test sites by using* Macintosh HD:Library:WebServer:Documents *as the server root.*

Putting everything in the server root has the following advantage:

■ The web server automatically recognizes any new subfolders inside the server root, eliminating the need for any further setup.

There are, however, two significant disadvantages:

■ All files need to be in the same parent folder, so if your web files are scattered in different parts of your system, you need to move them all before working with a server-side language like PHP.

■ Because each site is in a subfolder of the server root, you cannot test pages locally if they use links *relative to the site root*. This is particularly important if you use include files for navigation systems and other site-wide features that include links.

> **Site-root–relative and document-relative links:** *Dreamweaver 8 lets you choose whether all links are relative to the document (the default setting) or to the site root. Since Dreamweaver automatically updates links whenever you move pages, images, or other assets, the prime reason for choosing links relative to the site root is if you use server-side includes on a site that has a hierarchy of folders. Site-root–relative links always begin with a forward slash, like this:*
>
> ```
> <a href="/admin/quote_insert.php">Insert quote</a>
> ```
>
> *In* www.example.com, *this will always resolve to* www.example.com/admin/quote_insert.php, *even in a subfolder of* admin *(a document-relative link would need to be* ../quote_insert.php*). A document-relative link in an include file will break if used in folders higher or deeper in the site structure. When demonstrating server-side includes in Chapters 5 and 6, I use document-relative links, but keep them at the same level, so they don't break.*
>
> *The only time you need to worry about using site-root–relative links is if you are building a site with a hierarchy of folders and want to use the same include file(s) in different levels of the site.*

Working with virtual hosts If you use a hosting company for your website, it's almost 100 percent certain that it's located on a virtual host. Without getting into too many technical details, what this means is that, even though the files are not inside the server root, the web server treats them as though they're in a dedicated server root of their own. You can emulate this type of setup on your own development computer so that instead of http://localhost/phpdw/, the address for the same site set up as a virtual host becomes simply http://phpdw/. This has two main advantages:

- It doesn't matter whether your web files are scattered in different parts of your system—as long as each individual site is inside a single parent folder.
- Because a virtual host is treated as a dedicated server root, there is no problem with testing links relative to the site root.

There are no prizes for spotting that the advantages of virtual hosts overcome the disadvantages associated with keeping everything together in the server root. So why don't I just tell you to create virtual hosts, and forget all about the server root? Three reasons:

- Virtual hosts are slightly more complicated to set up. Each new one needs to be added to the web server's main configuration.
- To support virtual hosts with IIS, you must have a Windows Server. The version of IIS that runs on a Windows Workstation (the vast majority of personal computers) supports only virtual directories, which are not the same as virtual hosts.
- Even if you never put anything in the server root, you still have to create one.

Don't worry if you're not sure which to choose. Using the server root is simpler, faster, and adequate for most local development. Use virtual hosts if any of the following apply:

- Your sites are scattered all over your system, and you don't want to move them.

- You need to use links relative to the site root.

- Your folder structure is such that designating a parent folder as the server root would result in the inclusion of non-web files. Figure 3-3 illustrates the type of setup that would cause problems. If Clients were made the server root, confidential information such as invoices and contracts would be included along with the web files. This may not matter on a local development computer, but by definition, all files in a server root are publicly available through a browser. Any lapse in security on your local firewall, and your confidential files could literally be exposed to the world.

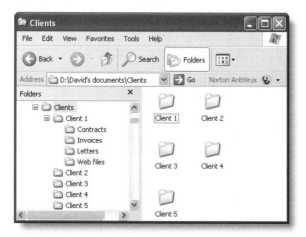

Figure 3-3. Even though all web files are in a common parent folder, this type of setup is better suited to virtual hosts.

Instructions are given for both types of setup later in this chapter, but now it's time to get to work installing the necessary software. First, Windows. Mac users should skip ahead to the section titled "Setting up on Mac OS X."

New versions of open source software are released much more frequently than commercial programs. I recommend that you check this book's errata page at www.friendsofed.com before starting installation. Even if there are no mistakes (and I certainly hope there aren't any), important changes to the installation process will be detailed there.

Setting up on Windows

Dreamweaver 8 requires a minimum of Windows 2000 or later. Make sure you're logged on as an Administrator.

By default, most Windows computers hide the three- or four-letter filename extension, such as .doc or .html, so all you see in dialog boxes and Windows Explorer is thisfile, instead of thisfile.doc or thisfile.html. The ability to see these filename extensions is essential for working with PHP.

Getting Windows to display filename extensions

If you haven't already enabled the display of filename extensions on your computer, open My Computer (it's a desktop icon on Windows 2000, but on the Start menu on more recent versions of Windows). Then from the menu at the top of the window, choose Tools ➤ Folder Options ➤ View. Uncheck the box marked Hide extensions for known file types, as shown in Figure 3-4. Click OK.

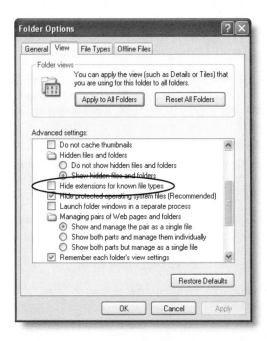

Figure 3-4. Setting Windows so that it automatically displays the extension on all filenames

I recommend you leave your computer permanently at this setting, as it is more secure—you can tell if a virus writer has attached an EXE or SCR executable file to an innocent-looking document.

Choosing the right web server

If you're not careful, the seemingly simple decision of choosing a web server can become horrendously complicated, so I'm going to make it simple for you. **Use Apache: It's the web server of choice for PHP.**

Why don't I recommend Microsoft IIS (Microsoft Internet Information Services), even though it's capable of serving PHP, ASP, and ASP.NET pages simultaneously, and is readily available on many (but not all) Windows installation disks? There are several reasons:

- Most hosts run PHP on Apache, so running Apache on your local computer will reproduce more closely the conditions on your remote server.

- Using PHP with IIS on a live Internet server requires important security measures best left to a specialist. As long as your development computer is behind a firewall, this shouldn't be a problem, but unless you actually *need* IIS, I recommend not using it.

- Most Windows installations don't allow you to create multiple virtual hosts, whereas Apache imposes no such restrictions.

- Windows XP Home and XP Media Center don't support IIS, so it's not an option for many users. There are ways of hacking it, but they're not recommended.

If you are developing with ASP or ASP.NET, and already have IIS installed, you can either run IIS and Apache in parallel on different ports (instructions are given later in the chapter), or install PHP on top of IIS. If you plan to do the latter, skip ahead to the section "Downloading and installing PHP on Windows."

Installing Apache on Windows

For a long time, the PHP development team issued dire warnings against using Apache 2.0 with PHP, but those days are now thankfully behind us. You should install the latest version of Apache 2.0.

If you already have Apache 1.3 installed, there is *no need* to move up to Apache 2.0. However, if you decide that you want to, you must first remove Apache as a Windows service, because Apache 2.0 is installed as a completely separate program, and not as an upgrade to an existing one. Do this by opening a Windows Command Prompt window, and typing NET STOP APACHE. When Apache has stopped, type the following commands, both followed by pressing *ENTER*:

```
cd c:\program files\apache group\apache
apache -u -n 'Apache'
```

You can then uninstall Apache 1.3 through Control Panel ➤ Add or Remove Programs. Although your original Apache configuration file, httpd.conf, will remain intact, do not attempt to use it for Apache 2.0, as many of the configuration commands are different. Delete the original Apache folder and all its contents before installing Apache 2.0.

If you're planning to run Apache in parallel with IIS on the same machine, you must either close down IIS temporarily, or accept the option in step 6 to start Apache manually on port 8080. This is because both servers use port 80 to listen for requests for web pages. To stop IIS, open the Windows Control Panel, double-click Administrative Tools, *and then double-click* Services. *In the Services window, highlight* IIS Admin, *and click* Stop. *Once Apache has been installed, you can choose the port on which you want to run each server, and restart both of them.*

If necessary, uninstall Apache 1.3. Then follow these steps to install Apache 2.0:

1. Go to `http://httpd.apache.org/download.cgi`. Scroll down to the section for Apache 2.0.*xx*, and select the file marked Win32 Binary (MSI Installer), as shown. The xx in the number represents the most recent version of the 2.0 series (at the time of this writing, it was 2.0.54). The download is approximately 4.6MB. Save the file to a temporary folder on your hard disk.

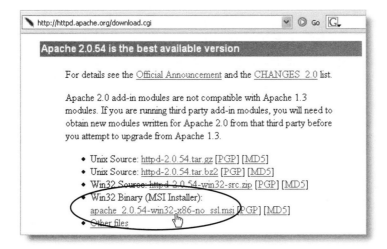

2. Apache comes in a Windows installer package, and is installed like any other software. Close all open programs, and temporarily disable virus-scanning software. Double-click the Apache installer package icon.

3. A wizard will take you through the installation process. Click Next to start. The first thing to appear is the Apache License agreement. Read the conditions and terms of use, select the Accept terms radio button, and click Next.

4. The following dialog box contains information about Apache. Read it, and click Next.

5. The Server Information dialog box, as shown in the next screenshot, follows. This is where you enter the default settings for your web server. In the Network Domain and Server Name fields, enter localhost, and in the last field, enter an email address. The localhost address tells Apache you will be using it on your own computer. The email address does not need to be a genuine one. It has no bearing on the way the program runs and is normally of relevance only on a live production server.

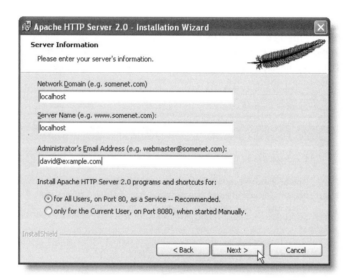

6. Select the option labeled for All Users, on Port 80, as a Service. That way, Apache runs in the background and you don't need to worry about starting it. Click Next.

> *If you plan to run IIS in parallel with Apache, and you have not turned off IIS, you must select the option labeled* only for the Current User, on Port 8080, when started Manually.

7. The next dialog box asks you to select the setup type. Select the Typical option, and click Next to continue.

8. You are then given an opportunity to change where Apache will be installed. The default location, C:\Program Files\Apache Group, is fine. Click Next. The final dialog box gives you an opportunity to go back and change any of your options. Assuming you're happy with your selections, click Install to finish the Apache installation.

9. The process is quite quick, but don't be alarmed if you see a Command Prompt window open and close several times while the program is being installed. This is perfectly normal. If you have a software firewall, such as Norton Internet Security (NIS), installed, you will probably see a warning message like the one shown here:

Although NIS recommends blocking all connections, accepting this recommendation will prevent Apache from working correctly. Either select the option to allow all connections, or—if you're feeling particularly cautious—create your own security rules manually. Manual settings will depend on your individual setup.

10. If you're running a local network, Windows may also attempt to block Apache. If you see a dialog box similar to the one shown here, choose the Unblock option.

11. Open a browser, and type http://localhost/ into the address bar. If all has gone well, you should see the following test page.

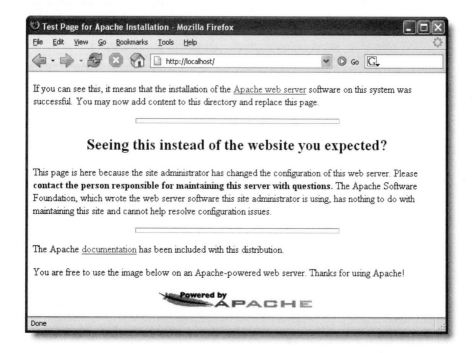

12. If you get an error message, it probably means that the Apache server is not running. Start up the server as described in the next section, and try again. If you still get problems, check C:\Program Files\Apache Group\Apache2\logs\error.log. If you chose the option to start Apache 2.0 on port 8080, you need to use the address http://localhost:8080/.

Starting and stopping Apache on Windows

The default installation of Apache runs the web server as a Windows service. This means it starts up automatically when you turn your computer on, and it runs unobtrusively in the background. It takes up very few resources, and most users simply forget that it's there. There are times, though, when you may need to stop Apache running, either temporarily or on a longer-term basis. You also need to restart Apache whenever you make any changes to its configuration (as you will do as soon as PHP has been installed).

Apache 2.0 places a tiny icon like a red feather with a white circle in the tray (or notification area) at the right end of the Windows taskbar. This is the Apache Service Monitor, which shows you at a glance whether Apache is running. If it's running, there is a green, right-facing arrow in the white circle. When Apache has stopped, the arrow turns to a red dot (see the screenshots below).

Click once on the icon with the left mouse button, and you will be presented with a context menu, as shown in the screenshot here. This provides a quick way of starting, stopping, and restarting Apache.

If you double-click the icon, the Apache Service Monitor will display a fuller interface. As you can see from the following screenshot, it looks rather empty on a single machine, and offers very little in the way of extra functionality. The top pane shows which Apache services are installed, and the bottom pane displays any messages from Apache—usually nothing more exciting than that the service is stopping or starting in response to you having clicked Start, Stop, or Restart. This is what the other buttons do:

- **OK:** Minimizes the Apache Service Monitor to the taskbar tray
- **Services:** Launches the Windows Services panel
- **Connect:** Connects to other computers on your network, so you can control Apache services installed on them
- **Disconnect:** Disconnects from another computer on your network
- **Exit:** Closes the Apache Service Monitor, and removes the icon from the taskbar tray (you can relaunch it from the Windows Start button ➤ All Programs ➤ Apache HTTP Server ➤ Control Apache Server ➤ Monitor Apache Servers)

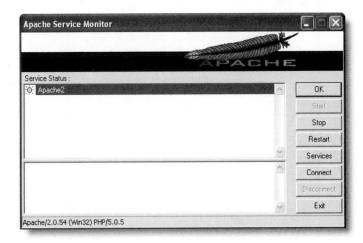

The most useful of these buttons is Services, a shortcut to the Windows Services panel. If you ever want to stop Apache from starting automatically every time the computer is switched on, or if you want to disable Apache temporarily, this is where you need to go.

Changing startup preferences or disabling Apache

If you stop developing PHP sites for a while, or decide you want to experiment with IIS, you don't need to uninstall Apache. You can either switch it to manual operation or disable it until you make up your mind. Either course of action is very simple.

1. Open the Windows Services panel either by using the Apache Services Monitor as described in the previous section, or by selecting Start ➤ Control Panel ➤ Administrative Tools ➤ Services.

2. When the Windows Services panel opens, highlight Apache or Apache2 (depending on which version you have installed), right-click, and select Properties.

3. From the Startup type drop-down menu, select Automatic, Manual, or Disabled. If you want to start or stop Apache at the same time, click the appropriate Service status button before clicking OK.

If you installed Apache 2.0, the Apache Service Monitor will continue to be displayed in the taskbar tray every time your computer starts, even if you switch to manual operation or disable Apache, making it easy to change your options at any time by following the same procedure.

Downloading and installing PHP on Windows

Now that you have a web server (either Apache or IIS) running, you need to get hold of the necessary software to run PHP. The basic installation process is identical for both servers. Actually, "installation" isn't really the right word, because all you do is copy the PHP files to a dedicated folder on your system, and then tell both Windows and the web server how to find them.

These instructions are for a completely new installation of PHP. The recommended method of installing PHP on Windows changed in August 2004, and it no longer involves copying DLL files and the php.ini configuration file to the Windows system folders. If PHP has never been installed on your computer, simply follow the instructions.

If you are upgrading an earlier version of PHP, you need to remove any PHP-related files from your main Windows folder (C:\WINDOWS or C:\WINNT, depending on your system) and the system32 subfolder. Changing the contents of the Windows system folders is not to be undertaken lightly, so I suggest that, rather than just deleting them, you cut and paste them to a temporary folder. Then, if anything goes wrong, you can easily restore them. The PHP files you need to remove are php.ini (in the main Windows folder) and php4ts.dll or php5ts.dll in the system32 subfolder. You should also remove any other PHP-related DLL files from the system32 subfolder. They are easy to recognize because they all begin with php.

If there's a copy of libmysql.dll in your Windows system folder, remove that, too.

1. Go to www.php.net/downloads.php and select the Windows binaries ZIP file for the latest stable version of PHP 5. At the time of this writing, it was PHP 5.0.5, but the PHP 5.1 series was also in an advanced stage of beta testing. Use the most recent stable release, even if your hosting company is still running PHP 4. With the exception of Chapter 12, all the scripts in this book are backwards compatible with PHP 4.3.0 or later. The version you download should be marked PHP 5.*x.x* zip package, and it's about 7.5MB.

I'm sure many of you will be tempted by the sight a few lines lower on the PHP download page of a Windows installer. **Resist the temptation.** Even though it says it automatically configures IIS, the PHP Windows installer runs PHP in a very restricted way and is likely to cause you considerable problems. The method I am about to show you makes no changes to either your operating system or web server, so in the unlikely event that anything goes wrong, it can be removed completely safely.

When you click the download link, you will be presented with a list of mirror sites. Choose the one closest to your location, and download the ZIP file to a temporary folder on your hard disk.

2. Unzip the contents of the ZIP file to a new folder called C:\php5. Check that the new folder contains about 30 files and several folders at the top level, as shown here. If everything is inside a single folder, move the contents of that folder into the php5 folder. The path to php5apache2.dll should be C:\php5\php5apache2.dll.

You can choose a different location from C:\php5, *but this is where PHP will be run from, so you will need to substitute the name of your new folder in all later steps. If possible, you should avoid locating the PHP files in a folder that contains spaces in either its name or pathname, because this can create problems with the Apache configuration.*

3. If you look in the php5 folder you have just unzipped, you will notice that there is a file called php.ini-dist and another called php.ini-recommended. You need to make a copy of one of these, and rename it php.ini, which Windows will use to configure PHP each time you start up your web server. Although the "recommended" version sounds a better choice, the other file, php.ini-dist, is more suitable for a development environment. It's a good idea to keep a backup in case anything goes wrong, so make a copy of php.ini-dist inside the php5 folder, and rename the copy php.ini.

4. As soon as you rename the file, its associated icon in Windows Explorer will change as shown alongside, indicating that it's an INI file—a configuration file that can be opened and edited in any text editor, such as Notepad. Double-click the icon of your new php.ini file, and take a quick look. You'll see that it's written in plain text. You may also notice that it's extremely long—more than 1,000 lines in fact.

If you've never worked with PHP before, this may fill you with dread, but a large part of the file consists of explanatory comments. An even larger part of the file consists of standard settings that you don't need to worry about. Getting PHP ready to work with Dreamweaver involves just a few changes.

> Although you can edit php.ini in Notepad, you may find it easier to open the file in a dedicated script editor—such as TextPad (www.textpad.com) or even Dreamweaver—that displays line numbers. This will make finding the relevant sections much easier. PHP is under constant development, so the line numbers given in the following steps should be taken only as a rough guide. Also note that the line numbers shown in the screenshots have been generated by a script editor. They are not part of php.ini.
>
> Lines that begin with a semicolon (;) are treated as comments in php.ini, so make sure any changes you make in the following steps are to configuration settings and not to comments.
>
> If you are upgrading from PHP 4, do not be tempted to copy your old php.ini. Make a new one based on the version distributed with PHP 5. Although the PHP 4 and PHP 5 configuration files are very similar, there are some important differences.

5. Scroll down (or use a search facility—*CTRL+F* in Notepad and Dreamweaver or *F5* in TextPad) until you find the following line (around line 288):

```
error_reporting  =  E_ALL & ~E_NOTICE & ~E_STRICT
```

Change it to

```
error_reporting  =  E_ALL
```

This sets error reporting to the highest level, and it will help you debug your PHP scripts. As the following screenshot shows, this is one of the cases where there is an identical line in a comment about 12 lines above. Make sure you edit the second one (marked here with an arrow), which does not begin with a semicolon.

```
272  ;  Examples:
273  ;
274  ;     - Show all errors, except for notices and coding standards warnings
275  ;
276  ;error_reporting = E_ALL & ~E_NOTICE & ~E_STRICT
277  ;
278  ;     - Show all errors, except for notices
279  ;
280  ;error_reporting = E_ALL & ~E_NOTICE
281  ;
282  ;     - Show only errors
283  ;
284  ;error_reporting = E_COMPILE_ERROR|E_ERROR|E_CORE_ERROR
285  ;
286  ;     - Show all errors except for notices and coding standards warnings
287  ;
288 ▶error_reporting  =  E_ALL & ~E_NOTICE & ~E_STRICT
289
```

6. About seven lines further down, there should be a setting for display_errors. It's important to be able to see the output of any error messages during development, so make sure it looks like this:

display_errors = On

7. As you scroll down, you will notice a setting called register_globals in the Data Handling section (around line 385):

register_globals = Off

This is the default setting, and under no circumstances should you be tempted to alter it. Even though turning register_globals on makes PHP scripts easier to run, it also gives malicious users an open invitation to crack into your site. A lot of scripts you will find online and in older books were written on the assumption that register_globals was On, so they no longer work. I will show you in Chapter 6 how to adapt such scripts and keep your site more secure.

8. A few lines further down (around line 411), you will see this line:

magic_quotes_gpc = On

Opinions are divided as to whether this setting should be On or Off. When On, it automatically inserts backslashes in front of quotes. This is designed to make life easier for beginners, because quotes need special handling when working with programming languages. However, it does have some drawbacks, so some developers insist that this setting should be turned off. Fortunately, the code generated by Dreamweaver is designed to work properly regardless of how this is set.

Leave the setting On for the time being, and check the setting used by your hosting company or production server. If you ever want to change the way quotes are handled, you can always come back and adjust the setting later.

9. In the Paths and Directories section, locate the final line in the following screenshot (marked here with an arrow):

```
435  ;;;;;;;;;;;;;;;;;;;;;;;;;;;;;;;
436  ; Paths and Directories ;
437  ;;;;;;;;;;;;;;;;;;;;;;;;;;;;;;;
438
439  ; UNIX: "/path1:/path2"
440  ;include_path = ".:/php/includes"
441  ;
442  ; Windows: "\path1;\path2"
443  ;include_path = ".;c:\php\includes"
444
445  ; The root of the PHP pages, used only if nonempty.
446  ; if PHP was not compiled with FORCE_REDIRECT, you SHOULD set doc_root
447  ; if you are running php as a CGI under any web server (other than IIS)
448  ; see documentation for security issues.  The alternate is to use the
449  ; cgi.force_redirect configuration below
450  doc_root =
451
452  ; The directory under which PHP opens the script using /~username used only
453  ; if nonempty.
454  user_dir =
455
456  ; Directory in which the loadable extensions (modules) reside.
457 ▶extension_dir = "./"
```

Change it to

extension_dir = **"C:\php5\ext\"**

This is the name of the folder where PHP will look for any extensions. This assumes you extracted the PHP files to the recommended location. If you chose a different location, change the path accordingly.

10. Scroll further down until you come to Dynamic Extensions. You will see a long list titled Windows Extensions (around line 559), all of them commented out. These extensions add extra features to the core functionality of PHP. You can enable any of them at any time simply by removing the semicolon from the beginning of the line for the extension you want, saving php.ini, and restarting Apache (or IIS). This is a lot easier, incidentally, than on Mac OS X or Linux, where enabling a new extension usually means completely reinstalling PHP.

Locate the four lines marked with an arrow in the screenshot (most extensions are listed alphabetically, but php_mbstring.dll is at the top of the list).

Enable them by removing the semicolon from the beginning of their respective lines, like this:

```
extension=php_mbstring.dll
extension=php_gd2.dll
extension=php_mysql.dll
extension=php_xsl.dll
```

This is what each of the extensions is for:

- The php_mbstring.dll extension enables support for multibyte character sets. Normally, you don't need this if you work exclusively in English, but MySQL 4.1 now stores identifiers in UTF-8 (Unicode), which is a multibyte character set.

- The php_gd2.dll extension enables the GD library, which you will use in Chapter 11 to manipulate images.

- The php_mysql.dll extension enables the code library needed to work with MySQL. If you have worked with PHP 4 before, this is an important change. MySQL is no longer enabled by default in PHP—something that has caused a lot of confusion when upgrading from PHP 4 to PHP 5.

- The php_xsl.dll extension is required for the new XSL Transformation server behavior in Dreamweaver 8, which will be covered in Chapter 12.

```
559  ;Windows Extensions
560  ;Note that ODBC support is built in
561  ;
562
563► ;extension=php_mbstring.dll
564  ;extension=php_bz2.dll
565  ;extension=php_cpdf.dll
566  ;extension=php_curl.dll
567  ;extension=php_dba.dll
568  ;extension=php_dbase.dll
569  ;extension=php_dbx.dll
570  ;extension=php_exif.dll
571  ;extension=php_fdf.dll
572  ;extension=php_filepro.dll
573► ;extension=php_gd2.dll
574  ;extension=php_gettext.dll
575  ;extension=php_ifx.dll
576  ;extension=php_iisfunc.dll
577  ;extension=php_imap.dll
578  ;extension=php_interbase.dll
579  ;extension=php_java.dll
580  ;extension=php_ldap.dll
581  ;extension=php_mcrypt.dll
582  ;extension=php_mhash.dll
583  ;extension=php_mime_magic.dll
584  ;extension=php_ming.dll
585  ;extension=php_mssql.dll
586  ;extension=php_msql.dll
587► ;extension=php_mysql.dll
588  ;extension=php_oci8.dll
589  ;extension=php_openssl.dll
590  ;extension=php_oracle.dll
591  ;extension=php_pdf.dll
592  ;extension=php_pgsql.dll
593  ;extension=php_shmop.dll
594  ;extension=php_snmp.dll
595  ;extension=php_sockets.dll
596  ;extension=php_sybase_ct.dll
597  ;extension=php_tidy.dll
598  ;extension=php_w32api.dll
599  ;extension=php_xmlrpc.dll
600► ;extension=php_xsl.dll
601  ;extension=php_yaz.dll
602  ;extension=php_zip.dll
```

11. There is one extension that you need to add to the list, which will avoid problems when working with MySQL. It's php_mysqli.dll, which enables the MySQL Improved extension.

Copy the line containing php_mysql.dll and paste it on the line immediately below. Amend the second line so they look like this:

```
extension=php_mysql.dll
extension=php_mysqli.dll
```

> *The settings in the next two steps are not essential for running PHP, but will be used for testing the mail application in Chapter 6 on your local computer. The explosion of spam has resulted in many ISPs rejecting mail that doesn't come from an identifiable source, so even if you make the changes in steps 12 and 13, you may still need to test the mail application on your remote server instead. Skip them if you don't have the necessary details to hand.*

12. In the Module Settings section immediately following the list of extensions, look for the code shown below. Change the line shown in the screenshot as line 618 to the name of the SMTP server you normally use for sending email.

```
616  [mail function]
617  ; For Win32 only.
618▶ SMTP = localhost
619  smtp_port = 25
620
621  ; For Win32 only.
622▶ ;sendmail_from = me@example.com
```

If your email address is, for instance, david@example.com, your outgoing address is most probably smtp.example.com. In that case, you would change the line like this:

SMTP = **smtp.example.com**

13. Remove the semicolon from the beginning of the command shown on line 622, and put your own email address in place of me@example.com:

sendmail_from = *your email address*

This puts your correct email address in the From: field of emails sent through PHP.

14. The final change you need to make to php.ini is considerably further down (around line 889). Locate the line at the bottom of this screenshot:

```
882  ; The file storage module creates files using mode 600 by default.
883  ; You can change that by using
884  ;
885  ;     session.save_path = "N;MODE;/path"
886  ;
887  ; where MODE is the octal representation of the mode. Note that this
888  ; does not overwrite the process's umask.
889▶ ;session.save_path = "/tmp"
```

Remove the semicolon from the beginning of the line, and change the setting in quotes to your computer's Temp folder. On most Windows computers, this will be C:\WINDOWS\Temp:

session.save_path = **"C:\WINDOWS\Temp"**

15. Save php.ini, and close it. Leave it inside the C:\php5 folder.

Adding PHP to your Windows startup procedure

The installation of PHP is complete, but it still needs to be added to your Windows startup procedure.

1. Open the Windows Control Panel (Start ➤ Settings ➤ Control Panel or Start ➤ Control Panel). Double-click the System icon. Select the Advanced tab, and click Environment Variables, as shown in the following screenshot.

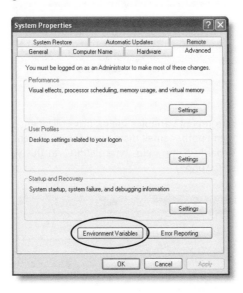

2. In the System variables pane at the bottom of the dialog box that opens, highlight Path as shown and click Edit.

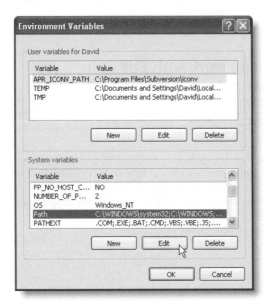

3. This will open a smaller dialog box. Click inside the Variable value field, and move your cursor to the end of the existing value. Type a semicolon followed by the name of the PHP folder you created in step 2 of the previous section (;C:\php5). As shown in the screenshot, there should be no spaces following the existing value or in the new pathname.

4. Click OK. With the Environment Variables dialog box still open, click New in the System variables pane. This will open another small dialog box for you to enter the details of the new system variable. In the Variable name field, type PHPRC. In the Variable value field, enter the path of the PHP folder (C:\php5).

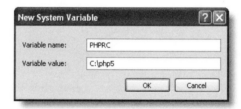

5. Click OK to close all the dialog boxes. The next time you restart your computer, Windows will know where to find all the necessary files to run PHP. You still need to make some changes to your web server configuration before restarting your computer. If you are using Apache, continue with the next section. Otherwise, skip ahead to "Configuring IIS to work with PHP."

Configuring Apache to work with PHP

Now that all the configuration settings have been made for PHP, you need to make some adjustments to the main configuration file for Apache. These instructions are based on Apache 2.0, but they indicate any differences that apply to Apache 1.3. When using Apache 1.3, all references to the Apache2 folder should be replaced by Apache.

> *Note that all the pathnames in the Apache configuration file use **forward** slashes, instead of the Windows convention of backward slashes. So, c:\php5 becomes c:/php5. Any path- or filenames that contain spaces must be enclosed in quotes.*

1. The Apache configuration file, httpd.conf, is located in C:\Program Files\Apache Group\Apache2\conf. You can either use Windows Explorer to locate the file directly and open it in a script editor or select Start ➤ All Programs ➤ Apache HTTP Server ➤ Configure Apache Server ➤ Edit the Apache httpd.conf Configuration File. Like php.ini, httpd.conf is a very long file composed mainly of comments, which in this case can be distinguished by a pound or hash sign (#) at the beginning of the line.

2. **This step applies only to parallel Apache/IIS installations**. If you are running Apache *on its own, without IIS*, skip straight to step 3.

   By default, both Apache and IIS listen for requests on port 80, but they cannot share the same port. So you must switch one of them to listen on a different port; 8080 is a good choice. If your main focus is on ASP or ASP.NET, you should leave IIS on port 80 and change the default setting for Apache.

   Locate the line indicated by the arrow in the following screenshot:

   ```
   116  # Change this to Listen on specific IP addresses as shown below to
   117  # prevent Apache from glomming onto all bound IP addresses (0.0.0.0)
   118  #
   119  #Listen 12.34.56.78:80
   120 ▶Listen 80
   121
   ```

   Change it to this:

   Listen 80**80**

   If you want to concentrate mainly on PHP, leave the settings for Apache unchanged, and reset IIS as described in the section titled "Configuring IIS to listen on port 8080" later in the chapter. (In Apache 1.3, the Listen command is commented out by default. You should use the Port command around line 268 instead. Set it to Port 80**80**.)

3. Scroll down until you find a long list of items that begin with LoadModule (many of them will be commented out). At the end of the list, add the following on a new line, as shown:

   LoadModule php5_module c:/php5/php5apache2.dll

   ```
   164  #LoadModule rewrite_module modules/mod_rewrite.so
   165  LoadModule setenvif_module modules/mod_setenvif.so
   166  #LoadModule speling_module modules/mod_speling.so
   167  #LoadModule status_module modules/mod_status.so
   168  #LoadModule unique_id_module modules/mod_unique_id.so
   169  LoadModule userdir_module modules/mod_userdir.so
   170  #LoadModule usertrack_module modules/mod_usertrack.so
   171  #LoadModule vhost_alias_module modules/mod_vhost_alias.so
   172  #LoadModule ssl_module modules/mod_ssl.so
   173
   174 ▶LoadModule php5_module c:/php5/php5apache2.dll
   175
   176  #
   177  # ExtendedStatus controls whether Apache will generate "full"
   ```

   For Apache 1.3, use php5apache.dll instead of php5apache2.dll.

   You want this and all following settings to work, so do *not* put a # at the beginning of the line. The pathname assumes you've installed PHP in c:\php5. Change it accordingly, if you used a different installation folder, and don't forget to use forward slashes in the pathname. Enclose the path in quotes if there are spaces in any of the folder names.

4. Scroll down again until you find the section shown in the following screenshot:

```
226  # DocumentRoot: The directory out of which you will serve your
227  # documents. By default, all requests are taken from this directory, but
228  # symbolic links and aliases may be used to point to other locations.
229  #
230 ▶DocumentRoot "C:/Program Files/Apache Group/Apache2/htdocs"
231
232  #
233  # Each directory to which Apache has access can be configured with respect
234  # to which services and features are allowed and/or disabled in that
235  # directory (and its subdirectories).
236  #
237  # First, we configure the "default" to be a very restrictive set of
238  # features.
239  #
240  <Directory />
241      Options FollowSymLinks
242      AllowOverride None
243  </Directory>
244
245  #
246  # Note that from this point forward you must specifically allow
247  # particular features to be enabled - so if something's not working as
248  # you might expect, make sure that you have specifically enabled it
249  # below.
250  #
251
252  #
253  # This should be changed to whatever you set DocumentRoot to.
254  #
255 ▶<Directory "C:/Program Files/Apache Group/Apache2/htdocs">
256
```

As explained earlier, a web server needs a folder designated as the **server root**. The two lines indicated by an arrow (lines 230 and 255 in the screenshot) tell Apache which one to use. In a browser, this becomes the equivalent of http://localhost/.

Unless you create virtual hosts, this folder is where all your web files will be stored. It's not a good idea to keep them in the same place as your vital program files. So, whenever I set up a new computer, I always create a dedicated folder called htdocs at the top level of my C drive, and put all my websites in subfolders of htdocs. You can either do the same, or you can configure Apache to look for your websites wherever you normally keep them (as long as they're all within a single parent folder). Change both lines to indicate the same location. In my case, they will look like this:

DocumentRoot "C:/**htdocs**"
#
Omitted section
#
<Directory "C:/**htdocs**">

5. Scroll down a bit further until you come to the following command (around line 323):

DirectoryIndex index.html index.html.var

This setting tells web servers what to display by default if a URL doesn't end with a filename, but contains only a folder name or the domain name (for instance, www.friendsofed.com). Apache will choose the first available page from a space-delimited list. The whole purpose of this book is to work with PHP, so you need to add index.php to the list. If you have files created in an earlier version of Dreamweaver, you may also want to add index.htm to the list, as follows:

DirectoryIndex index.html index.html.var **index.php index.htm**

> *You may be wondering what* index.html.var *means. It's used in a specialized feature known as content negotiation, which can automatically serve up different language versions of the same page by detecting the default language of the computer's operating system (see* http://httpd.apache.org/docs-2.0/content-negotiation.html). *Although content negotiation can be very useful, you should never use it as the only means of selecting a language. Just imagine your frustration at not being able to switch to your native language when viewing your favorite website in an Internet café in a different country. Apache 1.3 doesn't support content negotiation, so if you're using that version, this line won't include* index.html.var.

6. Close to the end of httpd.conf, you will find a section that includes several commands that begin with AddType. Add the following line in that section on a line of its own, as shown:

AddType application/x-httpd-php .php

```
756  AddType application/x-compress .Z
757  AddType application/x-gzip .gz .tgz
758
759 ▶AddType application/x-httpd-php .php
760
```

7. Save and close httpd.conf.

8. You now need to create a test file in the folder you designated as server root in step 4. Open Dreamweaver, and select File ➤ New. In the New Document dialog box that opens, select Dynamic Page and PHP, as shown here:

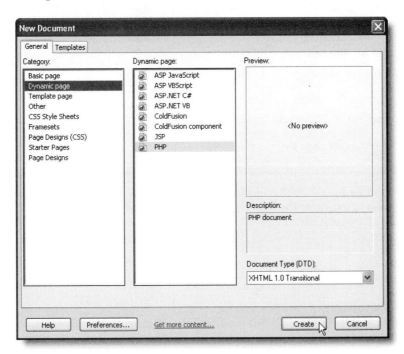

9. Switch to Code view, delete all the code automatically inserted by Dreamweaver, and type the following (it should be the only thing in your page):

```
<?php phpinfo(); ?>
```

10. Save the file as `index.php` in the server root (if you decided to follow my setup, you will need to create a new `htdocs` folder). Because you chose PHP as the page type in the previous step, Dreamweaver will automatically add the `.php` filename extension if you just type `index` in the File name field of the Save dialog box.

11. Restart your computer. Apache should start automatically as part of the Windows startup process. If you opted to control Apache manually, start it as described in the "Starting and stopping Apache on Windows" section earlier in the chapter.

If you have made any mistakes in `httpd.conf`, Apache will refuse to start. Depending on the version you have installed, you may get a helpful message in a Command Prompt window that tells you what the problem is and which line of `httpd.conf` it occurred on. Reopen `httpd.conf` and correct the error (probably a typo). On the other hand, Windows may simply display the very unhelpful message shown below.

Check the Apache error log for clues as to what went wrong. Alternatively, open a Command Prompt window (select Start ➤ Run, and then type cmd in the Open field and click OK). Inside the Command Prompt window, change to the appropriate Apache folder by typing the following command (assuming you accepted the default installation location) and pressing *ENTER*. The command for Apache 2.0 is as follows:

cd c:\program files\apache group\apache2\bin

The command for Apache 1.3 is as follows:

cd c:\program files\apache group\apache

Then type this (followed by *ENTER*):

apache

The reason for the failure should appear onscreen, usually with a line number pinpointing the problem in `httpd.conf`. The following screenshot shows what happened when I mistyped the location of `php5apache2.dll`.

If you encounter problems with Apache 1.3, you may need to add the following command to httpd.conf:

AddModule mod_php5.c

This command isn't always needed, but if you have problems with Apache 1.3 and PHP, add it at the end of a list of existing items that all begin with AddModule. (This is *not* required for Apache 2.0.)

After you correct any problems in httpd.conf, resave the file and restart Apache using the Apache Service Monitor or selecting Control Apache Server from the Apache listing on the Start menu.

If you type apache *in the Command Prompt window, and nothing seems to happen, it doesn't mean that Apache has hung. It indicates that Apache has started normally. However, while Apache is running, it doesn't return you to the command line, and if you close the window, Apache will crash. To close Apache gracefully, open another Command Prompt window, change directory to the* apache2\bin *or* apache *folder, and type the following command:*

apache -k shutdown

You can then restart Apache using the Apache Service Monitor.

There is also a Test Configuration *option on the Apache menu that can be accessed from the* Start *button. It displays the same information as in the method just described. On some systems, however, it snaps closed after 30 seconds. Opening a Command Prompt window involves more typing, but gives you the chance to read the results at leisure—something that's often very important if you're unfamiliar with Apache.*

12. Once Apache has restarted, open your browser and type http://localhost/ into the address bar (or http://localhost:8080/ if you chose the option to start Apache manually on port 8080). You should see a page similar to the one shown in Figure 3-5. Welcome to the world of PHP!

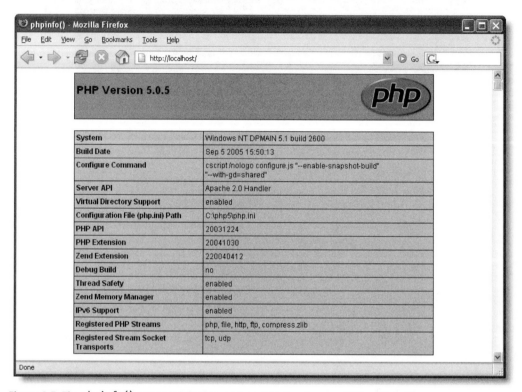

Figure 3-5. The phpinfo() command displays copious data showing your PHP configuration.

13. In the unfortunate event that anything goes wrong, check the next section. If that's not the answer, retrace your steps and make sure you have followed the instructions precisely. Check the short piece of code in step 9, and make sure there is no gap in the opening <?php tag. Try an ordinary HTML page in the same folder (remember, it must be the folder you designated as the server root in step 4). If the ordinary HTML page displays correctly, there's something wrong with the PHP part of your installation. If it doesn't display, then the problem lies in the way you configured Apache.

14. Assuming everything is running smoothly, skip ahead to the section titled "Checking your PHP configuration (Windows and Mac)."

Avoiding the "Cannot load mysqli extension" error

This is one of the most common error messages after installing PHP 5. It occurs because the web server cannot find the correct code library for the PHP MySQL Improved extension (mysqli). It's located in libmysql.dll, which should be in C:\php5. However, some third-party programs install libmysql.dll directly into the Windows\system32 folder.

The problem arises if the version used by the third-party program is older than the one in C:\php5. Wherever possible, you should avoid littering the system32 folder with DLL files, so remove libmysql.dll from system32. However, if this causes problems with the third-party program, you have little alternative but to copy the more recent version from the php5 folder to system32. When you install MySQL in Chapter 7, you will always find the most up-to-date version of libmysql.dll in the MySQL bin folder, although it's rarely necessary to use it instead of the one bundled with PHP 5.

Configuring IIS to work with PHP

I don't normally recommend running PHP on IIS, for reasons already explained earlier in the chapter, but it's something a lot of readers have asked for. These instructions assume that you are familiar with IIS basics, and already have it installed and running on your computer. You should also have completed the sections titled "Downloading and installing PHP on Windows" and "Adding PHP to your Windows startup procedure."

1. Open the Internet Information Services panel (Start ➤ Control Panel ➤ Administrative Tools ➤ Internet Information Services).

2. Expand the folder tree in the left panel, and highlight Default Web Site, as shown in the screenshot. Right-click, and select Properties from the context menu.

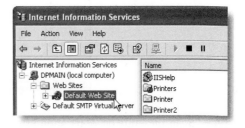

3. In the Default Web Site Properties dialog box, select the Home Directory tab, and set Execute Permissions to Scripts only, as shown here. Then click Configuration.

4. This opens the Application Configuration dialog box, as shown. Select the Mappings tab, and click Add.

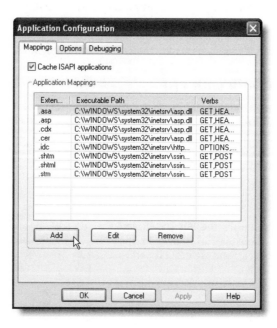

5. In the Add/Edit Application Extension Mapping dialog box that opens, enter the full path to php5isapi.dll in the Executable field. If you used the default location for the PHP files recommended earlier, this will be C:\php5\php5isapi.dll. Enter .php in the Extension field. **Don't forget the period at the front of the extension**—this is very important. Make sure that Script engine is checked, and leave the other settings unchanged.

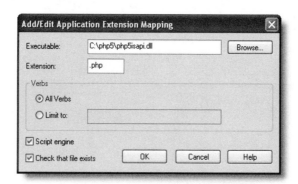

If you click the Browse *button to navigate to the location of your PHP files in step 5, make sure that the drop-down menu labeled* Files of type *at the bottom of the Open dialog box is set to* Dynamic Link libraries (*.dll) *or All files (*.*).* Otherwise, you won't be able to locate the correct file.

6. Click OK twice to close the Add/Edit Application Extension Mapping and Application Configuration dialog boxes. This should bring you back to the Default Web Site Properties dialog box. Select the Documents tab, and click Add. In the dialog box that opens, type index.php in the Default Document Name field, and click OK. Use the up and down arrows to move index.php to the position you want in the list. IIS uses the list to serve up a default document whenever you enter a URL in the browser address bar that doesn't include a filename (such as www.friendsofed.com). Make sure that Enable Default Document is checked.

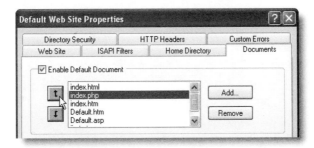

7. If you plan to run IIS in parallel with Apache on the same computer, and you want IIS to listen on port 8080, follow the instructions in the next section ("Configuring IIS to listen on port 8080") before proceeding with step 8.

8. Click OK to close the Default Web Site Properties dialog box. Before your changes can take effect, you need to restart IIS. Open the Services panel (Start ➤ Control Panel ➤ Administrative Tools ➤ Services). Highlight IIS Admin, and click Restart the service, as shown here.

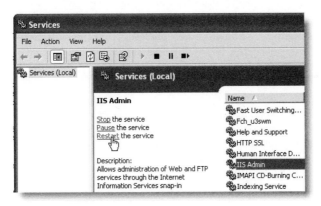

75

9. Create a PHP test file in Dreamweaver. Select New from the File menu. In the New Document dialog box that opens, select Dynamic page and PHP, as shown here:

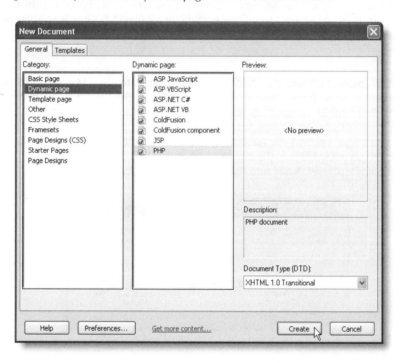

10. Switch to Code view, delete all the code automatically inserted by Dreamweaver, and type the following code (it should be the only thing in your page):

```
<?php phpinfo(); ?>
```

11. Save the file as phptest.php in C:\Inetpub\wwwroot or one of your virtual directories in IIS. Because you chose PHP as the page type in step 9, Dreamweaver will automatically add the .php filename extension if you just type phptest in the File name field of the Save dialog box.

12. Open a browser and type http://localhost/phptest.php in the address bar (adjust the address accordingly if you saved the file in a virtual directory). You should see exactly the same PHP information page as shown in Figure 3-5 in the section on configuring Apache to work with PHP. If you have configured IIS to listen on port 8080, adjust the address to http://localhost:8080/phptest.php.

If the page fails to display, test an ordinary web page in the same location. If both fail to display, there is something wrong with your IIS installation (check that it's running). If just the PHP page fails to display, retrace your steps through this section, as well as the sections on installing PHP. In my experience, IIS doesn't always recognize PHP after a simple restart, but rebooting the computer usually does the trick.

13. Once you have everything running smoothly, skip ahead to the section titled "Checking your PHP configuration (Windows and Mac)."

Configuring IIS to listen on port 8080 The following instructions show you how to change the default port for IIS. Follow them *only* if you want to run both IIS and Apache in parallel on the same computer, and you have left Apache on the default port 80. There is no need to make this change if you are running IIS on its own, or you set up Apache to listen on port 8080.

1. If the Default Web Site Properties dialog box is not already open, open it as described in steps 1 through 3 of the previous section, and select the Web Site tab.

2. Change the value of TCP Port to 8080, as shown in the following screenshot.

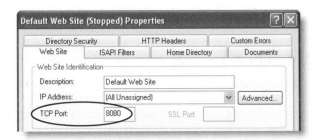

3. Continue with step 8 of the previous section.

Upgrading and uninstalling Apache and PHP on Windows

When new versions of PHP or Apache are released, you will probably want to upgrade. There may also be circumstances where you need to uninstall them, such as if you are at a college and need to leave the computer clean for the next course.

> *These instructions assume you have installed both programs as described in this chapter. They may not be appropriate for other installations, particularly if PHP was installed using the method generally recommended until August 2004. For instructions on removing an old-style installation of PHP, see the highlighted note at the beginning of the section titled "Downloading and installing PHP on Windows."*

Upgrading PHP The great advantage of the revised method of installing PHP is that all you need to do to upgrade is rename your C:\php5 folder C:\php5-old, and then unzip the latest version of the PHP Windows binaries to C:\php5. Then, copy php.ini from C:\php5-old to C:\php5. That's it! You can then delete C:\php5-old.

Upgrading Apache on Windows Although you cannot upgrade directly from Apache 1.3 to Apache 2.0, installing a later version of Apache 2.0 automatically replaces an older one, but leaves the Apache configuration file, httpd.conf, *unchanged*. If the Windows installer refuses to upgrade an existing installation of Apache 2.0, use the Apache Services Monitor to stop Apache, and then uninstall Apache through the Windows Control Panel. When you install the new version, it will automatically use the existing configuration.

Uninstalling PHP To remove PHP from your system, simply delete the C:\php5 folder and all its contents. You should also undo the steps outlined in the section titled "Adding PHP to your Windows startup procedure." You can simply delete the PHPRC environment variable. Take care, however, when editing the Path variable. Make sure you remove only what you added in the first place (;C:\php5).

Uninstalling Apache Uninstall Apache in the normal way through Start ➤ Control Panel ➤ Add or Remove Programs. The uninstall process for Apache 2.0 automatically removes Apache as a Windows service, so there is no need to remove it manually. However, it does *not* remove either the configuration files or server logs. These need to be removed manually from C:\Program Files\Apache Group\Apache2. They are located in the conf and logs folders. If you are sure no other programs are located in the Apache Group folder, you can remove it.

Setting up on Mac OS X

After leafing through so many pages of Windows instructions, you may be surprised that this section is considerably shorter. That's because Apache is preinstalled on Mac OS X; all you have to do is start it. PHP is also preinstalled, but it's not enabled, and the default version at the time of this writing is not suitable for working with the latest version of MySQL. Fortunately, an excellent Mac PKG file is available for free download, and it will provide you with a full-featured, up-to-date version of PHP 5.

Most of the setup is done through the familiar Mac interface, but you need to edit some configuration files. Although these are ordinary text files, they are normally hidden, so you can't use TextEdit to work with them. Instead, you need a specialist text editor—such as BBEdit—capable of editing hidden files.

> *If you don't own a suitable text editor, I suggest that you download a copy of TextWrangler from www.barebones.com/products/textwrangler/. TextWrangler is a cut-down version of BBEdit; it has fewer features but is perfectly adequate for what's required here—and it's free. It also works with the File Compare feature described in the previous chapter. All the instructions have been tested on both BBEdit and TextWrangler.*

Starting Apache and testing PHP

To make changes to the Apache and PHP configuration files, you must be logged into Mac OS X with Administrative privileges. These instructions have been tested on Mac OS X 10.3 and 10.4. They do *not* cover Mac OS X Server.

1. Open System Preferences and double-click Sharing in Internet & Network.

2. In the dialog box that opens, click the lock in the bottom-left corner, if necessary, to allow you to make changes, and enter your password when prompted. Highlight Personal Web Sharing on the Services tab, as shown in Figure 3-6, and then click the Start button on the right. A message will appear informing you that personal web sharing is starting up. Once it's running, the label on the button changes to Stop. Use this button to stop and restart Apache whenever you install a new version of PHP or make any changes to the configuration files. Click the lock again, if you want to prevent accidental changes.

Figure 3-6. The Apache web server on a Mac is switched on and off in the Sharing section of System Preferences.

3. Open your favorite browser and type http://localhost/~*username*/ into the address bar, substituting your own Mac username for *username*. You should see a page like that shown in Figure 3-7, confirming that Apache is running. (If you use just http://localhost/ as the address, you will see the same screen as shown in step 11 of the "Installing Apache on Windows" section. It doesn't matter which you see; all you're interested in is confirming that Apache is working correctly.)

Figure 3-7. Confirmation that Apache is running successfully on Mac OS X

4. At the time of this writing, the default installation of PHP is neither enabled nor is it suitable for working with this book. However, things may have changed by the time you read this, and it's worth doing a quick test. Open BBEdit or TextWrangler, and enter the following code in a new document:

```
<?php phpinfo(); ?>
```

5. Save the document as index.php in your Sites folder (Macintosh HD:Users:*username*:Sites).

6. Reopen your browser and change the URL to http://localhost/~*username*/index.php. If you see a PHP configuration page similar to Figure 3-8, it means PHP has been enabled. Skip ahead briefly to the section "Checking your PHP configuration (Windows and Mac)" later in the chapter to determine whether your installation has all the necessary features. If it doesn't, come back and carry on with the next section.

If, on the other hand, you see the same raw code that you entered in step 4, you have no choice but to upgrade. Continue with the next section.

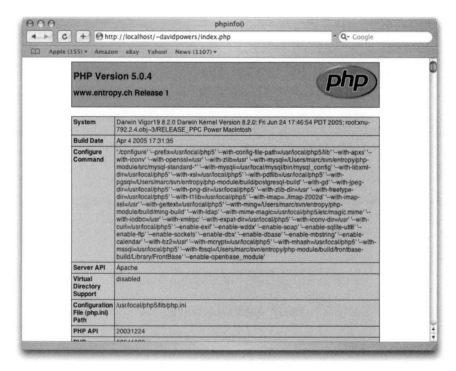

Figure 3-8. The PHP configuration page reveals whether your installation is basic or full-featured.

Upgrading PHP on Mac OS X

The engine underlying Mac OS X is Unix, a very stable multitasking operating system that's been around for more than 30 years. While that's a good thing, it means that installing PHP the traditional way involves compiling it from source code. Without a solid understanding of Unix, this can turn into a nightmare if anything unexpected happens.

Thankfully, it's a route you don't have to take. A software engineer named Marc Liyanage is highly respected in the Mac PHP community for the packages he creates for all major upgrades of PHP. Marc's packages are not only easy to install, he takes the trouble to configure them to support a wide range of extra features. The only drawback is that they involve a large download (some 28MB). Even if you have a slow Internet connection, the large download is worth it. You get a full-featured version of PHP that works "straight out of the box." If you run into problems, there's a searchable support forum on Marc's website, where answers tend to be fast and accurate. It should be your first port of call in case of installation problems.

> *PHP relies heavily on the availability of external code libraries. It is essential that you have installed all the latest Apple system software updates before proceeding.*

1. Marc Liyanage creates different packages for Apache 1.3 and Apache 2. The default installation in Mac OS X at the time of this writing is Apache 1.3, but it's important to check whether it's the same in your case. In Finder, open the Utilities folder within the Applications folder, and launch Terminal.

2. A window like that shown here will open.

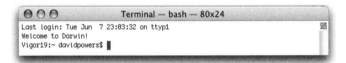

It doesn't look very impressive, but if you've ever worked on a Windows or DOS computer, it should be familiar as the Command Prompt, and it performs the same function. All instructions to the computer are inserted as written commands at what's known as the **shell prompt**. This is the final line in the preceding screenshot, and it looks something like this:

```
Vigor19:~ davidpowers$
```

The first part (before the colon) is the name of your Macintosh hard disk. The tilde (~) is the Unix shorthand for your home directory (or folder). This should be followed by your username and a dollar sign. As you navigate around the hard disk, your location is indicated in place of ~. All commands in Terminal are followed by *RETURN*.

3. To find out which version of Apache is running on your Mac, type the following command:

httpd -v

After pressing *RETURN*, you should see something like this:

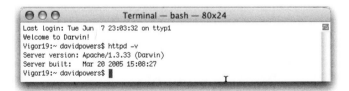

This tells you the version of Apache, and the date it was built. You need the first two numbers of the server version—in this case, 1.3—to ensure that you download the correct PHP package.

4. Go to www.entropy.ch/software/macosx/php/, scroll about halfway down the page, and select the version of PHP 5 for Mac OS X 10.3/10.4 that doesn't require a commercial license for PDFLib (unless you have a license key) and that also matches the version of Apache running on your computer. Read any installation instructions on the site, as they'll contain the most up-to-date information about special requirements or restrictions.

5. When the download is complete, the disk image should automatically mount the contents on your desktop. If it doesn't, just double-click it. The Extras folder contains either the commercial or the noncommercial version of the PDFLib library, neither of which is required for this book. Copy the Extras folder to your hard disk, and explore it later. Double-click the PHP PKG file and follow the instructions onscreen.

6. Your upgraded version of PHP will become available as soon as you restart Apache, but before you do that, you need to make a minor change to the PHP configuration file, php.ini.

Configuring PHP to display errors on Mac OS X

Marc Liyanage's package for PHP uses a version of php.ini that automatically turns off the display of error messages. Although no one likes seeing error messages, when using PHP for development, it's essential to see what's gone wrong and why.

1. Open BBEdit or TextWrangler. From the File menu, choose Open Hidden, and navigate to Macintosh HD:usr:local:php5:lib:php.ini. Because php.ini is a protected file, you need to select All Files from the Enable drop-down menu at the top of the Open dialog box. Click Open.

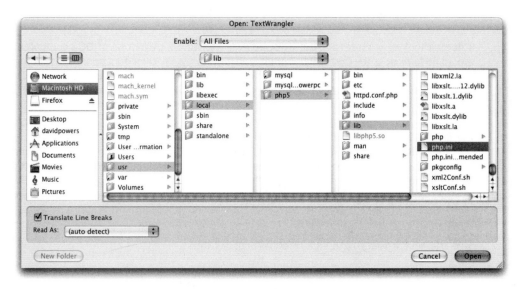

2. When php.ini opens in your text editor, you'll see that it's a long text file, and that most lines begin with a semicolon. This means they are comments; the configuration commands are on lines that don't have a semicolon at the beginning.

To make it easier to identify the correct place in the files you edit, choose Preferences from the BBEdit or TextWrangler menu, and then select Text Status Display. Make sure the Show Line Numbers check box is selected. Close the Preferences dialog box, and scroll down until you see the command shown on line 353 in the screenshot shown alongside:

3. The icon of a pencil with a line through it (shown at the top left of the previous screenshot) indicates that this is a read-only file. To edit it, click the pencil icon. You will see the following prompt:

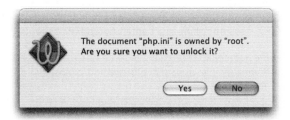

4. Click Yes, and change the command shown on line 353 as follows (use the line number just as a guide—it may be different in a later version of PHP):

```
display_errors = On
```

5. About 10 lines further down, locate the following command:

```
log_errors = On
```

Change it to

```
log_errors = Off
```

6. From the File menu, choose Save, and enter your Mac administrator password when prompted. Close php.ini.

7. Restart Apache and test PHP as described in the section titled "Starting Apache and testing PHP" earlier in the chapter. This time you should see a PHP configuration page like that shown in Figure 3-8.

> You may have noticed that Figure 3-8 shows PHP 5.0.4, whereas Figure 3-5 in the Windows section shows PHP 5.0.5. Marc Liyanage compiles the Mac PKG files on an entirely voluntary basis. As a result, Mac versions usually lag a short time behind the official PHP release.

As a result of these two small changes, error messages will now be displayed onscreen instead of being written to a log file. If you ever need to make further adjustments to your PHP configuration, follow the same procedure to edit php.ini, and restart Apache for the changes to take effect.

Checking your PHP configuration (Windows and Mac)

The screen full of information produced by phpinfo(), as shown in Figures 3-5 and 3-8, is a useful way of checking your configuration, and it provides a lot more detail than you would get by studying php.ini. What's more, it's in a very user-friendly format; everything is grouped together logically and usually in alphabetical order. The problem for beginners is that it feels like information overload. The following is a quick guide to the most important information, to help you check whether your installation is set up correctly to work through the rest of this book.

Version number The section at the top of the page contains two vital pieces of information: the PHP version number, and the path to php.ini. You should be using a minimum of PHP 4.3.0, and preferably PHP 5.0.5 or above. (PHP 5 is required for Chapter 12.)

Configuration File Path The location of php.ini depends on your system, but the important thing to check is that the value of Configuration File (php.ini) Path actually ends in php.ini. If your installation of PHP on Mac OS X does not point to a configuration file, it should be upgraded.

Windows users sometimes complain that changes to php.ini have no effect. This normally happens after upgrading from a version that used the old method of installation, and it means they have a duplicate of php.ini in their Windows system folder, which is taking precedence. The value of Configuration File (php.ini) Path tells you which file Windows is reading at startup. Remove the one from the Windows folder, and restart your web server.

PHP Core This long list shows the values of the main configuration settings. In most cases, the default settings are fine. Table 3-1 lists the settings that you need to check for this book, together with the recommended values.

Table 3-1. Recommended PHP configuration settings

Directive	Local value	Remarks
display_errors	On	Essential for debugging mistakes in your scripts. If set to Off, errors result in a completely blank screen, leaving you clueless as to the possible cause.
error_reporting	2047	This displays all levels of error message, apart from E_STRICT (a specialist type of error of interest mainly to advanced users). Although displayed as a number in the PHP configuration page, the setting in php.ini should be E_ALL.
extension_dir	See remarks	This is the location of Windows DLL files for extensions that expand the core functionality of PHP. If you installed PHP 5 to the location recommended in this chapter, this should be C:\php5\ext\. The value is unimportant on a Mac.
file_uploads	On	Self-explanatory. Allows you to use PHP for uploading files.
log_errors	Off	With display_errors set on, you don't need to fill your hard disk with an error log.

Directive	Local value	Remarks
magic_quotes_gpc	See remarks	The default in Windows is On, and Off in a Mac. Both are acceptable, because Dreamweaver code is designed to cope with either value. The significance of this setting, together with a strategy to cope with it when writing your own PHP, will be explained in Chapter 6.
register_globals	Off	This is an extremely important security setting. This setting is turned off by default. Do not listen to anyone who tells you life will be easier if you turn register_globals on. This issue will be dealt with in detail in Chapter 6.

The rest of the configuration page shows you which PHP extensions are enabled. Mac users will have many more listed than the average Windows user because extensions need to be built in at compile time on the Mac. Windows users can turn extensions on and off very quickly by editing the Dynamic Extensions section of `php.ini` and restarting their web server.

To work with this book, you need the following extensions enabled:

- gd (should be at least version 2)
- mbstring
- mysql (the Client API version should preferably be at least 4.1)
- mysqli (not available on PHP 4)
- pcre
- session
- xsl (not available on PHP 4)

> *Your computer reads the PHP configuration file only when the web server first starts up, so any changes to* `php.ini` *always require Apache or IIS to be restarted for them to take effect.*

Setting up virtual hosts

This section is entirely optional. If you don't need to set up virtual hosts as described earlier in the chapter, skip ahead to the section "Defining a PHP site in Dreamweaver." You can come back and set up virtual hosts at any time.

Creating virtual hosts on your local computer is a two-step process: First you need to tell the operating system the names of the virtual hosts; then you need to tell the web server where to find the files.

Registering virtual hosts on Windows

Most desktop versions of Windows do not support the creation of multiple virtual hosts on IIS. You need to be running a minimum of IIS 6 on a Windows Server System. You can, however, use virtual directories, described in the section "Registering virtual directories on IIS" later in this chapter.

Apache imposes no such restrictions, and allows you to create as many virtual hosts as you want. It's a two-stage process. First, you tell Windows the names of the virtual hosts, and then you tell Apache where the files will be located. This is how you do it:

1. Open `C:\WINDOWS\system32\drivers\etc\hosts` in Notepad or a script editor.

2. It's normally a very short file. Look for the following line at the bottom:

   `127.0.0.1   localhost`

   127.0.0.1 is the IP address that every computer uses to refer to itself.

3. On a separate line, enter 127.0.0.1, followed by some space and the name of the virtual host you want to register. For instance, to set up a virtual host for this book, enter the following:

   `127.0.0.1   phpdw`

4. Add any further virtual hosts you want to register, each on a separate line and pointing to the same IP address. Save the `hosts` file, and close it.

5. Open `C:\Program Files\Apache Group\Apache2\conf\httpd.conf` in a text editor, scroll right down to the bottom, and locate the following section:

```
939  #
940  # Use name-based virtual hosting.
941  #
942 ▶#NameVirtualHost *:80
943
944  #
945  # VirtualHost example:
946  # Almost any Apache directive may go into a VirtualHost container.
947  # The first VirtualHost section is used for requests without a known
948  # server name.
949  #
950  #<VirtualHost *:80>
951  #     ServerAdmin webmaster@dummy-host.example.com
952  #     DocumentRoot /www/docs/dummy-host.example.com
953  #     ServerName dummy-host.example.com
954  #     ErrorLog logs/dummy-host.example.com-error_log
955  #     CustomLog logs/dummy-host.example.com-access_log common
956  #</VirtualHost>
957
```

6. Uncomment the line marked in the screenshot with an arrow. This enables virtual hosting, but disables the main server root, so the first virtual host you create needs to reproduce the original server root. Use the example (on lines 945–56) as a guide. It shows all the commands that can be used, but only DocumentRoot and ServerName are required. If your server root is located, like mine, at `C:\htdocs`, the definition will look like this:

```
NameVirtualHost *:80

<VirtualHost *:80>
  DocumentRoot c:/htdocs
  ServerName localhost
</VirtualHost>
```

> *Don't forget that Apache requires forward slashes in pathnames. You don't need all the settings shown in the example in* httpd.conf, *but you do need to take care that you get the spelling of the commands correct. Apache is case-sensitive, and it doesn't take kindly to unexpected spaces in commands, such as* VirtualHost.

7. Immediately below the definition in step 6, add definitions for any new virtual hosts, using the location of the site's web files as the value for DocumentRoot, and the name of the virtual host for ServerName. If the path contains any spaces, enclose the whole path in quotes. For example:

```
<VirtualHost *:80>
   DocumentRoot "d:/David's documents/Friends of ED/books/phpdw"
   ServerName phpdw
</VirtualHost>
```

8. Save httpd.conf, and restart your computer. All sites in the server root will continue to be accessible through http://localhost/sitename/. Anything in a virtual host will be accessible through a direct address, such as http://phpdw/.

Registering virtual hosts on Mac OS X

This is a two-stage process. First you register the names of any new hosts in NetInfo Manager, and then you add the details of where to find them to the Apache configuration file.

1. In Finder, open NetInfo Manager, which is in the Utilities subfolder of Applications.

2. Click the lock at the bottom left of the dialog box that opens, and enter your administrator's password when prompted.

3. Select machines, then localhost, and click the Duplicate icon. When prompted, confirm that you want to make a copy.

4. Highlight the copy, and double-click the name in the lower pane, as shown in the screenshot alongside.

5. Change localhost copy to whatever you want to call the virtual host. For example, to create a virtual host for this book, enter phpdw.

6. Click any of the other entries in the left column of the top pane. The operating system will ask you twice if you really want to make the changes. You do. This registers the name of the virtual host with your computer. The next stage is to tell Apache where to find the web files.

7. Repeat steps 3 through 6 for any other virtual hosts you want to create. When you have finished, click the lock in the bottom-left corner of the NetInfo Manager, and close it.

8. Open BBEdit or TextWrangler, and select File ➤ Open Hidden. In the Open dialog box, select All Files from the Enable drop-down menu, and open Macintosh HD:etc:httpd:httpd.conf.

9. Scroll right down to the bottom, and locate the following section:

```
1073  #
1074  # Use name-based virtual hosting.
1075  #
1076  #NameVirtualHost *:80
1077
1078  #
1079  # VirtualHost example:
1080  # Almost any Apache directive may go into a VirtualHost container.
1081  # The first VirtualHost section is used for requests without a known
1082  # server name.
1083  #
1084  #<VirtualHost *:80>
1085  #     ServerAdmin webmaster@dummy-host.example.com
1086  #     DocumentRoot /www/docs/dummy-host.example.com
1087  #     ServerName dummy-host.example.com
1088  #     ErrorLog logs/dummy-host.example.com-error_log
1089  #     CustomLog logs/dummy-host.example.com-access_log common
1090  #</VirtualHost>
```

10. Click the pencil icon at the top left of the editor window, and confirm that you want to unlock the document, entering your administrator password when prompted. Uncomment the command shown on line 1076 in the screenshot by removing the hash sign (#). This enables virtual hosting, but disables the main server root, so the first virtual host needs to reproduce the Mac's server root. The example (on lines 1084–90) is there to show you how to define a virtual host. The only required commands are DocumentRoot and ServerName. After uncommenting the NameVirtualHost command, your first definition should look like this:

```
NameVirtualHost *:80

<VirtualHost *:80>
  DocumentRoot /Library/WebServer/Documents
  ServerName localhost
</VirtualHost>
```

11. Add any further definitions for virtual hosts. For instance, to create one for this book, I used the following:

```
<VirtualHost *:80>
  DocumentRoot /Users/davidpowers/Sites/phpdw
  ServerName phpdw
</VirtualHost>
```

12. Save httpd.conf, and restart Apache. All sites in your Sites folder can still be accessed using http://localhost/~username/sitename/, but named virtual hosts can be accessed directly, such as http://phpdw/. Of course, the site must exist in the location you defined before you can actually use a virtual host.

Registering virtual directories on IIS

Virtual directories are not as useful as virtual hosts because `localhost` always remains the basic address of the web server, so you cannot use them with links relative to the site root. They do come in useful, though, by avoiding the need to locate all web files in the default IIS server root at `C:\Inetput\wwwroot`. This means you can leave your sites wherever they are on your hard disk, but still get IIS to parse your PHP scripts when viewed through a browser.

To set up a virtual directory in IIS, open the Internet Information Services panel (Start ➤ Control Panel ➤ Administrative Tools ➤ Internet Information Services), highlight Default Web Server, right-click, and select New ➤ Virtual Directory. A wizard will appear and step you through the process.

Defining a PHP site in Dreamweaver

If you're a regular Dreamweaver user, I don't need to tell you the importance of site definition; it's how Dreamweaver organizes your web files and makes sure that links point to the right place. If you're in a hurry, and working with static web files, Dreamweaver will let you create a quick page without saving it within a defined site. That won't work with PHP pages. Dreamweaver uses the site definition to determine which tools to make available to you. Unless you choose the correct server model, all the PHP server behaviors will be inaccessible.

> It's also important to locate your PHP files in a folder that your web server recognizes as being within the server root, a virtual host, or a virtual directory, as described earlier in this chapter. The only exception is if you decide not to install a web server and PHP on your local computer.
>
> If you decide to use your remote server as the testing server, you will still be able to use Dreamweaver Live Data view, but only while actively connected to the Internet. You will also need to upload your files to the remote server every time you want to test them or preview them in a browser.

The following instructions show you how to set up a new site, but the procedure is almost identical for converting an existing site definition to support PHP. I suggest you create a new folder called `phpdw` in your server root (or as a virtual host or virtual directory), and use these instructions to define the site for the case study that you'll start work on in the next chapter.

1. Choose New Site from the Dreamweaver Site menu. This is a small, but very welcome, change in Dreamweaver 8, as it takes you directly to the Site Definition dialog box, instead of going through an intermediate step.

   To convert an existing site, choose Site ➤ Manage Sites, select the site name from the list, and click Edit.

2. When the Site Definition dialog box opens, select the Advanced tab, and make sure Local Info is highlighted in the Category column on the left. This is where you enter details of all the files related to a specific site, so that Dreamweaver knows where to find all the web pages, images, and PHP scripts on your local computer. Figure 3-9 shows the settings I used for the files in this book on both Windows and Mac OS X.

The value for Site name can be a descriptive name that includes spaces, but remember that it will be displayed in the drop-down menu in the Files panel, so should be relatively brief.

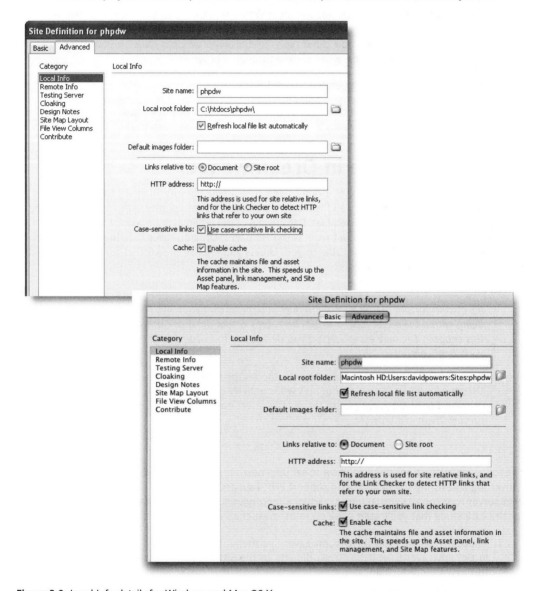

Figure 3-9. Local Info details for Windows and Mac OS X

Mac users should, of course, use their own username in the Local root folder field.

The Local Info category has two settings that are new to Dreamweaver 8. They both set site-wide options for the handling of links. The first lets you choose whether links are set relative to the document (the default) or to the site root. To avoid problems with include files, you should normally leave this option on the default Document when working with a PHP site. The other new option allows you to specify case-sensitive link checking. Although this is not checked by default, I recommend that you select it. Most PHP hosts run on Linux or Unix servers, which are case-sensitive. Choosing this option will help eliminate problems with using the wrong case in filenames.

I have not entered a URL in the HTTP address field because I don't intend putting the files on a live site, but you can fill in your own URL. I've also left Default images folder blank because this is an optional setting. The Refresh local file list automatically and Cache check boxes are selected by default, and I suggest you leave them selected.

3. Select Remote Info from the Category list. This is where you enter the details of how to connect to your remote server, and it is exactly the same as for a static website. Choose the upload method you plan to use from the Access drop-down menu, and fill in the appropriate fields. For Windows users only, the options for uploading to your remote server have been expanded in Dreamweaver 8 to include Microsoft Visual SourceSafe.

There is no need to fill in this section at this stage, even if you plan to use your remote server as the testing server. You can come back to this later when you're ready to deploy your site on the Internet. If you need any help filling in the Remote Info details, click the Help button at the bottom of the dialog box. This opens the Dreamweaver help files at the correct page with detailed instructions for the information required in each field.

4. Select Testing Server from the Category list. **This is probably the most important dialog box when building dynamic sites in Dreamweaver**. It's quite easy to fill in, but if you get the details wrong, Dreamweaver will be unable to communicate with any of your databases.

When you first open the Testing Server category, it should look like the following screenshot (the Mac version is identical, so I'll show only the Windows version):

Normally, the Server model drop-down menu will display None, but if you have ColdFusion installed on your computer, it may "helpfully" preselect that choice for you. Whatever value is displayed, open the menu, and select PHP MySQL.

The Access drop-down menu determines how you will communicate with the testing server. If you have set up a local test environment on your own computer or another computer that you can access over a LAN, choose Local/Network. If you don't have a local testing environment, choose FTP.

Depending on your choice, Dreamweaver will display a different set of further options for you to fill in. If you chose Local/Network, follow the instructions in steps 5 and 6. If you chose FTP, skip to step 7.

5. When using your local computer or another one on the same LAN, Dreamweaver presents you with the following options, and attempts to fill in the details for you:

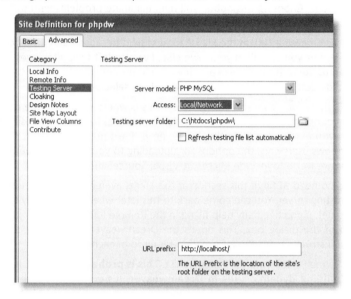

The value entered in Testing server folder will normally be correct. It should be the same folder that you selected as the Local root folder in step 2. In this example, it would be C:\htdocs\phpdw\ on Windows, or Macintosh HD:Users:*username*:Sites:phpdw: on a Mac. Note that in both cases, the pathname ends with a trailing backslash (or colon on the Mac). This is very important. If, for some reason, the wrong folder is displayed here, use the folder icon to the right of the field to browse to the correct location. That way, you can be sure that Dreamweaver will use the correct syntax.

Select the Refresh testing file list automatically check box immediately below.

The correct value for URL prefix depends on your operating system and configuration. Assuming that the site is called phpdw, choose the appropriate URL prefix from the following:

- If the site is in a subfolder of the server root of the same machine on Windows: http://localhost/phpdw/

- If the site is in a subfolder of your Sites folder of the same machine on a Mac: http://localhost/~*username*/phpdw/

- If the site is in a subfolder of Macintosh HD:Library:WebServer:Documents on the same Mac: http://localhost/phpdw/

- If the site is in a virtual host called phpdw on either Windows or a Mac: http://phpdw/

- If the site is in an IIS virtual directory: http://localhost/phpdw/

- If the site is on a different computer on a LAN: substitute localhost with the correct IP address of the other computer

Note that all the preceding examples include a trailing slash at the end of the URL prefix. Do *not* omit the trailing slash.

Unless you need to change the settings in any of the other categories of the Site Definition dialog box, click OK, and then click Done.

6. You will probably be presented with an alert box like the one shown alongside, warning you that the URL prefix specified in the previous step doesn't match the HTTP Address in Local Info. This matters only if you create links that are relative to the site root. As noted earlier, you should avoid doing this with PHP sites unless you have defined a virtual host on your testing server, so you can ignore this warning. Even if you do want to take heed of it, a bug in the first release of Dreamweaver 8 makes the choice of buttons meaningless. Even if you click Cancel, Dreamweaver goes ahead and creates the site definition, which is now complete.

7. If you decide you want to use a remote server to test all your files, Dreamweaver presents you with the following dialog box, requesting a similar set of details to those required for uploading your files:

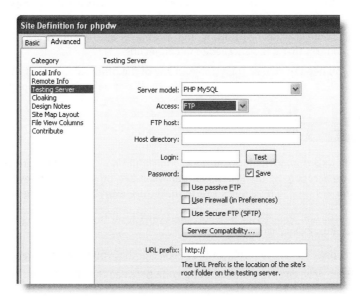

Even if you have filled in the Remote Info category, it's necessary to fill it in again here, although Dreamweaver is intelligent enough to copy across the main details. When using a remote server as your testing server, it's a good idea to create a dedicated test folder on your remote server, and use that as the setting for Host directory. For instance, if my main site is located in /home/dpowers/htdocs/, I would create a subfolder called phptest inside htdocs, and set the Host directory for the phpdw site as /home/dpowers/htdocs/phptest/ (don't forget the trailing slash).

Your next instinct will probably be to click the Test button to make sure that you can connect successfully to the host directory. If you do, you'll get a lengthy error message like this:

Before checking that you can connect, you must set the URL prefix. You must also create the folder for the host directory on the remote server yourself—Dreamweaver cannot create it for you. The value of the URL prefix is simply the URL for the site that you are testing. So if your domain name is www.example.com, and the test site is to be located in a folder called phptest, the correct URL prefix will be http://www.example.com/phptest/. Again, don't forget the trailing slash.

You can now click the Test button, and as long as all the details are correct, Dreamweaver should confirm that it has succeeded in connecting.

Unless you need to change the settings in any of the other categories of the Site Definition dialog box, click OK, and then click Done. Your PHP site definition is complete.

Testing your PHP site

If you have followed the instructions carefully, you should now have a PHP site within Dreamweaver that will give you access to all the PHP server behaviors and other PHP features. Before moving on to the next chapter, it's wise to do a quick test to make sure everything's working as expected.

1. In Dreamweaver, select File ➤ New, and in the New Document dialog box choose Dynamic Page ➤ PHP, and click Create.

2. Save the page as datetest.php in the phpdw site that you have just created.

3. Open Split view, and type the following code between the <body> tags:

```php
<?php
echo date('l, F jS, Y');
?>
```

Make sure you copy the code exactly (the first character after the opening quote is a lowercase L), or copy and paste it from the download files for this book. Don't worry about the meaning of the script. You'll soon see what it does.

The first thing you should notice is that Dreamweaver displays the opening and closing PHP tags in a bold red font, while echo and date are pale blue. If this doesn't happen, check that your filename ends with .php. Also select View ➤ Code View Options, and make sure that there's a check mark next to Syntax Coloring. If there isn't, click Syntax Coloring to toggle the setting on. The significance of the coloring will be explained in Chapter 5.

4. Click inside the Design view section of the page, and a gold shield labeled PHP should appear, as shown alongside. This marks the location of your PHP script.

5. Click the Live Data view button, as shown alongside or press CTRL+SHIFT+R/SHIFT+⌘+R. As long as your web server is running, you should see today's date displayed in Design view. It will be highlighted in a different color (the default is pale yellow) to indicate that it's dynamically generated output. You'll learn about the first part of the script—echo—in Chapter 5; it's one of the most basic commands in PHP that is used all the time. The rather cryptic aspects of the rest of the script will be covered in Chapter 6 when we delve into the mysteries of working with dates in PHP.

As soon as you click the Live Data view button again, the date will disappear and be replaced by the PHP gold shield.

Points to watch when using a remote server for testing

Dreamweaver tries to make everything seamless, regardless of whether you use a local or a remote web server for testing. However, there are several important differences that you should be aware of when using a remote testing server.

- It will take some time before Live Data view displays the output, because it needs to transfer the script across the Internet, rather than just handle it locally.

- If you check your remote server after completing the previous exercise, you will see that datetest.php isn't there. Dreamweaver uses the remote server to parse the script, and then stores it in a temporary file on your local computer. This temporary file remains hidden in the Files panel on Windows but is displayed on a Mac. Any such temporary files are removed automatically when you switch to another site in Dreamweaver or close the program. If you test a file that's in a new folder, Dreamweaver will create a folder with the same name on the remote server, but not the file itself.

■ If you decide to preview a file in a browser, the absence of a local server to parse the file means that Dreamweaver must first upload it to the remote server. It will do this even if you haven't entered any details in the Remote Info category of the Site Definition dialog box. Whenever you select File ➤ Preview in Browser (*F12/OPT+F12*), you will be warned—as shown in the screenshot—that your action may affect anyone else working on the file (because it will overwrite whatever version is on the remote server). This is important only if you're part of a team working on the same set of files.

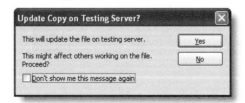

■ If you accept updating the file on the testing server, you will be given the choice to upload any dependent files, such as images. Unless you click Yes within the time specified, only the web page itself will be uploaded.

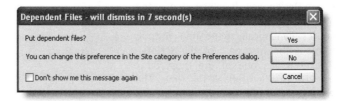

■ If you're on dial-up, and have chosen to use your remote server for testing, be aware that Dreamweaver automatically connects to the Internet every time you use Live Data view, and it doesn't automatically disconnect when you toggle Live Data view off. Unless you take care, you could end up with very large communications charges.

Now you're set to go . . .

This has been a long chapter—and deliberately so. If you decided to set up a local testing environment, you should now have the following:

■ A web server (Apache or IIS)

■ PHP 5 correctly configured to work with Dreamweaver 8 and all the exercises in this book

■ A file system within the server root, virtual hosts, or virtual directories ready for processing by the PHP engine

Whether testing locally or using a remote server, you should also have a properly defined PHP site within Dreamweaver. Fortunately, the setup process is something you need to go through only occasionally. Once you have worked through this chapter, you shouldn't need to come back to it unless you want to change your configuration or migrate to another computer, or perhaps refresh your memory about site definition.

There's one more element you need to set up—the MySQL database and a useful graphical interface for MySQL called phpMyAdmin. Rather than burden you with setting up more software at this stage, I want to get on with building a dynamic website in Dreamweaver 8. The next chapter is relatively short, and it shows you how to set up the case study around which the rest of this book is based. Then in Chapters 5 and 6 I'll show you how to put PHP through its paces, using such features as including data from external files and emailing the contents of an online form to your mailbox.

Chapter 4

GETTING READY FOR THE CASE STUDY

What this chapter covers:

- Introducing the East-West Seasons case study
- Making the best use of the download files
- Installing a handy extension for filler text
- Converting a graphic layout to CSS
- Building the basic pages
- Creating sites that degrade gracefully in legacy browsers
- Using `<link>` and `@import` to attach stylesheets
- Using conditional comments in place of CSS hacks

Throughout the rest of the book, you'll work on a case study that I've called "East-West Seasons." The idea for the site came from some photographs that I took at different times of the year in Britain, where I live, and in Japan, a country that I worked in for many years as a journalist. Figure 4-1 shows what the front page of the site looks like.

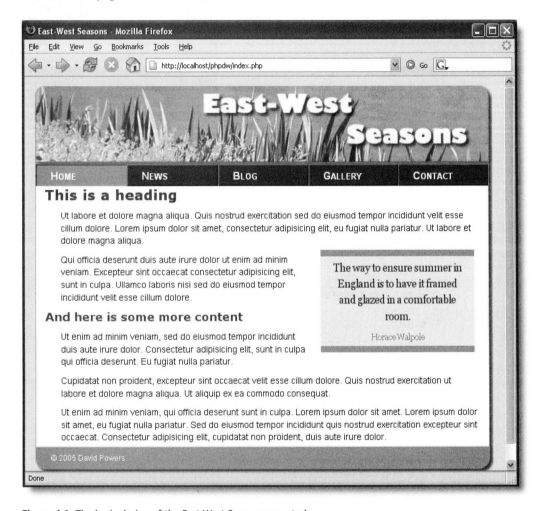

Figure 4-1. The basic design of the East-West Seasons case study

It's a generic website that can be adapted to a variety of uses. I hope that you'll work through each part of the case study, but you can just pick and choose those elements that you need. By the time you have finished, you will have learned how to do the following:

- Use PHP includes for common page elements and frequently changed text (Chapter 5)
- Create dynamic text that displays only when certain conditions are met (Chapter 5)

- Automatically change the design at random or depending on the time of the year (Chapter 6)
- Activate an online contact form that validates the details before emailing them to you (Chapter 6)
- Install a MySQL database system (Chapter 7)
- Build a random quotation generator (Chapter 8)
- Insert, update, and delete records in a multiple-table database (Chapter 9)
- Password-protect your content management system and other parts of your site (Chapter 10)
- Create a blog, and build an online gallery of photos (Chapter 11)
- Display a live news feed with Dreamweaver 8's new XSLT server behavior (Chapter 12)

You may be thinking, "But I don't want to create a random quotation generator; what I need is to create an online catalog that will display my company's products." No problem. An online catalog involves exactly the same principles as any other database-driven site. What's important is storing the information in a database, and knowing how to get it out again. Similarly, you may not want to create a photo gallery, but you almost certainly will need to know how to manage images in a database.

Creating the basic structure of East-West Seasons

There are two ways of approaching the design of a dynamic website. One might be called the "CSS Zen Garden approach" (after the CSS showcase at www.csszengarden.com), whereby you begin by creating content that's totally unstyled, and then add the design only at the final stage. This gives you the freedom to concentrate on the PHP and MySQL programming side, without having to worry about the final look of the site. Although your web pages *should* look logical without any styling, it's an approach that doesn't come easily to most design-oriented people. So, the alternative is to create a static design, and then slot in the dynamic elements.

For the front end of the East-West Seasons site, I've decided to take the second approach—not only because it's easier, but also because it gives me the chance to show you how to adapt an existing site to take advantage of the dynamic techniques you'll learn throughout this book.

Organizing the download files for the case study

All the files for this book can be downloaded from www.friendsofed.com/downloads.php. To enable you to concentrate on creating the dynamic code, the files include each page as it should be at the start of the chapter (except where you begin with a blank page, as in this chapter), as well as at the main stages of development, so you can pick up at almost any point.

> *All the photos in the download files were taken by me, and are there to help you complete the exercises in this book. If you want to use them for anything else, please contact me through friends of ED for terms and written permission. There is no restriction on the use of the code or CSS design.*

When you unzip the download files, you will find six main folders. Copy them and all their contents into the phpdw site that you defined in the previous chapter. Together with the datetest.php file that you created in Chapter 3, you should then have a site structure like that shown alongside. This is what the folders contain:

- **examples**: Most of the book is dedicated to working on the case study, but from time to time I will include basic examples of working with PHP. To make the examples easy to find, they are organized in subfolders according to the chapter they appear in.

- **extensions**: I have included a small number of Dreamweaver extensions that you can install to cut down on typing.

- **images_blog**: These are images for the blog in Chapter 11.

- **images_common**: These are the main images for the East-West Seasons case study.

- **images_gallery**: These are images for an online gallery in Chapter 11.

- **site_check**: This contains all the files for the East-West Seasons case study, organized by chapter.

The reason I have organized things this way is so that you will have two local copies of each file—the original download copy in the site_check folder and the version that you create as you work through the book. This way, you can use Dreamweaver 8's new built-in file compare feature (described in Chapter 2) to quickly identify any differences between your files and mine. So, when things go wrong, you won't need to pore over your code line by line, trying to spot what's causing the problem.

Create a new folder called testarea at the root level of your site, and move datetest.php into it. I suggest you use testarea to create your own copies of any example files. This will leave the root level of the phpdw site free for you to work on the main case study. As you progress through each chapter, you can find all the files for the case study in the relevant subfolder of site_check. Where a file goes through several stages of development during a chapter, each stage is indicated by a number at the end of the filename. So, for instance, you will find four versions of index.php in the ch08 folder, numbered index_01.php through index_04.php.

> *The best way to learn anything is by doing it yourself, but if you just want to read through the code and test it, copy the appropriate file from the site_check folder and paste it in the root level of the phpdw site. If Dreamweaver prompts you to update the links, choose Don't Update—the links are already correct. For the navigation links to work, you will also need to change the filename to remove the underscore and number. So index_04.php needs to be renamed index.php. Again, choose Don't Update when prompted to update any links.*

Installing Lorem and More

Inside the `extensions` folder, you'll find Lorem and More, a Dreamweaver extension that I created a few years ago. It's Dreamweaver-approved, so you can install it with confidence that it won't do any damage to your program. It simply speeds up the process of creating dummy text for the design stage of a website.

To install it, double-click the `Lorem_andMore1_21.mxp` icon in Windows Explorer (or Finder on a Mac). Click Accept in the dialog box that opens, and make sure the drop-down menu in the Extension Manager displays Dreamweaver 8. Alternatively, you can launch the Extension Manager  independently or from within Dreamweaver by selecting Manage Extensions from either the Commands or Help menu, and choose File ➤ Install Extension to browse to the MXP file's location. After the extension has been installed, you need to restart Dreamweaver before you can access it.

> *Access to the Extension Manager is now available on both the* Commands *and the* Help *menus in Dreamweaver 8 for greater conformity with Flash and Fireworks. That's a trivial change, but one that's very welcome is that the Extension Manager now lists all the extensions you had installed in a previous version of Dreamweaver. All you have to do is place a check mark in the* On/Off *check box to activate those extensions that you want to migrate to Dreamweaver 8.*
>
> *On a Mac, double-clicking the MXP file sometimes opens the Extension Manager, but fails to install the extension. If this happens, click the* Install *icon in the Extension Manager toolbar or select* File ➤ Install Extension.

Analyzing the main page layout

If you look at Figure 4-1, you can see that the page consists of four basic areas—a title area containing an image, a navigation area, the main body of the page, and a footer. The pull quote on the right will be added in Chapter 8, so you can ignore that for the time being.

I designed the page in Fireworks, the companion graphics program to Dreamweaver, but instead of using Fireworks to slice the images and export a series of nested tables, I decided to reproduce the same effect with CSS. By dividing the page into a series of blocks, which can be styled as `<div>`s, I was able to build the page with just four images. Figure 4-2 shows how I sliced up the design.

Figure 4-2. How the basic design was exported as four JPG images from Fireworks

Here is a brief description of each of the images:

- **bluebells_bg.jpg**: This is a 50-pixel square that will be tiled right across the main background.
- **bluebells_top.jpg**: This is the main title image with rounded corners at the top that blend in with the background. The photograph itself is 732 pixels wide, but I added a drop shadow to the whole design in Fireworks, bringing the overall width of the image to 738 pixels.
- **bluebells_footer.jpg**: Like the main title image, this has rounded corners designed to blend in with the background. With the drop shadow, it is also 738 pixels wide.
- **bluebells_side.jpg**: This is just 10px wide by 15px high, and will be used to continue the drop shadow down the side of the main content area. Modern browsers allow you to specify the position of background images, so there's no need to make it the full width of the page.

"What about images for the navigation buttons?" you may be asking. There aren't any; the buttons—complete with rollover effect—are built entirely with CSS.

The underlying structure of the page is shown in Figure 4-3. As you can see, everything is enclosed in a wrapper <div>, which simply holds everything together and makes it easy to center the whole design in the browser viewport.

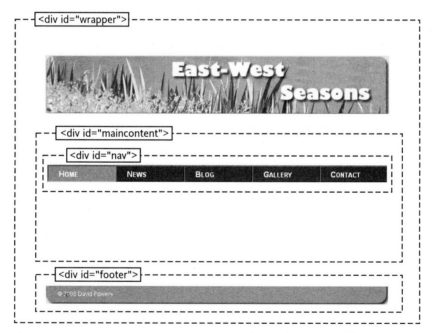

Figure 4-3. The underlying structure of the basic design consists of four <div>s nested inside a wrapper <div>.

If you're used to designing with tables, you may wonder, why bother? This design uses less code, is more accessible, and can be styled much more flexibly with CSS—that's why.

Building the East-West Seasons pages

You can find the completed pages for this chapter in the ch04 subfolder of site_check. I recommend, however, that you build the pages yourself, as the following exercise introduces you to some important changes to this version of Dreamweaver.

1. From the File menu, select New; and in the New Document dialog box, select Dynamic Page and PHP as shown in the following screenshot. Also make sure that Document Type (DTD) is set to XHTML 1.0 Transitional. If you prefer to use HTML, don't forget that all the code shown in this book will conform to XHTML rules, so you will have to make your own adjustments accordingly. Click Create.

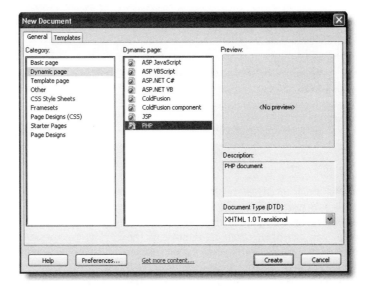

2. Give the page a title, such as "East-West Seasons," and save it in the site root as index.php.

3. The increased focus on CSS design in Dreamweaver 8 means that it's a lot easier to insert a <div> now. Instead of hiding the Insert Div Tag icon in the Layout category of the Insert bar, it's been brought out to a place of honor in the Common category (although it's still there in the Layout category for those who find it hard to break old habits). Make sure your cursor is inside Design view, and click the Insert Div Tag icon on the Common Insert bar, as shown alongside. It will bring up the following dialog box:

If you ever used Insert Div Tag in Dreamweaver MX 2004, you'll notice that there's an additional button on the dialog box now—New CSS Style—that provides a shortcut to the dialog boxes for defining CSS styles. One of the many CSS improvements in Dreamweaver 8 is that the New CSS Style dialog box will automatically select the class or ID of the current element. Unfortunately, the class or ID for your new <div> doesn't yet exist, and won't be picked up if you click the New CSS Style button here, so it's more efficient to create the style rules later.

The important things to concentrate on here are the values of the Insert and ID fields. Since your cursor was in an empty page in Design view, the default value of At insertion point is exactly what you want. In the ID field, type wrapper, and click OK.

4. If you open Split view, your page should now look like this:

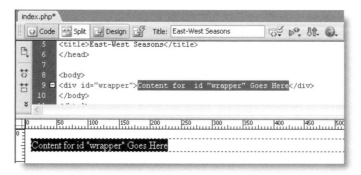

As you can see, a pair of <div> tags has been inserted, together with an ID attribute in the opening tag, and some filler text. Because only the text between the tags is highlighted, you can press *DELETE* to remove it. The <div> tags should remain, with your cursor placed between them. The new visual aids in Dreamweaver 8 also show the <div> is still there by placing a dotted outline around it in Design view. If you can't see a dotted outline, click the Visual Aids icon at the far right of the Document toolbar, and make sure that CSS Layout Outlines has a check mark next to it. (You can also access Visual Aids from the View menu.)

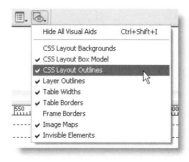

5. Click Insert Div Tag again. You want all the other <div>s to go inside the wrapper <div>, so accept At insertion point as the value for Insert, and type titlebar in the ID field. Click OK.

6. Press *DELETE* to remove the filler text, and insert bluebells_top.jpg from the images_common folder. Whichever method you use to insert an image—by clicking the image icon on the Common Insert bar, by choosing Insert ➤ Image, by dragging the image filename from the Files panel, or by pressing *CTRL+ALT+I/OPT+⌘+I*—Dreamweaver 8 now presents you by default with an extra dialog box for accessibility attributes. Normally, you only need to fill in the Alternate text field. This sets the alt attribute (often incorrectly called the "alt tag") inside the <img> tag to provide a text alternative for anyone not using a visual browser or who has images turned off. The recommended length for alternate text is a maximum of 50 characters. Type in something suitable, like "East-West Seasons," as shown here:

The Long description field sets the longdesc attribute, which should contain the URL of a text file with a more detailed description of the image. The longdesc attribute is not required, unless you need to comply with strict accessibility guidelines. Even then, it's only required if the image is complex, like a graph, and needs further explanation. Dreamweaver 8 automatically inserts http:// in the field as a hint. There is no need to remove it. When you click OK, Dreamweaver 8 will ignore Long description unless you have entered a different value.

> You can prevent the display of this dialog box by clicking the change the Accessibility preferences *link at the bottom. This opens the* Accessibility *category of* Preferences, *where you can deselect the* Images *option for* Show attributes when inserting. *Before taking that step, remember that the* alt *attribute is required for all images. To insert a "null"* alt *text (*alt=""*), open the drop-down menu in the* Alternate text *field and select* <empty>. *If you decide to disable this dialog box, and want to restore it, open* Preferences *from the* Edit *menu (or the* Dreamweaver *menu on a Mac), choose* Accessibility, *and reselect* Images.

7. Click Insert Div Tag again. If the code for the image you have just inserted is still highlighted, the value of the Insert field will be Wrap around selection. You don't want the maincontent <div> to be wrapped around the image, so open the drop-down menu for the Insert field, and select After tag. This will activate a new drop-down menu alongside the Insert field, listing all the <div>s on the page that have IDs. Select <div id="titlebar">. Type maincontent into the ID field, as shown here, and click OK.

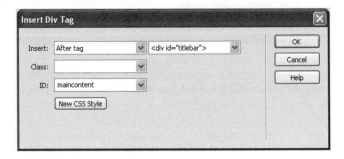

8. This time, *don't* delete the filler text for the maincontent <div>. Each page in the site will have different content, so it's useful to keep the filler text in place.

107

9. If you look back at Figure 4-3, you'll see that the nav <div> is nested inside maincontent. This means you either need to position your cursor in the right part of the code—immediately after <div id="maincontent">—or you can get Dreamweaver to do it for you. This is how: Click the Insert Div Tag button. You want the new <div> after the start tag of the maincontent <div>, so select After start of tag from the Insert drop-down menu. Dreamweaver offers you four choices. Choose <div id="maincontent">, as shown in the following screenshot. Type nav in the ID field and click OK.

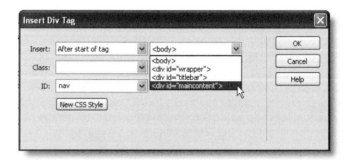

10. Check that your page looks like this in Split view:

11. Replace the filler text for the nav <div> with an unordered list (click the Unordered List button in the Property inspector, or select Text ➤ List ➤ Unordered List) of the following items:

- Home
- News
- Blog
- Gallery
- Contact

12. Highlight Home, and use the Property inspector to create a link to index.php. Highlight each other item in turn and link it to a PHP page of the same name as the link. For instance, link News to news.php, and so on. The pages don't exist yet, but you'll create them soon.

13. Now create the footer <div> by clicking Insert Div Tag. Select After tag from the Insert drop-down menu. You want the footer to go after the maincontent <div>, so choose <div id="maincontent"> from the second drop-down menu that appears. Type footer in the ID field, and click OK.

14. Replace the filler text for the footer <div> with the copyright symbol (it's in the drop-down menu at the far right of the Text Insert bar, or select Insert ➤ HTML ➤ Special Characters ➤ Copyright) followed by the year, and your name. Turn it into a paragraph by selecting Paragraph from the Format option in the Property inspector.

15. Save index.php. Then save four copies of the page as news.php, blog.php, gallery.php, and contact.php. In case you're wondering, I have deliberately avoided using Dreamweaver templates. Once you start working with PHP and databases, the need to handle editable and non-editable regions would make the case study unnecessarily complex. As you will see in the next chapter, PHP includes (the PHP equivalent of SSI, or server-side includes) offer a fascinating alternative to templates, and they can reduce dramatically the number of pages that need to be uploaded whenever you change part of the basic design.

16. Make sure that you're working in index.php. Remove the filler text for maincontent by highlighting it in Design view and pressing DELETE. Keep Split view open to make sure that you select only the text, and not any of the surrounding tags. Then, without moving the position of your cursor inside the code, click the Lorem and More icon (see the screenshot alongside). If you installed the extension as described in the "Installing Lorem and More" section earlier in this chapter, it should be at the far right of the Common Insert bar.

The dialog box that opens explains all the various options for filler text. It's self-explanatory, so I won't go into details. For the purposes of this page, the default settings are fine. Just click OK, and five paragraphs of Lorem Ipsum filler text will be inserted into the maincontent <div>.

17. Complete the filler text by adding a level 1 heading at the start of the paragraphs that you have just inserted. Do this as you normally would by positioning your cursor in Design view at the beginning of the first paragraph, and pressing ENTER/RETURN. Type a dummy heading, and select Heading 1 from the Format field in the Property inspector. The dotted borders around the <div>s in Design view should indicate whether your heading is outside the maincontent <div>. If it is, delete it, and use Split view to check the position of your cursor before retyping the headline. Add a level 2 heading after the second paragraph.

18. Save index.php, and press F12/OPT+F12 to view your handiwork in a browser. It should look like Figure 4-4. It's not very beautiful, but the layout is logical and accessible without a stylesheet—in some countries this is now a legal requirement for all websites; and in the United States, it's required for sites covered by Section 508 legislation.

> *Mac users should note that the keyboard shortcut for previewing a page in your primary browser has been changed from F12 to OPT+F12. This is because F12 is used by Mac OS X 10.4 (Tiger) to launch Dashboard.*

Figure 4-4. The unstyled design of the site is still fully comprehensible and accessible.

19. Switch back to Dreamweaver, and select Design view. If you select CSS Layout Backgrounds from the Visual Aids menu (at the far right of the Document toolbar or on the View menu), the different <div>s will be highlighted in various colors. This should only be used as a quick guide to your layout; it should be turned off most of the time.

Perhaps more useful is the way each <div> is surrounded by a thick blue border when you select its name in the Tag selector at the bottom of the workspace. As the screenshot alongside shows, selecting <div#maincontent> in the Tag selector places a thick border around both the navigation and main content areas, helping verify that they are correctly nested. I cannot stress enough the importance of creating properly structured documents. Not only will it affect the way your CSS works; once you start adding dynamic elements, bad structure can turn into a nightmare.

Styling the page with CSS

Even though there are now five pages in the site, I'm going to attach stylesheets only to index.php. (You'll see why in the next chapter.) Since the purpose of this book is to focus on using PHP with Dreamweaver 8, I'll keep my comments about the CSS for this design as brief as possible.

Deciding whether to support legacy browsers

I'm sure most of you know exactly what I mean by "legacy browsers." It mainly refers to Netscape 4—an excellent browser when it first came out, but with terrible CSS-rendering problems. For years, the Dreamweaver forum was full of questions about how to overcome the problems; and then whether it was still worth supporting. Most professional designers now respond: "I gave up supporting that old dinosaur years ago." Few of them reveal what they mean by "not supporting" Netscape 4.

Even though the proportion of people using Netscape 4 is now very tiny, they do exist; and if their choice of browser is dictated by the organization that provides their Internet access (such as a library or school), it's unrealistic to tell them to upgrade. Fortunately, Netscape 4 doesn't understand the @import method of attaching a stylesheet. So, as long as you use @import, you can create sophisticated styles in the confident knowledge that no harm will be done to users still stuck with Netscape 4.

> *Leaving pages unstyled in Netscape 4 is fine. Failing to hide from Netscape 4 any CSS styles that might cause it to crash is the sign of poor design.*

Because Netscape 4 does understand basic CSS, you *can* be nice by creating two stylesheets, and using the <link> method to attach just basic styles, while hiding the problematic ones with @import. That's what I propose to do with this case study—not only because I'm a generous sort of guy, but also because one of the objects of this chapter is to show you how to use PHP to serve up different stylesheets. I'm going to put all the styles that remain constant in one stylesheet, and those that change will go in three others. The basic stylesheet doesn't make any concessions to Netscape 4. It simply contains rules that would be in the main stylesheet anyway. By a stroke of good luck, they happen to do no harm to Netscape 4, so there's no point in not giving N4 users the benefit of them.

Internet Explorer 5 and 5.5 are also rapidly disappearing from the scene, but still have to be catered for. Fortunately, the main problem with them is the way they incorrectly interpret the CSS box model, which results in the width of block elements, such as <div>s, paragraphs, and lists shrinking if any padding or border is added. (You can see the effect in Figure 4-5 later in the chapter.) Perhaps the most well-known way of getting around this is Tantek's hack, which uses voice-family and a complex cocktail of quotes, braces, and backslashes (http://tantek.com/CSS/Examples/boxmodelhack.html). It works, but it's complicated. To my mind, the incorrect rendering of width is a Microsoft problem, and the best way of dealing with it is with a Microsoft solution called conditional comments. I'll explain their use after dealing with the main styles.

Attaching the basic styles with <link>

The full listing of basic style rules that will be served up to all browsers, including Netscape 4, follows. Inline comments explain the main purpose of each style block. I tend to hand-code my own CSS, rather than use Dreamweaver's dialog boxes, so the layout is not necessarily the same as Dreamweaver might produce. I also favor the use of shorthand styles. To get a deeper understanding of what the rules mean, study *Cascading Style Sheets: Separating Content from Presentation, 2nd edition,* by Owen Briggs and others (friends of ED, ISBN 1-59059-231-X) or *Web Designer's Reference: An Integrated Approach to Web Design with XHTML and CSS* by Craig Grannell (friends of ED, ISBN 1-59059-430-4). Come to think of it, study them both.

Create a `styles` folder at the root level of the `phpdw` site, and save the following rules in a page called `basic.css`. Alternatively, copy `basic.css` from the `styles` subfolder of `site_check`. Remember, do *not* let Dreamweaver update the links, as they are already correctly set for the new location.

```css
/* set page background to white and text to very dark gray
 * html is included because this is the root element for
 * pages served as application/xhtml+xml */
html, body {
  background: #FFF;
  color:#373737;
  margin: 0;
  padding: 0;
  font-family:Arial, Helvetica, sans-serif;
  }
/* set width of wrapper to same width as title image
 * no top or bottom margin
 * auto on both sides will center wrapper in modern browsers */
#wrapper {
  width: 738px;
  margin: 0 auto;
  }
/* set 15px top margin for titlebar, other margins set to zero */
#titlebar {
  margin: 15px 0 0;
  }
/* maincontent width is 1px smaller to account for left border */
#maincontent {
  width: 737px;
  border-left: #BFBCCB solid 1px;
  margin: 0;
  padding: 0;
  font-size: 85%;
  }
/* set margins, padding, and line height for maincontent paragraphs */
#maincontent p {
  margin: 0 25px 0 40px;
  padding: 5px 0;
  line-height:1.4;
  }
```

```
/* set dimensions for level 1 and 2 headings in maincontent */
#maincontent h1, #maincontent h2 {
   margin: 0 0 5px 15px;
   padding: 5px 0 0;
   font-family:Verdana, Arial, Helvetica, sans-serif;
   color: #396632;
   }
#maincontent h1 {
   font-size: 155%;
   }
#maincontent h2 {
   font-size: 135%;
   }
```

There are several ways to attach a stylesheet to a page in Dreamweaver 8. Perhaps the quickest is to select Attach Style Sheet from the Style drop-down menu in the Property inspector. Alternatively, open the CSS panel by clicking the new CSS button in the center of the Property inspector (if the button is grayed out, click anywhere inside the web page to make it selectable), or by choosing Window ➤ CSS Styles, or by pressing *SHIFT+F11* (Windows only). Then click the Attach Style Sheet icon at the bottom right of the panel, as shown alongside. It looks like a chain—a reference to the <link> tag used for stylesheets. Finally, you can select Attach Style Sheet by clicking the option menu icon at the top right of the CSS panel.

Dreamweaver appears to have been caught napping (daydreaming, maybe) by changes to Mac OS X 10.3 and above, which assigns function keys F9 through F11 to Exposé. This has disabled the keyboard shortcuts on the Mac for the Snippets (SHIFT+F9), History (SHIFT+F10), and CSS Styles (SHIFT+F11) panels. Although you can create your own shortcuts by selecting Keyboard Shortcuts from the Dreamweaver menu, it's probably much easier to open the panels directly or from the Window menu. The Windows version of Dreamweaver is not affected.

If you have upgraded from Dreamweaver MX 2004, you'll recognize the first two items in the Attach External Style Sheet dialog box. File/URL is where you set the path to the stylesheet, and Add to is where you specify how you want to attach it to your page using <link> or @import. Click Browse to navigate to basic.css in the styles folder, and then select the Link radio button.

Dreamweaver 8 now also lets you choose the media attribute. This specifies the type of devices to which the style rules will be applied. It's good practice these days to create a separate set of rules for printing, so let's apply these rules only to visual browsers. Select screen from the Media drop-down menu. If you want to specify multiple media types, the field is editable, and lets you enter a comma-delimited list.

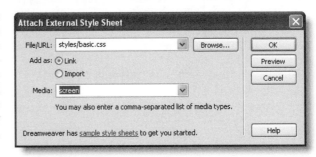

The other new feature in Dreamweaver 8 is the Preview button on the right of the dialog box. If you click the button, the new styles will be immediately reflected in Design view. Once you click Preview, however, you can't deselect it—the only remaining options are OK or Cancel. If you click Cancel, all the changes are discarded, and the dialog box closes. So the preview feature is really only of use where you have a lot of stylesheets in the same folder, and are not sure whether you have picked the right one. With only one stylesheet so far, you're not exactly spoiled for choice, so just click OK.

If you save index.php and preview it in a modern browser, you will see just a few cosmetic changes, such as the centering of the page, plus the border down the left side of the maincontent <div>. If you view the page in Netscape 4, you will see that the border is missing, and that the page isn't centered, but it displays with the bare minimum of styling. That's all it's going to get.

Attaching the remaining styles with @import

The more sophisticated styles add background images and restyle the unordered navigation list as a series of inline buttons. The buttons have different color borders to give them a three-dimensional effect.

The styles should be saved in bluebells.css in the styles folder. To save typing them all out yourself, you can find them in bluebells_01.css in the site_check/styles folder. I won't go into the details of the individual styles, but the inline comments should make clear what they're for.

```css
/* the height spawns a vertical scrollbar on all pages
 * to prevent short pages jumping to the left on Firefox
 * add a color and tiled image background to the page */
html, body {
  height: 101%;
  background: #ECF6CC url(../images_common/bluebells_bg.jpg);
  }
/* this next rule prevents Firefox adding a space beneath the title
 * image when displayed as application/xhtml+xml */
#titlebar img {
  display: block;
  }
/* set the maincontent background to white, and add a drop shadow
 * image to the right border */
#maincontent {
  background: #FFF url(../images_common/bluebells_side.jpg) top right repeat-y;
  }
/* styles for the nav menu - remove padding, margin and bullets */
#nav ul {
  margin: 0;
  padding: 0;
  list-style: none;
  }
/* float each list  element inline */
#nav li {
  float: left;
  display: inline;
  }
/* style the links in the nav list */
#nav a {
```

```
      display: block;
      margin: 0;
      height: 1em;
      padding: 7px 0 7px 22px;
      width: 120px;
      text-decoration: none;
      font-variant: small-caps;
      font-weight: bold;
      font-size: 120%;
      }
#nav a:link, #nav a:visited {
   background-color: #524872;
   color: #FFF;
   border-left: #908AA5 solid 2px;
   border-top: #908AA5 solid 2px;
   border-right: #2C263D solid 2px;
   border-bottom: #2C263D solid 2px;
}
#nav a:hover, #nav a:active {
   background-color: #DFECD9;
   color: #524872;
   border-left: #EBF3E7 solid 2px;
   border-top: #EBF3E7 solid 2px;
   border-right: #777E74 solid 2px;
   border-bottom: #777E74 solid 2px;
   }
/* special style for link to identify current page */
#thispage a:link, #thispage a:visited,
#thispage a:hover, #thispage a:active {
   background-color: #A8B2A3;
   border-left: #5B6058 solid 2px;
   border-top: #5B6058 solid 2px;
   border-right: #B1B7AE solid 2px;
   border-bottom: #B1B7AE solid 2px;
   color: #FFF;
   }
/* footer styles - set to height and width of the footer image */
#footer {
   background: url(../images_common/bluebells_footer.jpg) top left no-repeat;
   width: 738px;
   height: 40px;
   margin: 0;
   padding: 0;
   color: #FFF;
   font-size: 75%
   }
#footer p {
   margin: 0;
   padding: 10px 15px 0 25px;
   clear: both;
   }
```

To attach this stylesheet to index.php, follow the same steps as for basic.css. However, select the Import radio button this time. As soon as you click OK, you should notice a dramatic change in Design view—the unordered list will have been transformed into a row of 3D buttons, and the page should look very similar to Figure 4-1.

If you open Split view, you will see that basic.css has been attached to the page using a <link> tag, while bluebells.css has been placed in a <style> block and attached using @import, as shown in the following screenshot. If Design view looks hideously psychedelic, deselect CSS Layout Backgrounds in the Visual Aids menu at the top right of the document toolbar.

Strictly speaking, the HTML comments shown on lines 8 and 10 in the screenshot are not required; they are a hangover from the days when it was necessary to hide certain elements, such as @import, from older browsers that didn't understand them. However, although all modern browsers at the time of this writing will correctly interpret the @import statement inside the HTML comments, they are not *required* to do so. Consequently, it is advisable to remove the comment tags surrounding the @import statement.

> *Attaching a stylesheet using any of the methods described earlier always results in the selected stylesheet being attached to the page in addition to any existing ones. It does not replace them. When using more than one stylesheet, the order in which they appear in the code affects the way that style rules are interpreted. Dreamweaver normally inserts the code for each new stylesheet after any existing ones, but you should always keep Split view open when attaching stylesheets, and adjust the order by hand if necessary.*

If you ever need to remove a stylesheet, there are two ways to do it. If you're happy messing about in code, the quick and dirty way is to open Code view, highlight the <link> tag or <style> block surrounding @import, and press DELETE. To select the whole of a <link> tag or <style> block accurately, simply position your cursor anywhere inside, and click the Collapse Full Tag button (illustrated alongside) on the Coding toolbar.

The other—perhaps more elegant—way to remove a stylesheet is through the CSS panel. Open the panel directly, or press SHIFT+F11 (the keyboard shortcut is for Windows only) and select the All button at the top of the panel. You can then select the stylesheet that you want to remove by highlighting it in the All Rules field. To remove the stylesheet, click the trashcan icon at the bottom right of the CSS panel, as shown in the screenshot. If you realize immediately that you've deleted the wrong stylesheet, you can restore it by pressing CTRL+Z/⌘+Z. This works only if you haven't made any other changes to the page in the meantime. If you have, just restore it by using Attach Style Sheet again.

There's just one little quirk with using the trashcan method to remove stylesheets. Although <link> elements are removed cleanly, the <style> tags and HTML comments are left behind when you use it to remove @import directives. However, Dreamweaver is smart enough to use the same set of <style> tags if you add any other stylesheets with @import, so the only time you need to clean up after Dreamweaver is if you don't plan to replace the stylesheet that you have removed this way.

Identifying the current page

It's common practice to signal to users which page they're on by using a down-state image for the current page's navigation button. Since the navigation menu is built entirely with CSS, you need to create the same effect by a different means. I learned this technique—along with many others—from Al Sparber of Project Seven (www.projectseven.com), a company that develops some of the best menu-creation extensions (both free and commercial) and website design packs for Dreamweaver. Like most of the best techniques, it's disarmingly simple.

One of the first tricks that most people learn with CSS is how to create different colored links on the same page by assigning an ID to a <div>, and creating a set of link style rules for that ID. For example, bluebells.css uses #nav a to style the links in the navigation menu, and make them look like buttons. Since the menu is actually an unordered list, each item is enclosed in <li> tags. So, by applying an ID to the <li> tag for the current page, you can create a completely separate style for just one link within the menu.

Things should come clearer once you make the necessary change to index.php.

1. Place your cursor inside the HOME link in nav <div>.

2. In the Tag selector at the bottom of the Document window, select the <li> tag, right-click/*CTRL*-click, and choose Set ID. Choose thispage from the list of IDs that is displayed, as shown in the following screenshot.

3. As soon as you select the thispage ID, the HOME link in Design view should change from a deep purple to an olive color, and look as though it is indented.

4. Save index.php, and press *F12/OPT+F12* to preview the page in a browser. Apart from the absence of the pull quote on the right of the screen, it should look like Figure 4-1. In Netscape 4, it will look no different from before.

You could apply the thispage ID manually to the appropriate link for each of the four other pages. However, in Chapter 6 I'll show you a technique that automates the whole process in PHP.

Adjusting for the Internet Explorer 5 box model

If you look at the page in Internet Explorer 5 or 5.5 for Windows, the navigation bar and first heading will be incorrectly displayed, as shown in Figure 4-5. This is because both browsers apply the wrong interpretation to the CSS box model, and include padding and borders in the overall width of an element. Not only that, but the page is also not centered.

Figure 4-5. Internet Explorer 5 and 5.5 for Windows get the CSS box model wrong.

> *If you don't have Internet Explorer 5 or 5.5 for Windows, you can simulate the same effect in IE6 by adding an HTML comment (<!-- -->) above the DOCTYPE declaration. Remember to remove it afterwards—otherwise your page will display incorrectly in what's currently the world's most popular browser!*

Since this is a Microsoft-only problem, a Microsoft proprietary solution seems the most appropriate:

1. Open index.php in Code view, and locate the end of the <style> block containing the @import statement. If you removed the HTML comments around the @import statement, it should be on line 8.

2. Add the following code (the surrounding code is shown for clarity, with the new code highlighted in bold):

```
@import url("styles/bluebells.css");
</style>
<!--[if IE 5]>
<style>
body {text-align: center;}
#wrapper {text-align: left;}
#nav a {width: 146px;}
</style>
<![endif]-->
</head>
```

The addition of this simple piece of code will cause IE5 and 5.5 for Windows to display the page as intended. Because it is wrapped in a Microsoft **conditional comment**, only those browsers will see it.

> *It's important to place the conditional comment block after the links to the main stylesheets, because it relies on the cascade to override the rules that other browsers obey.*

Visit http://msdn.microsoft.com/workshop/author/dhtml/overview/ccomment_ovw.asp to learn more about Microsoft conditional comments.

PHP, here we come

The setup process has been quite lengthy, but good foundations are important for building a solid structure. Even if you have been using Dreamweaver for some time, the changes in Dreamweaver 8 are so extensive that you risk missing out on a lot of productivity improvements if you assume it's just "business as usual." The familiar looks are very deceptive.

Over the next two chapters, I intend to build further on those solid foundations by showing you how to incorporate PHP into the East-West Seasons site, so that you can change the design automatically at different times of the year or day. You'll also build an online form for the contact page that will validate the content and email it to your inbox. In addition, you'll convert the navigation menu so that you'll only ever need to change a single page to update it on every page. And if you're thinking I've forgotten about adding the stylesheets to the rest of the site—that'll be handled by PHP, too.

119

Chapter 5

INTEGRATING PHP INTO YOUR SITE

What this chapter covers:

- Using PHP includes for common page elements
- Including text from an external file
- Understanding PHP error messages
- Displaying PHP output with Live Data view
- Learning the basics of PHP
- Creating pages that make decisions for themselves

Something I have never really understood is why so many PHP books feel obliged to begin by demonstrating how to display "Hello, world" or "Hi, Mom!" onscreen. It's something you'll never want to do in real life—unless you plan to write a textbook on PHP, maybe. I'm going to begin your practical introduction to PHP with something genuinely useful: including code from an external file, or **server-side includes** (SSI).

Then I'll explain some of the basic principles of PHP, so that you understand what's happening with the code later in the book. Even if you already have some knowledge of PHP, I hope you'll get value out of this chapter by working with practical examples to add dynamic features to your sites.

Including text and code from other files

At the end of the previous chapter, only index.php had any styles. The obvious way to rectify that would be to attach both stylesheets, and copy the Microsoft conditional comment from index.php into the <head> of each page. But there is another, more powerful way of doing it—with PHP includes.

Using includes to apply styles

If you created your own files in the previous chapter, continue working with them. Alternatively, copy the files with names ending in _01.php from the site_check/ch05 folder into the phpdw site root. Also copy basic.css and bluebells_01.css from site_check/styles to a folder called styles at the site root level. If Dreamweaver asks you whether you want to update the links in the files, click Don't Update—the links in all the download files are the way they should be in the finished version.

> *As noted, many of the download files show the pages at different stages of development, and they have filenames numbered in sequence, such as* index_01.php, index_02.php, *and so on. If you want to use the download files instead of building your own, always copy—don't move—the file to the site root or named folder, and change the filename to remove the number—so, for instance,* index_01.php *becomes* index.php. *By making a copy, you will always have the original download file to check against, using Dreamweaver 8's File Compare feature.*

1. Open index.php, switch to Code view, and highlight the code from the beginning of the <link> tag to the end of the Microsoft conditional comment, as shown in the following screenshot. (If you are using your own file from the previous chapter, note that I have removed the HTML comments surrounding the @import statement.)

```
5    <title>East-West Seasons</title>
6    <link href="styles/basic.css" rel="stylesheet" type="text/css" media="screen" />
7    <style type="text/css" media="screen">
8    @import url("styles/bluebells.css");
9    </style>
10   <!--[if IE 5]>
11   <style>
12   body {text-align: center;}
13   #wrapper {text-align: left;}
14   #nav a {width: 146px;}
15   </style>
16   <![endif]-->
17   </head>
```

2. Cut (*CTRL*+*X*/⌘ +*X*) the highlighted code to the clipboard.

3. Select File ➤ New, and create a new PHP document.

4. Open Code view, and delete all the code in the new document. You want a completely empty file. Paste (*CTRL*+*V*/⌘ +*V*) into the empty file the code that you cut from index.php.

5. Save the file in the site root as style_rules.php. It should look like this:

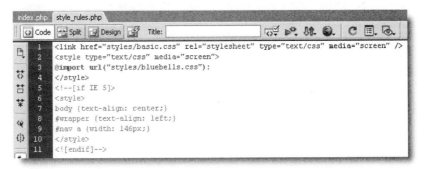

> It is crucial that the file contains nothing else. One of the most common mistakes in creating server-side includes is to leave in the DOCTYPE declaration or the <html> and <body> tags. Normally, your main file will already have these elements. You mustn't include them again.

6. Switch back to index.php, and select Split view. If you click in the Design view part of the page, you will see that it is no longer styled. Position your cursor in the Code view section of the page at the point where you removed all the style rules (about line 6). Select the PHP category of the Insert bar, and click the Include icon, as shown here.

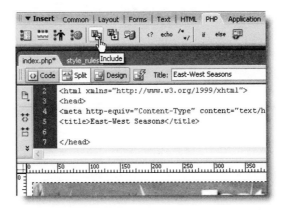

7. This will insert the following code wherever your cursor was positioned:

```
<?php include(); ?>
```

8. Your cursor will automatically be left between the parentheses, ready for you to insert the name of the file that you want to include—in this case, style_rules.php. The filename must be enclosed in quotes, so the code should look like this:

```php
<?php include('style_rules.php'); ?>
```

> *The quotes surrounding the filename can be either single or double quotes, as long as they're a matching pair. My personal preference is to use single quotes, because PHP handles single and double quotes in subtly different ways. More about that later in the chapter.*

When the include file is in the same folder, it's quicker to just type the filename directly. However, when you need to include a file from another folder, it's important to get the relative URL correct. The safest way to do this is to type the opening quote inside the parentheses, and right-click/*CTRL*-click to bring up a context menu. Select Code Hint Tools ➤ URL Browser, and then click Browse. Navigate to the file in the dialog box that opens. Make sure that the Relative to field at the bottom of the dialog box is set to Document. Click OK, and finally enter the closing quote. It's a rather fiddly way to have to do things, but it ensures the include path is accurate. Hopefully, the next version of Dreamweaver will bring up the Browse prompt automatically. The correct sequence of events is shown in the following screenshots.

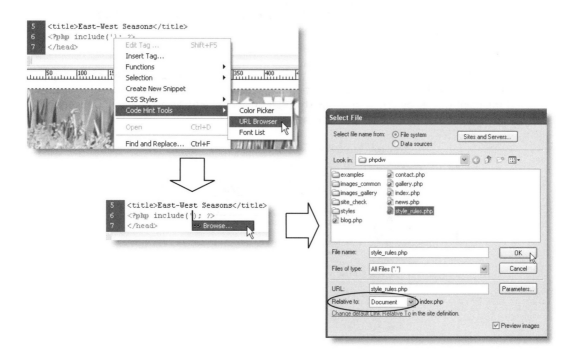

When using the URL Browser to select an include file, the URL must always be relative to the document. If you set it as relative to the site root, PHP may not be able to find the file. As long as you always move files within the Files panel, Dreamweaver automatically keeps track of includes and include files. Accept the option to update links when Dreamweaver prompts you.

9. Click inside the Design view section of the workspace. You should see the styles immediately reapplied to the page.

10. Highlight the line of code you created in steps 7 and 8, copy it, and paste it in the same position in the other four pages: `blog.php`, `contact.php`, `gallery.php`, and `news.php`.

11. Save the pages, and test them in a browser. (Remember, you should always test PHP pages using *F12/Opt+F12*, because they need to be parsed by the PHP engine.) The entire site should now be properly styled.

If you're used to using Dreamweaver templates or library items, you may question the advantage of using a PHP include like this. What makes it so much more powerful is that whenever you change the contents of the include file (in this case, `style_rules.php`), it is immediately reflected in every other file. What's more—and this is the key point—you need to upload only one file to your remote server. With Dreamweaver templates and library items, the changes are made to each individual file, and all of them need to be uploaded. This makes a huge difference on a site that contains a large number of pages that share common elements.

Includes can be used for a wide variety of purposes. Another practical use is to allow nonspecialists to add small amounts of content to a page.

Adding frequently changed content to a page

You can find the completed code for this exercise in `site_check/ch05/index_02.php`.

1. Open `index.php`, and position your cursor at the beginning of the first paragraph in Design view. Press *ENTER/RETURN* to enter a new, empty paragraph.

2. Open Split view, and remove the   (nonbreaking space) that Dreamweaver has inserted between the <p> tags of the new paragraph.

3. Click the Include icon in the PHP Insert bar. Type 'newtext.txt' between the parentheses after `include`, so the entire line of code looks like this:

```
<p><?php include('newtext.txt'); ?></p>
```

4. Select File ➤ New. In the New Document dialog box that opens, select Other and Text, and click Create. Type a sentence or two in the blank document, and save it as `newtext.txt`.

5. Switch back to `index.php`, save it, and click inside Design view. As the following screenshot shows, the content of `newtext.txt` is included inside the page. Because the include command is between <p> tags, the text is styled like any other paragraph.

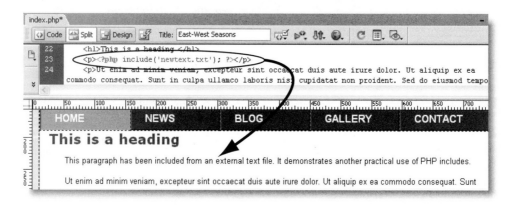

So, if you wanted to include a short paragraph on your site for frequently changing announcements, this might be an ideal way to do it.

Of course, you needn't stop there. You can include large chunks of HTML markup, and it will all be displayed as though it were part of the same page. The only important thing to remember is that the content of the external file will be included exactly as it is, and in exactly the position within the page where the include command has been inserted. So it's vital that the external file makes sense—not only from the point of view of content, but also any code must fit syntactically into the page.

For instance, you can't nest a <p> element inside another one. So, if your include looks like this,

```
<p><?php include('newtext.txt'); ?></p>
```

and the content of `newtext.txt` looks like this,

```
<p>This paragraph has been included from an external text file. It
demonstrates another practical use of PHP includes.</p>
```

the two together will produce this:

```
<p><p>This paragraph has been included from an external text file. It
demonstrates another practical use of PHP includes.</p></p>
```

The page will still display in most browsers, but it produces invalid XHTML. Just say, however, that the include file contained an opening <p> tag, but not a closing one (perfectly valid in HTML). As I warned you in Chapter 2, if the page is served as application/xhtml+xml, any mistake in coding will prevent the whole page from displaying. The result will be like this:

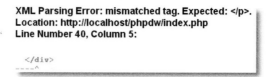

> *Includes are very powerful, but they can also make a complete mess of your page if you're not careful about what they contain.*

Using require() instead of include()

Sitting next to the Include button on the PHP Insert bar is the Require button, as you can see in the illustration alongside. They look almost identical, except that the Require button includes an exclamation mark. The best way to explain the difference between them is with a little experiment.

Exploring the difference between include() and require()

Continue working with the files from the previous exercise, or use site_check/ch05/index_02.php and site_check/ch05/newtext.txt.

1. In index.php, click anywhere inside the included text in Design view. Because it comes from an external file, this should select the whole section. If you open Split view, you will see that the whole of the include command, together with the surrounding PHP tags, has been selected, as shown in the following screenshot.

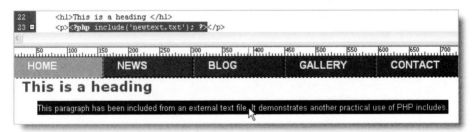

2. Press *DELETE*. This will remove the block of code highlighted in line 23 of the previous screen-shot. *It does not delete the external file*—only the link between index.php and the external file is removed.

3. Dreamweaver will place a nonbreaking space ( ) between the <p> tags in the Code view section of the page. Remove this, and leave your cursor between the <p> tags.

4. Click the Require button on the PHP Insert bar, and type the name of the external file between the parentheses. As before, the name of the file should be in quotes. Your line of code should now look like this:

```
<p><?php require('newtext.txt'); ?></p>
```

5. Save index.php and press *F12/OPT+F12* to view the file in a browser. It should look identical to when you used include(). So, what's the difference? Normally, very little. However, there is a major difference when things go wrong.

6. Change the filename between the parentheses to a non-existent file, save `index.php`, and view it in a browser again. You should see something like this (you can also use Live Data view to test the page—the only difference is that the error messages will be displayed in a Dreamweaver dialog box):

7. I'll explain the meaning of the warning messages in a moment. But first, change the command to `include()`, still with the incorrect filename. Save `index.php`, and view it in a browser again. This time, instead of being truncated at the point of failure, the rest of the page will display as normal, as you can see in the next screenshot.

What this little experiment demonstrates is that an error with require() brings everything to a screeching halt because "require" is used in the sense of "must have." As soon as it realizes a vital element is missing, the PHP parser stops processing the script. On the other hand, the parser carries on regardless when a file called using include() can't be found. On a server that has display_errors turned off in php.ini, visitors to the site would probably not realize anything was missing if an include() command failed, whereas it would be a complete show-stopper with require().

> *If you want to see the effect for yourself, you can turn off the display of errors for an individual page by adding the following code at the very top of the page:*
>
> ```php
> <?php error_reporting(0); ?>
> ```

For all practical purposes, there's little point worrying about the difference between the two, and many developers—including myself—use the generic term "include" to cover both require() and include(). If you use includes, you presumably want the contents of the external files inside your page, so that page will fail anyway if the external file is missing.

When you start working with databases later, you will see that Dreamweaver uses a closely related construct—require_once()—to include database connection details into each page that needs them. As the name suggests, this makes sure that the details are included only once during the running of a PHP script. This is marginally more efficient, and it ensures that any functions or variables in the external file are not redefined. There's an equivalent for include()—include_once().

Points to remember when using includes

Using includes is easy if you remember several simple rules:

- Use include() if you want the script to continue even if the external file is missing, but remember to switch off the display of errors as described earlier.

- If in doubt, use require_once().

- The external file doesn't need a .php extension unless it contains PHP code. (At the moment, style_rules.php doesn't contain any PHP code, but it will later.)

- PHP expects a document-relative path to the external file, although an absolute path is also acceptable. Site root–relative paths may not work as expected unless your testing site is in a virtual directory.

- You can use a full URL to include files from another server, as long as allow_url_fopen is turned on in php.ini. Although this is the default setting, some hosts disable this option. (You should never include files from another server unless you have the permission of the owner.)

- The contents of an external file are treated exactly the same as if they were part of the original document, so they should not contain anything that might cause problems when both files are merged—such as a second DOCTYPE declaration or XHTML tags that would be invalidly nested.

- Output to the browser is displayed at the point of the include command.

- A PHP function or variable in an external file cannot be used until the external file has been included. Consequently, it's good practice to include common function libraries right at the start of a page.

"Failed to open stream" and other error messages

Newcomers to PHP are frequently puzzled by error messages that appear on screen. "Failed to open stream" simply means that the file could not be opened.

Error messages report the line where PHP discovered a problem. Sometimes, as in the preceding exercise, this indicates where the error actually lies. In this case, the error is obvious, because you deliberately inserted the name of a non-existent file on line 23 of index.php. But what if the filename is spelled correctly? One reason for the failure could simply be that you forgot to upload the required file to your remote server. Another cause could be that the wrong permissions have been set on the file—it's there, but the web server isn't able to open it.

The following illustration shows the structure of a typical error message.

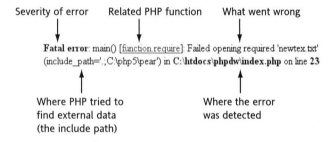

The first thing an error message tells you is the severity of the problem. There are four main categories, presented here in descending order of importance:

- **Fatal error:** Any XHTML output preceding the error will be displayed, but once the error is encountered—as the name suggests—everything else is killed stone dead. A fatal error is normally caused by referring to a non-existent file or function.

- **Parse error:** This means there's a mistake in PHP syntax, such as mismatched quotes, or a missing semicolon or closing brace. Like a fatal error, it stops the script in its tracks, and doesn't even allow any XHTML output to be displayed. PHP syntax is the subject of much of the rest of this chapter.

- **Warning:** This alerts you to a serious problem, such as a missing include file. However, the error is not serious enough to prevent the rest of the script from being executed.

- **Notice:** This advises you about the existence of a potential problem, such as the use of deprecated code or a nondeclared variable. Although many developers disregard notices, you should always try to eliminate them. Any error is a threat to your output.

Although fatal and parse errors are equally devastating, a script with a fatal error is syntactically correct—there are no mistakes in it, but there's a vital part missing. A parse error is caused by a mistake in the code that you have written—often much more difficult to track down. Although the line number reports where PHP discovered a problem, in the case of a parse error, the actual cause of the problem is—more often than not—*before* that line. For instance, if you omit the semicolon at the end of a line, PHP won't realize there's a problem until the next line or—if the next section of code is XHTML—considerably later. So, if you can't find the error on the line itself, you need to start working backwards from that point.

If the error is related to a built-in PHP function, the name of the function will be indicated inside square brackets. Although the name of the function is displayed as a hyperlink, you need to download the PHP manual and configure it correctly for the link to work. Since PHP is constantly under development, it is usually more efficient to visit the PHP online manual at www.php.net/manual/en/ and to search the function list for the relevant entry. The first warning message in both experiments referred to a non-existent function called main. A reference to main or main() simply means PHP itself.

If your script relies on external files, the error message will normally display the value of include_path in your PHP configuration. All code in this book is stored within your main site, so there is no need to take any notice of this information when deciphering error messages. It would be nice to say you won't need to worry about error messages, but I'm afraid they're a constant fact of life—particularly in the early stages of learning PHP.

Displaying PHP output with Live Data view

Now that you have a PHP site and some content to work with, you can try out the code that I showed you in Chapter 1, which automatically displays the correct year in the copyright notice.

Showing the current year

Continue working with the same file from the previous exercise, or use index_02.php from site_check/ch05.

1. In Design view, scroll down to the bottom of index.php, and place your cursor immediately after the year. Press BACKSPACE to delete the final number, and change it to last year, followed by a hyphen. I'm writing this in 2005, so I've changed it like the image to the right.

2. With your cursor still next to the hyphen, click the Echo button on the PHP Insert bar. This will automatically open Split view, or change the active view to Code view, and place a short block of PHP code into the underlying code, as shown here.

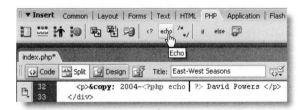

3. Dreamweaver automatically shifts the focus to the underlying code, and places your cursor in the correct position for you to insert whatever it is that you want PHP to display (echo displays output directly to the browser). Start typing date(. The first three letters (dat) will display in black, but as soon as you add the final "e," "date" will turn light blue, to indicate that it's a PHP keyword. (If it doesn't change color, check that Syntax Coloring is selected on the View ➤ Code View Options menu.)

When you add the opening parenthesis, a code hint will pop up like this:

The section of the code hint in bold type tells you what information the function expects you to enter. Each section of a code hint normally consists of two words—in this case, string format. The first word tells you the datatype required (**string** is the expression used in computer languages to mean text, which is always enclosed in quotes). The second word gives you a clue as to what type of information is required. So, in plain English, this code hint is telling you that date() expects you to enter a format for the date, and that it must be presented as a string. The date() function has a large number of preset formats, but the one you need on this occasion is an uppercase Y, which will format the year as a four-digit number. Because date() expects the format as a string, you must enclose it in quotes. Again, it doesn't matter whether you use single or double quotes, but I prefer single for reasons that I'll explain later in the chapter. So type 'Y' immediately after the opening parenthesis.

If you look at the code hint, you'll see that string format is followed by a comma. Type a comma, and the next part of the code hint ([int timestamp]) will be highlighted in bold type. Dreamweaver keeps track of what you have entered, and keeps reminding you of what's expected next. Anything enclosed in square brackets is optional, and on this occasion you don't need the second piece of information. I'll explain the various datatypes, and how the date() function works later; for the moment, just delete the comma, and type a closing parenthesis followed by a semicolon.

The code hint will disappear, and the code shown on line 32 in the preceding screenshots should now look like this:

```
<p>&copy; 2004-<?php echo date('Y'); ?> David Powers</p>
```

4. If you click inside the Design view side of the page, you will see that the new code is represented in your page as a gold shield labeled PHP.

5. Just seeing a gold shield isn't very helpful when you're trying to assess the overall effect of your design, so let's enter Live Data view. Click the Live Data button on the Document toolbar and, after a short pause, Dreamweaver should display the current year in place of the gold shield, as shown in the screenshot alongside.

You may find the date difficult to read because Dreamweaver highlights live data in pale yellow. I changed the color temporarily to make it stand out better for this book. If necessary, test the page in a browser to see that it displays the correct date.

> *If you want to change the default color for live data, open* Preferences *from the* Edit *menu (or the* Dreamweaver *menu on a Mac), and select the* Highlighting *category. Choose a different color for* Live data: Translated.

6. Live Data view is toggled on and off by clicking the Live Data button. Displaying the output of your PHP code like this can be quite processor-intensive, so it's always a good idea to switch off Live Data view after checking your layout. If you are using FTP to connect to a remote testing server, you need to be connected to the Internet every time you use Live Data view. If you get an error message, check the code. In particular, make sure that the filenames of the include files from the previous exercises are correct.

7. In Design view, select the gold PHP shield. This gives you another way to inspect the code. As shown alongside, the PHP code (without the surrounding PHP tags) is displayed in the Property inspector.

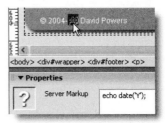

8. You can also edit code in the Property inspector. Replace the uppercase Y with a lowercase one, and see the result either in Live Data view or in a browser. It should have changed the year from a four-digit number to just the final two digits.

As I'm sure you've noticed, there's an unsatisfactory aspect to this last exercise. I asked you to change the static date to last year. What if you're building a new site, and you want the date to show just this year, but update automatically on New Year's Day? It's very simple to do, but it requires the use of PHP control structures. So before I can show you how, it's a good idea to explain the fundamental structures that are used in PHP.

Introducing the basics of PHP

The exercises in this chapter have now given you a little taste of how PHP integrates with XHTML. As I explained in Chapter 1, anything between an opening <?php tag and closing ?> tag will be interpreted by the PHP engine. Anything outside these tags is treated as plain XHTML.

> *You may come across PHP scripts in other books or in online tutorials that use* <? *instead of* <?php. *The shorter form is no longer recommended, and is disabled on some servers. The* <?php *version always works, so it is much safer.*

If you're completely new to PHP, you may find the following sections difficult to absorb at a single sitting. Don't worry. You don't need to learn all of this by heart. Skim through it, and do the exercises. Then come back to it later if you need to refresh your memory about the basics of PHP.

Using the correct filename extension

The opening and closing PHP tags tell the server to treat that part of the page differently. The other important signal to the server is the .php filename extension. A lot of people ask whether it's possible to get a server to treat .html (or any other filename extension) as PHP. The answer is yes, but it's not recommended, because doing so places an unnecessary burden on the server. If you're on a shared server, you're unlikely to persuade your host to do the necessary reconfiguration. Another strong argument against using a nonstandard filename extension for PHP files is that Dreamweaver won't recognize them as PHP files.

It's perfectly acceptable to mix (X)HTML and PHP files in the same site. In fact, you can even mix ASP and ColdFusion files with PHP ones—as long as your server supports all the necessary server-side languages. What you cannot do is mix different server-side languages in the same *page*.

When building a new PHP site, it's a good idea to create all pages with a .php extension, even if they don't contain dynamic code. Admittedly, this can lead to sending static pages unnecessarily to the PHP engine, but it means you can always add dynamic content to a page without worrying about the need to redirect visitors from an .html page. If you are converting an old site, you can leave the main home page as a static page, and use it to link to your PHP pages.

The best solution in both cases, though, is to use the appropriate filename extension, and implement a permanent redirect for any pages that need to be changed from .html to .php or vice versa. A permanent redirect tells the browser that the page has moved permanently, and this solution is very search engine–friendly. You can find instructions for how to do this with an .htaccess file on an Apache server at www.tamingthebeast.net/articles3/spiders-301-redirect.htm. If you're on a Windows server, contact your host for instructions.

The core components of PHP syntax

Just as human languages have rules called grammar, computer languages like PHP have similar rules, normally referred to as **syntax**. Fortunately, the rules of PHP syntax are a lot easier to learn than those of English or Spanish grammar, and there are far fewer exceptions to the rules. The most important elements of PHP syntax are as follows:

- **Variables:** These act as placeholders to represent values you don't know in advance. PHP variables always begin with a dollar sign.

- **Literals:** These are values that you know in advance. They're called literals because they literally represent themselves. Text literals (or **strings**) are always in quotes; numbers are not surrounded by quotes.

- **Functions:** These can be regarded as the verbs of PHP—they get things done. PHP has a vast array of built-in functions. You've already met date(), which displays a date according to the instructions (or **arguments**) that you pass to it. You can also create your own custom functions. Functions always end with a pair of parentheses, and arguments are passed to a function by placing them between the parentheses in the order that the function expects.

- **Control structures:** These enable PHP to make decisions. They are mainly based on simple human logic—*if* this is true, do something, *else* do something different. Other control structures *do* something continuously *while* a certain condition is true. The words in italics are actually used by PHP, so a lot of the code is very easy to follow.

Handling unknown values with variables

We work with variables all the time in our daily lives. Perhaps the simplest example is your bank balance. Payments come in and go out of your bank account all the time (for some reason, they often seem to go out more often than come in). Yet, if you ever want to know how much money you've got (or owe), you just ask for your "balance." The word "balance" is fixed, but the value is variable. Hence the concept of variables in PHP and other programming languages. Variables are simply a handy way of storing information. You know what sort of information it will be—an address, a price, or a name—but not the precise value.

The value of a variable may be assigned (fixed) once during a PHP script, or it may change many times—in just the same way as your bank balance changes. The name remains the same, but the value is always the one most recently assigned or calculated.

As noted earlier, all variables in PHP begin with a dollar sign, but forgetting this simple rule is a common beginner's mistake. Don't confuse the dollar sign with an uppercase *S*. PHP won't play ball if you use the wrong one.

Some other important things to note about variable names:

- Names can consist only of alphanumeric characters (a–z, A–Z, and 0–9) and the underscore.
- The first character after the dollar sign cannot be a number (you can use the underscore, but this is best avoided, as predefined PHP variables often use it).
- No spaces are allowed.
- Choose names that help you make sense of your script—$b is a lot easier to type than $balance, but will you understand what $b means in six months' time?
- Although you can mix uppercase and lowercase letters, variables are case-sensitive, so PHP treats $totalPrice and $totalprice as completely different.

Table 5-1 shows these rules in practice, with examples of what you can and cannot do when naming variables.

Table 5-1. Examples of legal and illegal variable names

Variable name	Validity
$total price	illegal—contains a space
$total_price	legal—contains an underscore
$total-price	illegal—contains an illegal character (-)
$totalPrice	legal
$totalprice	legal
$total+tax	illegal—contains an illegal character (+)
$address2	legal

Continued

Table 5.1. *Continued*

Variable name	Validity
$2address	illegal—starts with a number
$_2address	legal, but unadvisable—begins with an underscore (even if PHP doesn't use a variable with the same name, you may choose one by accident that is adopted by PHP at some future date)

A lot of people use camel-case notation (capitalizing the first letter of second or subsequent words in variables) to make them easier to read. Others prefer separating words with an underscore (this is the style adopted by Dreamweaver-generated code). Choose whichever suits you best. And remember, although there is no limit on the length of variables, the longer they are, the more difficult they are to type—and the easier to misspell:

```
$totalPriceAfterDiscountButIncludingTax
```

It says exactly what it's for, but it is probably not a good idea.

Finally, don't use $this as a variable. It's a reserved word, used only in those aspects of PHP related to object-oriented programming (OOP). Dreamweaver provides a visual warning by highlighting $this in light blue, indicating that it is part of the PHP core language.

> *Although PHP is not an object-oriented language, it does have extensive object-oriented features, which underwent a major revision in PHP 5. To learn more about OOP in PHP, read Beginning PHP 5 and MySQL 5: From Novice to Professional, 2nd Edition, by W. Jason Gilmore (Apress, ISBN: 1-59059-552-1).*

Assigning values to a variable

Since the whole idea of using variables is to handle values that you don't know in advance, you may be wondering where those values come from. They can come from a variety of sources, such as these:

- User input gathered from an online form
- Information retrieved from a database
- Predefined values set either by PHP or by yourself
- The result of logical or arithmetic calculations

You will see all of these in action as you progress through this book. Whenever you want to assign a new value to a variable, you use the **assignment operator** (=) like this:

```
variable = value;
```

Yes, it's an equal sign, but get into the habit of thinking of it as meaning "is set to" rather than "equals." This is because PHP uses *two* equal signs (==) to mean "equals"—something that catches out a lot of beginners. I'll explain the significance of this distinction later in the chapter in the exercise titled "Mixing up the assignment and equality operators."

Use the following rules when assigning a value to a variable:

- Strings *must* be enclosed in quotes
- Variables are not enclosed in quotes, unless combined with a string
- Numbers are not enclosed in quotes—enclosing a number in quotes turns it into a string

Here are few simple examples:

```
$greeting = "Hello,";    // string in double quotes
$name = 'Dolly';         // string in single quotes
$num1 = 2;               // number
$num2 = 4;               // number
$num1 = $num2;           // $num1 now has the same value as $num2 (4)
```

Getting to know the various datatypes

Many programming languages have very strict rules about the type of data you can store in variables, forcing you to make a decision up front, and then stick to it. PHP isn't like that. It's what's known as a loosely typed language, which means variables can hold any type of data without you having to specify it beforehand. Still, you need to know what datatypes are used in PHP to understand the meaning of code hints.

PHP uses eight different datatypes, as follows:

- **String:** Text enclosed in single or double quotes.
- **Integer:** Whole numbers, such as 42, 999, or 23. They can be positive or—if preceded by a minus sign—negative. You should not enclose integers in quotes, nor should you use commas or other separators between the digits. For instance, one million must be written as 1000000, and not as 1,000,000. Dreamweaver code hints use the abbreviation int to signify an integer.
- **Floating-point number (double):** These are numbers that contain a decimal fraction, and can be written using a decimal point, such as 2.1, or in scientific notation, such as 0.314E1. Like integers, they should not be enclosed in quotes. Code hints use float to indicate this type of number.
- **Boolean:** A true or false value. The following are treated as false in PHP:
  - The keywords false and NULL
  - The integer 0 and floating-point number 0.0
  - Zero as a string ('0' or "0")
  - An empty string ('' or "" with no space in between)
  - An array with zero elements

  Everything else is treated as true.

  Code hints use bool to indicate a Boolean datatype.

> *Beware of putting quotes around the keywords* false *and* NULL. *If enclosed in quotes, they become strings and are treated by PHP as* true.

- **Array:** These are variables that hold multiple values, rather like lists. One of the most important uses of arrays in Dreamweaver is to hold the results of a database query. They will be covered in more detail in Chapter 6.

- **Object:** These are used in object-oriented aspects of PHP, and are not used in this book.

- **Resource:** When PHP accesses an external resource, such as a database or file, you need to store a reference to the connection in a variable.

- **NULL:** This has one value only—the case-insensitive keyword NULL. It is used to set a variable to have no value. It must not be enclosed in quotes.

Indenting code and use of white space

Just like XHTML, PHP normally ignores white space within code. The previous examples look a lot neater—without affecting their functionality—by lining up the assignment operators like this:

```
$greeting = "Hello,";    // string in double quotes
$name     = 'Dolly';     // string in single quotes
$num1     = 2;           // number
$num2     = 4;           // number
$num1     = $num2;       // $num1 now has the same value as $num2 (4)
```

Spacing out your code, and indenting it to keep logical blocks together, is a good habit to get into, because it makes your code easier to understand and maintain. There are no hard and fast rules about how much white space to use. Dreamweaver's auto indent feature helps keep scripts tidy.

Separating commands with the semicolon

PHP is able to ignore white space and new lines because it expects a semicolon at the end of each **statement** (or instruction). PHP is made up of a series of statements, usually single instructions to do something.

```
Find the date;
Display this message;
Multiply number of items by item price;
```

Forgetting the semicolon at the end of each statement is a common beginner's mistake—and the cause of major headaches. PHP is not like JavaScript or ActionScript, where the semicolon is optional. Miss one, and everything comes to a grinding halt. The only time you can omit the semicolon at the end of a statement is when it's the only one in a PHP code block. Still, it's always good practice to include the semicolon, even when there's only a single statement. That way, you won't run into problems if you add an extra statement later.

Commenting scripts for clarity and debugging

Even if you are an expert programmer, code is not always as immediately understandable as something written in your own human language. That's where comments can be a lifesaver. You may understand what the code does five minutes after creating it, but when you come back to maintain it in six months' time—or if you have to maintain someone else's code—you'll be grateful for well-commented code.

In PHP, there are three ways to add comments. The first will be familiar to you if you write JavaScript or ActionScript. Anything on a line following a double slash is regarded as a comment, and will not be processed.

```
<?php
  // Display the current year
  echo date('Y');
?>
```

You can also use the hash sign (#) in place of the double slash.

```
<?php
  # Display the current year
  echo date('Y');
?>
```

Either type of comment can go to the side of the code, as long as it doesn't go onto the next line (to save space from now on, I won't always surround code samples with PHP tags).

```
echo date('Y');     // This is a comment
echo date('Y');      # This is another comment
```

The third style allows you to stretch comments over several lines, by sandwiching them between /* and */ (just like CSS comments).

```
/* You might want to use this sort of comment to explain
the whole purpose of a script. Alternatively, it's a
convenient way to disable part of a script temporarily.
*/
```

As the previous example explains, comments serve a dual purpose: They not only allow you to sprinkle your scripts with helpful reminders of what each section of code is for; They can also be used to disable a part of a script temporarily. This is extremely useful when you are trying to trace the cause of an error. New features in Dreamweaver 8 make the insertion and removal of such comments very easy.

Experimenting with PHP comments

Continue working with the same page as in previous exercises, or use `index_02.php` from the download files for this chapter.

1. Open `index.php` in Code view, and locate the following code (it should be around line 6):

```
<?php require('style_rules.php'); ?>
```

It doesn't matter whether the code uses `include()` instead of `require()`. The purpose of this exercise is to experiment with PHP comments.

2. Highlight the whole line, and click the Apply Comment button on the Coding toolbar. You will be offered five choices, as shown in the screenshot alongside. Of these five, only three are applicable to PHP scripts, but even these three are not appropriate in every circumstance.

3. Click Apply /* */ Comment. The line of code will be surrounded by CSS-style comments, but remain highlighted. Click anywhere else in the page to remove the highlighting. This is where Dreamweaver syntax coloring comes in very useful. PHP code that has been rendered inactive by commenting is displayed by default in orange. You will see that the PHP code has not turned orange. In other words, the comments have had no effect.

Why? It's because the comments are outside the PHP tags. If you save the page, and preview it in a browser, you will see that the stylesheets are still applied, and that most browsers display the comment tags in the top left of the browser window (Safari ignores the comment tags entirely).

4. Highlight the whole line again in Code view, and click the Remove Comment button on the Coding toolbar. The comment tags will be removed.

5. To apply this style of comment tag correctly, you need to highlight the code inside the PHP tags. Highlight the code shown here in bold type, and select Apply /* */ Comment again:

```
<?php require('style_rules.php'); ?>
```

6. Click elsewhere in the code, and you should see that the highlighted code has turned orange. If you switch to Design view or preview the page in a browser, you will see that the stylesheets have been disabled.

7. Highlight the same code and the surrounding comment tags, and click the Remove Comment button to remove them. Now place your cursor immediately before `require`, and click the Apply Comment button. This time select Apply // Comment.

8. This type of comment applies to the rest of the line, so it has the same effect as the comment you applied in step 5.

9. Click the Remove Comment button. Nothing happens. It doesn't matter what you try, you cannot remove this type of comment if any other code precedes it on the same line.

10. Use the keyboard to remove the // comment, and separate the code onto three lines like this:

```php
<?php
require('style_rules.php');
?>
```

11. Position your cursor in front of require again, and select Apply // Comment.

12. Now move your cursor so that it is anywhere within the code that has just been commented out. Click Remove Comment. This time, the comment is removed correctly. Try steps 11 and 12 again with the middle line of PHP code indented several tab spaces. It still works. So this technique is best suited to single lines.

13. After you have removed the // comment, scroll down to the bottom of the page, and highlight the entire PHP code block that enters the current year in the copyright notice, as shown here.

14. Select Apply <?php /*?> <?php */?> Comment. The effect of this is to comment out all the code inside the PHP block, but to place two active PHP tags around the entire section. The effect is the same as in steps 5 and 6; it's just a different way of doing it.

> You should use Apply <?php /*?> <?php */?> Comment only to complete PHP code blocks, including their opening and closing tags. If you apply it inside a PHP code block, you will nest PHP tags incorrectly, and generate syntax errors. Use Apply /* */ Comment when working inside a PHP block.

15. Switch back to Code view, and remove the comment tags. There is another way to add CSS-style tags. It's on the PHP Insert bar, as shown in the screenshot.

16. The PHP Insert bar has no option to remove comments, but you can use the Remove Comment button on the Coding toolbar. One slight curiosity of the Insert bar comments is that Dreamweaver leaves an extra space on either side when they are removed. But since white space is ignored by PHP, this is nothing to worry about.

17. You probably know enough about comments now to last you a lifetime, but if you're a context menu fan, there's one final way. Highlight a section of code, right-click/*CTRL*-click, and choose Selection from the menu that appears. All the options you have just explored are available here, as you can see from the screenshot. (There are actually many more, as I haven't shown the full menu.)

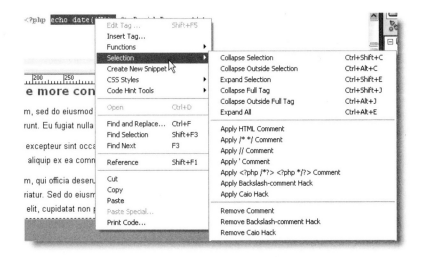

Although extremely useful for debugging, remember that the main purpose of comments is not to disable sections of code, but to explain what the code is for. You'll find that Dreamweaver-generated code is liberally sprinkled with comments. Even if you don't understand all the code in detail, the comments will help you identify more quickly the section that needs tweaking to meet your own requirements.

> *When learning, you may want to rush ahead without bothering with comments. Don't do it. A few minutes spent writing comments now will save you a lot of time later. Get into the habit early.*

Handling text and other output in PHP

The whole point of creating dynamic pages is so that you can change the content, so it's important to know how PHP handles text—or strings, as they're called. Sometimes text is stored in variables. At other times, you may just want to display some text in your web page. The normal way to display output that's not stored in a variable is to close the PHP code block, go back to XHTML, and open another PHP code block when you need to work with variables again. Sometimes, the amount of plain text (which can include XHTML tags) is so short, it's a lot easier to get PHP to output it to the browser.

You have already used echo to display output. It has a close counterpart called **print**, which also sends output to a browser (and *not* to a printer). There are some subtle differences between echo and print, but you can regard them as being equivalent to each other. The creator of PHP, Rasmus Lerdorf, has provided the official explanation for the incurably inquisitive at www.faqts.com/knowledge_base/view.phtml/aid/1/fid/40. I prefer echo for the following reasons:

- echo is one fewer character to type
- echo is marginally faster than print (but the difference is so small, you would never notice)
- echo is the form preferred by Dreamweaver

Both echo and print take an optional pair of parentheses to enclose the output they send to the browser. So, the PHP code to display the current year in index.php could be written in any of the following ways:

```
echo date('Y');
echo (date('Y'));
print date('Y');
print (date('Y'));
```

If you use parentheses, you can also omit the space after echo or print.

```
echo(date('Y'));
print(date('Y'));
```

All the above produce exactly the same output. Adding parentheses serves no real use, but it's useful to know that this is valid PHP if you ever come across it in other scripts.

> You may come across <?= in some scripts. This is the same as <?php echo. It can only be used when the PHP code block contains a single command. It's also likely to fail on some servers, so you should always replace it with the longer version.

Because date('Y') is a PHP function, it can stand on its own, but if you want to use a string with echo or print, you must enclose it in quotes. Either single or double quotes will do, but there is a difference between them.

Choosing single or double quotation marks

If all you're concerned about is what ends up on the screen, most of the time it doesn't matter which quotes you use, but behind the scenes, PHP uses single and double quotes in very different ways.

- Anything between single quotation marks is treated as plain text
- Anything between double quotation marks is processed

Experimenting with quotes

In index.php, you used echo to display the value of date('Y') directly in the page, but you might have got the date from somewhere else, such as a database or user input from an online form. To achieve the same effect, you can assign the value of date('Y') to a variable. Let's call it $year.

1. Copy the following code into a new PHP page, or use examples/ch05/quotes.php from the download files for this chapter, and then view it in a browser:

```php
<?php
$year = date('Y');
echo 'Single quotes: The year is $year<br />';
echo "Double quotes: The year is $year";
?>
```

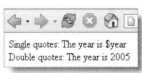

Single quotes: The year is $year
Double quotes: The year is 2005

As you can see from the screenshot alongside the code, $year is treated as plain text in the first line, but is correctly processed in the second line, which uses double quotes.

> *To get the output to display on separate lines, you have to include XHTML tags, such as*
 , because echo *outputs only the values passed to it—nothing more.*

2. Change the text slightly in lines 3 and 4 of the code, as follows:

```php
echo 'Single quotes: This year it's $year<br />';
echo "Double quotes: This year it's $year";
```

As you type, the change in Dreamweaver syntax coloring should alert you to a problem, but save the page nevertheless, and view it in a browser (it's quotes2.php in the download files). You should see something like this:

http://localhost/phpdw/examples/ch05/quotes2.php

Parse error: syntax error, unexpected T_STRING, expecting ',' or ';' in C:\htdocs\phpdw\examples\ch05\quotes2.php on line 11

As far as PHP is concerned, an apostrophe and a single quote are the same thing, and quotes must always be in matching pairs. What's happened is that the apostrophe in it's has been regarded as the closing quote for the first line; what was intended as the closing quote of the first line becomes a second opening quote; and the apostrophe in the second line becomes the second closing quote. All quite different from what was intended—and if you're confused, is it any wonder that PHP is unable to work out what's meant to be going on?

3. To solve the problem, insert a backslash in front of the apostrophe in the first sentence, like this (see quotes3.php in the download files):

```php
echo 'Single quotes: This year it\'s $year<br />';
```

You should now see the syntax coloring revert to normal. If you view the result in a browser, it should display correctly like this:

Single quotes: This year it's $year
Double quotes: This year it's 2005

Using escape sequences in strings

Using a backslash in this way is known as an **escape sequence**, which tells PHP to treat a character in a special way. Double quotes within a double-quoted string? You guessed it—escape them with a backslash.

```
echo "Swift's \"Gulliver's Travels\""; // displays the double quotes
```

The next line of code achieves exactly the same thing, but by using a different combination of quotes:

```
echo 'Swift\'s "Gulliver\'s Travels"';
```

> When creating strings, the outside pair of quotes must match—any quotes of the same style inside the string must be escaped with a backslash. However, putting a backslash in front of the opposite style of quote will result in the backslash being displayed. To see the effect, put a backslash in front of the apostrophe in the doubled-quoted string in the previous exercise.

So what happens when you want to include a literal backslash? You escape it with a backslash (\\).

The backslash (\\) and the single quote (\') are the only escape sequences that work in a single-quoted string. Because double quotes are a signal to PHP to process any variables contained within a string, there are many more escape sequences for double-quoted strings. Most of them are to avoid conflicts with characters that are used with variables, but three of them have special meanings: \n inserts a new line character, \r inserts a carriage return (needed mainly for Windows), and \t inserts a tab. Table 5-2 lists the main escape sequences supported by PHP.

Table 5-2. The main PHP escape sequences

Escape sequence	Character represented in double-quoted string
\"	Double quote
\n	New line
\r	Carriage return
\t	Tab
\\	Backslash
\$	Dollar sign
\{	Opening curly brace
\}	Closing curly brace
\[	Opening square bracket
\]	Closing square bracket

> *The escape sequences listed in Table 5-2, with the exception of \\, work only in double-quoted strings. If you use them in a single-quoted string, they will be treated as a literal backslash followed by the second character.*

Double quotes are obviously very useful, so why not use them all the time? A lot of people do, but the official recommendation is to use the quoting method that uses the least processing power—and that's usually single quotes. Whenever PHP sees an opening double quote, it tries to process any variables first. If it finds none, it goes back and treats the string as plain text. On short scripts, such as those you're creating in this book, the difference in processing time is negligible, but it can make a difference on long, complex scripts.

Joining strings

It's often necessary to join together two strings—usually when at least one of them is stored in a variable. In technical terms, this is called **concatenation**, and the symbol used to do this is known as the **concatenation operator**. PHP's choice of concatenation operator may come as a surprise—it's a period (.) or dot.

When concatenating two strings, PHP takes no notice of white space (except within a quoted string). The following example illustrates what this means.

```
$greeting = 'Hello,';
$name = 'Dolly';
echo $greeting.$name // Displays "Hello,Dolly"
```

The result remains the same even if you change the last line like this:

```
echo $greeting. $name; // Still displays "Hello,Dolly"
```

To get white space between concatenated strings, you have three options:

- Use a double-quoted string
- Add the white space as a separate string
- Include the white space in one of the strings

```
echo "$greeting $name.";        // "Hello, Dolly."
echo $greeting.' '.$name.'.';   // "Hello, Dolly."
$greeting = 'Hello, ';
echo $greeting.$name.'.';       // "Hello, Dolly."
```

Double quotes usually have a clear advantage when you need to incorporate variables in a string, although there are exceptions that you will learn about later in the book.

The concatenation operator can be difficult to spot in a long script in a book or on your computer screen, so if your script generates unexpected errors, it's one of the first things to check. If seeing the concatenation operator becomes a problem in Dreamweaver, go to Edit ➤ Preferences (Dreamweaver ➤ Preferences on a Mac), select the Fonts category, and change the size of the font for Code view.

Adding to an existing string

The examples in the preceding section only join the strings temporarily. You'll often find that you want to add to an existing string and store the new value in the same variable. The obvious way is like this:

```
$tweedledee = "'The time has come,' the Walrus said,\n";
$tweedledee = $tweedledee."'To talk of many things:\n";
$tweedledee = $tweedledee."Of shoes, and ships, and sealing wax,\n";
$tweedledee = $tweedledee."Of cabbages, and kings,\n";
$tweedledee = $tweedledee."And why the sea is boiling hot,\n";
$tweedledee = $tweedledee."And whether pigs have wings.'";
echo $tweedledee;
```

Typing out the same variable twice for every assignment statement gets rather tedious, so PHP has a handy piece of shorthand known as a **combined assignment operator**. You place the concatenation operator directly in front of the assignment operator, like this:

```
$tweedledee =  "'The time has come,' the Walrus said,\n";
$tweedledee .= "'To talk of many things:\n";
$tweedledee .= "Of shoes, and ships, and sealing wax,\n";
$tweedledee .= "Of cabbages, and kings,\n";
$tweedledee .= "And why the sea is boiling hot,\n";
$tweedledee .= "And whether pigs have wings.'";
echo $tweedledee;
```

You can compare both blocks of code in concatenated.php and combined.php in the download files for this chapter. The effect is identical. The next screenshot shows combined.php as seen in a browser, and also as seen in the browser's page source view.

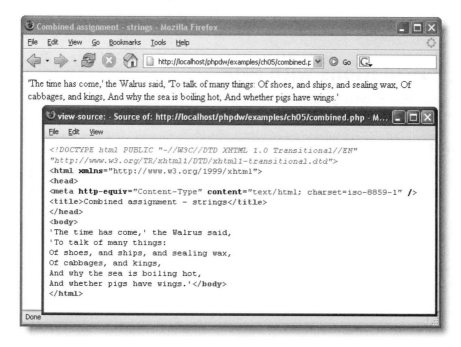

Note how the PHP code uses the \n escape sequence to insert a new line character at the end of each line. When viewed in a browser, the new lines are apparent only in the source code. Ifa you want the text to be displayed on separate lines in the browser, you need to hard-code <br /> tags into the string. Alternatively, you can pass the string to a PHP function called nl2br(), which converts all new line characters into <br /> tags. All that's needed is to change the final line of code like this:

```
echo nl2br($tweedledee);
```

This illustrates a powerful—and sometimes confusing—aspect of PHP: the nesting of functions. (Technically speaking, echo isn't a function, but it performs an almost identical role, so you can regard it as one here.) Even though echo comes first, PHP looks at the whole statement, and realizes that nl2br() needs to add the <br /> tags before the content of $tweedledee is sent to the browser. You could write the same code like this:

```
$brTagsAdded = nl2br($tweedledee);
echo $brTagsAdded;
```

However, the single-line version is a lot more compact, and it's the way most experienced PHP developers would favor. Don't worry if you find it difficult to use this sort of shortcut yourself until you gain more experience. The important thing is to write code that *works*. You'll pick up the skill to write more compact script as you become more familiar with the language. You'll also discover that the sometimes odd names for functions do have a logic behind them. The function you have just used stands for **n**ew **l**ine **2** (to) **br**eak—obvious, really!

> *How long can a string be? As far as PHP is concerned, there's no limit. In practice, you are likely to be constrained by other factors, such as server memory; but in theory, you could store the whole of* War and Peace *in a string variable.*

Doing calculations with PHP

PHP is highly adept at working with numbers, and can perform a wide variety of calculations, from simple arithmetic to complex math.

Arithmetic operators

The standard arithmetic operators all work the way you would expect, although some of them look slightly different from those you learned at school. For instance, an asterisk (*) is used as the multiplication sign, and a forward slash (/) is used to indicate division.

Table 5-3 shows examples of how the standard arithmetic operators work. To demonstrate their effect, the following variables have been set:

```
$x = 20;
$y = 10;
$z = 4.5;
```

Table 5-3. Arithmetic operators in PHP

Operation	Operator	Example	Result
Addition	+	$x + $y	30
Subtraction	-	$x - $y	10
Multiplication	*	$x * $y	200
Division	/	$x / $y	2
Modulo division	%	$x % $z	2
Increment (adds 1)	++	$x++	21
Decrement (subtracts 1)	--	$y--	9

You may not be familiar with the modulo operator. This returns the remainder of a division, as follows:

```
26 % 5     // result is 1
26 % 27    // result is 26
10 % 2     // result is 0
```

A practical use of the modulo operator is to work out whether a number is odd or even. $number % 2 will always produce 0 or 1. In Chapter 11, I'll show you how to use this to create a table with different background colors for alternating rows.

The increment (++) and decrement (--) operators can come either before or after the variable. When they come before the variable, 1 is added to or subtracted from the value before any further calculation is carried out. When they come after the variable, the main calculation is carried out first, and then 1 is either added or subtracted. Since the dollar sign is an integral part of the variable name, the increment and decrement operators go before the dollar sign when used in front:

```
++$x
--$y
```

Calculations in PHP follow exactly the same rules as standard arithmetic. Table 5-4 summarizes the precedence of arithmetic operators.

Table 5-4. Precedence of arithmetic operators

Precedence	Group	Operators	Rule
Highest	Parentheses	( )	Operations contained within parentheses are evaluated first. If these expressions are nested, the innermost is evaluated foremost.
Next	Multiplication and division	* / %	These operators are evaluated next. If an expression contains two or more operators, they are evaluated from left to right.
Lowest	Addition and subtraction	+ -	These are the final operators to be evaluated in an expression. If an expression contains two or more operators, they are evaluated from left to right.

If in doubt, use parentheses all the time to group the parts of a calculation that you want to make sure are performed as a single unit.

Combining calculations and assignment

You will often want to perform a calculation on a variable and assign the result back to the same variable. PHP offers the same convenient shorthand for arithmetic calculations as for strings. Table 5-5 shows the main combined assignment operators and their use.

Table 5-5. Combined arithmetic assignment operators used in PHP

Operator	Example	Equivalent to
+=	$a += $b	$a = $a + $b
-=	$a -= $b	$a = $a - $b
*=	$a *= $b	$a = $a * $b
/=	$a /= $b	$a = $a / $b
%=	$a %= $b	$a = $a % $b

- Don't forget that **the plus sign is used in PHP only as an arithmetic operator**.
- **Addition:** Use += as the combined assignment operator
- **Strings:** Use .= as the combined assignment operator

Making decisions with PHP

Earlier in the chapter, I got you to use the previous year's date to demonstrate how static text can be combined with dynamic data, but a far more satisfactory solution would be to show the actual year in which a website was launched, and add any further years automatically. You know the starting date—that's a fixed value. So all that's necessary is to compare the current date with the starting date. In terms of human logic:

> *If the current year is the same as the starting year*
>   *Display the starting year only*
> *Else*
>   *Display both*

And that is almost exactly how you would do it with PHP.

Improving the copyright notice

Continue using the same copy of index.php as in earlier exercises, or use index_02.php from site_check/ch05. The finished version is in index_03.php and copyright.php.

1. Scroll down to the bottom of the page, and place your cursor anywhere inside the copyright notice. Open Split view, and click the <p> tag in the Tag selector to highlight the entire paragraph, including the surrounding <p> tags, as shown here. Cut the highlighted section to the clipboard.

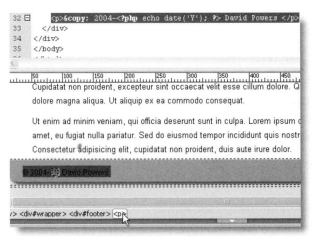

151

2. Close up any space between the footer `<div>` tags, and create an include for the copyright page, which you will create in the next step. The code should look like this (you can use any of the include() or require() commands):

```
<div id="footer"><?php include('copyright.php'); ?></div>
```

3. Create a new PHP file, and save it in the site root as copyright.php. Click in Design view, and paste the copyright paragraph from the clipboard. Highlight the copyright paragraph as in step 1, and then switch to Code view.

4. Hold down the *ALT/OPT* key, and click the Collapse Section button (shown along-side) on the Coding toolbar. This will collapse all the code *outside* the highlighted paragraph. You should end up with the page looking like this:

5. Click inside both collapsed sections of code in turn, and press *DELETE*. You should be left with just the line of code that you originally cut to the clipboard, and the line number that it's on should have changed to 2.

> *This isn't the only way to cut and paste a section of code into an empty PHP page, but I chose it for two reasons: to demonstrate how to leverage some of the new features on the Coding toolbar, and because using paste directly into Code view would have resulted in © **2004-** **David Powers** without any of the associated XHTML tags or PHP code. Even though you saw everything highlighted in Split view, cutting to the clipboard was done in Design view. Consequently, to preserve all the underlying code, it's necessary to be in Design view when pasting it back.*

6. Amend the code in copyright.php so that it looks like this (new code is in bold type):

```
<p>&copy;
<?php
// define the starting year
$startYear = 2005;
// calculate the current year
$thisYear = date('Y');

if ($startYear == $thisYear) {
  // if both are the same, just show the starting year
  echo $startYear;
  }
else {
  // if they're different, show both
  echo "$startYear-$thisYear";
  }

?> David Powers</p>
```

Normally, you don't need to write such detailed comments for every line of code, but I've done so here to help you understand what's going on. I've also chosen descriptive variable names. Often, the choice of variable names is sufficient to describe the purpose of code without comments. Such code is referred to as **self-commenting**.

7. Save `copyright.php`, and press *F12/OPT+F12* to view it in a browser. As long as you've not made any typing errors, you should see a copyright notice with the current year displayed. If you do get errors, check your code against the version in the download files.

8. Change the value of $startYear, and view the page again. This time, you should see the range of years displayed as before. Note that the hyphen between $startYear and $thisYear in line 14 does *not* perform a subtraction. The double quotes treat it as a literal hyphen, and not as a minus sign. Remove the double quotes, and you'll see PHP display the result of the calculation instead. After experimenting with the quotes, restore the code to the way it looks in step 6, and save `copyright.php`.

9. Amend the footer `<div>` on the four other pages so that the code is the same as in step 2.

When you view `index.php`, the copyright notice should now display only the current year, but it will automatically display a range of years from January 1. If there's no space separating the date or name from the surrounding characters, add the necessary white space in the code. I left a space after © in line 1, and between the closing PHP tag and my name in the final line.

Now that you've seen how it works, I'll explain the theory.

Using if . . . else conditional statements

What you have just used is called a **conditional statement**—it performs an action or series of actions only if a certain condition is satisfied. The condition being tested is placed in parentheses, and the actions are surrounded by curly braces. The basic structure looks like this:

```
if (condition is true) {
  // Execute this code
  }
else {
  // Do this instead
  }
```

If you want to consider more than two options, the intermediate ones are introduced by elseif (this is normally written as one word in PHP):

```
if (condition is true) {
  // Execute this code
  }
elseif (alternative condition is true) {
  // Do this instead
  }
else {
  // Do this as a last resort
  }
```

You can have as many elseif clauses in the sequence as you like. PHP will consider each one in turn, and execute the first one that matches. If you only want to do something when a particular condition is met, you can run an if statement on its own:

```
if (it's between December 1 and 24) {
    Display the number of days to Christmas
    }
```

That conditional statement would run only in the final run-up to Christmas, and would be ignored at any other time of the year.

You *can* omit the braces when there's only one statement to be executed, but it's not a good idea. The braces make the logic of your code much easier to follow. It's also easy to forget to restore the braces if you later add any further statements.

Often, decisions are made by comparing two or more values. PHP uses comparison and logical operators to handle this sort of situation.

Using comparison operators

Comparison operators are used to compare two values (known as **operands** because they appear on either side of an operator). If both values meet the criterion being tested for, the expression evaluates to true—or to use the technical expression, it **returns** true; otherwise, it returns false. Computers make decisions on the basis of whether two values are equal, whether one is greater than the other, and so on. "Well, maybe" doesn't cut any ice. Table 5-6 lists the comparison operators used in PHP.

Table 5-6. PHP comparison operators used for decision-making

Symbol	Name	Use
==	Equality	Returns true if both operands have the same value; otherwise, returns false.
!=	Inequality	Returns true if both operands have different values; otherwise, returns false.
<>	Inequality	This has the same meaning as !=. It's rarely used, but has been included here for the sake of completeness.
===	Identical	Determines whether both operands are identical. To be considered identical, they must not only have the same value, but also be of the same datatype (for example, both floating-point numbers).
!==	Not identical	Determines whether both operands are not identical (according to the same criteria as the previous operator).
>	Greater than	Determines whether the operand on the left is greater in value than the one on the right.

Symbol	Name	Use
>=	Greater than or equal to	Determines whether the operand on the left is greater in value than or equal to the one on the right.
<	Less than	Determines whether the operand on the left is less in value than the one on the right.
<=	Less than or equal to	Determines whether the operand on the left is less in value than or equal to the one on the right.

As I mentioned earlier in the chapter, one of the most common beginner mistakes is to think of the equal sign as meaning "is equal to." When comparing two values, you must always use the equality operator (==), the identical operator (===), or their negative equivalents (!= and !==).

Mixing up the assignment and equality operators

This is such a common mistake, it's important for you to see the effect of using = instead of ==.

1. Open copyright.php, and change the value of $startYear to any year other than the current one:

   $startYear = **1776**;

2. Remove the second equal sign from the comparison in line 8, so it looks like this:

   if ($startYear = $thisYear) {

3. Save the page and press *F12/OPT+F12* to view it in a browser. This is what you'll see:

4. Change the value of $startYear to something completely different. For instance, assign a string like this:

   $startYear = **'Rebel colonies break free'**;

5. Save the page, and view it in a browser again. You should get the same result. It doesn't matter what you change the value of $startYear to, you will always get the same result.

6. Restore lines 4 and 8 to their original state, and save copyright.php.

Why does it happen? A single equal sign is the assignment operator, so the change in line 8 results in the values of $startYear and $thisYear no longer being *compared*. Instead, what happens is that the value of $thisYear is *assigned* to $startYear.

But since they're no longer being compared, why does the if statement succeed? It's because an if statement tests whether the condition inside the parentheses returns true. The successful assignment of the value of one variable to another will always return true, so the if statement will always succeed.

There's a natural tendency when typing = to think "is equal to," so this causes problems even to experienced PHP developers. It's one of the first things you should check if your scripts produce unexpected results.

Testing more than one condition

Frequently, comparing two values is not enough. PHP allows you to set a series of conditions using **logical operators** to specify whether all, or just some, need to be fulfilled.

All the logical operators in PHP are listed in Table 5-7. **Negation**—testing that the opposite of something is true—is also considered a logical operator, although it applies to individual conditions rather than a series.

Table 5-7. Logical operators used for decision-making in PHP

Symbol	Name	Use
&&	Logical AND	Evaluates to true if both operands are true. If the left-hand operand evaluates to false, the right-hand operand is never tested.
and	Logical AND	Exactly the same as &&, but it takes lower precedence.
||	Logical OR	Evaluates to true if either operand is true; otherwise, returns false. If the left-hand operand returns true, the right-hand operand is never tested.
or	Logical OR	Exactly the same as ||, but it takes lower precedence.
xor	Exclusive OR	Evaluates to true if only one of the two operands returns true. If both are true or both are false, it evaluates to false.
!	Negation	Tests whether something is not true.

Technically speaking, there is no limit to the number of conditions that can be tested. Each condition is considered in turn from left to right, and as soon as a defining point is reached, no further testing is carried out. When using && or and, every condition must be fulfilled, so testing stops as soon as one turns out to be false. Similarly, when using || or or, only one condition needs to be fulfilled, so testing stops as soon as one turns out to be true.

```
$a = 10;
$b = 25;
if ($a > 5 && $b > 20) // returns true
if ($a > 5 || $b > 30) // returns true, $b never tested
```

The implication of this is that you should always design your tests with the condition most likely to return false as the first to be evaluated. If any of your conditions involve complex calculations, place them so they are the last to be evaluated. Doing so will speed up execution.

If you want a particular set of conditions considered as a group, enclose them in parentheses.

```
if (($a > 5 && $a < 8) || ($b > 20 && $b < 40))
```

> *Operator precedence is a tricky subject. Stick with && and ||, rather than and and or, and use parentheses to group expressions to which you want to give priority.*

The xor operator is rarely used.

You'll see the negative operator in action later in the book, but let's finish this chapter with an example of testing two conditions.

Testing for the existence of an external file

Continue working with index.php, or use index_03.php from the download files for this chapter.

1. Save index.php as index_iftest.php, and continue working with the new file.

2. Locate the footer <div>, and open Split view. Position your cursor after the opening PHP tag, and amend the code like this:

```
<div id="footer"><?php $includeFile = 'copyright.php';
  if (file_exists($includeFile) && is_readable($includeFile)) {
    include($includeFile);
    }
?></div>
```

The second line of this code uses two PHP built-in functions that have self-explanatory names: The first checks for the existence of a file, and the second tests whether it's readable. Using && in the if statement indicates that *both* conditions must be true for the code between the curly braces to be executed. Consequently, if the file doesn't exist, or if it exists, but doesn't have the right permissions, the include command will be ignored.

3. Save index_iftest.php, and view the page in a browser. If you have typed the code correctly, it should display exactly the same as before. If you get an error, check your code against index_iftest.php in site_check/ch05.

4. Change the value of $includeFile to the name of a non-existent file, save index_iftest.php, and view it in a browser again. This time, you won't get any error notices; the copyright section just won't appear.

5. Change line 3 in step 2 to use require() instead of include(). Even though you're still using a non-existent filename, the page will still display correctly. This is because all the code inside the curly braces of an if statement is ignored if the test conditions aren't matched. The require statement never runs, so it cannot trigger a fatal error.

Although I have assigned the filename of the external file to $includeFile, you could use the actual filename (in quotes) in each of the functions. The point of using a variable is that there's less chance of misspelling the filename. It also makes the code reusable. You could use this same block of code for all three include commands on the page, just changing the value of $includeFile in each one. $includeFile will always have the most recently assigned value, so it can represent different files at different times. Yes, but what if I misspell the variable name? Try it.

6. Change one of the instances of $includeFile to $includefile (all lowercase), and preview the page in a browser. You should see something like this:

> Notice: Undefined variable: includefile in **C:\htdocs\phpdw\index_iftest.php** on line **32**

This should serve as a timely reminder that PHP is case-sensitive, and that PHP notices serve a valuable purpose. It tells you that includefile is undefined (PHP error messages remove the $ from the beginning of variable names)—usually a sign that you have misspelled the name of a variable.

You could change all the includes in the East-West Seasons site to use this technique, but it has the disadvantage that includes are no longer automatically displayed in Dreamweaver Design view. This would prevent the CSS displaying. Although you could use Design Time Style Sheets (Text ➤ CSS Styles ➤ Design-time) instead, I propose to leave the includes in their current form. Performing a change like this is something you should consider doing just before finally deploying a site on the Internet.

Solid foundations

I hope you found that both interesting and practical. It's just a taster of the way in which PHP can make your sites not only dynamic, but also more efficient. You've also covered most of the basics of PHP syntax. In the next chapter, I'll cover the remaining basic aspects of the language, which should give you the confidence to adapt Dreamweaver's code to your own specific requirements and, hopefully, to start experimenting with PHP on your own. Among the things I'll show you are how to change the overall look of the East-West Seasons site automatically at different times of the year, and how to activate an online contact form.

Chapter 6

GETTING FEEDBACK FROM AN ONLINE FORM

What this chapter covers:

- Gathering user input and sending it by email
- Using Dreamweaver's accessibility features for forms
- Organizing related information in arrays
- Validating user input on both the client and server
- Displaying errors without losing user input
- Formatting dates and extracting date parts
- Automatically changing the site's style
- Using loops and custom-built functions

Armed with the knowledge from the previous chapter, you're now in a position to put PHP to really practical use. In this chapter, I'll show you how to gather information from a contact form, check that all the required fields have been filled in, and then send the user's input to your mailbox.

To be honest, sending an email from an online form is just the sort of task that Dreamweaver should automate, but unfortunately it doesn't. Commercial extensions are available to automate the process for you, such as MX Send Email in the MX Kollection 3 suite of Dreamweaver extensions from InterAKT, which is available as a trial version from www.interaktonline.com/Products/Bundles/MXKollection/Try-Download. However, not everyone will have—or want to buy—a commercial extension in addition to Dreamweaver 8, so I think it's important to show you how to hand-code this vital feature. At the same time, it will give me the opportunity to cover the remaining control structures in PHP, as well as other basic elements of the language, such as arrays and functions.

After building the contact form, I'll show you how to change the look of the site automatically with the passing seasons, and a way of building the navigation menu with a custom-built PHP function.

Designing the feedback form

Figure 6-1 shows what the finished feedback form looks like in a browser. It contains just three fields—for the visitor's name, email address, and a message.

Figure 6-1. The completed contact form as viewed in a browser

I've deliberately kept the form simple; exactly the same technique is used whether your form has three fields or thirty. The content of each field is combined into one long string in PHP, and sent as the body of an email. The escape sequences that you learned about in the previous chapter will rearrange everything into a readable format. But first things first—before you can get down to scripting the PHP, you need to build the online form in XHTML.

Laying out the feedback form

Continue working with the files from the previous chapter, or copy contact_01.php, style_rules_01.php, and copyright.php from site_check/ch06 into your phpdw site root. If using the download files, always remember to rename the file so contact_01.php becomes contact.php, and so on. Just in case you think there's something missing, the Contact button on the navigation menu will not appear in the down state, as shown in Figure 6-1, until the end of the chapter.

1. In contact.php, highlight the placeholder text for the maincontent <div>, as shown in the screenshot, and select Heading 1 from the Format field in the Property inspector. You need to replace the placeholder text with something more suitable, such as "Send us your comments." However, the footer <div> will shift disconcertingly to the right if you delete the existing text first. So, with the placeholder text still highlighted, type in your new heading, and everything should stay firmly in place.

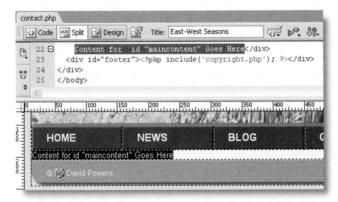

2. Press ENTER/RETURN to create a new paragraph, and insert a couple of lines about welcoming feedback. Alternatively, use the Lorem and More extension that you installed in Chapter 4 to add some filler text. To create just one paragraph with Lorem and More, enter 1 in the Amount field.

3. The feedback form needs to go immediately after the paragraph, so you'll probably do what I've always done—press ENTER/RETURN and then use the Forms Insert bar or Insert ➤ Form ➤ Form to insert the <form> tags. The only problem is that you end up with an empty paragraph below the form, which leaves an unwanted gap that needs to be removed manually later. There's a much simpler way . . .

If you don't already have Split view open, select it now, so that you can follow what happens to the underlying code. Click at the end of the paragraph in Design view; in Code view, you should be able to see that your cursor is just to the left of the closing </p> tag. In other words, it's still inside the paragraph. However, Dreamweaver is smart enough to realize that the form should go outside. Click the Form button on the Forms Insert bar (or use the Insert menu).

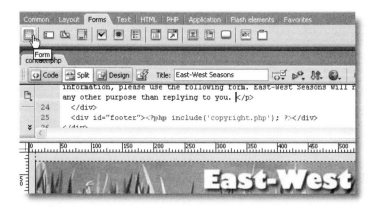

4. The <form> tags will appear in the correct position outside the paragraph, but still inside the maincontent <div>, as shown here. Note that this happens *only* if the focus of your page is in Design view. If you click inside Code view, you will be presented with the Tag Editor, which is a lot less user-friendly, and the resulting form will be inserted exactly where your cursor was. Although you will dip in and out of Code view for the rest of this section, always make sure the focus is in Design view when inserting a new form element from the Forms Insert bar.

```
    any other purpose than replying to you. </p>
24      <form id="form1" name="form1" method="post" action="">
25      </form>
26      </div>
```

> *Dreamweaver will create the form wherever your cursor happens to be. So if it's not at the end of the paragraph, Dreamweaver splits the current paragraph by inserting a closing </p> tag, followed by an opening one, with the form in-between.*

5. In the Property inspector, insert contactForm in the Form name field, and leave all other settings at their default values.

6. I decided to create the layout shown in Figure 6-1 by putting each input element in a separate paragraph. It sounds easy, but changes to the way Dreamweaver 8 creates forms have resulted in some odd, and not always user-friendly, behavior. Dreamweaver displays forms in Design view as an area surrounded by a red dotted line. Click inside this area, and press *ENTER/RETURN* to create a new paragraph. Instead of creating just one, Dreamweaver normally creates two, and leaves your cursor inside the second one. You need four paragraphs in all, so press *ENTER/RETURN* two more times.

7. Use your keyboard up arrow or mouse pointer to return to the first paragraph inside the form, and then click the Text Field button on the Forms Insert bar (immediately to the right of the Form button). By default, Dreamweaver 8 now brings up an accessibility dialog box. Although this inserts important tags, the way it works leaves a lot to be desired. Like the accessibility dialog box for images that you encountered in Chapter 4, the Input Tag Accessibility Attributes dialog box provides a direct link to the Preferences panel for you to prevent it appearing in future. You may decide that's the best course of action, but first give it a try.

The first field in the Input Tag Accessibility Attributes dialog box inserts a label for your text field. Type Name followed by a colon, and select Attach label tag using 'for' attribute. You'll see what this is for in the following steps.

The lower half of the dialog box has settings for Position, Access Key, and Tab Index. Position simply determines whether the label comes before or after the form item. You want it before, so select the appropriate radio button. For the purposes of this exercise, you can leave Access Key and Tab Index blank. You can learn more about these accessibility attributes in *Web Designer's Reference* by Craig Grannell (friends of ED, ISBN 1-59059-430-4).

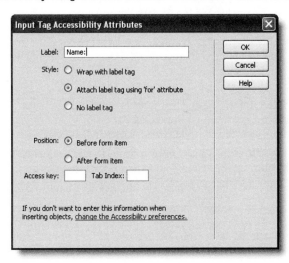

8. Click OK. The code that has been inserted should look like this in Split view:

The for attribute of the <label> tag provides important accessibility details for the visually impaired by clearly identifying which input element it relates to. To do so, it needs to have the same value as the name and id attributes of the <input> tag. At the moment they all have the same value, but it's the default, and not the one you want. The Dreamweaver team really missed a great opportunity here to make everything work smoothly by allowing you to set the value through the previous dialog box. Instead, you have to dig into the code itself.

165

9. Click inside Code view, and change the code shown on line 26 of the preceding screenshot like this (new code is shown in bold text):

```
<label for="name">Name:</label>
```

10. Click back in Design view, and select the text field. This will highlight the <input> tag on line 27 of the preceding screenshot. You can now use the Property inspector to change the name of the text field to name. By using the Property inspector, Dreamweaver automatically assigns the same value to the field's id attribute. If you make the change directly in Code view, you need to change both the name and id attributes manually.

11. Still in Design view, click between the label and the text field, and press SHIFT+ENTER/SHIFT+RETURN to insert a line break (<br />).

12. Move your cursor into the empty paragraph below, and repeat steps 7 through 11 to insert a second text field with Email as its label, and email as its name/ID.

13. Move your cursor into the third paragraph, and select the Text Area button on the Forms Insert bar. Apply the label Message: and change the for, name, and id attributes to message in the same way as for the text fields. Set the Char width and Num Lines fields in the Property inspector to 60 and 6, respectively. The actual values are unimportant because CSS style rules will ultimately control the size of the text area. However, the cols and rows attributes created by these two settings are required elements in (X)HTML, so they should not be left out even when their role is superseded by CSS.

14. Move your cursor down into the final paragraph, and insert a submit button. Unlike the previous fields, the button doesn't need a text label in front of it, because you can change the label on the button directly. So, when the Input Tag Accessibility Attributes dialog box opens, leave the Label field blank, and select No label tag as the Style. Click OK.

15. In the Property inspector, change the button name to ewComments. To change the label that appears on the button, set the Value field to Send comments.

16. Open Code view. The code for your form should look like this:

```
<form id="contactForm" name="contactForm" method="post" action="">
  <p>
    <label for="name">Name:</label>
    <br />
    <input type="text" name="name" id="name" />
  </p>
  <p>
    <label for="email">Email:</label>
    <br />
    <input type="text" name="email" id="email" />
  </p>
  <p>
    <label for="message">Message:</label>
    <br />
    <textarea name="message" id="message"></textarea>
  </p>
  <p>
    <input name="ewComments" type="submit" id="ewComments"
➥ value="Send comments" />
  </p>
</form>
```

17. Open styles/bluebells.css, and add the following style rules at the bottom of the existing ones. Because each form input element has an ID, it will pick up the appropriate style, as will all the labels. The warning class will be used later in the chapter to display error messages in the same font as the form labels. A separate rule for the warning class also sets the color of the text to red.

```
/* styles for contact form */
form {
  margin: 10px 25px 0 50px;
  }
#name, #email {
  width: 200px;
  }
#message {
  width: 500px;
  height: 150px;
  }
label, .warning {
  font-family:Verdana, Arial, Helvetica, sans-serif;
  font-weight: bold;
  }
.warning {
  color: #F00;
  }
```

18. Save both contact.php and bluebells.css (if you don't want to type out the new style rules yourself, just use bluebells_02.css from site_check/styles, and rename it). View contact.php in a browser. It should look like Figure 6-1, although the Contact button on the navigation menu won't yet be styled to indicate that it's the current page.

Activating the feedback form

If you have used a CGI script, such as FormMail, to process a form, you will know that you set the action attribute in the opening <form> tag to the address of the script. With PHP, it's often more efficient to process everything in the same page.

Understanding how the contact form works

When creating an online form, there are two important settings in the Property inspector:

- **Action:** Where to send the form for processing
- **Method:** How the form should be processed

I told you to leave Action empty, because this is going to be a self-processing form. You'll add the necessary PHP code for this in a moment.

Method has three options available in a drop-down menu: Default, GET, and POST. In spite of what you might think, the first option is *not* the Dreamweaver default—it tells the browser to use its own default method, which is normally GET. Dreamweaver defaults to POST, which is the method you want.

> GET *sends the form values as part of the URL, whereas* POST *sends them directly to the processing script. Normally, you should use the* POST *method, because it doesn't have any limitation on the length of material that can be sent, and it's marginally more difficult for others to hijack the content. The* GET *method is used mainly for sending short pieces of information, such as the ID of a database record, or when you want to be able to bookmark the results of a database search.*

Figure 6-2 shows what happens when a visitor to the site clicks the submit button on the form.

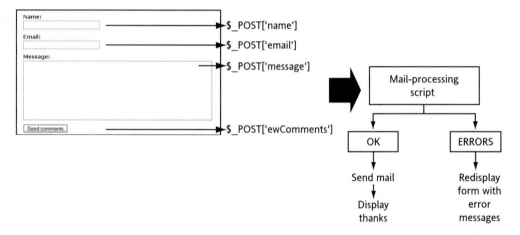

Figure 6-2. How the self-processing contact form works

PHP gathers the information from each input field in a special variable known as the **POST array**, which belongs to an important group known as superglobal arrays. I'll explain superglobals in more detail later, but first you need to know what arrays are, and how they work.

Organizing related values in arrays

Basically, arrays are variables that can hold more than one value. The classic example is a shopping list:

1. *milk*
2. *bread*
3. *cookies*
4. *butter*

PHP puts the number in square brackets after the variable; but instead of starting at 1, it starts counting at 0. So, my shopping list would look like this in PHP:

```
$shoppingList[0] = 'milk';
$shoppingList[1] = 'bread';
$shoppingList[2] = 'cookies';
$shoppingList[3] = 'butter';
```

The number in square brackets is called the **array key** or **index**, and it is used to identify individual items within an array. You refer to the entire array by the variable on its own and to individual items by the array variable followed by its key, like this:

```
$shoppingList    // the whole array
$shoppingList[2] // my favorite - cookies!
```

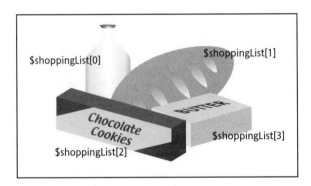

Arrays can contain more than one level. One packet of cookies is never enough, so I need another list:

```
$cookies[0] = 'chocolate digestives';
$cookies[1] = 'chocolate chip';
$cookies[2] = 'Jaffa cakes';
$cookies[3] = 'chocolate wafers';
```

Although there are now two arrays, they're both really part of the same shopping list, so in computer terms, you could replace the string cookies in the $shoppingList array with the $cookies array:

```
$shoppingList[2] = $cookies;
```

In other words, you have created an array within an array—a **multidimensional array**.

An array that uses numbers as the array key is technically known as an **indexed array**. But while computers are happy to work with numbers, we humans usually find it easier to work with names, so you can use a string in place of a number for each array key. This is known as an **associative array**, and it is something you will come across a great deal when working with the PHP code that Dreamweaver generates. The POST array is a good example of an associative array. Although it's possible to create an array that uses both numbers and strings as the array keys, it's a recipe for disaster. *Don't even think of doing it.*

So, to summarize—there are three types of arrays:

- **Indexed array:** An array that uses numbers as the array key
- **Associative array:** An array that uses strings as the array key
- **Multidimensional array:** An array that contains other arrays

After that brief excursion into my passion for chocolate cookies, it's back to the mail-processing script.

Identifying elements in the POST array

The **superglobal arrays** contain predefined variables that gather information from the server, such as the path of the current file, details passed through the URL, or input fields of a form. As mentioned earlier, when the form's method is set to post, the values are gathered in the POST array. (And if the method is set to get, it will come as little surprise to know the values are gathered in the GET array.)

Like all PHP superglobals, the POST array begins with $_. The entire array is contained in a variable called $_POST, and the key for each element is simply the name of the input element in the form. So, as Figure 6-2 shows, the value of the text field called name is assigned to $_POST['name'], and so on. You don't need the value of the submit button, but you do need to know whether it has been set. By testing for the existence of $_POST['ewComments'], you can control whether the mail-processing script should run when the page loads. (The GET array is stored in a variable called $_GET, which works identically.)

> *Because they are strings, the keys of an associative array should always be enclosed in quotes. The only exception is when you use an associative array variable within a double-quoted string, when the quotes around the array key should be omitted. This is a strange quirk of PHP that can cause an apparently perfect script to fail. Some developers get round this by omitting the quotes around array keys all the time, but this is bad practice.*

Keeping secure with the superglobal arrays

The superglobal arrays also play an important role in keeping your site secure. In Chapter 3, I warned you about a setting in php.ini called register_globals. This has been turned off by default since 2002, but you will often come across "advice" online that you should turn it back on for scripts to work properly. This is utter nonsense. The default is off, which means you will have no control over the setting on shared hosting, and turning register_globals on leaves a gaping security hole in your code.

In the days when the Web was a more innocent place, PHP used the name attribute of form fields and automatically converted them into PHP variables. So the content of a form input field called email became available in your scripts as $email. The same happened with values passed through a query string at the end of the URL. It was very convenient, but it meant that malicious users could inject values into your scripts with the greatest of ease. Turning off register_globals put an end to all that.

If you ever need to work with an old PHP script that relies on register_globals being turned on, all you need to do is convert variables that gather data from external sources to the appropriate superglobal array. In the case of forms, this is usually $_POST or $_GET. You may also come across old scripts that use $HTTP_POST_VARS and $HTTP_GET_VARS. These should now be replaced with $_POST and $_GET, respectively (www.php.net/manual/en/language.variables.predefined.php).

You'll encounter another of the superglobal arrays in this next section, but that's more than enough theory for the time being. Let's get on with building the form-processing script.

Scripting the feedback form

Continue working with same page as before, or use contact_02.php from site_check/ch06.

1. Open Split view, and use the Tag selector to select the entire form. This should bring the opening tag of the form into view in the Code view section of the workspace. Click inside Code view so that your cursor is between the quotes of the action attribute. Although you can set the action for the form through the Property inspector, doing so in Code view greatly reduces the possibility of making a mistake.

2. From the PHP Insert bar, click the Code Block button, as shown here. This will insert a pair of PHP tags between the quotes of the action attribute.

3. Dreamweaver positions your cursor in the correct place to start typing. To set the action attribute of the form to process itself, you need to use a variable from the SERVER superglobal array. As noted before, superglobals always begin with $_, so type just that between the PHP tags. Dreamweaver automatically presents you with a pop-up menu containing all the superglobals, as shown alongside.

4. You can navigate this pop-up menu in several ways: Continue typing "server" in either uppercase or lowercase until SERVER is highlighted, or use your mouse or the arrow keys to highlight it. Then double-click or press ENTER/RETURN. Dreamweaver will then present you with another pop-up menu. Locate PHP_SELF as shown, and either double-click or press ENTER/RETURN.

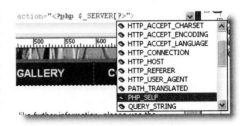

5. Although it's not strictly necessary for a single command, get into the habit of ending all statements with a semicolon, and type one after the closing square bracket (]) of the superglobal variable that's just been entered. The code in the opening <form> tag should look like this (new code is highlighted in bold type):

```
<form id="contactForm" name="contactForm" method="post"
➥ action="<?php $_SERVER['PHP_SELF']; ?>">
```

6. You now need to add the mail-processing script at the top of the page. From this point onward, it will be easier to work in Code view. Switch to Code view, and insert the block of PHP code shown in the following screenshot *above* the DOCTYPE declaration:

```
1   <?php
2   if (array_key_exists('ewComments', $_POST)) {
3       // mail processing script
4       echo 'You clicked the submit button';
5   }
6   ?>
7   <!DOCTYPE html PUBLIC "-//W3C//DTD XHTML 1.0 Transitional//EN"
    "http://www.w3.org/TR/xhtml1/DTD/xhtml1-transitional.dtd">
```

This uses the PHP function array_key_exists() to check whether the POST array contains a key called ewComments, the name that you gave to the submit button in the form. If you don't want to type out the function name yourself, don't forget that you can press *CTRL+SPACE* to bring up an alphabetical list of all PHP functions. Type just the first few letters, and then use your arrow keys to select the right one. When you press *TAB* or *ENTER/RETURN*, Dreamweaver finishes the rest of the typing, and pops up a code hint. Alternatively, you can just type the function name directly, and the code hint will appear as soon as you enter the opening parenthesis after array_key_exists:

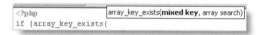

The mixed datatype refers to the fact that array keys can be either numbers or strings. In this case, you are using a string, so enclose ewComments in quotes, and then after a comma, type $_POST. Because it's a superglobal, you will be presented with the same pop-up menu as in step 3. If you select POST, Dreamweaver will assume that you want to add the name of an array key, and will automatically add an opening square bracket after the T. On this occasion, you want to check the whole POST array, not just a single element, so remove the bracket by pressing *BACKSPACE*. Also make sure that you use two closing parentheses—the first belongs to the function array_key_exists(), and the second encloses the condition being tested for by the if statement.

If the ewComments array key exists, the submit button must have been clicked, so any script between the curly braces will be executed. Otherwise, it will be ignored. Don't worry about the fact that echo will display text above the DOCTYPE declaration. It's being used for test purposes only, and will be removed eventually.

> Remember, an if *statement doesn't always need to be followed by* else *or* elseif. *When the condition of a solitary* if *statement isn't met, PHP simply skips to the next block of code.*

7. Save contact.php, and test it in a browser. It should look no different from before.

8. Click the submit button. A message should appear at the top of the page saying "You clicked the submit button." Since it's above the DOCTYPE declaration, the CSS will be messed up in Internet Explorer 6, but that's only a temporary problem.

9. You now need to test what happens when the page is loaded again normally. Click a link to any of the other pages in the navigation bar, and then click Contact to return to the page. The message should disappear. This confirms that any code inside the curly braces will run *only* if the submit button has been clicked.

10. Change the block of code that you entered in step 6 so that it looks like this:

```php
<?php
if (array_key_exists('ewComments', $_POST)) {
    // mail processing script
    // initialize variables
    $to = 'me@example.com'; // use your own email address
    $subject = 'Feedback from East-West Seasons';

    // build the message
    $message = 'From: '.$_POST['name']."\n\n";
    $message .= 'Email: '.$_POST['email']."\n\n";
    $message .= 'Comments: '.$_POST['message'];

    // send the email
    mail($to, $subject, $message);
}
?>
```

The script creates three variables: $to, $subject, and $message. The first is for the email address to which you want the content of the form to be sent (use your own email address). If you want to send the email to more than one address, list the email addresses as a comma-separated string. The second variable contains the subject line that will appear in the email, and the third contains the body of the message. There is nothing magical about these variable names. I've chosen them because they describe what's contained in each one, making much of the script self-commenting.

As you can see, I have used the combined concatenation operator (.=) to build the message from the elements of the POST array, and escape sequences to add new line characters between each section. The combined concatenation character and escape sequences were both covered in the previous chapter. I have also avoided the problem with quoting the keys of associative array elements by using the concatenation operator (.) to join the strings and variables together.

Finally, all that's needed to send the email is to pass the three variables in the correct order to the mail() function. It's as easy as that!

11. Now it's time to test your script. Mac users should be able to send a test email from their local computer, but Windows users will need to have set up the correct SMTP setting in php.ini, as described in steps 12 and 13 of the "Downloading and installing PHP on Windows" section in Chapter 3.

Save the page, load it into a browser, and send yourself a test email. If all has gone well, you should receive your message in your email inbox after a short while. If you don't receive anything, don't panic. The proliferation of spam has made ISPs far more selective about the sources of email they will accept. It's quite possible that your email has been sent, but has been rejected, and there's nowhere to bounce it back to. Try uploading it to your remote server, and test it again. The script still needs quite a bit of refinement, so even if it still doesn't work, just carry on to the next section.

12. Check your code so far against `contact_03.php` from `site_check/ch06`.

Two things that may go wrong at this stage depend on how mail is handled by your host. Some mail servers object to new line characters that are not accompanied by carriage returns. If you receive a warning that includes SMTP server response: 451, change the escape sequences in the section that builds the message like this:

```
$message = 'From: '.$_POST['name']."\r\n\r\n";
$message .= 'Email: '.$_POST['email']."\r\n\r\n";
```

Some SMTP servers also require user authentication before accepting mail. This will produce SMTP server response: 530. The PHP `mail()` function is designed to work directly with a mail transport agent (MTA), such as Sendmail, located on the same server, so doesn't support SMTP authentication. You can get around this by using a free script called PHPMailer (`http://phpmailer.sourceforge.net`), but this should not be necessary once you upload the contact form to your remote server. So, if you're having problems with SMTP authentication, I suggest testing `mail()` exclusively on your remote server.

Adding additional headers to the email

When typing the code in step 10, you may have noticed that the code hint for the `mail()` function shows that it can take two more optional arguments. The first of these two is particularly useful, because it allows you to add additional headers to the email message. You can find a full list of additional email headers at `www.faqs.org/rfcs/rfc2076`, but some of the most well-known and useful ones enable you to send copies of an email to other addresses (cc and bcc), to add a return address, or to change the encoding (often essential for languages other than Western European ones).

> *Poorly designed scripts that use additional headers can lay your contact form open to what's known as an email injection attack (see "Avoiding email injection attacks" later in the chapter). A spate of such attacks in mid-2005 resulted in some hosts disabling the use of additional headers. If the code in the following section fails to work, check your hosting company's instructions for setting the From header in PHP mail(). You will probably be restricted to using your own email address, and may not be allowed to add any other headers.*

1. Continue with the same file as in the previous section, or use contact_03.php.

2. Create two headers immediately above the line that sends the email, and add the fourth argument to the mail() function like this:

```
//build the additional headers
$additionalHeaders = "From: E-W Seasons<feedback@example.com>\r\n";
$additionalHeaders .= 'Reply-To: '.$_POST['email'];

// send the email
mail($to, $subject, $message, $additionalHeaders);
```

Like the body of the email, you need to store all additional headers in a single variable. Each header must be on a new line separated by a carriage return and new line character. This means using the \r and \n escape sequences in double quotes after each additional header, except the final one, which requires nothing at the end.

Make sure you use a genuine email address in the first line of $additionalHeaders, because many ISPs seem to use this to determine whether to accept messages. The format of the address can either be of the type feedback@example.com, or as shown in the preceding code lines with a plain text name followed by the email address in angle brackets.

3. Save contact.php, and test it again. If you still receive nothing, test it from your remote server. If it still doesn't work, contact your hosting company to make sure that mail() has been enabled (it's a core part of PHP, so there's no reason it should be disabled), and that masquerading has been correctly configured for your domain.

> *Masquerading is a setting that a hosting company must enable for multiple domains to send email from a shared server. Your PHP mail may be rejected if it has been set incorrectly.*

4. Assuming that your mail gets through, click the reply button on your mail program. Instead of sending the reply to your web server, the email address entered in the email field of the contact form should be displayed—a nifty use of additional headers.

Other useful additional headers In addition to From and Reply-To, the most useful headers are as follows:

- **Cc:** This sends a copy to each additional email address in a comma-separated list.
- **Bcc:** This is like cc, but it doesn't reveal the addresses to other recipients of the message.
- **Content-Type:** This is used to set the encoding of the email.

As noted before, each additional header must be on a new line created by the \r and \n using the PHP "\r\n" escape sequence. The name of the additional header should be followed by a colon and the required value. In the case of Cc and Bcc, only one value is permitted, so all additional addresses for each heading must be in a single comma-separated list. Content-Type is slightly more complex. The following examples show the settings for Unicode and Japanese, respectively:

```
Content-Type: text/plain; charset=utf-8
Content-Type: text/plain; charset=iso-2022-jp
```

To set a different language encoding, change the value of charset to the appropriate language setting, which should be the same as in a web page <meta> tag.

> *Older Unix-type servers interpret the "\r\n" escape sequence incorrectly, so if you experience problems with additional headers, try separating each line with "\n" instead of "\r\n".*

Improving the feedback form

You should now have a fully working feedback form, but it's far from perfect. You may find unexpected backslashes in your messages, and there's no way of preventing someone from sending a blank email. More importantly, there's a danger of being exploited by email injection attacks. The following sections will address each of these issues.

Getting rid of unwanted backslashes

The first problem will be apparent to most people using Windows if they included an apostrophe or any quotes in their test messages. As noted in Chapter 3, a PHP configuration setting called magic_quotes_gpc, which automatically escapes quotes and apostrophes, is set opposite ways in Windows and the Mac. As a result, Windows users may get unwanted backslashes in their emails. It's not just a simple Windows/Mac problem, though. Mac users are just as likely to find that their hosting companies have turned on magic quotes. Consequently, you need a universal solution.

Fortunately, the PHP online manual at www.php.net/manual/en/security.magicquotes.disabling.php has the answer. I have adapted it slightly, and created a Dreamweaver snippet, so that you can drop the ready-made script into any page that needs it. It's part of a collection of snippets that I've created for this book and packaged as a Dreamweaver extension so they can be installed in a single operation.

Installing the PHP snippets collection

If Dreamweaver is open, you will need to close and restart the program after installing the snippets, so save any files that are open.

1. If Dreamweaver is open, access the Extension Manager by choosing Manage Extensions from the Help menu. If Dreamweaver is closed, open the Extension Manager from the Windows Start menu or Finder (it's in the Macromedia folder).

2. Select Dreamweaver 8 in the drop-down menu on the Extension Manager toolbar, and choose File ➤ Install Extension, or click the Install button. Alternatively, press *CTRL+I* on Windows or ⌘ *+O* on the Mac.

3. In the dialog box that opens, navigate to Foundation_PHP_DW8.mxp in the extensions folder of the download files, and click Install.

4. After the extension has been installed, close Dreamweaver if it's open. The snippets will be available in the PHP-DW8 folder of the Snippets panel the next time you open the program.

Using the POST stripslashes snippet

1. Open `contact.php` in Code view. Position your cursor on line 4, just under the `mail processing script` comment. Open the Snippets panel by clicking the Snippets tab in the Files panel group or selecting Window ➤ Snippets. On Windows, you can also use the keyboard shortcut *SHIFT+F9*, but this doesn't work on the Mac version. Highlight the new POST stripslashes snippet in the PHP-DW8 folder, as shown alongside, and double-click it or click the Insert button at the bottom of the panel.

2. This will insert the following block of code into your page:

```
// remove escape characters from POST array
if (get_magic_quotes_gpc()) {
  function stripslashes_deep($value) {
    $value = is_array($value) ? array_map('stripslashes_deep', $value)
➥ : stripslashes($value);
    return $value;
    }
  $_POST = array_map('stripslashes_deep', $_POST);
  }
```

Lying at the heart of this code is the PHP function `stripslashes()`, which removes the escape backslashes from quotes and apostrophes. Normally, you just pass the string that you want to clean up as the argument to `stripslashes()`. Unfortunately, that won't work with an array. This block of code checks whether magic quotes have been turned on; and if they have, it goes through the POST array and any nested arrays, cleaning up your text for display either in an email or in a web page.

3. Save `contact.php`, and send another test email that includes apostrophes and quotes in the message. The email that you receive should be nicely cleaned up. If you have any problems, check your page against `contact_04.php` in `site_check/ch06`.

> *Many PHP servers have magic quotes turned on by default because it's essential to escape quotes and apostrophes when entering records in a database. Dreamweaver ensures everything is properly escaped when working with a database, but it doesn't have any method of removing unwanted backslashes on pages that display text in a web page or email. There should be no problem using this snippet on the same page as Dreamweaver code that interacts with a database, but it should be inserted after the database script.*

Checking required fields for valid input

The feedback form won't be much use if visitors forget to fill in required fields. Dreamweaver has a built-in JavaScript function that performs basic checks before the form is submitted, but that won't work if the visitor has JavaScript disabled. With PHP, though, you can prevent the email being sent unless all the required fields have been filled in. It's also vital to reject any input that might be used to compromise the security of your online form.

Avoiding email injection attacks

Although adding additional headers to an email through the optional fourth argument of the `mail()` function is extremely convenient, unless you're careful, it can be *too* convenient—for a malicious user, that is. What happens is that the attacker probes your form to see if any field is used as an additional header, and then uses that field to inject more headers. In this way, your form can be hijacked and turned into a spam relay.

To avoid this type of attack, you must validate the input of any field that will be used as an additional header, and make sure that it doesn't contain any characters that could be used to inject further headers. You can then implement this very simple strategy (in pseudocode):

```
if (illegal code detected) {
  reject the mail
  }
else {
  send it
  }
```

As explained before, each header must be on a new line separated by a carriage return and a new line character. So testing the `email` field of the contact form for those characters alone should be sufficient. For extra safety, I suggest checking for blank spaces, commas, semicolons, and quotes. None of these are allowed in an email address, so you can safely reject any input in the `email` field that contains them.

In common with many other computing languages, PHP uses a very powerful tool called regular expressions (regex) to describe patterns of text and other characters. Defining a regex for an email address is notoriously difficult, so the one I have created for the Email address check snippet concentrates on rejecting all illegal characters while checking for the two things an email address must have: an @ mark in the middle, and at least one period surrounded by characters in the second half. Used in combination with the error test in step 10 of "Validating the form on both client and server," it prevents this type of attack from succeeding.

Regular expressions are a fascinating subject, but not one for the faint-hearted. Fortunately, you don't have to learn how to build them yourself (unless you're slightly crazy, like me). Some of the most useful regular expressions can be found ready-made in an excellent online repository at http://regexlib.com. Nathan A. Good has also compiled a useful compendium of regular expressions in *Regular Expression Recipes: A Problem-Solution Approach* (Apress, ISBN 1-59059-441-X).

Validating the form on both client and server

Continue working with the same page, or use `contact_04.php` from `site_check/ch06`.

1. Switch back to Design view, and highlight the form either by clicking the dotted red outline or by selecting <form#contactForm> on the Tag selector.

2. Open the Behaviors panel (*SHIFT+F4*), click the plus button, and select Validate Form.

3. The dialog box that opens automatically displays the names of the three fields in the form. Highlight each one in turn, and select Value: Required. This will ensure that at least something is entered into the field. Choose Accept: Anything for the name and message fields, and Accept: Email address for the email. Your selections should be reflected by the addition of R in parentheses after name and message, and RisEmail after email, as shown in the following screenshot. Click OK when you have finished.

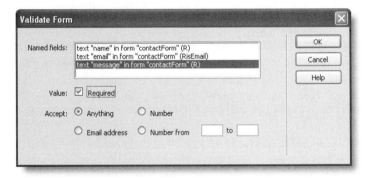

> The Dreamweaver form-validation behavior has a very limited range of choices. A free, third-party extension with a much wider range of validation options is available from `www.yaromat.com/dw/?ex=Check%20Form%20MX`.

4. This will place the necessary JavaScript code in the <head> of your web page. The Behaviors panel will also show the form-validation behavior and its associated JavaScript event. (In XHTML, all JavaScript events must be written in lowercase. Although Dreamweaver displays onSubmit in the Behaviors panel, it uses the correct lowercase format if you have selected an XHTML DTD.)

   If you ever want to remove this behavior, highlight the form, select the behavior in the Behaviors panel, and click the minus button to remove all the code cleanly.

   Although this simple behavior will prevent a completely empty form from being submitted, it has very limited value. When Dreamweaver says accept anything, it means just that—pressing the space bar a couple of times is enough to bypass the validation. With PHP, you can stop nuisance messages like that in their tracks.

179

5. Open Code view, and insert the following code immediately below the POST stripslashes snippet that you inserted in the previous section:

```
// validate the input, beginning with name
$name = trim($_POST['name']);
if (empty($name)) {
  $error['name'] = 'Please enter your name';
  }
```

This passes the value of $_POST['name'] to the PHP function trim(), and assigns the result to $name. The trim() function does pretty much what you might expect—it trims any white space characters (including tabs and new lines) off both ends of a string. The if statement then passes the result to another function called empty(), which tests—yes, you've guessed it—whether the variable is empty. If empty() returns true, an appropriate error message is assigned to $error['name'], and is stored for display later.

6. The next part of the form that needs to be validated is the email address. This is the most important validation check, because the address will be used as an additional header in the mail() function, and it could lay you open to an email injection attack. The Dreamweaver form-validation behavior performs only the crudest of tests: If the field contains the @ character at least once, it's considered to be a valid email address. Clearly, you need something far more robust.

Position your cursor on a new line immediately below the code in step 5, and assign the value of $_POST['email'] to a shorter variable, followed by the shorter variable on a line of its own, like this:

```
$email = $_POST['email'];
$email
```

7. Highlight the $email variable on the second line of the previous step, and open the Snippets panel. Select the Email address check snippet that you installed in the PHP folder earlier in the chapter. Double-click the snippet name, or click the Insert button at the bottom of the Snippets panel. The snippet code will wrap itself around the $email variable like this (the original variable is highlighted in bold):

```
// check for valid email address
$pattern = '/^[^@]+@[^\s\r\n\'";,@%]+$/';
if (!preg_match($pattern, trim($email))) {
  $error['email'] = 'Please enter a valid email address';
  }
```

The regex assigned to $pattern on the second line is designed to reject any of the illegal characters listed previously in the "Avoiding email injection attacks" section. PHP supports two types of regex—Perl-compatible (PCRE) and POSIX—each of which has its own related set of functions (PCRE-related functions all begin with preg_; POSIX-related ones begin with ereg_ or eregi_). I prefer PCRE because they are more efficient.

The next line uses preg_match() and the negative operator (an exclamation mark preceding the element to which it applies) to check whether the email address supplied matches $pattern. The negative operator is used because you want to set an error message if the match fails.

> *If you insert the* Email address check *snippet without first highlighting a variable, Dreamweaver will leave your cursor in the correct position between the parentheses of* trim() *for you to type the name of the variable.*

8. The final check is on the contents of the message text area to make sure it contains at least something. The code is identical to that in step 5, except for the variable names and error message. Add the following immediately after the code in the preceding step:

```
// check the content of the text area
$messageBody = trim($_POST['message']);
if (empty($messageBody)) {
  $error['message'] = 'Please enter your message';
  }
```

This time, I have used a slightly different variable ($messageBody) to which to assign the trimmed value. This is because $message is used in the existing code to build the whole email. Unless you use a different variable, the next few lines of code will overwrite the contents of $message.

9. Each of the validation checks assigned the POST variables to ordinary variables, using the array key as the basis for the name. I could have used the POST variables throughout, but doing it this way involves less typing. You could leave the POST variables in the rest of the script—they still exist. All you have done is to trim off any white space and copy the values to new variables. However, let's tidy up the rest of the script by using the new variables. Change the section of the code that builds the message and sends the mail like this:

```
// build the message
$message = "From: $name\n\n";
$message .= "Email: $email\n\n";
$message .= "Comments: $messageBody";

//build the additional headers
$additionalHeaders = "From: E-W Seasons<feedback@example.com>\r\n";
$additionalHeaders .= "Reply-To: $email";
```

See how much neater the code now is? Each string is now enclosed in a single pair of double quotes instead of a mixture of double and single quotes, and is much easier to read. And before you ask, yes, this is the way I would do it from the start. The reason I did it the other way first was to show you a quick method of sending form input by email. Once you start manipulating the content of the POST array, it makes more sense to reassign the values to ordinary variables that are easier to type and incorporate into double-quoted strings.

10. If you look back at Figure 6-2, you'll see that the plan is to send the email only if there are no errors. If the tests you entered in steps 5 through 8 find any problems, they assign values to named elements of an array called $error. If, as you hope, they find no problems, the array $error will never be created. So, all you need to do is check whether it has been created (or set). You do this with a function called isset(), and since you want to know if it hasn't been set, you use the negative operator (!). Change the section of code that sends the mail like this:

```
// send the email if there are no errors
if (!isset($error)) {
  mail($to, $subject, $message, $additionalHeaders);
  }
```

> Make sure you don't forget the closing curly brace. There's another one that comes on the following line that belongs to the existing code.

11. The isset() function is also used to determine whether to display the error messages. If you're familiar with reading XHTML code, scroll down to the <label> for name. Alternatively, switch to Design view, place your cursor immediately to the right of Name:, and then switch back to Code view. Position your cursor immediately after the closing </label> tag in the following line of code (it should be around line 100):

```
<label for="name">Name:</label>
```

12. Amend the code like this (leaving a single space between the closing </label> and opening PHP tags):

```
<label for="name">Name:</label> <?php if (isset($error['name'])) { ?>
<span class="warning"><?php echo $error['name']; ?></span>
<?php } ?>
<br />
```

This may look complex, but it's quite simple once you understand what's going on. The PHP block in the first line checks whether $error['name'] has been set, and it is followed by the opening curly brace that will hold the code to be executed if the test returns true. Then comes a closing PHP tag, taking you back to XHTML in the next line. But where's the closing curly brace? It's in the third line.

What this means is that the whole of the second line, even though it contains two sections of plain XHTML, will be ignored unless $error['name'] has been set.

13. This concept is often difficult to grasp when you first encounter it, so save contact.php, and load the page into a browser. Then select View Source or Page Source from your browser's View menu. The underlying code should look like this:

14. Now try to send the form by entering just a series of spaces in the name field. You should see a warning message like this one.

15. View the page source again. The underlying code will have changed like this:

The only clue that a server-side language like PHP has been at work is the unconventional spacing of the XHTML tags. That's where the PHP `if` statement was in the code, but PHP code is never sent to the browser—only the output generated by PHP is displayed. If `$error['name']` hasn't been set, the `<span>` and the warning message are never displayed. The reason for using a `<span>` is to apply the warning class that was added to the CSS rules earlier in the chapter, and to make the message stand out in bold red text.

It's important that you learn to recognize this way of mixing PHP and XHTML, because it's the way that Dreamweaver will automatically generate a lot of the code in the second half of this book. By understanding where to find the closing brace of a section of code, you will avoid making disastrous mistakes when customizing Dreamweaver's code to your own needs.

16. Repeat steps 11 and 12 for the `email` and `message` fields, using `$error['email']` and `$error['message']` as appropriate.

17. Save and test your page. It's beginning to look great, but there's a huge drawback. Let's say someone writes a long message, and then makes a mistake in one of the other fields. The entire message disappears. You have one very unhappy visitor to your site. This problem is easily remedied, because each value is still stored in the variables from the mail-processing script.

18. Locate the following line in Code view (it should be around line 104):

```
<input type="text" name="name" id="name" />
```

If you have difficulty finding it, switch to Split view, and highlight the name text field in the Design view section of the workspace. The underlying code will automatically be highlighted in Code view.

19. You need to add a conditional statement to the `<input>` tag that displays any existing value in the text field. Since the mail-processing script stores the user input in $name, all you need to do is add the value attribute to the `<input>` tag, and wrap it in an `if` statement like this:

```
<input type="text" name="name" id="name"
<?php if(isset($error)) {echo "value='$name'";} ?> />
```

This time the `if` statement tests to see whether *any* error message has been generated. If you test for `$error['name']`, the echo command won't run unless there's a mistake in the name field, which is the opposite of what you want. It's when there's a mistake in the *other* fields that you want to redisplay the existing value of $name.

183

20. Change the code for the email field in the same way, like this:

```
<input type="text" name="email" id="email"
<?php if(isset($error)) {echo "value='$email'";} ?> />
```

21. You need to handle the message text area slightly differently, because the <textarea> tag doesn't have a value attribute. Instead, you place the if statement between the opening and closing <textarea> tags, like this:

```
<textarea name="message" id="message"><?php if(isset($error))
➥ {echo $messageBody;} ?></textarea>
```

Although the page width of this book means that the code has had to be split over two lines, make sure that you keep everything on one line, with no spaces between the <textarea> tags and the PHP code block. Otherwise, you will end up with blank space in the text area when the feedback form is displayed in a browser.

22. Save and test the page. Try omitting some of the fields, or entering an invalid email address. You should now have a very user-friendly form that warns users of missing information, but doesn't destroy any information that has already been entered.

23. Finally, send an email to yourself. This time, as long as no errors are generated, the mail should be sent, and the input fields will be left blank. The if statements that you entered in steps 19 through 21 run the code between the curly braces only if they return true. Because $error won't have been set, they will all return false, leaving the form ready for a new message. You can check your code against contact_05.php from the download files if you experience any problems.

Improving the look of the email

The layout of the email that the feedback form sends is very basic. I deliberately kept it simple so that you could concentrate on the basics of activating the form and handling all the conditional statements. I also chose a simple layout because online forms are often used for surveys, and you want to be able to identify quickly the user's response to each question (although, for a survey, storing the results in a database would probably be more efficient).

You can format the content of the form input however you like by concatenating ordinary strings with the form variables. All that's required is that the final content of the message body is stored in a single variable to be passed to the mail() function. For instance, you could change the code from this:

```
$message = "From: $name\n\n";
$message .= "Email: $email\n\n";
$message .= "Comments: $messageBody";
```

to this:

```
$message = 'On '.date('l, M j, Y').' at '.date('g:ia').', ';
$message .= "$name ($email) wrote: \n\n";
$message .= $messageBody;
```

This combines some static text with the PHP date() function to make the email look a little less stark, as shown below. The mysteries of the date() function will be revealed a little later in the chapter. You can find the code in site_check/ch06/contact_06.php.

Feedback from East-West Seasons
E-W Seasons [feedback@example.com]

```
On Tuesday, Aug 2, 2005 at 6:07pm, David Powers
(david@example.com) wrote:

By combining standard text with PHP functions and user
input you can make your feedback form more informative and
easier to read.
```

You can even add HTML tags to the output if you include the appropriate MIME information as part of $additionalHeaders:

```
$additionalHeaders = "MIME-Version: 1.0\r\n";
$additionalHeaders .= 'Content-type: text/html; charset=iso-8859-1';
```

However, you should not normally use this technique to send HTML email to others, because it doesn't incorporate a plain text version for people whose email program can't handle HTML or who refuse to accept messages that use it.

The PHP mail() function is basically designed to handle plain text email only. If you want to use HTML email or to send attachments, you should investigate PHPMailer (http://phpmailer.sourceforge.net).

There's one final thing that needs to be done to the feedback form—it should display a message thanking the visitor. I'll deal with that shortly, but first a few words about the longevity of variables.

How long does a variable last?

Working with a self-processing form raises the question of how long a variable retains its value. After all, the same page will load at least twice if the form is successfully submitted; maybe more if any errors are detected. PHP is a server-side language, and the script is processed once—normally from top to bottom—when the page is loaded. The value of a variable is set the first time it is encountered, and it retains that value until it's changed, or the script ends. After that, it's gone. Although the POST and GET arrays are used to transmit values from one page to another, or to preserve the value in a self-processing page, once they have performed that role, they no longer exist. Every time you submit a form, the POST array is reset to reflect the latest content of the input fields.

It's important to realize that if you want to preserve the result of a script for future use, you need to store it. There are several ways of doing this, including using session variables, cookies, hidden form fields, or a database. Each of these methods, with the exception of cookies, will be described later in the book.

Acknowledging the feedback

To thank visitors for feedback, you can either display a message at the top of the form, or replace the form entirely. The only difference lies in what is displayed after the email has been sent.

Displaying a thank you message

Another conditional statement, in conjunction with what's known as a flag, controls the display. This flag is set to false at the beginning of the script, and is only set to true if the email is sent.

1. Continue working with contact.php, or use contact_06.php from site_check/ch06.

2. The variable used as a flag—$mailSent—needs to go right at the top of the PHP script, *outside* the if statement that encloses the mail-processing script. This is because the value of $mailSent is always needed, even if the mail-processing script doesn't run. Place it immediately after the opening PHP tag at the top of the page, like this:

```php
<?php
// set flag to indicate whether mail has been sent
$mailSent = false;
if (array_key_exists('ewComments', $_POST)) {
```

As explained in the previous chapter, false is a keyword. It must *not* be enclosed in quotes. Otherwise, it will paradoxically equate to true.

3. Change the code that sends the mail as follows:

```php
if (!isset($error)) {
  $mailSent = mail($to, $subject, $message, $additionalHeaders);
  // check that the mail was sent successfully
  if (!$mailSent) {
    $error['notSent'] = 'Sorry, there was a problem sending your mail.
➥ Please try later.';
  }
}
```

> *When showing sections of code that need to be changed, I normally show just the existing block, with the new elements in bold type. Take care when amending this block, as there is another closing curly brace on the line below, which belongs to the conditional statement nearly 50 lines higher up the script.*

Don't test the page just yet, because you need to add more code in the body of the page. Before doing that, let me explain the purpose of the $mailSent flag and the code that you have just inserted.

What happens is that if the email is sent successfully, the PHP mail() function returns true, so this resets the $mailSent flag. If it fails to send the email, the function returns false, leaving

$mailSent unchanged (still false), and an error message is assigned to $error['notSent'].
Figure 6-3 shows how the cascade of if statements controls the value of $mailSent. This type
of structure is often referred to as **code branching**, because the logic follows the branches of
a decision tree.

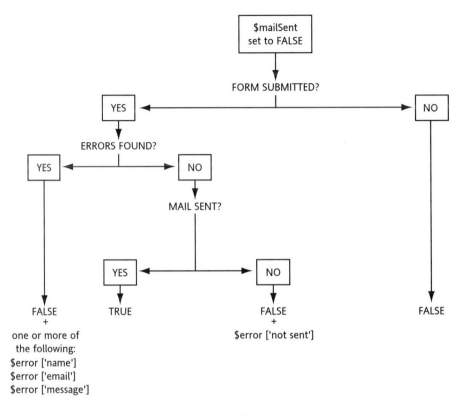

Figure 6-3. How the script knows whether the email has been sent

As Figure 6-3 shows, by the time the script gets to the end of the PHP block above the DOCTYPE
declaration, there are four possible scenarios. You have already dealt with the two outer ones.
If the form hasn't been submitted, you simply display the page ready to receive user input. If
the form has been submitted, but contains errors in the name, email, or message fields, you display the error messages and any existing input. The other two scenarios are that the mail has
been sent and $mailSent is set to true, so you need to display an acknowledgement; or that
the mail hasn't been sent (and $mailSent is false), and you need to display an apology. Let's
deal with this last (albeit unlikely) scenario first.

> *When PHP reports that the email has been successfully sent, it means the instruction to
> send the email has been passed on successfully from the PHP script. It does not guaran-
> tee the email will actually arrive at its intended destination.*

4. Switch to Design view. You will notice that Dreamweaver has surrounded the PHP blocks next to the form labels with Show If tags, as shown alongside. These tags are associated with the Show Region server behavior, which you may have discovered on the Insert ➤ Application Objects submenu. Unfortunately, you can't use the Show Region server behavior on an ordinary form like this. You either need to hand-code it, or create a server behavior of your own. I'll show you how to create your own server behavior in Chapter 10, but for the time being, it's easy enough to hand-code.

5. If $error['notSent']$ has been set, you need to change the heading and explanatory paragraph above the form. Position your cursor at the start of the level 1 heading, and press ENTER/RETURN to create a new line above. Use the up arrow on the keyboard to move your cursor into the empty line, which should automatically have been formatted as a level 1 heading. Type Server error, and press ENTER/RETURN to insert a new paragraph. Highlight the <p> tag in the Tag selector, and apply the warning CSS class to it. The top of your page should look like the screenshot alongside in Split view.

6. Replace the   shown on line 96 of the screenshot with the following code highlighted in bold:

```
<p class="warning"><?php echo $error['notSent']; ?></p>
```

7. You want the new heading and paragraph to be displayed only when $error['notSent']$ has been set, so you need to wrap them in an if statement. At the same time, wrap the original heading and introductory paragraph in an else statement. The final code should look like this (I have shortened the original paragraph for space reasons):

```
<?php if (isset($error['notSent'])) { ?>
<h1>Server error</h1>
<p class="warning"><?php echo $error['notSent']; ?></p>
<?php } else { ?>
<h1>Send us your comments</h1>
<p>We hope you have enjoyed this site... </p>
<?php } ?>
```

8. Save contact.php, and preview the page in a browser. It should look exactly the same as before. No? Did you get an error like the following on Windows?

Parse error: syntax error, unexpected $end in C:\htdocs\phpdw\
➥ contact.php on line 140

On a Mac, it will be slightly different:

Parse error: parse error, unexpected $ in Users/username/phpdw/
➥ contact.php on line 140

This is one of the most common—and infuriating—errors in PHP until you know what it means. Line 140 in my version of contact.php is a blank line after the closing </html> tag, so the error obviously can't be there. The Windows error message gives you a strong clue as to the problem: unexpected $end. The PHP parser has reached the end of the script unexpectedly. It's done so because a closing curly brace is missing. Searching for a missing brace may sound as hopeless as looking for a needle in a haystack, but the Balance Braces button on the Coding toolbar makes this a very simple operation. If you're stuck at this point, skip ahead to the section titled "Using Balance Braces" and come back when you've sorted out the problem.

9. Hopefully, the server error message that you created in step 6 should never be displayed, but you still need to check that it's working properly. Do this by disabling the mail() function temporarily by commenting it out like this:

```
//$mailSent = mail($to, $subject, $message, $additionalHeaders);
```

10. Save contact.php again, and send a test message. You should get a result like that shown alongside. As you can see, the original heading and paragraph have disappeared, and have been replaced by the error message. Because $error has been set, all the user input has been preserved, too, so the user can try to send the message again. Note, however, that the message is lost as soon as you go to another page. If necessary, compare your code with contact_07.php.

11. Remove the slashes that you inserted in step 9, to re-enable the mail() function.

12. All that remains now is to display an acknowledgement of the feedback. As Figure 6-3 shows, $mailSent will be set to true only if the email has been sent successfully. This means that you can now amend the conditional sequence in step 7 to this:

```
<?php if (isset($error['notSent'])) { ?>
<h1>Server error</h1>
<p class="warning"><?php echo $error['notSent']; ?></p>
<?php } elseif ($mailSent) { ?>
<h1>Thank you for your comments</h1>
<p>We appreciate your feedback, and will be in touch if necessary.</p>
<?php } else { ?>
<h1>Send us your comments</h1>
<p>We hope you have enjoyed this site... </p>
<?php } ?>
```

What this means in simple terms is this:

```
if (there has been an error) {
  display an error message
  } elseif (the mail has been sent) {
  display an acknowledgement
  } else {
  display the normal page
  }
```

Notice how $mailSent is used on its own in the elseif statement. This is equivalent to

```
<?php } elseif ($mailSent == true) { ?>
```

$mailSent has a Boolean value (true or false), so testing its value alone is sufficient.

> *There's an important difference between the first* if *statement, which uses* isset(), *and the* elseif *statement, which doesn't.* isset() *checks only whether a variable has been set—it takes no notice of its value. Since* $mailSent *has been set,* isset($mailSent) *will always return* true. *What you're interested in this time is whether the value of* $mailSent *is* true *or* false.

13. Save contact.php, and send a test message. This time, the section above the form should look like the following screenshot, and all the input fields will be cleared. If necessary, compare your code with contact_08.php.

14. As it stands, the script leaves the feedback form onscreen. If you want to create a much longer acknowledgement message, you could remove the form altogether. All that's necessary is to surround the form with another if statement. Insert the following code immediately before and after the opening and closing form tags (I have omitted most of the form code for space reasons):

```
<?php if (!$mailSent) { ?>
<form action=...
</form>
<?php } ?>
```

15. Save and test the page again. This time, the acknowledgement message will appear, but the form will not display unless you go to another page and return. You can compare the final code with contact_09.php.

The current acknowledgement message is probably too short on its own, but this demonstrates the great potential of dynamic pages—you can change the content at will, depending on circumstances.

Using Balance Braces

Even if you didn't encounter a problem in step 8 of the previous section, Balance Braces is a tool that you definitely need to know about. Like quotes, curly braces must always be in matching pairs, but sometimes the opening and closing braces can be dozens, even hundreds, of lines apart. If one of a pair is missing, your script will collapse like a pack of cards. Balance Braces matches pairs in a highly visual way, making troubleshooting a breeze.

Let's take a look at the section of code that I suspect will trip many people up. I deliberately removed a closing curly brace on line 50 of the screenshot below. That triggered the parse error, which reported an unexpected $end on line 140. This normally means only one thing—a missing closing brace. So I placed my cursor inside the final curly brace, and clicked the Balance Braces button in the Coding toolbar. As you can see, it highlighted all the code up to the inside of the matching opening brace on line 43. Because I have indented my code, it's easy to see that this forms a logical block.

So, the next thing I did was go right to the top of the script and position my cursor to the right of the opening curly brace at the end of line 4, which contains the following code:

```php
if (array_key_exists('ewComments', $_POST)) {
```

When I clicked the Balance Braces button again, nothing was highlighted, and my computer just made a hollow clunking sound. So there was the culprit. All I needed to work out was where the closing brace should go. Admittedly, it's fairly easy for me. I've not only been coding PHP for many years, I also designed the script, and created a deliberate mistake.

Nevertheless, you'll find Balance Braces is a great timesaver. It works not only with braces, but also with square brackets and parentheses. Just position your cursor inside any curly brace, square bracket, or parenthesis, and Balance Braces finds the other one of the pair. You may need to test several blocks of code to find the cause of a problem, but it's an excellent way of visualizing code blocks and the branching logic of your scripts. With Dreamweaver 8's code collapse feature, you can also use it to hide large sections of code while working on another part of a script.

You can also access Balance Braces through the Edit menu, and if you're a keyboard shortcut fan, the combination is *CTRL*+'/⌘+' (single quote).

If, like me, you use a UK keyboard, the Balance Braces shortcut won't work on Windows, nor will the shortcut to switch between Design and Code views, which uses CTRL+ ` (a backtick). Both are known bugs, which have apparently been corrected in non-English versions of Dreamweaver 8, so the problem should be eliminated when an updater is released for the English version. The Mac version is not affected.

Turning the email regular expression into a snippet

The Email address check snippet that you installed earlier in the chapter is designed to work with this particular case study. You may find it useful to create a separate snippet that contains just the regular expression, ready to drop straight into any other script. Using the Snippets panel to store pieces of code that you use on a regular basis, or that are hard to type, is a good practice, and it's very easy to do.

1. Open the Snippets panel, and select the PHP-DW8 folder. This will ensure that your snippet is stored in the right place.

2. Highlight the line containing the regular expression, right-click/CTRL-click, and choose Create New Snippet from the context menu, as shown here. Make sure you select the complete line of code, including the final semicolon.

3. The Snippet dialog box will open, with the code shown on line 21 in the previous screenshot already entered in the Insert before area. This reflects the fact that you can create two types of snippets: those that wrap code around anything already selected in Code view (like Email address check), and those that insert a single block of code (like POST stripslashes). If you want to wrap code around a selection, the first half goes in the Insert before area, and the second half in Insert after. On this occasion, you want the regular expression to be inserted as a single block, so for Snippet type select the Insert block radio button. The Insert before and Insert after areas will merge into one.

Whatever you type in the Name field will appear in the Snippets panel, so choose something short, but descriptive. As the screenshot shows, it can include spaces. The Description field is for a longer explanation of the snippet's purpose. This does appear in the Snippets panel, but can't be seen in the default layout unless you scroll to the right. Then the first few words appear, and the full description is displayed as a tooltip if you hover your mouse pointer over them.

The Preview type option lets you choose how to display the snippet contents in a window at the top of the Snippets panel. This is a code snippet, so choose Code.

That's all there is to making a snippet. If you ever want to edit or delete a snippet, use the appropriate buttons at the bottom of the Snippets panel.

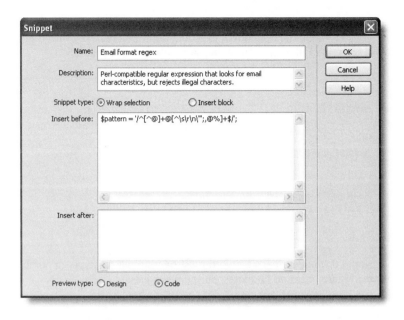

Changing the site's styles automatically

By now, you should be thoroughly familiar with the way if statements are used to control output to the browser. Technically speaking, there is no limit to the number of if . . . else decisions you can chain together, but PHP offers an alternative approach that's particularly useful when a large number of alternatives are involved. It's called the **switch statement**. To demonstrate its use, I'll show you how to change the site's stylesheets automatically depending on the time of year.

Using the switch statement for decision chains

The basic structure of a switch statement looks like this:

```
switch(variable being tested) {
  case value1:
    statements to be executed
    break;
  case value2:
    statements to be executed
    break;
  default:
    statements to be executed
  }
```

The case keyword indicates possible matching values for the variable passed to switch(). When a match is made, every subsequent line of code is executed until the break keyword is encountered, at which point the switch statement comes to an end. A simple example follows:

```
switch($myVar) {
  case 1:
    echo '$myVar is 1';
    break;
  case 'apple':
    echo '$myVar is apple';
    break;
  default:
    echo '$myVar is neither 1 nor apple';
}
```

The main points to note about switch are as follows:

- The expression following the case keyword must be a simple datatype—a number or a string. As always, strings are enclosed in quotes, but numbers aren't.

- You cannot use comparison operators with case. So case > 100: isn't allowed.

- Each block of statements should normally end with break, unless you specifically want to continue executing code within the switch statement.

- You can group several instances of the case keyword together to apply the same block of code to them (you will see this demonstrated later in the chapter).

- If no match is made, any statements following the default keyword will be executed. If no default has been set, the switch statement will exit silently and continue with the next block of code.

Building an automatic style changer

With a name like East-West Seasons, it would be a cool idea to change the overall look of the site with each changing season. There are 12 months in the year, so you could have 12 different stylesheets, and get PHP to change them automatically each month. So far, you have looked only at how to display the current year with date(), but it can be used to display the date in many different ways; or—and this is what we want—you can extract different parts of the current date.

Extracting date parts with date()

The date() function can be used to format any date if you pass it a Unix timestamp as the second, optional argument (see www.php.net/manual/en/function.mktime.php), but it's particularly useful for dealing with the current date. The function takes as its first required argument a string that indicates the format in which you want to display the date. There are quite a lot of format characters. Some are easy to remember, like Y for the year, but others seem to have no obvious reasoning behind them. You can find a full list at www.php.net/manual/en/function.date.php. Table 6-1 lists the most useful.

Table 6-1. The main format characters used in the date() function

Unit	Format character	Description	Example
Day	d	Day of the month with leading zero	01 through 31
	j	Day of the month without leading zero	1 through 31
	S	English ordinal suffix for day of the month	st, nd, rd, or th
	D	First three letters of day name	Sun, Tue
	l (lowercase L)	Full name of day	Sunday, Tuesday
Month	m	Number of month with leading zero	01 through 12
	n	Number of month without leading zero	1 through 12
	M	First three letters of month name	Jan, Jul
	F	Full name of month	January, July
Year	Y	Year displayed as four digits	2005
	y	Year displayed as two digits	05
Hour	g	Hour in 12-hour format without leading zero	1 through 12
	h	Hour in 12-hour format with leading zero	01 through 12
	G	Hour in 24-hour format without leading zero	0 through 23
	H	Hour in 24-hour format with leading zero	01 through 23
Minutes	i	Minutes with leading zero if necessary	00 through 59
AM/PM	a	Lowercase	am
AM/PM	A	Uppercase	PM

You can combine these format characters with punctuation to display the current date in your web pages according to your own preferences. For instance, the following code (also in dates.php in examples/ch06) produces output similar to that shown in the screenshot:

```
<p>American style: <?php echo date('l, F jS, Y'); ?></p>
<p>European style: <?php echo date('l, jS F Y'); ?></p>
```

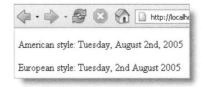

> *The* date() *function always outputs the names of the days and months in English. If you are working in a different language, use* strftime(), *which formats dates and times according to the web server's locale settings. See* www.php.net/manual/en/function.strftime.php *for details of both* strftime() *and how to change the locale for an individual script.*

With the help of Table 6-1, you can get the value of the current month like this:

```
$month = date('n');
```

Let's combine that with a switch statement to change the look of the website with the changing seasons.

Changing styles according to the month

Ideally, you would have a bigger selection of styles, but for the purposes of this exercise, I'm going to use just three. You will find all the necessary images in images_common, and the alternative stylesheets are in the styles folder of site_check.

> *Up to now, Dreamweaver has managed to preserve most of the layout in Design view. For the rest of the chapter, your page may look as though it's falling apart. This is because certain crucial elements will be stored in variables. As long as you follow the instructions, everything should be fine—and you always have the download files to check your progress against.*

1. Open style_rules.php in the working folder, and save it as style_rules_monthly.php. (If you just want to follow the code, use style_rules_monthly.php in site_check/ch06.)

2. Change the code like this (new code is shown in bold type):

```
<link href="styles/basic.css" rel="stylesheet" type="text/css"
➥ media="screen" />
<?php
// get current month as a number
$month = date('n');
// select theme for the month
switch($month) {
  case 10:
  case 11:
  case 12:
  case 1:
    $theme = 'maples';
    break;
  case 2:
  case 3:
  case 4:
```

```
      $theme = 'bluebells';
      break;
    default:
      $theme = 'tulips';
    }
 ?>
 <style type="text/css">
 /* apply the theme for the current month */
 @import url("styles/<?php echo $theme; ?>.css");
 </style>
 <!-[if IE 5]>
 <style>
 body {text-align: center;}
 #wrapper {text-align: left;}
 #nav a {width:146px;}
 </style>
 <![endif]->
```

What is happening here is remarkably simple. First, the date() function works out the number of the current month, and then the switch statement uses that information to set the value of $theme. From October through January, $theme will be maples; from February through April, it will be bluebells; and tulips at any other time of the year. The following line of code is the key to the style switcher:

```
@import url("styles/<?php echo $theme; ?>.css");
```

Once the value of $theme is set, echo is used to build the name of the appropriate stylesheet. In December, the value of $month is 12, so the switch statement sets $theme to "maples," and the @import statement becomes:

```
@import url("styles/maples.css");
```

For this to work, there must be *no* gaps on either side of the PHP block inside the @import statement. Also note the different style of commenting inside the <style> block—using two forward slashes won't work here.

3. Open contact.php in Code view, and change the filename of the include file from style_rules.php to style_rules_monthly.php. Use Edit ➤ Find and Replace (*CTRL+F/⌘ +F*), if you have difficulty locating it.

4. Switch to Split view, and click inside the Design view section. Only the styles from basic.css are still applied. This is because a PHP script now determines the main styles. Highlight the image in the titlebar <div> to select the underlying code, click inside Code view, and change the value of the src attribute like this:

```
<img src="images_common/<?php echo $theme; ?>_top.jpg"
```

5. Save `contact.php`. By now, your page will look totally unstyled until you preview it in a browser. Depending on the time of the year, you will get one of the three designs shown in Figure 6-4.

Figure 6-4. PHP code automatically changes the entire look of the site with the changing seasons.

6. Change the values in the `switch` statement to view all three designs. Compare your code with `contact_10.php` and `style_rules_monthly.php` if you run into any problems.

> *Because this style-switching mechanism prevents Dreamweaver from rendering the CSS correctly in Design view, I suggest that you wait until you have finished the rest of the site before applying these changes to other pages.*

Automating the navigation menu

Although PHP's 2,600 or more built-in functions offer more choice than you're ever likely to need, you'll frequently find that you want to use certain blocks of code over and over again. Rather than typing everything out each time you need it in a script, PHP allows you to create functions of your own. To finish this chapter—and, incidentally, your whirlwind tour of basic PHP—I'd like to show you how to turn the navigation menu into a custom-built function, which automatically inserts the ID for the current page. This also gives me an opportunity to show you the last set of control structures—loops.

Using loops to handle repetitive tasks

As the name suggests, a **loop** is a section of code that is repeated over and over again until a certain condition is met. Normally, the way you control a loop is by setting a variable to count the number of iterations, and increasing it by one each time the loop runs. When the variable gets to a preset number, it brings the loop to a halt. The other way loops are controlled is by running through each item of an array. When there are no more items to process, the loop stops.

> Even if you don't plan to do much PHP hand-coding, you need to recognize loops, because they are crucial to understanding how Dreamweaver displays your database results.

Loops using while and do . . . while

The simplest type of loop is called a while loop. Its basic structure looks like this:

```
while (condition is true) {
  do something
  }
```

The following code will display every number from 1 through 100 in a browser (you can test it in while.php in examples/ch06).

```
// set counter
$i = 1;
while ($i <= 100) {
  echo "$i<br />";
  $i++; // increase counter by 1
  }
```

A variation of the while loop uses the keyword do and follows this basic pattern:

```
do {
  code to be executed
  } while (condition to be tested);
```

The only difference between a do . . . while loop and a while loop is that the code within the do block will always be executed *at least once*, even if the condition is never true. The following code (in examples/ch06/dowhile.php) will display the value of $i once, even though it's greater than the maximum expected.

```
$i = 1000;
do {
  echo "$i<br />";
  $i++; // increase counter by 1
  } while ($i <= 100);
```

Dreamweaver frequently uses while and do . . . while loops, so you will come to recognize them a lot when customizing scripts later. The danger with while and do . . . while loops is forgetting to set a condition that brings the loop to an end, or setting an impossible condition. When this happens, you create an infinite loop that will either freeze your computer or cause the browser to crash.

The examples given here are very simple, but loops frequently contain conditional statements to handle a variety of situations. Sometimes you may want to bring a loop prematurely to an end when a certain condition is met. You do this by inserting the break keyword that you met earlier in the switch statement. As soon as the script encounters break, it will exit the loop. At other times, you may just want to skip an iteration of the loop when a certain condition is met. The continue keyword works in exactly the same way as break, except that instead of exiting the loop, it returns to the top of the loop and executes the next iteration.

The versatile for loop

The for loop looks rather strange at first encounter, but once you get used to it, you'll realize that it has the advantage of being less prone to generating an infinite loop. This is because you are required to declare all the conditions of the loop in the first line. The for loop uses the following basic pattern:

```
for (initialize counter; test; increment) {
  code to be executed
  }
```

The following code does exactly the same as the previous while loop, displaying every number from 1 to 100 (see forloop.php in examples/ch06):

```
for ($i = 1; $i <= 100; $i++) {
  echo "$i<br />";
  }
```

The three expressions inside the parentheses control the action of the loop (note that they are separated by semicolons, *not* commas):

- The first expression shows the starting point. You can use any variable you like, but $i is traditionally favored by PHP coders. When more than one counter is needed, $j and $k are frequently used, but this is no more than a convention.

- The second expression is a test that determines whether the loop should continue to run. This can be a fixed number, a variable, or an expression that calculates a value.

- The third expression shows the method of stepping through the loop. Most of the time, you will want to go through a loop one step at a time, so using the increment (++) or decrement (--) operator is convenient. There is nothing stopping you from using bigger steps. For instance, replacing $i++ with $i+=10 in the previous example would display 1, 11, 21, 31, and so on.

Looping through arrays with foreach

The final type of loop in PHP is used exclusively with arrays, and it is the technique that will be used to build the navigation menu. It takes two forms, both of which use temporary variables to handle each array element. If you only need to do something with the value of each array element, the foreach loop takes the following form:

```
foreach (array_name as temporary_variable) {
  do something with temporary_variable
  }
```

If you want to use both the key and value of each array element, it takes this slightly different form:

```
foreach (array_name as key_variable => value_variable) {
    do something with key_variable and value_variable
    }
```

It's easier to understand if you see it in action, but first you need to know how to create an array.

Creating arrays

Earlier in the chapter, I showed you a basic example of an array using $shoppingList:

```
$shoppingList[0] = 'milk';
$shoppingList[1] = 'bread';
$shoppingList[2] = 'cookies';
$shoppingList[3] = 'butter';
```

Although that's a perfectly valid way of creating an indexed array (one that uses numbers to identify each element), it's a nuisance to have to type out the variable name each time, so there's a much shorter way of doing it. You declare the variable name once, and assign all the elements by passing them as a comma-separated list to array(), like this:

```
$shoppingList = array('milk', 'bread', 'cookies', 'butter');
```

> The comma must go outside the quotes, unlike American typographic practice. For ease of reading, I have inserted a space following each comma, but it's not necessary to do so.

PHP numbers each array element automatically, beginning from 0, so the second example creates exactly the same array as the original one. To add a new element to the end of the array, use a pair of empty square brackets like this:

```
$shoppingList[] = 'coffee';
```

PHP simply uses the next number available, so this will become $shoppingList[4].

There is also a shorthand way of creating an associative array (one that uses strings to identify each element). It uses the same => operator as the foreach loop. The function you are about to build to automate the navigation menu uses an associative array comprising the filenames of each page and the menu label like this:

```
$pages = array('index.php' => 'Home', 'news.php' => 'News', 'blog.php'
➥ => 'Blog', 'gallery.php' => 'Gallery', 'contact.php' => 'Contact');
```

This has the same effect as building the array like this:

```
$pages['index.php'] = 'Home';
```

and so on.

201

Turning the navigation menu into a function

The final code for the navigation menu function can be found in navmenu.php in site_check/ch06.

1. Create a new PHP page in the site root, and save it as navmenu.php. Switch to Code view, and remove all the existing code. You want just a blank page to start with.

2. Insert the following code:

```php
<?php
$pages = array('index.php'   => 'Home',
               'news.php'    => 'News',
               'blog.php'    => 'Blog',
               'gallery.php' => 'Gallery',
               'contact.php' => 'Contact');

foreach ($pages as $listing) {
  echo $listing.'<br />';
  }
?>
```

> Be sure to write foreach as a single word. The script will fail if you put a space between for and each.

3. Switch to Design view, and click the Live Data view button. You should see the value of each element of the $pages array displayed on a separate line, as shown alongside. This demonstrates the first method of using a foreach loop—$listing is used as a temporary variable inside the loop to represent the value of each element.

4. Switch off Live Data view, and go back to Code view. Amend the foreach loop like this:

```php
foreach ($pages as $file => $listing) {
  echo "<li><a href='$file'>$listing</a></li>\n";
  }
```

This time, the key of each array element has been assigned to a temporary variable called $file, and the => operator indicates that $listing will be used as a temporary variable for each element's value. Inside the loop, <li> tags are used to create a list item, $listing is wrapped in a pair of <a> tags, and $file is used to populate the href attribute of the <a> tag. The entire string is enclosed in double quotes, so the values of the variables will be displayed. The string ends with a new line character. This is not strictly necessary, but it makes the XHTML that's eventually produced easier to read.

5. You can't see the results very well in Live Data view, so save navmenu.php, and preview it in a browser. Also take a look at the source code of the page. They should look like the screenshot below.

The key of each element in the $pages array is now the link, and the value of each element has become the label in the unordered list. The only things missing are the `<ul>` tags, and some method of inserting the thispage ID, which is used to style the down-state of the current page's navigation button (see "Identifying the current page" in Chapter 4).

6. Earlier in the chapter, $_SERVER['PHP_SELF'] was used to set the action of the form, and turn contact.php into a self-processing form. There's another member of the SERVER superglobal array called $_SERVER['SCRIPT_FILENAME'], which contains the complete pathname of the current file. You can use this in conjunction with a PHP function called basename() that will conveniently extract the filename from the path. So, to find the name of the current file, combine the two like this:

```
basename($_SERVER['SCRIPT_FILENAME'])
```

Now that you have a method of determining the current filename, it's just a question of comparing it with the value of $file. If they match, you need to add the thispage ID to the `<li>` tag. You could hard-code the name of the ID into the conditional statement, but I'm going to use a variable instead. Change the foreach loop in step 4 like this:

```
foreach ($pages as $file => $listing) {
  echo '<li';
  // if the current filename and array key match, insert ID
  if (basename($_SERVER['SCRIPT_FILENAME']) == $file) {
    echo " id='$pageID'><a href='javascript:;'>";
    }
  else {
    echo "><a href='$file'>";
    }
  echo "$listing</a></li>\n";
  }
```

What this code does is to add the ID inside the `<li>` tag, and create a JavaScript null link for the current page. All other pages are treated exactly as before. The reason for using a variable for the ID is that all the code is now controlled by variables, making it an ideal candidate for conversion into a custom-made function.

7. Amend the code in the previous step so that it looks like this:

```php
function insertMenu($pages, $pageID) {
  echo "<ul>\n";
  foreach ($pages as $file => $listing) {
    echo '<li';
    // if the current filename and array key match, insert ID
    if (basename($_SERVER['SCRIPT_FILENAME']) == $file) {
      echo " id='$pageID'><a href='javascript:;'>";
      }
    else {
      echo "><a href='$file'>";
      }
    echo "$listing</a></li>\n";
    }
  echo "</ul>\n";
  }
```

Apart from two echo commands outside the loop, the only changes are to wrap the code in curly braces, and precede the entire block with a function declaration:

```php
function insertMenu($pages, $pageID)
```

The keyword function tells PHP that this is a custom-built function; insertMenu is the name that you are giving the function; and the two variables inside the parentheses are the parameters (arguments) that will be passed to it. The $pages array that you created in step 2 should be outside the function. Check your code against navmenu.php in site_check/ch06 if you are unsure about anything.

8. Save navmenu.php, and open contact.php in Code view. Find the include command for style_rules_monthly.php, and create another one for navmenu.php on the following line like this (you can use either include() or require()):

```php
<?php include('style_rules_monthly.php'); ?>
<?php include('navmenu.php'); ?>
```

> The normal practice in PHP would be to enclose both includes within a single pair of PHP tags. Unfortunately, Dreamweaver is incapable of rendering PHP includes correctly in Design view unless each include command is in a separate PHP block. The development team is aware of this shortcoming; and it's to be hoped it will be rectified in a future version of Dreamweaver.

9. Locate the code for the unordered list inside the nav <div>, and replace it with a call to the insertMenu() custom-built function like this:

```php
<div id="nav">
<?php insertMenu($pages, 'thispage'); ?>
</div>
```

10. Save `contact.php` (or use `contact_11.php` from `site_check/ch06`), and preview it in a browser. It should look exactly the same as before, except that the down-state CSS style will be applied to the correct button in the navigation menu. If you check the source code, you will see that the custom-built function has inserted the correct ID and a JavaScript null link in the underlying code, as shown in Figure 6-5.

If you want, you can apply steps 8 and 9 now to the other pages in your site. However, the navigation bar will then disappear from Design view and be replaced by a PHP shield. The more dynamic elements you include in a page, the more difficult it becomes to visualize—even with the help of Live Data view, which gives you only an approximation of what your page will look like. You may find it easier to wait until you have finished building the other pages in the rest of the book before replacing the navigation menu with this custom function.

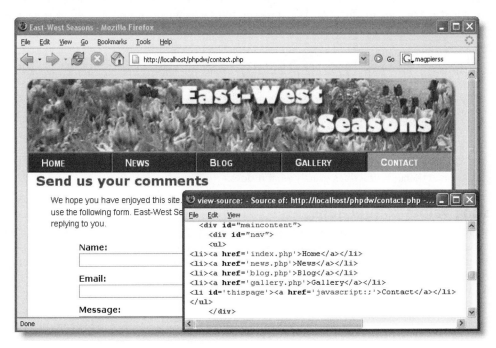

Figure 6-5. The `insertMenu()` function builds the menu from an array, and sets the down-state button style automatically.

Modularizing code with functions

As you have just seen, building your own functions in PHP is very easy. You simply wrap a block of code in a pair of curly braces, and use the `function` keyword to name your new function. The function name is always followed by a pair of parentheses, which may be either empty or contain a list of parameters to be supplied to the function. What parameters are and how you use them will be described shortly in the section titled "Passing values to functions."

There are no hard and fast rules as to when you should turn a block of code into a function, but if you find yourself using the same code over and over again, it's a fairly sure sign that a function would make your life easier, and your code a lot clearer to understand. The insertMenu() function that you have just created is an excellent example—it not only saves a lot of typing for each page of the East-West Seasons site, it can be used in any PHP site to create a navigation menu that inserts an ID in the <li> tag for the current page.

Naming functions

You can call a function almost anything you like. The basic rules are the same as for naming variables (see "Handling unknown values with variables" in Chapter 5), except that functions don't begin with the dollar sign. Also, you cannot use the name of any built-in PHP function. With PHP having more than 2,600, that may seem a tall order. Fortunately, Dreamweaver's syntax coloring will help you. If you choose the name of a built-in function, Dreamweaver turns it light blue by default, alerting you immediately to a conflict.

> *Although PHP is a case-sensitive language, function names are case-insensitive. However, Dreamweaver code hints and syntax coloring are case-sensitive. If you find that one of your custom-built function names triggers an error, try typing it all in lowercase to see if you've chosen the name of a built-in function by mistake.*

As with variables, it makes sense to give your functions names that are meaningful. The one you have just built, insertMenu(), describes exactly what it does.

Passing values to functions

Sometimes you just want a function to perform a routine task. For instance, you may just want to display your location and today's date. Although the date() function does it automatically for you, you may find it easier to create your own function, rather than having to remember the correct format characters all the time. Of course, you could store it in the Dreamweaver Snippets panel, but I just want to show a simple example like this:

```
function showDate() {
  echo 'London: '.date('l, jS F Y');
  }
```

I can now put

```
showDate();
```

anywhere in a PHP code block, and it will display "London:" followed by the date in European format.

Let's say, however, that I want to display the name of a visitor to my site. I have no way of knowing in advance what the name will be. Again, this next example is deliberately simple, and it doesn't really need a function, but it helps illustrate how to pass a value to a function.

```
function greet($name) {
  echo "Hi, $name, welcome to my site.";
  }
```

By placing $name between the parentheses of greet(), I have created a **parameter**—a value that the function will expect to be passed to it. Whatever value is passed to greet() will be used inside the function in place of $name. This is something that many people find difficult to grasp when first working with functions. It doesn't mean that you need to pass a variable called $name to the function. You could, for instance, do this:

```
greet($visitor);
```

If the value of $visitor is "Jason", what will appear onscreen is "Hi, Jason, welcome to my site."

> *When you declare a function, any values between the parentheses are called parameters. When you call (use) a function, they are called* **arguments**. *The two words are often used interchangeably, but a parameter is a variable waiting to be assigned a value, whereas an argument is usually a variable that already contains a value. When a function takes two or more arguments, separate them with a comma.*

It's also important to understand that variables inside a function remain exclusive to the function. This example should illustrate the point (the code is in scope.php in examples/ch06):

```
function doubleIt($number) {
  $number *= 2;
  echo "$number<br />";
  }
$number = 4;
doubleIt($number);
echo $number;
```

If you view the output of this code in a browser, you may get a very different result from what you expect. The function takes a number, doubles it, and displays it onscreen. Line 5 of the script assigns the value 4 to $number. The next line calls the function, and passes it $number as an argument. The function processes $number, and displays 8. After the function comes to an end, $number is displayed onscreen by echo. This time, it will be 4, and not 8.

What this demonstrates is that the variable $number that has been declared inside the function is limited in **scope** to the function itself. The variable called $number in the main script is totally unrelated to the one inside the function. To avoid confusion, it's a good idea to use variable names in the rest of your script that are different from those used inside functions. This isn't always possible, so it's useful to know that functions work like little black boxes, and don't normally have any direct impact on the values of variables in the rest of the script. But what if you do want a function to change the value of a variable?

Returning values from functions

There's more than one way to get a function to change the value of a variable passed to it as an argument, but the most important method is to use the `return` keyword, and to assign the result either to the same variable or to another one. This can be demonstrated by amending the doubleIt() function like this:

```
function doubleIt($number) {
  return $number *= 2;
  }
$num = 4;
$doubled = doubleIt($num);
echo "\$num is: $num<br />";
echo "\$doubled is: $doubled";
```

$num is: 4
$doubled is: 8

You can test this code in `return.php` in examples/ch06. The result is shown in the screenshot alongside the code. This time, I have used different names for the variables to avoid confusing them. I have also assigned the result of doubleIt($num) to a new variable. The benefit of doing this is that I now have available both the original value and the result of the calculation. You won't always want to keep the original value, but it can be very useful at times.

Halfway review

You're now roughly halfway through the book, so it's time to pause for breath and consider what you have achieved so far. This chapter and the previous one have contained a massive amount of material. Through hands-on experience, you have covered all the basics of PHP—working with variables, functions, and control structures. You have also learned about the different datatypes, including strings, numbers, and arrays. If you're a complete newcomer to PHP or programming, you may find it hard to remember everything from these two chapters after working through them just once. That's not important. The objective has been to give you a solid foundation that you will find invaluable when you start working with Dreamweaver's database-related server behaviors, as well as showing you how to make the best use of Dreamweaver 8's impressive coding features. Although you don't need to become an expert programmer, you do need to understand how functions, arrays, and other aspects of PHP work. Without that knowledge, you will find it hard to adapt the Dreamweaver code, or troubleshoot any problems that may arise.

The part of this chapter that I expect most readers will want to return to on a regular basis is the activation of the feedback form, and sending user input by email. It's a pity that the Dreamweaver development team hasn't made this an automated process, because it's such a fundamental part of building even a static website. However, building the contact form was also an important preparation for working with databases. Forms are required to insert and update records in a database, so you'll find yourself building quite a lot of them during the second half of this book.

An important feature of this chapter has been the emphasis on making sure that user input is valid. The test for illegal characters in an email address should prevent email injection attacks, but you should also be on your guard for other inappropriate input. Malicious users frequently use (X)HTML tags. You can sanitize such input by passing a string to `htmlentities()`, which converts any character that has an equivalent HTML entity to that entity. So, for instance, < becomes <. Another useful tool is the `strip_tags()` function, which strips out all (X)HTML tags from a string. Although malicious attacks are an unpleasant fact of life, you shouldn't become paranoid about them. Dreamweaver's server behaviors are designed to protect you against the most dangerous attack connected with database input—SQL injection. And as you'll discover in the coming chapters, one of the most important reasons for checking user input comes from the need to avoid careless mistakes. If you're on your guard against such mistakes, building security features into your PHP applications will become second nature.

I hope that you'll also find the automated changing of stylesheets and the navigation menu function equally useful. If you look at `contact.php` in Design view, you will realize that the disadvantage of using dynamic elements in pages is that it becomes harder and harder to visualize what the site looks like. This will become even more apparent when you start incorporating the results of database queries in your pages. Live Data view helps a lot, but you need to test your pages in a browser frequently to check how your pages really look.

The next chapter will guide you through the process of installing the MySQL database system and a graphical interface called phpMyAdmin. After that, it's databases and Dreamweaver automatic code generation all the way, with the occasional foray in to Code view to customize the output.

Chapter 7

PUTTING THE POWER OF A DATABASE BEHIND YOUR PAGES

What this chapter covers:

- Installing MySQL on Windows and Mac OS X
- Securing the database system
- Working at the command line with MySQL
- Exploring graphical interfaces to MySQL

Now that you've a good idea of the basic principles of PHP and put it to some practical use, it's time to bring on the big guns. Dynamic sites really come alive when teamed up with a database. Although PHP is capable of interacting with most popular databases (and some less well-known ones, too), Dreamweaver has made the choice for you. All the server behaviors are designed to work with MySQL—a good choice, because it's widely available, free, very fast, and offers an excellent range of features. I sang the praises of MySQL in Chapter 1, so I'll spare you the sales talk all over again.

If you have ever worked with Microsoft Access, your first encounter with MySQL might come as something of a shock. For one thing, it doesn't have a glossy interface. As Figure 7-1 shows, it looks like a throwback to the bad old days of DOS (although, to be honest, they weren't *really* so bad) before the friendly graphic interfaces of Mac and Windows. Its beauty lies, however, in its simplicity. What's more, most of the time you'll never see MySQL in its raw state like this. You'll either use Dreamweaver, or one of the graphic interfaces that I'll show you later in the chapter. Best of all, you'll be creating your own personalized interface by creating PHP pages.

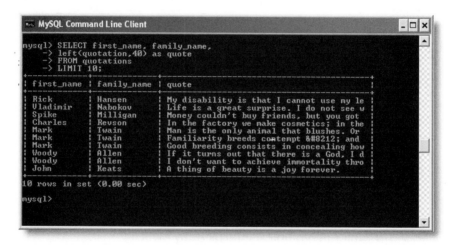

Figure 7-1. The unadorned interface of MySQL as seen in the Windows MySQL Command Line Client

The other thing that comes as a surprise to Access users is that your database is not kept in a single file that you can upload to your remote server. MySQL keeps all databases in a central data folder, and each database table normally consists of three separate files. The way you transfer data from one server to another is by creating a text file that contains all the necessary commands to build the database and its contents—in other words, a backup file. I'll show you how to populate a database from such a file in the next chapter, and instructions for creating backup files of your own are in Appendix B. All you need to know now is that there isn't "a database file"—there are lots of them, and you should never normally handle them directly.

Choosing the right version

Because of its open source background, new versions of MySQL are being released all the time. Most new versions add minor enhancements and fix bugs, but the development team has been working at a furious pace to add new features. Versions are indicated by three numbers separated by periods—for example, the stable version at the time of this writing is 4.1.14. The first two numbers are the most important: together they indicate which series the version belongs to. Changes in the final number indicate a minor upgrade or bug fix. Sometimes, the versions for Windows or Mac OS X will also have a letter on the end. For instance, version 4.1.13a was released for Windows about three weeks after 4.1.13 to fix a vulnerability in an external code library called zlib. The "a" does not stand for alpha; it simply indicates a fix for code not directly related to MySQL, but on which MySQL relies.

Data stored in MySQL is normally compatible with any version of the same series or later, but not with an earlier series. Fortunately, an option was added in MySQL 4.1 to create backwards-compatible files for backup or transfer to other computers. Consequently, if you have set up a local testing environment, I recommend installing MySQL 4.1 or later. Just as this book was going to print, a release candidate of MySQL 5.0 became available, so MySQL 5.0 is likely to have become the production version by the time you read this. If so, install the most recent version of MySQL 5.0.

It goes without saying that having the latest version on your development computer doesn't mean you'll be able to use all the latest bells and whistles if your remote server is still running a much older version, but at least you'll be able to create compatible files. Since many hosts still support only MySQL 3.23, I will always point out if a feature used in this book requires a later version.

Explaining the terminology

If you've not worked with a relational database before, you may find your head spinning with some of the names that crop up throughout the rest of the book. So here's a quick guide.

- **SQL:** Structured Query Language—the international standard behind all major relational databases. It's used to insert and otherwise manipulate data, and is based on natural English. For instance, to get the values of first_name and family_name from a database table called members, where username is equal to dpowers, you would use the following command (or SQL query):

```
SELECT first_name, family_name
FROM members
WHERE username = 'dpowers'
```

  As you can see, it's very human readable, unlike many other computer languages. Although SQL is a standard, all of the main databases have added enhancements on top of the basic language. If you have been using Access or Microsoft SQL Server, be prepared for some slight differences in the use of functions. Some people pronounce SQL "sequel," while others say "Ess-queue-ell." Both are right.

- **MySQL:** This refers to the entire database system created by MySQL AB of Sweden. It's always spelled in uppercase, except for the "y," and the official pronunciation is "My-ess-queue-ell." It's not just a single program, but also a client/server system with a number of related programs that perform various administrative tasks. The two main components are mysql and mysqld, with both terms entirely in lowercase.

- **mysqld:** This is the server (or, to give it its proper technical name, **daemon**) that runs in the background listening for requests made to the database. Once it has been started, you can ignore it.

- **mysql:** This has three distinct meanings. The first is the client program used to feed requests to the database. mysql is also the name of the main administrative database that controls user accounts, and on Windows it is the name of the Windows service that starts and stops the database server. Once you start working with MySQL, differentiating between the different meanings of "mysql" is not as confusing as it first seems.

So, let's press ahead and install MySQL. There are separate instructions for Windows and Mac OS X. If you plan to use a remote server as your testing server, and already have MySQL and phpMyAdmin set up, you can skip ahead to the next chapter.

Installing MySQL on Windows

Installing MySQL on Windows got a whole lot easier with the release of **Windows Essentials**, first introduced with MySQL 4.1.5. It contains all the important stuff, and certainly everything you need for this book. Although installation is automated through a Windows installer, the steps you need to take depend on whether you have an existing installation of MySQL, and if so, which version.

You can find out which version you're running by launching the MySQL monitor. As soon as you log on, you will be greeted with a message similar to the following:

```
Your MySQL connection id is 9 to server version 4.1.14-nt
```

The -nt at the end simply indicates that it's a version designed for Windows NT, 2000, XP or later. It's the numbers that are important.

If you're not sure how to start MySQL monitor, the other way to tell which version you have is to check the installation folder. If your installation folder is C:\mysql, you have a version prior to MySQL 4.1.5. Anything later than version 4.1.5 will be in C:\Program Files\MySQL\MySQL Server x.x, where x.x represents the first two numbers of the MySQL series (currently likely to be either 4.1 or 5.0).

Your next steps will depend on which version you have:

- If you have *never* installed MySQL before on your current computer, follow the instructions in the sections titled "Installing the Windows Essentials version of MySQL" and "Configuring MySQL Windows Essentials."

- If you have a version of MySQL prior to 4.1.5, *you must first remove it* by following the instructions in "Removing an older version of MySQL."

- If you have a version of MySQL later than 4.1.5, and are upgrading to a later version of the *same* series (for instance, from 4.1.8 to 4.1.14, or from 5.0.2 to 5.0.13), just run the Windows installer as described in "Installing the Windows Essentials version of MySQL." Do *not* run the Server Instance Configuration Wizard. The installer will automatically update your version of MySQL without changing any settings or affecting your existing databases.

- If you have MySQL 4.1.5 or later, and are upgrading to a *later* series (such as MySQL 5.0), follow the instructions in "Upgrading to a later series of Windows Essentials."

Removing an older version of MySQL

Because of the changes introduced by the new Windows Essentials version of MySQL, you must uninstall any version of MySQL earlier than MySQL 4.1.5.

1. Back up your existing data as described in Appendix B. You can restore the data later (instructions also in Appendix B).

2. Open a Windows Command Prompt.

3. Enter the following command and press ENTER to close down the MySQL server:

```
net stop mysql
```

4. If you get a message saying The specified service does not exist as an installed service, skip to step 5. Otherwise, remove MySQL as a service by typing the following commands, each followed by ENTER:

```
cd c:\mysql\bin
mysqld --remove
```

5. Open the Windows Control Panel from the Start menu, and double-click Add or Remove Programs. Locate your existing installation of MySQL, and click Remove.

> *If you have previously installed new versions of MySQL on top of existing ones, you may see more than one version of MySQL listed in the Control Panel. Unless the versions were installed in different folders, removing any one of them removes MySQL completely from your system. Although the other versions will remain listed in the Control Panel, this shouldn't cause any problems. The Windows Essentials version of MySQL has a new default installation folder, so there should be no danger of uninstalling your new version by mistake.*

Installing the Windows Essentials version of MySQL

Shortly before this book was about to go to print, MySQL AB announced the first release candidate of MySQL 5.0, and urged developers to start using it immediately. In the limited time I had for testing the release candidate (MySQL 5.0.13) with Dreamweaver 8 and the files in the remaining chapters, I encountered no problems and found it very stable. It is likely that MySQL 5.0 will have become the Generally Available (recommended) version by the time you read this. If so, that's the version you should install. However, even if MySQL 5.0 is still in the release candidate stage, there's a strong argument for choosing it, because it stores data in a completely different location from MySQL 4.1. By going straight to the new series, you avoid the need to move all your data when the final production version is released.

Although the screenshots in the following instructions are based on the production version at the time of this writing (MySQL 4.1.14), the installation process is identical to that used by the release candidate of MySQL 5.0. The only difference is in the default installation location. The 4.1 series is installed in C:\Program Files\MySQL\MySQL Server 4.1. The Windows Essentials version of MySQL 5.0 is installed in C:\Program Files\MySQL\MySQL Server 5.0.

These instructions assume that you have never installed MySQL on your current computer, or that you have followed the instructions in either "Removing an older version of MySQL" or "Upgrading to a later series of Windows Essentials."

1. Go to the MySQL downloads page at http://dev.mysql.com/downloads. Select the link for MySQL 5.0 or the Generally Available (recommended) release of MySQL database server & standard clients.

2. In the page that opens, scroll down to find the section marked Windows downloads. Choose Windows Essentials (x86), and click the download link. (It may say Download or Pick a mirror—either will do.)

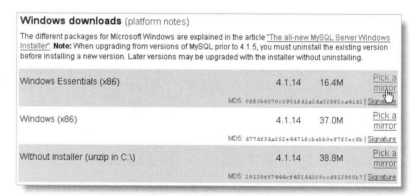

3. Follow the instructions onscreen, and download the MySQL file to your hard disk. It will have a name like mysql-essential-x.x.x-win32.msi, where x.x.x represents the version number.

4. Exit all other Windows programs, and double-click the icon of the file you have just downloaded. This is a self-extracting Windows Installer package.

5. Windows Installer will begin the installation process. If you are upgrading an existing version of the *same series* of Windows Essentials to a more recent one, the first dialog box will inform you that it has detected your current installation. You may also see extra dialog boxes connected with the upgrade process. Normally, they require no user input, but are there to inform you what is happening. Click Next to continue.

> *The installer will not treat the installation of a different series—say from MySQL 4.1 to MySQL 5.0—as an upgrade, because Windows treats each series as a separate program.*

6. The next dialog box gives you the opportunity to change the installation destination. Accept the default and click Next.

7. In the next dialog box, accept the default setup (Typical) and click Next.

8. If you're happy to go ahead with installation, click Install in the next dialog box. Otherwise, click Back and make any necessary changes.

9. Before launching into the actual installation, MySQL invites you to sign up for a free MySQL.com account. I suggest that you select Skip Sign-Up and click Next. After you've finished setting everything up, visit www.mysql.com/register.php to see if you're interested in the benefits offered. The main advantage is that you get automatic emails advising you of new versions, and links to helpful background articles about new features of MySQL. Signing up is quick and hassle-free.

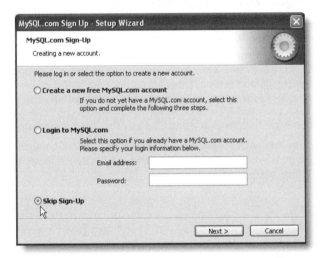

10. The actual installation now takes place and is normally very quick. When everything's finished, you're presented with a final dialog box, as shown.

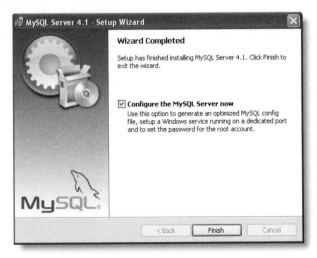

The Configure the MySQL Server now check box is selected by default.

- If this is a new installation, or you are upgrading from one series to another, leave the check box selected. Click Finish, and then move on to the next section.

- If you are simply upgrading to a later version of the same series (such as from 4.1.5 to 4.1.14, or from 5.0.2 to 5.0.13), deselect the check box before clicking Finish. Your version of MySQL should be ready to use, but will need to be restarted manually (see "Starting and stopping MySQL manually on Windows" later in the chapter). If you have a software firewall, such as Norton Internet Security, you may also be prompted to allow connections to and from MySQL.

Configuring MySQL Windows Essentials

If the configuration wizard fails to launch, or if you ever need to change any of the settings, you can access it any time by clicking the Windows Start button, and then choosing Programs ➤ MySQL ➤ MySQL Server x.x ➤ MySQL Server Instance Config Wizard where x.x represents the series number of your version of MySQL. There are quite a lot of dialog boxes to go through, although in most cases, all you need to do is accept the default setting. These instructions are based on version 1.0.5 of the configuration wizard, which offers exactly the same options for MySQL 4.1 and 5.0.

1. The configuration wizard opens with a welcome screen. Click Next to proceed.

2. The first dialog box asks whether you want a detailed or standard configuration. Unless you are confident you can handle manual configuration of MySQL, choose the default Detailed Configuration option and click Next.

> *You should choose the* Standard Configuration *option only on machines that do not already have MySQL server installed, because it will configure the server to use port 3306, which might cause conflicts with existing installations. No further instructions will be given for this option.*

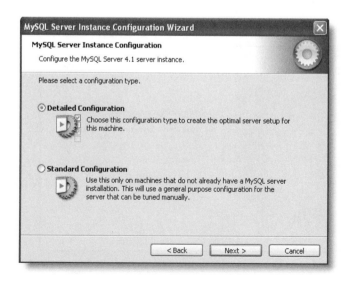

3. The three options on the next screen affect the amount of computer resources devoted to MySQL. The default Developer Machine allocates 12 percent of the available memory to MySQL, which is perfectly adequate. The two other options, Server Machine and Dedicated MySQL Server Machine allocate 50 percent and up to 95 percent, respectively, so use them only if the computer is going to be used as a live server. Otherwise, be prepared for all your other programs to slow down to a crawl. After making your choice, click Next.

4. The next dialog box asks you to select from the following three types of database:

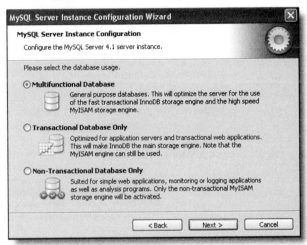

- Multifunctional Database: Allows you to use both InnoDB and MyISAM tables.

- Transactional Database Only: InnoDB tables only. MyISAM is disabled.

- Non-Transactional Database Only: MyISAM tables only. InnoDB is disabled.

Most hosting companies support only MyISAM tables, the MySQL default, and all the examples in this book will be built using MyISAM, so Non-Transactional Database Only seems the best choice. However, if you have access to your own server, or your host offers InnoDB, choose the Multifunctional Database option instead. This requires an extra 30MB of disk space, which MySQL reserves for the InnoDB tablespace.

> What's the difference between MyISAM and InnoDB? Both have their advantages and drawbacks. MyISAM is faster, and uses considerably less disk space to store data. The advantage of InnoDB is that it supports foreign key constraints and transactions—advanced features that are not expected to be available in MyISAM for some time. Foreign key constraints are useful in preserving the integrity of your data. Transactions ensure that a set of SQL queries is performed as a single operation—if one part fails, the whole operation is abandoned. This is important for databases that perform financial transactions, as it prevents money being transferred from one account to another if sufficient funds are not available.
>
> You can mix different table types in the same database, and it is very easy to convert an existing table from MyISAM to InnoDB and vice versa. If you're unsure what to do, select Non-Transactional Database Only. If you ever decide you need InnoDB tables, all that you need to do is run the configuration wizard again and choose Multifunctional Database.

Choose either Non-Transactional Database Only or Multifunctional Database, and click Next. If you choose Multifunctional Database, you will need to make a simple text edit to the MySQL configuration file later, as described in "Changing the default table type on Windows Essentials."

5. The next dialog box allows you to specify the location of the InnoDB tablespace. It will be grayed out if you are upgrading or if you chose Non-Transactional Database Only in the preceding step.

The InnoDB engine stores database files in a completely different way from MyISAM. Everything is kept in a single "tablespace" that acts as a sort of virtual file system. InnoDB files, once created, cannot be made smaller. The default location for the tablespace is C:\Program Files\MySQL\MySQL Server x.x\data.

If you want to locate your InnoDB tablespace elsewhere, the drop-down menu offers some suggested alternatives. The example shown in this screenshot would create a new folder called MySQL InnoDB Datafiles at the top level of your C drive. If you want to use a different drive, click the button with the three dots on it to select an alternative location. When you have made your choice, click Next.

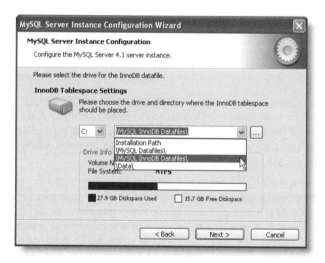

6. Unless you are configuring a live server that will encounter very heavy traffic, leave the next dialog box at its default setting of Decision Support (DSS)/OLAP, and click Next.

7. The MySQL server needs to communicate with Apache and your PHP scripts. By default, it does this through port 3306. Unless you want to run two different versions of MySQL simultaneously on the same computer, accept the default, and make sure Enable TCP/IP Networking is checked. Click Next.

> Instructions for running two different versions of MySQL simultaneously on the same computer are given in the next section, "Upgrading to a later series of Windows Essentials."

8. MySQL has impressive support for most of the world's languages. The next dialog box invites you to choose a default character set. In spite of what you might think, this has no bearing on the range of languages supported—all are supported by default. The character set mainly determines the order in which data is sorted. This is a complex issue that affects only developers with specialized needs, and it is covered in detail in Appendix A. Unless you have a specific reason for choosing anything other than the default Standard Character Set, I suggest you accept it without making any changes. You can always change it later. Click Next.

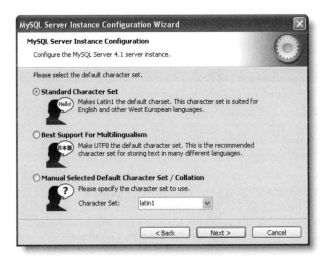

9. The recommended way of running MySQL is as a Windows service. If you accept the defaults as shown in the top half of the next dialog box, MySQL will always start automatically when you boot your computer, and it will run silently in the background. (If MySQL has already been installed as a Windows service, this section will be grayed out.) If, for any reason, you don't want MySQL to start automatically, uncheck the Launch the MySQL Server automatically option. You can easily change this option if you change your mind later (see the section "Starting and stopping MySQL manually on Windows").

The lower half of the dialog box gives you the option to include the bin directory in your Windows PATH. This will enable you to interact directly with MySQL and its related utilities at the command line without the need to change directory every time. You won't need to do this very often—if at all—but selecting this option makes life a little more convenient on the rare occasions you work at the command line. By the way, bin stands for binary; it has nothing to do with the Windows Recycle Bin. Make sure the check box is selected, and click Next.

If you get a warning message like the following one after clicking Next, it means MySQL is already installed as a Windows service. If you click Yes, the wizard will continue happily, but then fail at the final hurdle (I know—I found out the hard way). You must click No, and choose a different name from the drop-down menu in the Service Name field.

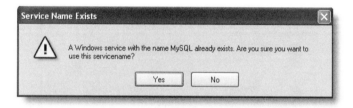

10. A fresh installation of MySQL has no security settings, so anyone can tamper with your data. MySQL uses the name "root" to signify the main database administrator who has unrestricted control over all aspects of the database. Choose a password that you can remember, and enter it in both boxes. In most cases, you should leave the Enable root access from remote machines check box unchecked. The only exception is if you access your development server from a different computer over a network.

Do *not* check Create An Anonymous Account. It will make your database very insecure. I'll explain MySQL user accounts and how they're set up in Chapter 8.

If you are upgrading an existing version of Windows Essentials, all options will be grayed out. Select the Modify Security Settings check box to make any changes.

Click Next when you have finished.

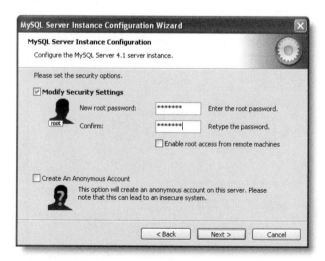

11. At long last, everything is ready. Click Execute.

If you have installed a software firewall, such as Norton Internet Security, it will probably warn you that MySQL is trying to connect to a DNS server and suggest that you always block it. You must allow the connection; otherwise, MySQL will never work. Configure your firewall to allow inward and outward connections on port 3306, or take the less paranoid view and allow MySQL to connect using all ports. Since MySQL is configured to work on port 3306 only, the less paranoid option is probably fine, but the choice is up to you.

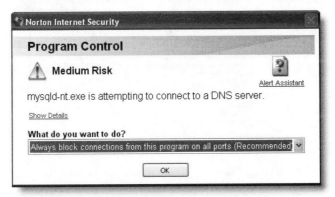

12. Assuming all was OK, you should see the following screen, which confirms that everything went smoothly. MySQL should now be running—even if you selected the option not to start automatically (the option applies only to automatic start on bootup).

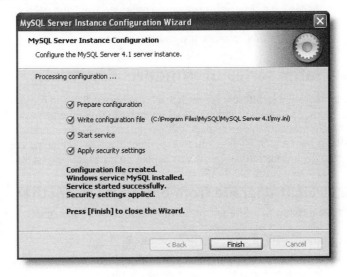

13. If you want to change the configuration at a later date, or to remove MySQL as a Windows service, launch the configuration wizard from the Windows Start button by choosing Programs ➤ MySQL ➤ MySQL Server x.x ➤ MySQL Server Instance Config Wizard. You will be presented with the following dialog box:

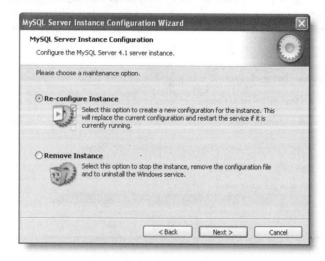

This dialog box gives you the option to change the various settings by going through all the dialog boxes again or to remove the server instance. This second option does not remove MySQL from your system, but it is intended for use if you no longer want Windows to start MySQL automatically each time you boot your computer. Unfortunately, it removes not only the automatic startup, but also the configuration file. The section "Starting and stopping MySQL manually on Windows" offers a less radical solution.

Upgrading to a later series of Windows Essentials

The default installation location is different for MySQL 4.1 and MySQL 5.0 (and presumably the same will apply to later series, too). As a result, Windows treats an upgrade to a different series as an installation of a completely separate program. In one respect, this is a nuisance because it doesn't provide a smooth upgrade path. On the other hand, it enables you to experiment with two different versions on the same computer. Fortunately, the installation process is very simple, so all it requires is a little planning.

Performing a straight upgrade from one series to another

Most people will not want to run two different versions of MySQL, and so should follow these instructions:

1. Back up your current data as described in Appendix B.

2. Uninstall MySQL using Start ➤ Control Panel ➤ Add or Remove Programs. This will remove not only the program files, but also MySQL as a Windows Service.

3. Since you no longer have MySQL on your computer, you can install and configure the new version as described earlier in the chapter.

4. Restore your old data as described in Appendix B.

5. Remove any old files not removed by the uninstall process.

Running two series in parallel

The following instructions are for the benefit of advanced users who want to experiment with a later series, without uninstalling the existing one. Since it involves running one version on a nonstandard port, you should not attempt this unless you understand the principles involved, and are prepared to modify your scripts accordingly.

An alternative for less-experienced readers is to disable the existing version of MySQL, as described in "Stopping and starting MySQL manually on Windows," and install the later version as normal. Everything should work fine as long as only one version is running at any given time.

> *If you decide to install two versions, the data files will be entirely separate. Any changes made while connecting to MySQL 4.1 will not be reflected in your MySQL 5.0 databases or vice versa. You should also be aware that running two versions of MySQL in parallel will consume more memory resources, and could adversely affect performance of other programs.*

1. Install the new version of MySQL as described in "Installing the Windows Essentials version of MySQL" earlier in the chapter.

2. Configure the new version as described in "Configuring MySQL Windows Essentials." When you get to step 7, activate the Port Number drop-down menu, and select 3307 or one of the other numbers available, as shown in the following screenshot. This is necessary because only one device can listen on a particular port.

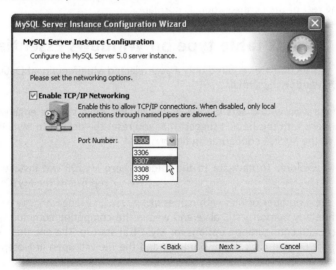

3. Perform step 8 as before.

4. In step 9, activate the Service Name drop-down menu, and select the name that matches the version of MySQL you are installing. This will enable both versions to run in parallel as Windows services. The precise name is unimportant, as long as it's not already in use as the name of a Windows service, but choosing the correct series number makes it easier to control each one independently.

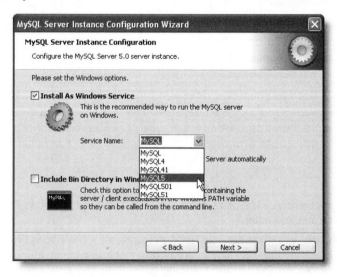

5. Continue the rest of the configuration as normal.

Changing the default table type on Windows Essentials

The instructions in this section are required only if you selected Multifunctional Database in step 4 of "Configuring MySQL Windows Essentials."

The Windows configuration wizard sets InnoDB as the default table storage engine for a multifunctional database. To work with this book, I suggest that you reset the default to MyISAM. All it requires is a simple change to the MySQL configuration file, my.ini.

1. Use Windows Explorer to navigate to the folder where MySQL was installed. The default is C:\Program Files\MySQL\MySQL Server x.x where x.x represents the MySQL series number.

2. You should see a number of files with names like my.ini, my-huge.ini, my-small.ini, and so on. (Yes, schoolboy humor is still alive and well in the computing community.) Most of these files are suggested configuration options for MySQL at startup. The one that actually does anything is my.ini. Double-click the my.ini icon, and the file will open in Notepad (alternatively, right-click and select a text editor of your choice).

3. Approximately 80 lines from the top, you should find a line that reads

default-storage-engine=INNODB

Change it to

default-storage-engine=**MyISAM**

4. Save the file and close it. To make the change effective, restart MySQL. MySQL will now create all new tables in the default MyISAM format. You can still use InnoDB tables, and you can change the table type any time you want. Details of how to do that are in Appendix B.

Starting and stopping MySQL manually on Windows

Most of the time, MySQL will be configured to start up automatically, and you can just forget about it entirely. There are times, though, when you need to know how to start or stop MySQL manually—whether for maintenance, to conserve resources, or because you're paranoid about security (a physical firewall is probably a much better solution).

1. Select Control Panel from the Windows Start menu. Double-click the Administrative Tools icon, and then double-click the Services icon in the window that opens. Alternatively, if you're running Apache 2, you can open the Services panel through the Apache Service Monitor, as described in Chapter 3.

2. In the Services panel, scroll down to find MySQL, and highlight it by clicking once. You can now use the video recorder–type icons at the top of the panel to stop or start the server as shown. The text links on the left of the panel do the same.

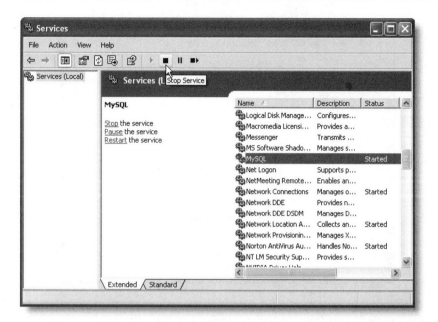

3. To change the automatic startup option, highlight MySQL in the Services panel, right-click to reveal a context menu, and choose Properties.

4. In the dialog box that opens, activate the Startup type drop-down menu, and choose Automatic, Manual, or Disabled. Click OK. That's all there is to it.

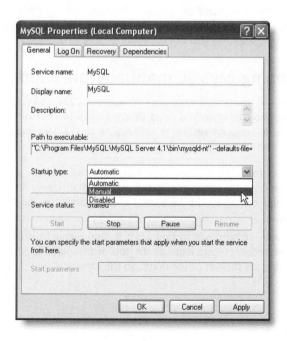

If you have two versions of MySQL on the same computer, you can set one service to Automatic and the other to Manual. Only the service set to Automatic will be invoked when you start up your computer. When you want to switch to the other version, stop the one that's running and start the other.

Introducing the MySQL monitor on Windows

Although most of your interaction with MySQL will be through Dreamweaver or one of the graphic interfaces described later in this chapter, you need to know how to access MySQL the traditional way, through the MySQL monitor.

Starting a session

From the Windows Start button, select Programs ➤ MySQL ➤ MySQL Server x.x ➤ MySQL Command Line Client. This will open the Command Line Client and ask you for your password. Type in the root password you chose in step 10 of the section "Configuring MySQL Windows Essentials," and press *ENTER*. As long as the server is running—and you typed your password correctly—you will see a welcome message similar to the one shown here.

If you get your password wrong, your computer will beep and close the window. If you find this happening repeatedly, even though you're sure you typed in your password correctly, there are two likely explanations. The first is that your *CAPS LOCK* key is on—MySQL passwords are case-sensitive. The other is that the MySQL server isn't running. Refer back to the previous section on how to control MySQL manually before doing too much damage by banging your forehead on the keyboard.

> *Being unable to connect to MySQL because the server isn't running is probably the most common beginner's mistake. The MySQL server runs in the background, waiting for requests. Opening the Command Line Client does not start MySQL; it opens the MySQL monitor, which is a channel for you to send instructions to the server. Equally, closing the Command Line Client does not stop MySQL. The server continues running in the background until the computer is closed down or you stop it manually.*

Ending your session

When you have finished working with the MySQL monitor, type exit or quit at the mysql> prompt, followed by *ENTER*. The MySQL Command Line Client window will automatically close.

Now take a well-earned rest while I get the good Mac folks sorted out. Skip ahead a few pages to the section "Working with the MySQL monitor on Windows and Mac."

Setting up MySQL on Mac OS X

After leafing through so much Windows-centric material, you'll be relieved to learn that installing MySQL on the Mac is a breeze. It's available as a Mac PKG file, so everything is taken care of for you, apart from some minor configuration. That's the good news. The bad news is that according to MySQL AB, the Mac OS X installer "does not yet offer the functionality required to properly upgrade previously installed packages." This isn't as bad as it sounds, but it means you *must* back up any existing MySQL databases *before upgrading*. If you fail to do so, your old data will be locked in the previous version, and no longer accessible.

Downloading and installing the software

> *The following instructions assume that you're installing MySQL for the first time. If you have an existing installation of MySQL and don't want to lose your existing data, you must perform a backup as described in Appendix B before going any further.*

1. Go to www.mysql.com/downloads.

2. Just as this book was about to go to print, MySQL AB announced the first release candidate for MySQL 5.0 and strongly urged everyone to upgrade. Although I would normally recommend you to exercise caution and use only the latest stable release, the tests I have done on Mac OS X 10.4 with MySQL 5.0.13 and Dreamweaver 8 have not revealed any problems. Moreover, the installation instructions are identical for MySQL 5.0 and the current stable release (MySQL 4.1.14). So, select the link either for the latest version of MySQL 4.1 or 5.0. Both should work equally well.

   Scroll down to the Mac OS X downloads section, and choose the standard installer package. Make sure you get the right one for your version of Mac OS X. (Since version 4.1.13, there have been separate packages for Jaguar, Panther, and Tiger.) The size of the download file is approximately 24MB.

3. When the download is complete, the disk image will automatically mount the contents on your desktop, as shown here. (If this doesn't happen automatically, double-click the DMG icon.) The actual number of files contained in the disk image may vary, depending on the version you downloaded.

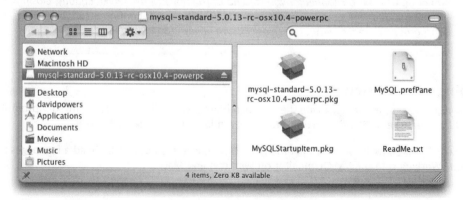

4. Double-click the mysql-standard-x.x.x.pkg icon to start the installation process (the precise name of the file will depend on the version downloaded). This opens the Mac OS X installer. Follow the instructions on the screen.

5. Open a Finder window and drag the MySQL.prefPane icon onto Applications ➤ System Preferences. This will install a MySQL control panel in your System Preferences. A dialog box will appear asking whether you want the control panel to be available just to yourself or to all users. Make your choice, and click Install.

Once installed, the control panel will open automatically and should start the MySQL server. Occasionally the first-time startup incorrectly reports The MySQL Server Instance is running, but the button on the right-hand side of the control panel still says Start MySQL Server. Click the button and enter your Mac administrator password when prompted. If this fails to solve the problem, restart your computer. Before restarting, I recommend you select the option to have the MySQL server start automatically whenever your computer starts up. Unfortunately, even if you select the automatic startup option, there appears to be a bug with its operation on Tiger. Currently, you need to open System Preferences ➤ MySQL and start it manually each time you restart your Mac.

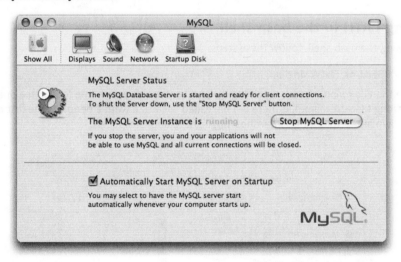

The installation process will add the MySQL icon shown alongside to the Other section of System Preferences. Use this whenever you need to start or stop the MySQL server.

6. You can now discard the disk image, although it's a good idea to keep the ReadMe.txt in case of problems.

Adding MySQL to your PATH

Most of the time, you will access MySQL through Dreamweaver or a graphical interface called phpMyAdmin (introduced later in this chapter), but there will be times you need to access it directly in Terminal. To avoid having to type out the full path to the correct directory every time, you can add it to the PATH in your environmental variables. If you have a new installation of Panther or Tiger, Terminal will use what is known as the "bash shell." If you have upgraded from Jaguar using Archive and Install, you will almost certainly be using the "tcsh shell." The only way to make sure is to open Terminal (in Applications ➤ Utilities) and check the title bar. It will either say Terminal — bash, as shown in the following screenshot, or Terminal — tcsh. Use the appropriate set of instructions.

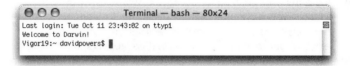

Amending PATH in the bash shell

If you are using the bash shell, follow these steps:

1. Open BBEdit or TextWrangler.

2. From the File menu, choose Open Hidden, and browse to your home folder (the one that uses your long Mac username). If there is a file called .profile (with a period as the first character), as shown in the following screenshot, highlight it, and click Open.

3. The file will only exist if you have already made changes to the way Terminal operates. If `.profile` doesn't exist, click Cancel, and open a blank file.

4. If you have opened an existing version of `.profile`, add the following code on a separate line at the end. Otherwise, enter it in the blank page.

`export PATH="$PATH:/usr/local/mysql/bin"`

5. Select File ➤ Save, and save the file as `.profile` in your own home folder. The period at the beginning of the filename should provoke the following warning:

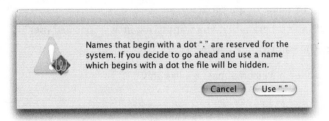

6. Select Use "." and close your text editor. The next time you open Terminal, the MySQL program directory will have been added to your PATH.

Amending PATH in the tcsh shell

If you are using the tcsh shell, follow these steps:

1. Open Terminal and enter the following command at the shell prompt:

`echo 'setenv PATH /usr/local/mysql/bin:$PATH' >> ~/.tcshrc`

Make sure you copy everything exactly, including the quotes and spacing as shown.

2. Press *RETURN* and close Terminal. The next time you open Terminal, the MySQL program directory will have been added to your PATH.

Securing MySQL on Mac OS X

Although you have a fully functioning installation of MySQL, by default it has no security. If you're the only person working on your computer, you may think there's no need to add any password protection, but that's a bad decision. When you eventually deploy your databases on a live Internet server, communication between your PHP pages and MySQL will depend on the use of a named user and password, so you need to set up a similar system on your development computer. MySQL lets you set up as many user accounts as you like (you'll learn more about them in the next chapter), but there's one important account that exists by default on all MySQL servers. It's called "root," and it is the main database administrator with unlimited powers over database files. When you first install MySQL, access to the root account isn't password-protected, so you need to block this gaping security hole.

> *Mac OS X is Unix-based, and it has a totally unrelated root user of its own, which has equally unlimited powers over the operating system and can do irreparable damage in inexperienced hands. Because of this, the Mac OS X root user is disabled by default. Enabling root for MySQL has no effect on the OS X root user, so you can do this without fear.*

Setting the MySQL root password

Setting the root password involves opening the MySQL monitor in Terminal. All commands in Terminal and the MySQL monitor are followed by *Return*.

1. Open Terminal and type the following command:

mysql -u root

The command contains three elements:

- **mysql**: The name of the program
- **-u**: Tells the program that you want to log in as a specified user
- **root**: The name of the user

2. You should see a welcome message like this:

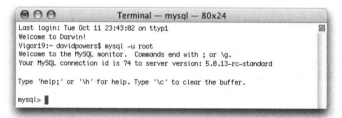

3. The most common problem is to instead get an error message like the following one:

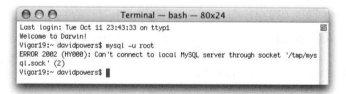

This means that mysqld, the MySQL server, is not running. If you installed the MySQL control panel in System Preferences, use it to start the server.

Another common problem is for Terminal to report command not found. That means you have either mistyped the command, or that you haven't added the MySQL program files directory to your PATH, as described in the previous section.

4. As explained earlier, the root user has unlimited powers over database files, but you have just logged in without a password! Assuming you have logged in successfully, as described in step 2, type the following command at the mysql> prompt:

use mysql

5. This tells MySQL you want to use the database called mysql. This contains all the details of authorized users and the privileges they have to work on database files. You should see the message Database changed, which means MySQL is ready for you to work on the files controlling administrative privileges. Now enter the command to set a password for the root user. Substitute *myPassword* with the actual password you want to use. Also make sure you use quotes where indicated, and finish the command with a semicolon.

UPDATE user SET password = PASSWORD('*myPassword*') WHERE user = 'root';

6. Next, remove anonymous access to MySQL:

DELETE FROM user WHERE user = '';

The quotes before the semicolon are two single quotes with no space in between.

7. Tell MySQL to update the privileges table:

FLUSH PRIVILEGES;

The sequence of commands should produce a series of results like this:

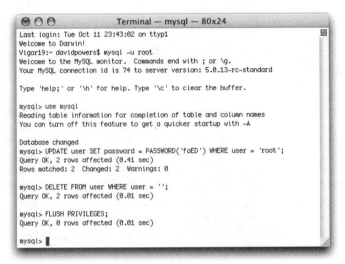

```
Last login: Tue Oct 11 23:43:02 on ttyp1
Welcome to Darwin!
Vigor19:~ davidpowers$ mysql -u root
Welcome to the MySQL monitor.  Commands end with ; or \g.
Your MySQL connection id is 74 to server version: 5.0.13-rc-standard

Type 'help;' or '\h' for help. Type '\c' to clear the buffer.

mysql> use mysql
Reading table information for completion of table and column names
You can turn off this feature to get a quicker startup with -A

Database changed
mysql> UPDATE user SET password = PASSWORD('foED') WHERE user = 'root';
Query OK, 2 rows affected (0.41 sec)
Rows matched: 2  Changed: 2  Warnings: 0

mysql> DELETE FROM user WHERE user = '';
Query OK, 2 rows affected (0.01 sec)

mysql> FLUSH PRIVILEGES;
Query OK, 0 rows affected (0.01 sec)

mysql>
```

8. To exit the MySQL monitor, type exit, followed by *RETURN*. This simply ends your session with the MySQL monitor. *It does not shut down the MySQL server.*

9. Now try to log back in, using the same command as in step 2. MySQL won't let you in. Anonymous and password-free access have been removed. To get in this time, you need to tell MySQL that you want to use a password:

mysql -u root **-p**

10. When you press *RETURN*, you will be prompted for your password. Nothing will appear onscreen as you type, but, as long as you enter the correct password, MySQL will let you back in. Congratulations, you now have a secure installation of MySQL.

Working with the MySQL monitor on Windows and Mac

From this point on, 99.9 percent of everything you do is identical on both Windows and Mac OS X. If you are used to working exclusively with a GUI like Windows or Mac OS, it can be unsettling to work at the command line with MySQL. It's not difficult, and you should get used to it quite quickly. Here are a few pointers to make you feel more at home:

- When you work inside the MySQL monitor, most commands need to end with a semicolon (;). The only exceptions are use *databaseName* and exit. The MySQL monitor is quite happy if you use a semicolon after these two commands, so the simple rule is this: *If in doubt, put a semicolon on the end of each command.*

- If you forget to put a semicolon at the end of a command that needs one, the MySQL monitor will assume that you want to break your command over more than one line, and that you haven't finished typing. It will patiently wait for you to do so, like this:

```
mysql> use mysql
Reading table information for completion of table and column names
You can turn off this feature to get a quicker startup with -A

Database changed
mysql> UPDATE user SET password = PASSWORD('foED') WHERE user = 'root'
    ->
```

This enables you to spread long queries over a number of lines. Not only is this easier to read onscreen, it's also useful if you make an error. The MySQL monitor remembers previous commands line by line, and you can retrieve them by pressing the up and down arrow keys on your keyboard. Once a previous command has been redisplayed, you can use your left and right arrow keys to move along the line and edit it in the normal way. Once you have completed the command, just type a semicolon and press *ENTER/RETURN*. The MySQL monitor will then process it.

- If you spot a mistake before pressing *ENTER/RETURN*, use your left and right arrow keys to edit the current line. If the mistake is on a previous line, there is no way to go back. Abandon the command by typing \c. The MySQL monitor will ignore everything you have entered and present you with the mysql> prompt.

- By convention, SQL queries are written with SQL commands in uppercase. This is nothing more than a convention to make them easier to read. *SQL is case-insensitive.* The following commands have exactly the same meaning and effect:

```
UPDATE user SET password = PASSWORD('myPassword') WHERE user = 'root';
update user set password = password('myPassword') where user = 'root';
```

- Putting SQL keywords in uppercase can seem a bit tiresome, but it does make it easier to distinguish keywords from the names of tables, columns, and other data. Dreamweaver will automatically generate a lot of SQL for you, and it always follows the convention of uppercase for SQL keywords.

- Although SQL keywords can be written in any combination of uppercase or lowercase, *database names and table names are case-sensitive in MySQL on all systems except Windows.* The Windows version of MySQL now automatically creates all database and table names in lowercase. Since most hosting companies offering PHP and MySQL use Linux servers, Windows users should stick to lowercase names on both systems to avoid problems.

Using MySQL with a graphical interface

Working with the MySQL monitor at the command line may be good for the soul, but—let's face it— if there's a more intuitive interface, most of us are likely to jump at it. The message has been taken to heart by MySQL AB, and in 2004 two programs were released that aim to give MySQL an easy-to-use graphical interface. One is called MySQL Administrator, which handles the administrative side of database management—creating user accounts, databases, and tables, running backups, and so on. The other is MySQL Query Browser, which enables you to inspect the content of your databases and run test queries. They're closely integrated with each other, and they look very slick. Eventually, I'm sure they will become the standard interface to MySQL, but as of this writing, the Windows and Mac versions still have shortcomings that hold me back from giving them wholehearted endorsement. I'll describe them briefly a little later, and encourage you to try them. By the time you read this, the bugs may have been ironed out.

The graphical interface that I suggest you install is phpMyAdmin, since many hosting companies provide it as the standard interface to MySQL.

phpMyAdmin: A golden oldie

As the name suggests, phpMyAdmin is a PHP-based administrative system for MySQL. It has been around since 1998, and it constantly evolves to keep pace with MySQL developments. It works on Windows, Mac OS X, and Linux, and it currently supports all versions of MySQL from 3.23.32 to 5.0.

Obtaining and installing phpMyAdmin

phpMyAdmin is open source software and is free, although the project also accepts donations to help support development. You will use it in later chapters, so I suggest you go ahead and install it now.

1. Go to the project's website at www.phpmyadmin.net and download the latest stable version. The version number of phpMyAdmin is frequently followed by "pl" and a number. The "pl" stands for **patch level** and indicates a fix for a bug or security problem. The files can be downloaded in three types of compressed file: BZIP2, GZIP, and ZIP. Choose whichever format you have the decompression software for. In the case of Windows users, this is most likely to be ZIP (2.8MB). Mac OS X users should be able to choose any format. BZIP2 is the smallest download (1.6MB).

2. Unzip the downloaded file. It will extract the contents to a folder called phpMyAdmin-x.x.x, where x represents the version number.

3. Highlight the folder icon and cut it to your computer's clipboard. Paste it inside the folder where you keep all your PHP sites (the folder designated as your web server root in Chapter 3). If you're on a Mac, and want phpMyAdmin to be available to all users, put the folder in Macintosh HD:Library:WebServer:Documents, rather than in your own Sites folder.

4. Rename the folder you have just moved phpMyAdmin.

5. You need to create a short configuration file called config.inc.php within this folder to tell phpMyAdmin your MySQL login details. You can use any text editor to create the file. Alternatively, open Dreamweaver, create a new PHP file, switch to Code view and delete all the default code so that you are left with a blank page.

6. If you are the only person who uses your computer and you don't need to password-protect access to phpMyAdmin, type the following code into the blank document:

```php
<?php
$cfg['Servers'][$i]['extension'] = 'mysqli';
$cfg['Servers'][$i]['password']  = 'mysqlRootPassword';
?>
```

Use your own MySQL root password in place of *mysqlRootPassword*. I find this the most convenient way to work on my development computer, but it may not be appropriate for everyone because it gives anyone using your computer full access to all your MySQL databases, including the power to alter and delete existing data.

7. If your circumstances dictate the need to password-protect access to phpMyAdmin, use the following code instead of that shown in step 6:

```php
<?php
$cfg['Servers'][$i]['extension'] = 'mysqli';
$cfg['Servers'][$i]['auth_type'] = 'http';
?>
```

You will be prompted for a username and password each time you launch phpMyAdmin. Log in the first time as root. After setting up individual user accounts and privileges as described later in the chapter, you can log in with a different username, but your privileges will be limited to those granted to that particular user.

8. Save the file as config.inc.php in the main phpMyAdmin folder.

9. Open a browser and enter http://localhost/phpMyAdmin/ in the address bar (on a Mac, if you put phpMyAdmin in your Sites folder, use http://localhost/ ~*username*/phpMyAdmin/).

   If you used the code in step 6, you should see the phpMyAdmin welcome screen right away, as shown in Figure 7-2.

   If you used the code in step 7, enter root as the username and your MySQL root password when prompted.

10. In the unlikely event that phpMyAdmin reports that it cannot auto-detect the correct URL, add the following line (shown in bold) to config.inc.php:

```php
<?php
$cfg['PmaAbsoluteUri'] = 'http://localhost/phpMyAdmin/';
$cfg['Servers'][$i]['extension'] = 'mysqli';
```

On a Mac, use http://localhost/~*username*/phpMyAdmin/ if you put phpMyAdmin in your Sites folder.

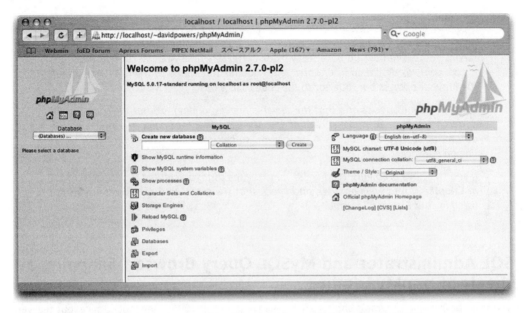

Figure 7-2. phpMyAdmin is a very user-friendly and stable graphical interface to MySQL.

11. If you are using MySQL 4.1 or above, a very important setting on this front page is the third item down in the right-hand column: MySQL connection collation. This determines the character encoding of connections to MySQL, which needs to match the character set used in your database tables. phpMyAdmin always chooses utf8_general_ci. If you chose a standard installation of MySQL, this value should be reset to latin1_swedish_ci. You may need to reset this every time you restart your computer, because phpMyAdmin forgets your change. Hopefully, this bug will be ironed out by the time you read this.

Collation is a new feature in MySQL 4.1. It's complex subject that most developers need never bother about except when first setting everything up, but it mainly affects the order in which records are sorted. For anyone working with languages other than English, collation is explained in greater detail in Appendix A.

12. If you opted for the http login method in step 7, you will find two more options listed at the bottom of the MySQL section of the front page, just beneath Export (see the screenshot). These are self-explanatory: they allow you to change your login password and to log out of phpMyAdmin once you have finished.

> *If phpMyAdmin fails to load correctly, check that you have entered the correct web address, and not the file path, in step 6. If it still fails to display on Windows, it probably means you did not set up* DirectoryIndex *correctly in the Apache configuration file,* httpd.conf, *as described in Chapter 3. Try adding* index.php *to the URL you enter in the browser address bar (but not to the code in step 6).*
>
> *If you get a message saying that the server is not responding, or that the socket is not correctly configured, make sure that the MySQL server is running. As noted earlier, automatic startup on Mac OS X Tiger seems to be problematic, even though it works fine on Panther.*
>
> *If you still have problems, load* index.php, *the file that you created in your server root in Chapter 3, into your browser, and check that the mysql and mysqli extensions are listed in your PHP configuration.*

MySQL Administrator and MySQL Query Browser: Snapping at the heels of phpMyAdmin

I first tried both these programs shortly after they came out in 2004. They looked nice, but felt very counterintuitive, and there was no documentation. A year later, they had improved greatly, but still not enough to recommend them as replacements for phpMyAdmin. Because they are part of the MySQL family, development is closely integrated with the database system, so I expect further rapid improvements, and suggest you give them a try to see if you like them. Like phpMyAdmin, they're free.

To obtain MySQL Administrator, go to http://dev.mysql.com/downloads/administrator/, select the appropriate file for your operating system (about 4.7MB for Windows and 3.1MB for Mac OS X), and install it like any other program.

Although the MySQL Administrator interface is quite intuitive, you may be overwhelmed if you select some of the options. That's because it's designed mainly for administrators of large installations. There's full documentation at http://dev.mysql.com/doc/administrator/en/index.html.

There are four sections of MySQL Administrator of interest to web developers:

- **User Administration:** This is called **Accounts** in the Mac version, and it is where you create user accounts and passwords, and grant user privileges.
- **Backup:** The name is self-explanatory; it creates backups of your data, and can be set to run at scheduled times to automate the process.
- **Restore:** This enables you to restore data from backup files.
- **Catalogs:** This rather unusually named section is where you'll find all your databases.

MySQL Administrator is purely an admin program. If you want to work with the contents of your databases, you need to install MySQL Query Browser as a separate program. This is a graphical interface designed to make it easy to run different SQL queries to check the results they produce, and to compare them with alternative queries. It's perhaps of less interest to beginners than MySQL Administrator, because Dreamweaver incorporates a similar (albeit less powerful) facility. Still, once you have a reasonable command of SQL, it's well worth giving a trial run, and it seems to be very reliable.

To get hold of a copy, go to http://dev.mysql.com/downloads/query-browser and select the version for your operating system. The video tutorials on the MySQL website at www.mysql.com/products/tools/query-browser are far more effective at showing you how it works than lengthy descriptions in a book, so I won't go into any more details.

Now to business

With MySQL up and running, you're ready to start building your first database. With the help of phpMyAdmin, it's not at all difficult, but you do need to understand the basic principles of database design. You also need to learn how to query your database tables with SQL. Throughout the rest of the book, I'll guide you through these issues, as well as putting all the main server behaviors in Dreamweaver through their paces. We'll start by creating a random quotation generator.

Chapter 8

BUILDING A RANDOM QUOTATION GENERATOR

What this chapter covers:

- Finding your way around phpMyAdmin
- Setting permissions for MySQL user accounts
- Defining a database table
- Deciding which column types to use
- Populating a database from a SQL file
- Creating a database connection in Dreamweaver
- Building a simple recordset
- Displaying database results in a web page
- Inserting, updating, and deleting records
- Creating a navigation bar to page through database results

One of the great temptations after installing database software for the first time is to try to build the "killer app" that you have always dreamed of having. For a time, it may go well. Then you realize that you want to do something slightly different with your data, and that you either don't have the faintest idea how to do so, or—even worse—that all your hard work has locked you into a rigid structure that makes it impossible. So it's better to start small and work your way up to bigger applications when you understand more about database design and web programming. I'm going to start with a simple database table that contains famous quotations (and some not so famous ones, as well), which can be selected at random for display on the front page of the East-West Seasons site.

To save you time (and typing), I've already created a sample database for you to work with, although the instructions for creating it are included in this chapter in case you want to follow the creation process through. By the end of this chapter, you will have learned how to select records from the database and display them in a web page. You will also build a simple content management system, which will enable you to insert new records, as well as update and delete existing ones. Before you can do all that, however, you need to create the necessary user accounts in MySQL—and for that, you'll use phpMyAdmin.

Finding your way around phpMyAdmin

phpMyAdmin is a frames-based web interface to MySQL. It's capable of carrying out an enormous range of operations on your databases, but is designed in a way that should be familiar to most web designers. If you set it up as described in the previous chapter, the address on Windows will be http://localhost/phpMyAdmin/. It will be the same on a Mac if you installed it for all users. Otherwise, it will be http://localhost/~*username*/phpMyAdmin/. If you have difficulty opening phpMyAdmin, follow the troubleshooting hints at the end of the previous chapter.

As shown in Figure 8-1, the left frame is used for navigation, and stays onscreen at all times. The main frame on the right displays screens that allow you to create databases, define tables, browse through records and edit them, perform backups, and much more. It does everything by creating the necessary SQL queries in the background, thereby saving you the need to learn all the administrative commands before you can get started. You'll use phpMyAdmin a lot, but you should regard it more as an administrative tool than as the main interface with MySQL. That's the job of what you'll start building in Dreamweaver shortly.

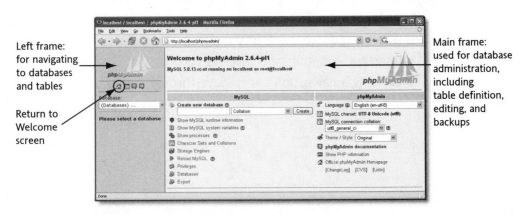

Figure 8-1. The left frame of phpMyAdmin stays onscreen at all times and is used for navigation, while the main frame is where all the work gets done.

The Welcome screen in the main frame is divided into two columns. The left column contains a simple form for creating a new database, followed by links that display a variety of MySQL settings. The most important of these is Privileges. You'll work with both of these in the next section.

The right column deals with phpMyAdmin settings. The Language setting at the top lets you choose from more than 50 languages to specify how you want the phpMyAdmin interface to display. It has no effect on MySQL. The most important setting in this column is MySQL connection collation. As I mentioned in the last chapter, phpMyAdmin currently sets this to utf8_general_ci. For most interaction with MySQL, this doesn't cause any problems. However, it's best to set it to latin1_swedish_ci, which is the default MySQL collation. Toward the bottom of the column is a useful link labeled Show PHP information, which displays details of your PHP configuration in a new browser window. Although you created a page to do this yourself in Chapter 3, this ready link is convenient whenever you need to check your setup.

The Database drop-down menu in the left frame is the main way to navigate through phpMyAdmin. Each name in the list is a hyperlink that can be used to load details of a particular table into the main · frame. On a brand new installation of MySQL 5.0, the drop-down menu will contain just three entries:

- information_schema (16)
- mysql (17)
- test (-)

The number in parentheses tells you how many tables the database contains. The test database is empty, but the other two—information_schema and mysql—already contain important data that define your setup. (The information_schema database is new to MySQL 5.0, so you won't see it if you decided to install an earlier version.) If you select mysql from the drop-down menu, a screen showing the database structure loads into the main frame, and links to all its tables are displayed in the navigation frame. Click on any of these links, and the structure of the selected table loads into the main frame. Further navigation is controlled by a tabbed interface across the top of the main frame, and by icons that appear within the various displays. It probably looks overwhelming at first glance, but you'll quickly start to find your way around it over the next few chapters.

The mysql database controls user access to all your databases, so don't make any changes while exploring. In fact, you should normally never work directly inside the mysql database, because phpMyAdmin has a much more user-friendly interface for administering user accounts.

Creating user accounts for MySQL

If you refer to Figure 1-4 in Chapter 1, you'll see that when web pages interact with a database, the PHP script sends a request to the MySQL server and waits for the response. Sadly, not everyone on the Internet these days has honorable intent, so you need to make sure that requests come from legitimate sources, particularly if they make any changes to your database records.

In the previous chapter, I told you not to allow anonymous access to MySQL, so any request will be rejected from a script that doesn't supply a recognized username and password. At the moment, your installation of MySQL has only one registered user—the superuser account called "root," which has complete control over everything. A lot of beginners think that once they have set up a password for the root user, they can start building databases. This is a big mistake. The root user should *never* be used for anything other than administration. Letting scripts on a public website use the root username and password is just as bad as leaving the door wide open with anonymous access. Moreover, if you're on shared hosting, you won't have access to your hosting company's root user account.

As I also explained, MySQL doesn't store your data in a single file that you can upload to your website. All databases are stored in a common directory. So, on shared hosting, your database—with all its precious information—will be rubbing shoulders with everyone else's databases. Clearly, there needs to be a way of preventing unauthorized people from seeing or altering your data. The answer is to create user accounts that have access only to specific databases, and that are limited in what they can do. The general principle when creating MySQL accounts is to give the user the fewest number of privileges necessary to perform essential tasks, preferably on a single database.

Your hosting company will have given you either a single user account, limited to a named database, or the right to create a specific number of user accounts. You need to create a similar setup on your local testing system. Even if you have your own dedicated server, you should still create named user accounts, because PHP scripts contain the MySQL username and password in plain text. If a malicious user manages to gain access to one of your scripts, the damage will be limited to a single database, rather than to your entire MySQL server.

> *Although named user accounts prevent unauthorized people from accessing your data on shared hosting, you should be aware that the hosting company controls the root account, and has full access to all databases at all times. You should never store sensitive data on any server that doesn't give you control over the root account and the freedom to change the root password. Once you have changed the password, give it only to people you trust implicitly.*

Granting the necessary user privileges

When you put a database online, you normally want visitors to your site to be able to see the information it contains, but not to change it in any way. However, as administrator of the site, you need to be able to insert new records, and update or delete existing ones. This involves four types of privileges, all named after the equivalent SQL commands:

- **SELECT:** Retrieves records from database tables
- **INSERT:** Inserts records into a database
- **UPDATE:** Changes existing records
- **DELETE:** Deletes records, but not tables or databases (the SQL command for that is DROP)

In an ideal setup, you would create two separate user accounts: one for administrators, who require all four privileges, and another one for visitors, limited to SELECT. That's the strategy that I'm going to adopt for this book, by creating an administrator account called dw8admin, and an account called dw8query to be used on public pages. However, if your hosting company gives you only one account name, you should use that, and set it up locally with the same privileges as dw8admin. Throughout the rest of the book, use your own account name in place of dw8admin and dw8query.

Before setting up the user accounts, you also need to create the database that the accounts will be working with. Since the site you'll be working with is called East-West Seasons, I've decided to call the database for this book seasons. If you have no choice of database name, substitute the one allocated by your hosting company whenever you see a reference to the seasons database from now on.

Setting up the database and user accounts

If you are using your remote server as your testing server, you can skip this section.

1. If it's not already open, launch phpMyAdmin in your browser. Click the little house icon in the left frame, if necessary, to display the Welcome screen in the main frame.

2. Type seasons in the Create new database field at the top left of the Welcome screen. Leave the Collation drop-down menu in its default position, and click Create. I will explain the significance of Collation shortly.

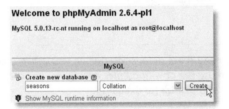

3. phpMyAdmin will then present you with a screen reporting that the seasons database has been created, and giving you the opportunity to create a new table. You'll do that a little later. First, you need to set up the user accounts. To do that, you need to return to the Welcome page. Click either the home icon (the little house in the left frame) or the localhost link at the top.

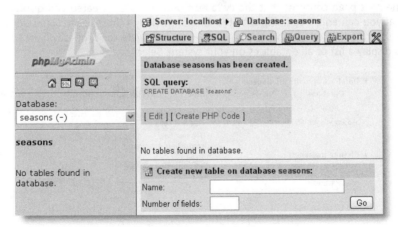

4. Click the Privileges link in the left column of the Welcome screen (it's the seventh item below Create new database in Figure 8-1). This opens the User overview screen. If you have never worked with MySQL before, you should have only one user: root. Click the Add a new User link halfway down the page.

5. In the page that opens, enter dw8admin (or the name of the user account that you want to create) in the User name field. Select Local from the Host drop-down menu. This will automatically enter localhost in the field alongside. Selecting this option means the dw8admin user will be able to connect to MySQL only from the same computer. Then enter a password in the Password field, and type it again for confirmation in the Re-type field. The Login Information table should look like the following screenshot:

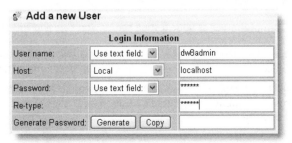

Dreamweaver will need these details later when you make a connection to the database. If you want to use the download files exactly as they are, use weaver *as the password for* dw8admin, *and* Vivaldi *for* dw8query.

6. Beneath the Login Information table is one labeled Global privileges. These give a user privileges on all databases, including the mysql one, which contains sensitive information. Granting such extensive privileges is insecure, so leave the Global privileges table unchecked, and click the Go button right at the bottom of the page.

7. The next page confirms that the dw8admin user has been created and displays many options that you can edit, beginning with the Global privileges table again. Scroll down below this to the section labeled Database-specific privileges. Activate the drop-down menu, as shown here, to display a list of all databases on your system. Select seasons.

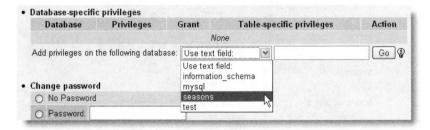

8. The next screen allows you to set the privileges for this user on just the seasons database. You want dw8admin to have all four privileges listed earlier, so click the check boxes next to SELECT, INSERT, UPDATE, and DELETE. (If you hover your mouse pointer over each option, phpMyAdmin will display a tooltip describing what the option is for.) After selecting the four privileges, click the top Go button, as shown. This will give dw8admin those privileges on any table in the seasons database.

Table-specific privileges, at the bottom of the page, allows you to set privileges in individual tables, and even specific columns, but you don't need that for this book.

> *phpMyAdmin frequently offers you a variety of options on the same page, each of which normally has its own Go button. Always click the one at the foot of or alongside the section that relates to the options you want to set.*

9. phpMyAdmin will present you with the following confirmation that the privileges have been updated for the dw8admin user account:

10. The page also displays the Database-specific privileges table again, in case you made a mistake and need to change anything. Assuming you got it right the first time, click the Privileges tab at the top right of the page. You should now see dw8admin listed along with root in the User overview.

If you ever need to make any changes to a user's privileges, click the Edit Privileges icon to the right of the listing, as shown. You can also delete users by selecting the check box to the left of the User column, and then selecting the method of deletion in Remove selected users before clicking Go. The default method just deletes the users, so they remain active until the privileges table is reloaded or the MySQL server is restarted.

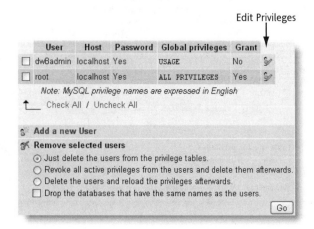

11. Click Add a new User, and repeat steps 5 through 10 to create a second user account called dw8query. This user will have much more restricted privileges, so when you get to step 8, check only the SELECT option this time.

Building the first database table

MySQL is what's known as a relational database system. All the data is stored in tables, very much in the same way as a spreadsheet stores data. In this chapter, you're going to build a simple random quotation generator that contains the quotation and the name of the person who originally said or wrote it. Although that sounds like two columns, you actually need four. Figure 8-2, which shows the first few rows of the table as seen in phpMyAdmin, should explain why.

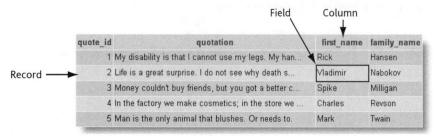

Figure 8-2. Information in a database table is stored in rows and columns, just like in a spreadsheet.

As you can see, the information in the table is organized into rows and columns. Each row contains an individual **record** of related data. The intersection of a row and a column, where the actual information is stored, is called a **field**. So, for instance, the first_name field for the second record in Figure 8-2 contains the value "Vladimir."

> The terms "field" and "column" are often used interchangeably, particularly by phpMyAdmin. A **field** holds one piece of information for a single record, whereas a **column** contains the same information for all records.

The first column, quote_id, contains a unique number known as a **primary key**. Although the primary key is rarely ever displayed, it's a vital tool when working with a relational database, because it identifies the record. When you come to work with multiple tables in the next chapter, you will see that the primary key of one table is frequently used in another table to create a direct link between them.

- A primary key doesn't need to be a number, but you cannot use the same value for more than one record in a table. *It must be unique.*

- Good examples of suitable values for a primary key are social security, staff ID, or product numbers, which may consist of a mixture of numbers, letters, and other characters, but are always different.

- MySQL will also generate a primary key automatically for you, which is the technique I use in this book.

Because a primary key must be unique, MySQL doesn't normally reuse the same number when a record is deleted. Although this leaves holes in the sequence, it doesn't matter. The purpose of the primary key is to identify the record. This behavior also makes it easier to identify the most recent entry into a database. (There are circumstances in which deleted numbers may be reused, such as when all records are deleted simultaneously, but in general terms it's safe to assume that numbers are not recycled.)

You'll also see that I have separated the names of each record into two columns: first_name and family_name. This is an important principle of a relational database:

Break down complex data into its component parts, and store each part separately.

It's not always easy to decide how far to break down data, but if you can give part of a larger entity an individual name, it's likely to be a good candidate for a separate database column. For instance, you might want to store contact details. Name, address, and phone number are good starting points, but you've already seen how names can be broken down. You might also want separate columns for title (Mr., Mrs., Ms., Dr., and so on), and for middle names or initials. Addresses can probably be better broken down into street, town, county, state, zip code, and so on. And phone numbers may also need to be split into categories such as business, home, fax, and mobile. Although it may be a nuisance to compartmentalize data like this, it's far easier to reassemble the individual elements than it is to try to extract them from a larger mass of data. For instance, if you want to run a search for all contacts in Berkeley whose family name begins with *C*, it's a lot easier to specify the city and family name than trying to pick those details out of an uncategorized system.

Although Figure 8-2 shows the similarity between a database table and a spreadsheet, there's an important difference. With a spreadsheet, you can enter numbers, text, dates, and so on, without the need to specify beforehand what type of data it is. That's not acceptable with a database—you must specify the datatype in advance.

So, let's create the structure for the table, which we'll call quotations.

Defining the quotations table

If you are using your remote server as the testing server, use the version of phpMyAdmin provided by your hosting company to create the quotations table either in your main database, or—if you can create new databases—in a new database called seasons. Otherwise, the instructions are the same for both remote and local testing environments.

1. Launch phpMyAdmin, if it's not already open, and select seasons from the Database drop-down menu in the left frame.

2. Create a new table called quotations by filling in Name and Number of fields as shown in the screenshot. Then click Go.

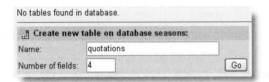

3. The next screen is where you define the name and datatype of each column. As noted earlier, phpMyAdmin uses "field" interchangeably with "column," so the column names are entered under Field. Fill in the values as shown in the following screenshot, in most cases selecting the appropriate option from a drop-down menu. The table is quite wide, and you may have to scroll horizontally to see everything on your monitor. Take particular care to select the Primary Key radio button on the right side of the screen for quote_id. You can identify it by the golden key icon shown alongside.

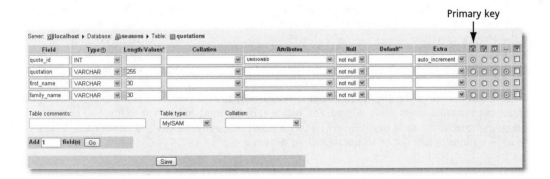

The values set for quote_id are as follows:

- INT: This sets the column datatype to INT (integer), so it will accept only whole numbers.
- UNSIGNED: This means that only positive numbers will be accepted.
- not null: This means that a value is not allowed to be NULL, so a value *must* be set in this column for each record.
- auto_increment: This instructs MySQL to select the next available number automatically.
- Primary Key: This designates the column as the table's primary key. Each table can have only one primary key, although in certain circumstances, two columns may be selected as a *joint* primary key.

The values for the other columns are much simpler. The datatype for all of them is VARCHAR. Prior to MySQL 5.0, this accepts a maximum of 255 text characters, so I have chosen 255 as the length for quotation, while first_name and family_name are set to 30, which should be adequate for even the longest name. If you subsequently enter a name that exceeds this length, it will be cut off at the 30th character, so when setting the length of a VARCHAR column, you should always choose a value that is going to be adequate. You can alter the size later, but that's not much use if you discover your column is too short after entering dozens of records.

The VARCHAR columns have also been set to not null. This has a different implication from the setting for the primary key, where it forces MySQL to assign the next available auto_increment value. As you might expect, "not null" means that there *must* be a value. That's exactly what I want in the case of the quotation column. There's no point in permitting a record to be stored in the database if the quotation field is empty. In the case of first_name and family_name, however, it might be useful to allow those fields to be empty. For instance, Voltaire and Le Corbusier don't have first names. The most logical choice would seem to be to set either or both of these columns to null. After all, "null" means no value. Unfortunately, it's not quite as simple as that.

What happens if you fail to insert a value for a column depends on how it has been defined. In the case of not null, MySQL uses the value assigned to Default. In the absence of a default, MySQL inserts an empty string (in other words, nothing) into text-type columns, or 0 into numeric columns. If a column is defined as null, the keyword NULL—an explicit way of indicating no value—is inserted. The problem with NULL is that you can't perform calculations or use most of MySQL's functions with it—and in the next chapter I plan to use a MySQL function with first_name and family_name. Consequently, not null is my only choice for these two columns as well, even though I may occasionally be happy for them to have no value.

Since MySQL simply inserts an empty string, what's the problem? Dreamweaver, that's what. If you define a column as not null, Dreamweaver's server behaviors treat it as a *required* field, and fail if no value is supplied. So, when designing tables, you should normally use the following rules:

- **Required fields:** set the column to not null
- **Optional fields:** set the column to null

However, as I have explained, that won't work in this particular case, so set all columns to not null. When using the insert and update forms later in the chapter, just insert a single space in any column that you want to leave empty. It's not an ideal solution, but it works, and it is a lot easier than trying to rewrite all of Dreamweaver's code. When you have set all the values, click the Save button at the bottom of the screen.

4. phpMyAdmin will create the table and display the following screen, showing the table structure. Check that the details are the same as shown here.

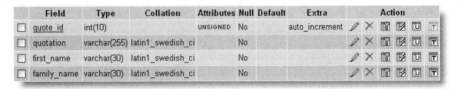

	Field	Type	Collation	Attributes	Null	Default	Extra	Action
☐	quote_id	int(10)		UNSIGNED	No		auto_increment	✏ ✕ 🛢 🔀 🔟 🔠
☐	quotation	varchar(255)	latin1_swedish_ci		No			✏ ✕ 🛢 🔀 🔟 🔠
☐	first_name	varchar(30)	latin1_swedish_ci		No			✏ ✕ 🛢 🔀 🔟 🔠
☐	family_name	varchar(30)	latin1_swedish_ci		No			✏ ✕ 🛢 🔀 🔟 🔠

You will see that quote_id is underlined, indicating that it's the table's primary key. Collation will also be set to latin1_swedish_ci for each of the text columns. This is the default setting for MySQL, and reflects the program's Swedish origins. Collation simply controls the order in which records are sorted. Swedish and English use the same sort order for unaccented characters, so this is a setting that you need never worry about if you work exclusively in English (or Swedish). Appendix A explains collation in more detail for anyone working with other languages.

> *Collation was first introduced in MySQL 4.1, so there is no point setting it to a different value from* latin1_swedish_ci *unless your remote server also uses MySQL 4.1 or later.*

If any of your settings don't match those shown in the screenshot, click the pencil-like icon in the appropriate row, change the values, and click Save again.

If you look at the tabs across the top of the screen in phpMyAdmin, you will see one labeled Insert. You could click this and start entering records in your new database table, but the table will be redesigned in the next chapter. Anyway, I want to save you all the typing, so I've created a file that will populate your table with 50 records in less than one second. But first, a few words about datatypes . . .

Choosing the right column type

You may have received a bit of a shock when selecting the datatype for the quote_id column just now. The Type drop-down menu in phpMyAdmin lists all available column types—there are 28 in MySQL 5.0. Like the massive number of functions in PHP, there are many that most people will never use, but it's useful to know that they're there if you ever need them. Rather than confuse you with unnecessary details, I'll explain just the most commonly used. If you need to find out about any of the others, they are all explained in the MySQL documentation at http://dev.mysql.com/doc/refman/5.0/en/column-types.html.

> *In October 2005, MySQL revised the structure of its online documentation to provide separate manuals for MySQL 4.1, MySQL 5.0, and MySQL 5.1 (currently at a very early stage of development). All the URLs in this book point to the MySQL 5.0 version. If you need to consult the documentation for the 4.1 series, replace the* 5.0 *in the URL with* 4.1. *The main index to all MySQL documentation is at* http://dev.mysql.com/doc/.

Storing text

The difference between the main text column types boils down to the maximum number of characters that can be stored in an individual field.

- **VARCHAR**: A variable-length character string. You must specify the maximum number of characters you plan to use in the Length/Values field in phpMyAdmin. Prior to MySQL 5.0, the limit is 255. This has been increased to 65,535 in MySQL 5.0.
- **CHAR**: A fixed-length character string. You must specify the required length in the Length/Values field. The maximum permitted value in all versions of MySQL is 255.
- **TEXT**: Stores text up to a maximum of 65,535 characters (equivalent to the text in about 20 pages of this book).

The important differences between CHAR and VARCHAR boil down to speed and the amount of storage space required. MyISAM handles CHAR columns more quickly than VARCHAR, but if your data is of varying lengths, fixed-length CHAR columns take up a lot more disk space. However, you cannot mix CHAR and VARCHAR columns in the same table prior to MySQL 5.0 (MySQL will automatically convert them all to VARCHAR, if you try to do so).

The TEXT column type is convenient because you don't need to specify a maximum size (in fact, you can't). Although the maximum length of VARCHAR is the same as TEXT in MySQL 5.0, other factors may limit the actual amount that can be stored. So TEXT remains the better option for long text.

> *Keep it simple: Unless your text is always of uniform length, use* VARCHAR *for short text items and* TEXT *for longer ones.*

You can't specify a default value for a TEXT column, whereas you can for both VARCHAR and CHAR. Other column types are available if you ever need to store larger amounts of text. Check the online documentation at the previously mentioned address for details.

> *The term "characters" here refers only to characters in the Latin1 (ISO-8859-1) character set—the default encoding for most Western European languages. If you decide to store your data in UTF-8 (Unicode), the limit is calculated in bytes. This has important consequences for Spanish, French, and other languages that use accented characters. Whereas accented characters in Latin1 require only one byte, they occupy two bytes in UTF-8.*

Storing numbers

Because databases are frequently used for calculations, MySQL offers a wide choice of numeric column types. The most frequently used are as follows:

- **INT**: Any whole number (integer) between −2,147,483,648 and 2,147,483,647. If the column is declared as UNSIGNED, the range is from 0 to 4,294,967,295.

- **FLOAT**: A floating-point number. You can optionally specify two comma-separated numbers in the Length/Values field. The first number specifies the number of digits before the decimal point, and the second specifies the precision to which the decimal portion should be rounded. Since PHP will format numbers after calculation, **I recommend that you use** FLOAT **without the optional parameters**.

- **DECIMAL**: A floating-point number *stored as a string. This column type is best avoided.*

DECIMAL has been listed here, not so much for its usefulness, but to warn you about its weird behavior. Its main use is intended to be for currencies, but you can't perform any calculations with strings inside a database. A far more practical way of storing currencies is to use an INT column. For instance, if you are working in dollars or euros, store currencies as cents; if you are working in pounds, use pence. Then use PHP to divide the result by 100, and format the currency as desired.

> *When inserting numbers into a database, do not use commas or spaces as the thousands-separator. Apart from numerals, the only characters permitted are the negative operator (-) and the decimal point (.). The commas in this section have been added purely for readability. When retrieving numbers from a database, you can use the MySQL* FORMAT() *function to insert commas automatically (*http://dev.mysql.com/doc/refman/5.0/en/miscellaneous-functions.html*).*

Storing dates and times

MySQL stores dates in the following format: YYYY-MM-DD. This comes as a major shock to many people, but it's the standard approved by the ISO (International Organization for Standardization), and avoids all the ambiguity inherent in different national conventions. If you're American, 7/4 means Independence Day. To me, as a European, it means 7 April. I'll return to the subject of dates in Chapter 11. The most important column types for dates and times are as follows:

- **DATE**: A date displayed in the format YYYY-MM-DD. The supported range is 1000-01-01 to 9999-12-31.

- **DATETIME**: A combined date and time displayed in the format YYYY-MM-DD HH:MM:SS.

- **TIMESTAMP**: A timestamp (normally generated automatically by the computer). Legal values range from the beginning of 1970 to partway through 2037.

> *MySQL timestamps are based on a human-readable date, and, since MySQL 4.1, use the same format as* DATETIME. *As a result, they are incompatible with Unix timestamps, which are based on the number of seconds elapsed since January 1, 1970. Don't try to mix timestamps generated by MySQL with those generated by the PHP function* mktime() *or by a Linux server.*

Storing predefined lists

MySQL lets you store two types of predefined list that could be regarded as the database equivalents of radio button and check box states:

- **ENUM**: This column type stores a single choice from a predefined list, such as "yes, no, don't know" or "male, female." The maximum number of items that can be stored in the predefined list is a mind-boggling 65,535—some radio-button group!

- **SET**: This column type stores zero or more choices from a predefined list. The list can hold a maximum of 64 choices.

While ENUM is quite useful, SET tends to be less so, mainly because it violates the principle of storing only one piece of information in a field. The type of situation where it can be useful is when recording optional extras on a car or multiple choices in a survey.

Storing binary data

Storing binary data, such as images, in a database is generally not a good idea. It bloats your database files, and you cannot display an image directly from a database. I'll return to this subject in Chapter 11, when showing you how to build a blog and display an online image gallery. If, for any reason, you do need to store binary data, you can use one of the delightfully named BLOB column types. There are four different sizes:

- **TINYBLOB**: Up to 255 bytes
- **BLOB**: Up to 64KB
- **MEDIUMBLOB**: Up to 16MB
- **LONGBLOB**: Up to 4GB

With such whimsical names, it's a bit of a letdown to discover that BLOB stands for **binary large object**.

Populating the database table

The SQL file that automatically populates the quotations table contains 50 handpicked gems of wit and wisdom from the ages (well, I like them, anyway). Since the name of the site is East-West Seasons, about half of them have a seasonal theme.

Loading data from a SQL file

I have created three versions of the SQL file. The main one, `quotations.sql`, is designed for MySQL 4.1 or later. Use `quotations_40.sql` or `quotations_323.sql` if your remote server is running MySQL 4.0 or 3.23, respectively.

1. Launch phpMyAdmin if it's not already open, and select the seasons database from the drop-down menu in the left frame. When the database structure loads into the main frame, click the SQL tab at the top of the page, as shown.In phpMyAdmin 2.7.0 or later, click the Import tab instead.

2. This opens a screen that lets you run SQL queries on your database. At the bottom of the screen is an option to browse for a text file (this option is at the top of the screen in phpMyAdmin 2.7.0 or later). Click the Browse button, and navigate to wherever you have saved `quotations.sql`. Click Go.

3. You should then see the following message reporting the successful execution of the SQL query. The contents of `quotations.sql`, in fact, comprise a series of SQL queries from a backup file. What you have just done is exactly the same procedure that you use to restore a database from a backup, or transfer it from one computer to another. Click the Structure tab at the top left of the screen.

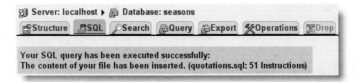

4. In the screen that opens, click the Browse icon, as shown alongside. This opens a page displaying the first 30 records in the quotations table in the same format as Figure 8-2. You can use the navigation buttons on the page to see the following 20 records.

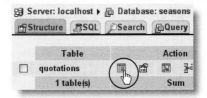

phpMyAdmin is very useful for doing a lot of the basic administration tasks with MySQL, and I encourage you to explore by clicking different tabs and icons. Even if you accidentally delete some data, you have seen how easy it is to restore from the quotations.sql backup file. A lot of the options may mean little to you at the moment, but most of phpMyAdmin is quite intuitive, so there's little need for explanation or detailed documentation.

Now that you have a database to experiment with, it's time to get back to working with Dreamweaver.

Displaying database content

Displaying content from a database in a web page with Dreamweaver involves a three-stage process:

- Create a connection to the database
- Query the database, and store the result in a recordset
- Insert dynamic data objects into your web page wherever you want to display your database content

Each step is straightforward, and completely automated through Dreamweaver dialog boxes. By the end of this section, the front page of the East-West Seasons site will display a random quotation from the database, as shown in Figure 4-1 in Chapter 4.

Creating a connection

The connection stores the username and password details of the MySQL user account. You need to create the connection files only once for each user account for each site.

1. Open index.php in the phpdw site root, or use index_01.php from site_check/ch08.

2. Open the Databases panel in the Application panel group (*CTRL+SHIFT+F10*/*SHIFT+⌘+F10*), click the plus button, and select MySQL Connection (it should be the only option) as shown alongside.

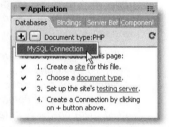

3. The dialog box that opens asks you for the following details:

- Connection name: You can choose any name you like, but it must not contain any spaces or special characters. I have entered seasonQuery.

- MySQL server: This is the address of the database server. If you have set up a local testing environment with MySQL on the same computer as Dreamweaver, you should enter localhost.

  If you are using your remote server as a testing server, use the address given to you by your hosting company. In most cases, this will also be localhost. Dreamweaver will upload hidden files to your remote server, and create a local connection there.

Some hosting companies locate the MySQL server on a different computer from your web files. If you are doing remote testing, and have been given a server name other than local-host, enter that name now. If you are testing locally, but know that your host doesn't use localhost, you will have to change this field when you finally upload your site to the remote server.

- User name: Enter the name of the MySQL user account that you want to use. This connection will be used for public pages, so I have entered dw8query. You will create another connection for the dw8admin account later in the chapter. If your hosting company permits only one user, create a connection for that user, and use the same one all the time.

- Password: Enter the password for the user account. I used Vivaldi (fans of classical music will know why).

- Database: Enter the name of the database that you want to use. You can also use the Select button to get Dreamweaver to show you a list of databases that the named user has access to.

Fill in the necessary details. The completed dialog box should look something like the screenshot alongside. When you have finished, click the Test button. If all goes well, Dreamweaver will tell you that the connection was made successfully.

This is the point at which many people start tearing out their hair, usually because they have incorrectly set up the testing server in the Dreamweaver site definition. You may get a lengthy error message about there being no testing server, or saying that the testing server doesn't map to a particular URL.

All communication between Dreamweaver and MySQL is conducted through two files, MMHTTPDB.php and mysql.php, located in a hidden folder called _mmServerScripts. Dreamweaver automatically creates the hidden folder and files in the site root of your testing server, and uploads everything to your remote server if necessary. (You don't need them on the remote server if you're testing locally.) However, the information in your site definition must be correct for Dreamweaver to put them in the right place. If it can't, the result is no communication with your database. If you run into this problem, go back to steps 4 through 7 of "Defining a PHP site in Dreamweaver" in Chapter 3. Make sure that the site root and URL prefix in the site definition are correct, and that they have a trailing slash on the end.

Other things to check are that MySQL and your web server are running. Also check your username and password—both are case-sensitive and will fail if you use the wrong case. (Make sure CAPS LOCK isn't on by accident.) A software firewall may also be blocking communication between Dreamweaver and MySQL. Try turning it off temporarily. If that solves the problem, adjust the firewall settings.

4. If you got the thumbs up from Dreamweaver, click OK to close both dialog boxes. If you failed to make the connection, cancel the connection setup, and check the points listed previously before trying again.

5. Look in the Databases panel, where you will see a database icon that has been created for seasonQuery. Expand the tree menu by clicking the tiny plus button (it's a triangle on the Mac) to the left of seasonQuery. It should look like the screenshot alongside. It displays the database features available to the seasonQuery connection, including a brief description of every column in the quotations table. The little key icon alongside quote_id indicates that it's the table's primary key. Both Stored procedures and Views are empty. Although MySQL 5.0 supports these features, support for them has not yet been implemented in Dreamweaver 8.

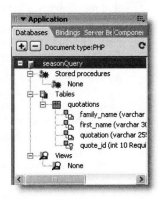

If you ever need to change the connection details, double-click the database icon in the Databases panel to reopen the MySQL Connection dialog box, make your changes, and click OK. Alternatively, you can right-click/*CTRL*-click on the connection name, and choose Edit Connection from the context menu.

Creating a recordset

Now that you have established a connection with the database, you can query it and retrieve data. Dreamweaver stores the results of a database query in what it calls a **recordset**. Although you can query databases in very sophisticated—and sometimes complex—ways, let's start off with something simple.

1. Continue working from the previous section, and open the Server Behaviors panel. It's in the same panel group as the Databases panel, so just click the Server Behaviors tab or press *CTRL*+F9/⌘+F9.

2. Click the plus button and choose Recordset. Alternatively, you can select the Recordset button on the Application Insert bar. Both open the same dialog box, as shown in the next screenshot. If you get a more complex dialog box, click the Simple button on the right (it's in the same position as the Advanced button in the screenshot).

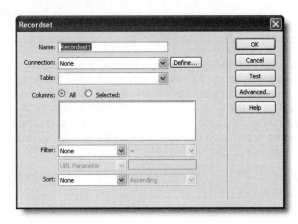

3. In the Name field, enter a name for the recordset. This will be used to create a PHP variable, so it must not contain any spaces. Some developers use a prefix like rst to indicate that it's a recordset, but I don't think that's really necessary. The important thing is to choose a name that makes sense. I'm going to use getQuote.

4. Activate the drop-down menu for Connection. It will list all available connections for the current site. There's only one to choose—seasonQuery. If you ever forget to create a connection, the Define button lets you create one without having to exit the Recordset dialog box.

5. As soon as you select the connection, the Table drop-down menu is automatically populated with the names of all available tables. Again, there is only one this time—quotations. The names of all the columns in the quotations table will appear in the Columns field, but they will not be selectable. This is because the All radio button is selected by default. They become selectable only if you choose the Selected radio button. On this occasion, you want to retrieve all columns, so leave the radio button on the default, All, and click Test. You should see a list of the first 25 records, as shown in the screenshot.

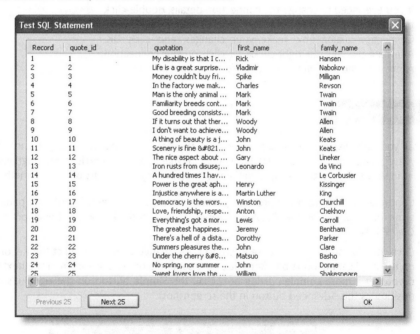

Since you have chosen all columns, the results shown in the Test SQL Statement panel are identical to the display in phpMyAdmin. Dreamweaver also displays a column labeled Record. This refers to the order in which the results will be stored in the recordset. The numbers are the same as in the quote_id column because the SQL query generated by Dreamweaver simply selects everything in the table, and the records will always be in the same order. But this is going to be a random quotation generator, so you need some method of jumbling the order. Let's see how the order can be changed. Click OK to close the Test SQL Statement panel.

6. In the Recordset dialog box, click the Advanced button. Don't panic, it's not as scary as it sounds. You should now see the following dialog box:

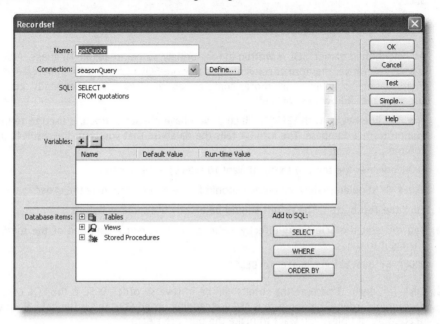

The advanced Recordset dialog box shows you the actual SQL query that will be used to build the recordset, and provides tools to build more sophisticated queries than those generated automatically by the simple Recordset dialog box.

> *The advanced and simple Recordset dialog boxes are two sides of the same coin. Dreamweaver opens whichever you used last. You can always switch from the simple Recordset dialog box to the advanced one by clicking the* Advanced *button. However, once you have started building a SQL query in the advanced Recordset dialog box, Dreamweaver normally won't let you switch back to the simple one.*

7. Expand Tables in Database items at the bottom of the dialog box to reveal all the columns in the quotations table, and select quote_id. Click the ORDER BY button, as shown.

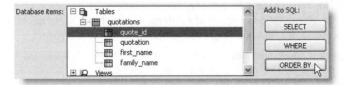

8. This will change the query in the SQL field like this:

```
SELECT *
FROM quotations
ORDER BY quotations.quote_id
```

As I mentioned earlier, SQL is written in reassuringly human-readable language. Although SQL is case-insensitive, the normal convention is to write SQL commands in uppercase, as it makes them easier to identify in more complex queries. All SQL commands generated by Dreamweaver follow this convention.

The first line begins with SELECT, which as you have already learned, is used to retrieve information from a database. The asterisk tells the database that you want the result to include all columns.

FROM indicates the table(s) that you want to select the results from.

ORDER BY stipulates which column(s) should be used in determining the order.

9. Click the Test button. The results should be exactly the same as before.

10. You can edit the SQL query directly, so insert your cursor at the end of the third line, and change it to this:

```
ORDER BY quotations.quote_id DESC
```

11. Click Test again. This time the results will be in reverse order. DESC is the SQL command for descending order. (The opposite is ASC—ascending order—but this is the default, so you don't need to use it unless you want to make the purpose clear.)

12. Reverse order is useful, but it's not what you want this time. Change the third line of the SQL like this:

```
ORDER BY RAND()
```

13. RAND() is a MySQL function that generates a random number. Click Test again, and the results should come up in random order. If you try it several times, they should always be in a different order.

14. You want only one quotation at a time, so let's limit the number to 1. That's done easily enough. Change the SQL so it now looks like this:

```
SELECT *
FROM quotations
ORDER BY RAND()
LIMIT 1
```

15. Click Test again. You should now get only one quotation. Try it several times, and you should get one of the 50 quotations chosen at random. Although the same quotation may come up twice in succession, it's highly unlikely to happen three times in a row.

16. The SQL query is now complete. Click OK to close the Recordset dialog box. The recordset will now be listed in the Server Behaviors panel as shown alongside.

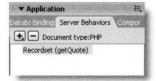

17. Switch to Code view. As you can see in the following screenshot, Dreamweaver has added the recordset code above the DOCTYPE declaration. You can see the SQL query on line 4, and the following lines contain calls to PHP functions that all begin with mysql_. These do all the hard work of getting the result from the MySQL database.

```
1    <?php require_once('../Connections/seasonQuery.php'); ?>
2    <?php
3    mysql_select_db($database_seasonQuery, $seasonQuery);
4    $query_getQuote = "SELECT * FROM quotations ORDER BY RAND() LIMIT 1";
5    $getQuote = mysql_query($query_getQuote, $seasonQuery) or die(mysql_error());
6    $row_getQuote = mysql_fetch_assoc($getQuote);
7    $totalRows_getQuote = mysql_num_rows($getQuote);
8    ?><!DOCTYPE html PUBLIC "-//W3C//DTD XHTML 1.0 Transitional//EN"
     "http://www.w3.org/TR/xhtml1/DTD/xhtml1-transitional.dtd">
```

18. The line above the recordset code contains an include command that points to a page called seasonQuery.php in the Connections folder. Dreamweaver inserted this when you created the seasonQuery connection in the previous section. If you open seasonQuery.php, you will see that it contains your MySQL user account name and password, together with PHP code that establishes the connection to the database. If you want to make sure that everything's OK, check your code against index_02.php in site_check/ch08.

> When you eventually upload your site to a remote server, you must always remember to upload the Connections folder and all its contents. Otherwise, your pages will not be able to connect to the database. This is one of the most common beginner mistakes.

Binding dynamic data to a web page

Now that your page can store the results of the database query in a recordset, you need to be able to display them in the appropriate part of the page. Continue working with the same page as before, or use index_02.php from site_check/ch08.

1. In Design view, place your cursor inside the first paragraph of index.php. (If your page still has the newtext.txt include from Chapter 5, use the paragraph following the include command.) Open Split view so you can check that your code will be inserted in the right place. Select the <p> tag in the Tag selector. Press the  right arrow key once, to move the cursor outside the closing </p> tag in the underlying code, and click the Text Indent button in the Property inspector. This will insert a pair of <block-quote> tags between the first and second paragraphs.

2. In the Property inspector, select Paragraph from the Format drop-down menu. In Split view, you should now see an empty paragraph inside the <blockquote> tags, as shown alongside. This is where the quotation will be displayed. There's no need to remove the . Dreamweaver will do that automatically in step 4.

However, if for some reason the paragraph tags fail to appear, insert them manually in Code view *without* , and position your cursor between them. The   isn't needed, but more importantly, Dreamweaver won't automatically replace it in step 4 if the focus is in Code view.

```
      pariatur. Ut labore et dolore magna aliqua.</p>
31        <blockquote>
32          <p> </p>
33        </blockquote>
34        <p>Qui officia deserunt duis aute irure dolo
```

3. Open the Bindings panel. It's in the same panel group as Databases and Server Behaviors, so just click the Bindings tab or press *CTRL+F10/⌘+F10*. Expand Recordset (getQuote) as shown alongside. If you can't see the names properly, position your mouse pointer over the vertical line between Source and Binding at the top of the panel, hold down your mouse button, and drag the Source column wider.

4. The lightning bolt icon alongside each of the column names indicates that this is dynamic data. You'll see this icon frequently as you work through the rest of this book.

Select quotation, and click the Insert button at the bottom of the Bindings panel. This replaces the   between the <p> tags in the underlying code with a block of PHP code, and inserts a dynamic content placeholder in Design view, as shown below. If you entered the <p> tags manually in step 2, the placeholder won't appear until you click back in Design view.

The code uses echo to display an array element called $row_getQuote['quotation']. As you can see, the array name is derived from the recordset name (getQuote), and the array key is the column name. This makes it easy to recognize what to look for whenever you want to customize the Dreamweaver output. Similarly, the dynamic content placeholder is made up of the recordset and column names separated by a period, and enclosed in curly braces. By default, the placeholder is highlighted in light blue.

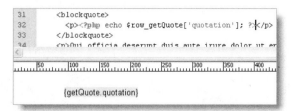

5. Click the Live Data view button, and you should see the dynamic content placeholder replaced by one of the quotations. Toggle Live Data view on and off several times, and you should see different quotations displayed.

6. Make sure Live Data view is off, and click to the right of the dynamic content placeholder in Design view. Press ENTER/RETURN to insert a new paragraph. Highlight first_name in the Bindings panel, and click Insert. Place your cursor to the right of the new dynamic content placeholder, and press SPACE. Then highlight family_name in the Bindings panel, and click Insert.

7. Turn on Live Data view, and you should now see not only the quotation, but also the name of the person who said or wrote it. Congratulations! You have built a random quotation generator. All that remains now is to make it look a bit smarter. If you encounter any problems, check your code against index_03.php in the download files.

Styling the displayed quotation

All the styling of the quotation is done by CSS. The colors are slightly different in the maples and tulips themes, but the versions of both maples.css and tulips.css used in Chapter 6 already contain the necessary rules for the complete site, so there is no need to update them.

1. Open bluebells.css, and add the following style rules at the bottom of the existing ones. (If you don't want to type the style rules yourself, you can find them in site_check/styles. Copy bluebells_03.css to the styles folder in the site root, and don't update the links when prompted by Dreamweaver. Then rename it bluebells.css to replace the existing stylesheet.)

```css
/* styles for random quote */
blockquote {
  border-top: 10px solid #A8B2A3;
  border-bottom: 10px solid #A8B2A3;
  background: #EFF0EE;
  width: 250px;
  text-align: center;
  margin: 0 30px 0 1em;
  padding: 0;
  font-family: georgia, serif;
  font-size: 130%;
  letter-spacing: -1px;
  line-height: 1.2;
```

```
  color: #555;
  float: right;
  }
#maincontent blockquote p {
  margin: 0 1em;
  }
#quote {
  margin: 0;
  padding: 20px 20px 10px 20px;
  }
#author {
  margin: 0;
  padding: 0 0 10px 0;
  color: #999;
  font-size: 80%;
  }
```

The styles make the `<blockquote>` 250 pixels wide, and float it to the right. Because the rules don't add any border or padding to the width, no compensation needs to be made for Internet Explorer 5.0 and 5.5. The rest of the rules just give the text a more elegant look with plenty of space all around.

2. Save `bluebells.css`, and switch back to `index.php`. Most of the changes should immediately be reflected in Design view. If they're not, run Live Data view, and then turn it off. That should refresh the display. Highlight the quotation dynamic content placeholder, and then right-click/*CTRL*-click the `<p>` tag on the Tag selector. Choose Set ID, and select quote from the pop-up menu, as shown. The quote ID was declared in the style rules that you created in step 1, and should be picked up automatically by Dreamweaver.

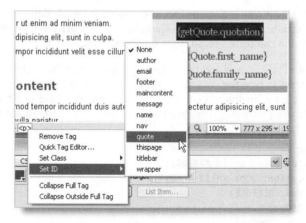

3. Select the `<p>` tag on the Tag selector for the paragraph containing the `first_name` and `family_name` placeholders, and set the ID to author.

4. Save `index.php`, and view the page in a browser. If the random quotation is just one line long, it will look the same as in Figure 4-1. However, a large number of quotations contain new lines. As you have already discovered, browsers ignore new lines in the underlying code, so you need to format the dynamic text in some way.

Once dynamic text has been inserted into a page, each instance is listed in the Server Behaviors panel, as shown alongside.

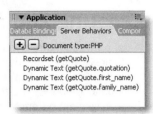

5. Highlight Dynamic Text (getQuote.quotation), and double-click it to open the Dynamic Text dialog box. The Format drop-down menu at the bottom of the dialog box offers a variety of preset formats, such as changing everything to uppercase (AlphaCase – Capitalize), or removing white space from either or both sides (Trim). The format that you want (changing new lines to <br /> tags) isn't available, but the final option on the drop-down menu gives the impression that you can add your own. Unfortunately, if you select Edit Format List, the appropriate dialog box opens, but it's broken. (It's a bug carried over from MX 2004, and still hasn't been fixed.) However, you can edit the code directly.

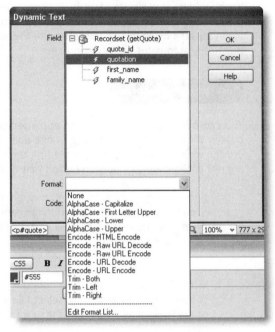

6. Close the Format drop-down menu, and make sure it's set to None. Then insert your cursor inside the Code field just to the left of $row_getQuote. Change the code like this, taking care not to forget to add a closing parenthesis before the semicolon:

```php
<?php echo nl2br($row_getQuote['quotation']); ?>
```

This uses the nl2br() function that you first met in Chapter 5. It converts new line characters to <br /> tags.

> *If you prefer, you can edit the code directly in Code view. The advantage of using the Dynamic Text dialog box is that it automatically selects the right section of PHP code for you. If you're a programming-minded person, you'll probably opt for working directly in Code view. Choose whichever method suits you better.*

7. Save index.php, and view it in a browser. The text will now move correctly onto a new line wherever a new line character appears in the dynamic text. Compare your code, if necessary, with index_04.php in site_check/ch08.

269

Creating and updating database records

phpMyAdmin offers you the means to insert new records and update existing ones in the quotations table. However, the interface can be rather overwhelming for non-experts, and it gives complete control over all your databases—something you should allow only trusted people to have. When creating a database-driven site for yourself or a client, it's far more usual to create a custom-made content management system to manipulate just the bits of data you are interested in for a particular web page or application. Dreamweaver provides an excellent set of tools to do just that—server behaviors that insert, update, and delete records. They work in a very similar way to the contact form that you created in Chapter 6. The form has a separate input field for each database column, but instead of sending everything by email, it's transferred to the appropriate database field. What's more, Dreamweaver practically automates the whole process.

Inserting new records

You can build your own forms and apply server behaviors to them, or you can use Dreamweaver's built-in wizards that do everything in one operation. I prefer to build my own, but in this chapter I'll use the wizards because some people find them easier. Apart from testing in a browser, *everything in the rest of this chapter is done in Design view or through Dreamweaver dialog boxes.*

> *Don't upload any content management pages to your remote server unless you put them in a password-protected folder. I'll show you how to protect your pages with PHP sessions in Chapter 10.*

1. In the Files panel, select Site - phpdw, right-click/*CTRL*-click, and select New Folder from the context menu. Alternatively, select File ➤ New Folder from the Option menu at the top right of the Files panel group. Call the new folder admin, and make sure it's in the root of your phpdw site.

2. Create a new PHP page called quote_insert.php, and save it in the admin folder.

3. Open the Databases panel (*CTRL+SHIFT+F10*/*SHIFT+⌘+F10*), click the plus button, and select MySQL Connection. Create a new connection called seasonAdmin for the dw8admin user. Fill in the dialog box as shown. (If you chose the same password as me for dw8admin, it's weaver.) If you are allowed just one user account, use the connection that you created earlier in the chapter (but make sure it has SELECT, INSERT, UPDATE, and DELETE privileges).

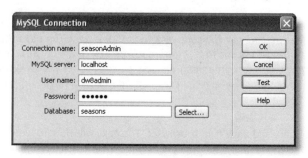

4. Give `quote_insert.php` a suitable title and heading. Make sure your cursor in the underlying code is outside the heading by selecting `<h1>` in the Tag selector at the bottom of the workspace, and pressing your right arrow key once. Then open the Application category of the Insert toolbar. (If you're not using the tabbed interface of the Insert toolbar, select Application from the drop-down menu on the left side of the toolbar.) Click the little down arrow to the side of the eighth button from the left, and select Record Insertion Form Wizard from the pop-up menu, as shown below.

5. In the Record Insertion Form dialog box that opens, select seasonAdmin from the Connection drop-down menu. Since there is only one table in the database, this will automatically select quotations for the Table field, and then populate the rest of the dialog box as shown in the following screenshot.

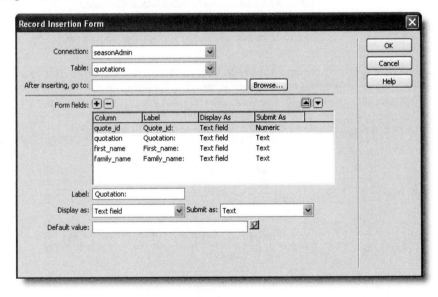

Dreamweaver uses the column names of the quotations table to suggest labels and appropriate types of input fields for the record insertion form. When you select an item in the Form fields area, the values are displayed at the bottom of the dialog box, where you can edit them. The wizard lays out the form in a table in the order shown in the dialog box, so you can use the arrow buttons to rearrange the fields. If you don't want to display a particular field, remove it by clicking the minus button. To restore a deleted item, click the plus button, and select it from the list displayed.

You can also specify where you want to go to after the record has been inserted. If you leave the option blank, the same page will be redisplayed ready for another record. That's fine for this form, but you need to edit the form fields.

6. Highlight quote_id, and click the minus button to delete it. When you created the quotations table, you specified auto_increment for the quote_id column, so MySQL will automatically insert the next available number when a new record is inserted.

7. Highlight quotation, and use the down arrow button to move it to the bottom of the list. The quotation can be up to 255 characters long, so select Text area from the Display as drop-down menu.

8. Highlight first_name, and edit the Label field to remove the underscore, so that it reads First name:—this is the label that will appear onscreen in the form.

9. Do the same for family_name.

10. Leave the Default value field blank for all of them. You need to use this only if you want to specify a default for a particular column. Check that the Form fields area looks like the following screenshot, and click OK.

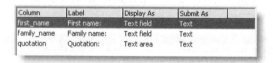

11. Save quote_insert.php and press *F12/OPT+F12* to view it in a browser. You should now have a ready-made form to insert a new quotation in the database. Type something suitable into each field, and click Insert record. The fields will clear, but your pithy quotation should now be in the database. The next step is to find out whether it really is. Check your code against quote_insert.php in site_check/ch08 if you have any problems.

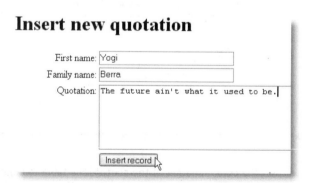

Creating a list of all records

You need to be able to create a list of all records in your database for several reasons. It's not only a useful way to check what it contains, but also you need to be able to select individual records to update or delete them.

1. Create a new PHP page in the admin folder, and save it as quote_list.php.

2. Give it a suitable title and heading. Insert a table below the heading (choose Table from the Common Insert bar or the Insert menu, or press *CTRL+ALT+T/OPT+⌘+T*). The table should have two rows and four columns. In the Table dialog box, I set Table width to 700 pixels, Cell padding to 4, and selected Top for Header. This last setting inserts <th> tags in the first row, instead of <td> tags. The screenshot shows the settings that I used.

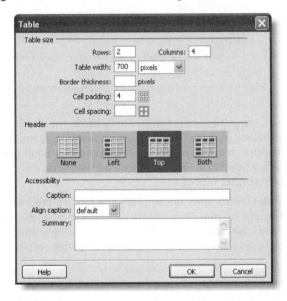

3. Type Name and Quotation in the first two cells of the first row. They will be automatically centered and displayed in a bold typeface because of the <th> tags. Type EDIT and DELETE in the last two cells of the second row. The page should look like this:

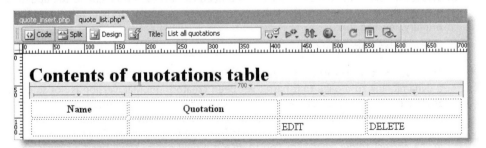

4. Click the Recordset button on the Application Insert bar (it's the first one on the left), and make sure you're using the advanced Recordset dialog box.

5. Name the recordset quoteList, and select the seasonAdmin connection. This recordset only performs a SELECT operation, but it's more consistent to use the same connection for all the pages in the admin folder.

6. Expand the Tables tree in Database items at the bottom of the Recordset dialog box, highlight quotations, and click the SELECT button. Then highlight family_name, and click ORDER BY. Next, highlight first_name, and click ORDER BY again. Finally, highlight quotation and click ORDER BY. The contents of the SQL field should now look like this:

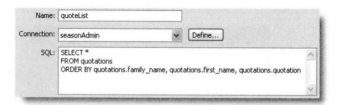

What this does is order the results first by family name, then by first name, and finally by quotation, all in alphabetical order. Click the Test button to verify the results. The columns will still be in the same order, but the contents will have been sorted in the order specified, with two quotations from Woody Allen at the top of the list. Click OK to close both the Test SQL Statement and Recordset windows.

7. The Bindings panel should open automatically. If it doesn't, press *CTRL+F10*/⌘ *+F10*, and expand the Recordset (quoteList) tree. Drag first_name from the Bindings panel into the first cell of the second row of the table, and insert a space. Then drag family_name, and place it alongside. Drag quotation into the second cell of the second row. The table should now look like this:

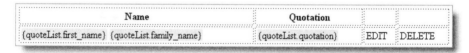

8. Select the text in the third cell (EDIT). You need to turn this into a link to the update page. To identify the correct record, the link needs to contain a query string that includes the record's primary key, like this:

quote_update.php?quote_id=9

This involves several steps. Although the Windows version of Dreamweaver allows you to build a dynamic link to a page that hasn't yet been created, the Mac version is not so cooperative. So, begin by creating a blank PHP page and saving it in the admin folder as quote_update.php. A quick way to do this is to highlight the admin folder or any of its contents in the Files panel, right-click/*CTRL*-click, and choose New File from the context menu. The new file will be created in the correct folder, ready for you to give it a new name. You'll need a similar page for the DELETE link, so create another page called quote_delete.php.

9. Click the Browse for File button to the right of the Link field in the Property inspector. In the Select File dialog box that opens, navigate to the admin folder, and select quote_update.php. Then click the Parameters button alongside the URL field, as shown.

10. In the Parameters dialog box, type quote_id in the Name field. Then press *TAB* to enter the Value field. (You need to press *TAB* twice on Windows, but just once on a Mac. If you over-shoot the Value field, use your mouse pointer to click inside it alongside the name that you have just entered.) The field needs to be populated with dynamic data, so click the lightning bolt icon on the right as shown.

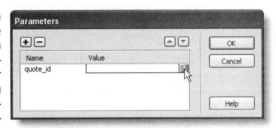

11. In the Dynamic Data dialog box, highlight quote_id, as shown in the screenshot, and click OK. Click OK to close the Parameters dialog box. Then click OK (Choose on the Mac) to close the Select File dialog box.

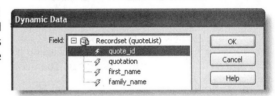

12. Save quote_list.php, and preview it in a browser. Only one record will be displayed. That's fine—you'll handle the display of the others shortly. Right now, you need to check that the query string has been correctly formed. Hover your mouse pointer over the EDIT link. The status bar of your browser should display something like this:

http://localhost/phpdw/admin/quote_update.php?quote_id=9

If necessary, check your code against quote_list_01.php in site_check/ch08.

13. You now need to create a similar link in the fourth cell of the second row. Repeat steps 9 through 12, this time selecting DELETE, and creating a link to quote_delete.php. The URL displayed in the status bar of your browser should look like this:

http://localhost/phpdw/admin/quote_**delete**.php?quote_id=9

14. Switch back to Dreamweaver, and position your cursor anywhere in the second row of the table in quote_list.php. Select <tr> on the Tag selector to highlight the entire row, and click the Repeated Region button in the Application Insert bar.

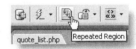

275

15. The dialog box that opens allows you to choose how many records to show at a time. The default is 10 records. Change that to 20, and click OK.

Note that if you have more than one recordset on the page, you need to select the correct one from the Recordset drop-down menu. On this occasion, there is only one, so the choice is automatic.

16. Dreamweaver will place a gray outline around the table row, together with a tag labeled Repeat, indicating that this is a repeated region.

If you click the Live Data view button, you should see 20 records displayed instead of just 1. If you need to check your code, compare your page with quote_list_02.php in site_check/ch08.

There's just one problem—you have a total of 51 items in the database, but only 20 are displayed. Well, it's not really a problem, because Dreamweaver has the answer in its Recordset Paging server behavior.

Creating a record navigation system

Frequently, the number of results from a database query will be too great to display on a single page. With a dynamic site, though, you can get the PHP code to select a subset of results, and navigate back and forth through the full set. The illusion is of displaying a series of pages, whereas, in fact, it's just different content in the same page. The Recordset Paging server behavior makes this complex operation a breeze.

1. Continue working with quote_list.php or use quote_list_02.php from site_check/ch08.

2. Position your cursor outside the table, immediately to the right of it, click the small down arrow next to the Recordset Paging button on the Application Insert bar, and select Recordset Navigation Bar, as shown.

3. The dialog box that opens has just two options: first, to choose the recordset that you want to navigate through (on this occasion, quoteList is the only one available), and whether to use text or images for the navigation bar. If you select Images, Dreamweaver will insert a set of standard arrow images in the same folder as the page. Even if you don't like the default images, you can later substitute others. So, select Images and click OK.

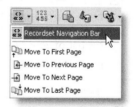

4. That's all there is to it! Save quote_list.php, and view the page in a browser. At the bottom of the page, you will see a set of navigation buttons that will page back and forth through the full set of records.

> *The Recordset Paging server behavior makes very light work of a complex operation. It has one slight drawback, however. It creates the navigation bar inside a table, using deprecated alignment attributes. This won't matter if you're using an HTML or XHTML Transitional DTD. If you're using a Strict DTD, and need your code to validate, you will need to go into Code view and remove the deprecated attributes from the underlying code. It's not difficult, but it's a picky job. Hopefully, the next version of Dreamweaver will create code that works with all DTDs.*

When you view the page in a browser, you will notice that the design looks a little ragged. Copy the admin.css stylesheet from site_check/styles to your main styles folder, and attach it to quote_list.php. If you reload the page in a browser, quote_list.php should look a lot tidier, like the screenshot alongside. The arrow images at the bottom of the page are automatically controlled by PHP code. When you view the next 20 items in the recordset, navigation images will also appear on the left side of the screen, and when you reach the final set of items, the buttons on the right will be automatically hidden.

Although it may be difficult for you to read in the screenshot, I can see that my new quotation has been entered. It's the fifth item from the top. All the quotations have been rearranged in alphabetical order of the family name; and where more than one quotation is attributed to the same person,

Contents of quotations table

Name	Quotation		
Woody Allen	I don't want to achieve immortality through my work... I want to achieve it by not dying.	EDIT	DELETE
Woody Allen	If it turns out that there is a God, I don't think that he's evil. But the worst that you can say about him is that basically, he's an underachiever.	EDIT	DELETE
Matsuo Basho	Under the cherry — blossom soup, blossom salad	EDIT	DELETE
Jeremy Bentham	The greatest happiness of the greatest number is the foundation of morals and legislation.	EDIT	DELETE
Yogi Berra	The future ain't what it used to be.	EDIT	DELETE
Robert Burns	Oh, my Luve's like a red, red rose That's newly sprung in June	EDIT	DELETE
Lewis Carroll	Everything's got a moral, if only you can find it.	EDIT	DELETE
Lewis Carroll	No! No! Sentence first, verdict afterwards.	EDIT	DELETE
Anton Chekhov	Love, friendship, respect do not unite people as much as common hatred for something.	EDIT	DELETE
Winston Churchill	Democracy is the worst form of government except all those other forms that have been tried from time to time.	EDIT	DELETE
John Clare	Summers pleasures they are gone like to visions every one.	EDIT	DELETE
Samuel Taylor Coleridge	The frost performs its secret ministry, Unhelped by any wind	EDIT	DELETE
Samuel Taylor Coleridge	Therefore all seasons shall be sweet to thee.	EDIT	DELETE
Leonardo da Vinci	Iron rusts from disuse; stagnant water loses its purity and in cold weather becomes frozen; even so does inaction sap the vigor of the mind.	EDIT	DELETE
John Donne	No spring, nor summer beauty hath such grace, As I have seen in one autumnal face	EDIT	DELETE
Albert Einstein	I never think of the future. It comes soon enough.	EDIT	DELETE
George Ellis	Snowy, Flowy, Blowy, Showery, Flowery, Bowery, Hoppy, Croppy, Droppy, Breezy, Sneezy, Freezy	EDIT	DELETE
Heyward & Gershwin	Summer time an' the livin' is easy, Fish are jumpin' and the cotton is high	EDIT	DELETE
HR Haldeman	Once the toothpaste is out of the tube, it is awfully hard to get back in.	EDIT	DELETE
Margaret Halsey	The English never smash in a face. They merely refrain from asking it to dinner.	EDIT	DELETE

they are also listed in alphabetical order. When building the SQL in the Recordset dialog box, it was important to select the ORDER BY columns in the correct sequence, because SQL sorts results in the same order as you specify the columns. If I had put first_name at the beginning of the sequence, quote_list.php would show a quotation by Le Corbusier first, because the first_name column for him is blank.

If you hover your mouse pointer over the EDIT links, you should see in the browser status bar that the quote_id number is different for each one. You're now ready to build the update page. If you need to check your code, compare it with quote_list_03.php in site_check/ch08.

Updating records

Updating a record is very similar to inserting a new one. You work with an almost identical form, and populate all the fields with the record that you want to edit. After you make any changes, the record is reinserted using an UPDATE SQL command. Again, let's use the Dreamweaver wizard.

1. Open quote_update.php, and give it a suitable title and heading.

2. Before you can update a record, you need to retrieve it from the database, so that means creating a recordset. Click the Recordset button on the Application Insert bar, and select the simple Recordset dialog box. Fill in the details as shown in the screenshot.

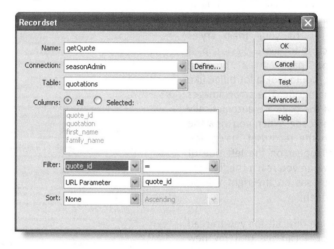

Because you are updating a specific record, you want to select only that one. The Filter settings at the bottom of the dialog box let you choose which column to use as the basis for the selection. Normally, this will be the table's primary key, so choose quote_id from the drop-down menu. The three other fields in the Filter settings set the criteria for the selection. You want quote_id to match the value in the query string, so choose the equal sign and URL Parameter. Dreamweaver will automatically suggest quote_id as the name of the parameter, which is exactly what you want, because the query string added to the URL always takes the form ?query_id=*number*.

If you press the Test button, you will be prompted for a test value for quote_id. Enter any number between 1 and 51, and click OK. The Test SQL Statement panel will display the single record identified by that number as its primary key in the quotations table. Close the Test SQL Statement panel, and click OK to create the recordset.

3. Click the little down arrow alongside the Update Record button in the Application Insert bar, and select Record Update Form Wizard.

4. The Record Update Form dialog box is almost identical to the one that you used to create the insert form. Make sure that you choose the connection with administrative privileges (seasonAdmin). You have got only one recordset on the page, so Dreamweaver automatically chooses getQuote as the value for the field labeled Select record from. It also automatically selects quote_id as the value for Unique key column, because it's registered in MySQL as the primary key for the quotations table. After updating the record, it's a good idea to display the full list of records, so browse to quote_list.php or enter it directly in the field labeled After updating, go to.

Rearrange the Form fields and edit the labels as you did in the Insert Record Form dialog box. This time, though, you will notice that Dreamweaver displays a block of PHP code in the Default value field. This is because you want the value from the recordset to be displayed in each input field of the form ready for editing. Check that your dialog box looks like the screenshot alongside, and click OK.

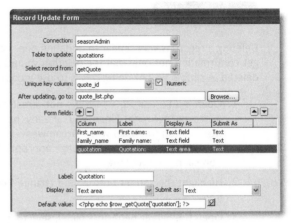

5. Dreamweaver builds the update form and the necessary PHP and SQL code using the information in the dialog box. The form should look almost identical to the one in quote_insert.php, except that it has dynamic content placeholders in each input field. Save quote_update.php, and load quote_list.php into your browser.

6. Choose one of the quotations, and click the EDIT link alongside it. This will load quote_update.php into your browser with the selected quotation displayed inside the form ready for editing, as shown here.

As you can see from the browser address bar, the URL has a query string attached to the end, which identifies the record that you want to edit and instructs the page to display the correct one.

279

7. Alter some of the words in the quotation, and click Update record.

8. You will be taken back to the full list of quotations, where any changes should be reflected. Repeat steps 6 and 7 to restore the original content of the quotation. Check your code against quote_update.php in site_check/ch08 if necessary.

Your content management system is almost complete. All you need to do is wire up the delete links in quote_list.php.

Deleting records

Deleting a record is very similar to updating one. However, it's an irreversible action, so it's essential to get confirmation not only that the deletion should go ahead, but also that the correct record is being deleted. A simple way of doing this is to use a copy of the update form.

1. Open quote_update.php if it's not already open. Select File ➤ Save As, and name the copy quote_delete.php. Since you already have a blank page with the same name, click Yes (Replace on the Mac) when Dreamweaver asks if you want to replace the existing file. Change the title and heading of the page appropriately, and add a paragraph warning that the operation cannot be undone.

2. Highlight the submit button, and change the Value in the Property inspector to Confirm deletion.

3. Open the Server Behaviors panel, select Update Record, and click the minus button to remove the server behavior and all related code cleanly from the page.

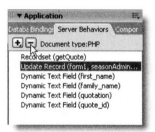

4. In the bottom-left corner of the form, you should see a small gold shield with the letter H on it, indicating the presence of a hidden form field. This was created by the Update Record Form Wizard, and it should still be there, even though you deleted the server behavior in the previous step. Select the shield, and confirm in Property inspector that the hidden field is called quote_id, and that the Value field contains dynamic text. The Delete Record server behavior will use this value to identify the record to delete. If the hidden field has the right settings (which it should), skip to step 6.

5. *This step is required only if the hidden form field is missing.* If you can't see the gold shield, open the Preferences panel from the Edit menu (Dreamweaver menu on a Mac), select Invisible Elements, and check that Hidden form fields has been selected. If the gold shield still doesn't appear, and Dynamic Text Field (quote_id) is not listed in the Server Behaviors panel, choose Insert ➤ Form ➤ Hidden Field. In the Property inspector, name the hidden field quote_id, and click the lightning bolt icon next to the Value field. In the Dynamic Data dialog box that opens, expand the getQuote recordset, select quote_id, and click OK.

6. Click anywhere inside Design view to deselect the hidden form field. Then click the Delete Record button on the Application Insert bar, as shown, to insert a Delete Record server behavior.

7. Fill in the Delete Record dialog box as shown in the next screenshot. Make sure that you choose the connection that has administrative privileges. Since quotations is the only table in the database, it will automatically be chosen. Dreamweaver should also automatically select quote_id as the Primary key column. However, the server behavior uses the hidden field to identify the correct record to delete, so make sure you select Form Variable as the Primary key value, and that quote_id is entered in the text field alongside. After the record has been deleted, it's a good idea to load the complete list, so enter quote_list.php in the final field labeled After deleting, go to. Click OK to insert the server behavior.

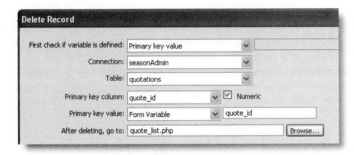

8. Save quote_delete.php, and load quote_list.php into your browser. Select a quotation to be sent to cyber-oblivion, and click the DELETE link alongside it. The selected quote should be displayed in quote_delete.php as shown.

Delete quotation

You are about to delete the following quotation from the database. This operation cannot be undone.

First name: Yogi

Family name: Berra

Quotation: The future ain't what it used to be.

Confirm deletion

9. To make sure that everything's working, click Confirm deletion. When you are returned to quote_list.php, the record will have gone. One thing missing from the form created by the wizard is a method of canceling the operation. You can add a link back to quote_list.php, or simply click the browser back button. Check your code against quote_delete.php in site_check/ch08 if you encounter any problems.

A great deal achieved

This has been an action-packed chapter with a lot of material to absorb. You have learned all the basic features of working with a database: creating user accounts, defining a table, and using the essential quartet of SQL commands—SELECT, INSERT, UPDATE, and DELETE.

To get a sense of how much hard work Dreamweaver has done for you, open any of the content management pages in Code view. You may get quite a shock at all the code that Dreamweaver has created on your behalf. It's not necessary to understand how all of it works, although in later chapters I'll show you how to dig into it to customize it. What is more important is learning the correct settings for each of the dialog boxes. Dreamweaver makes a lot of intelligent guesses, but once you start building more complex pages, you will need to pay greater attention to the options in each field. The reason Dreamweaver gets so much right at this stage is because you have only one table in the database, so there are few options for it to choose from.

The form-building wizards are extremely useful, but they're not very flexible. Once you click OK, the form is built automatically, and cannot be changed easily. They're also limited to working with single tables. The real power of a relational database like MySQL, however, lies in working with multiple tables, which just happens to be the subject of the next chapter. See you there.

Chapter 9

WORKING WITH MULTIPLE TABLES

What this chapter covers:

- Moving content from one table to another
- Linking related information in different tables with a foreign key
- Applying the rules of normalization to decide what to store in a table
- Building SQL queries with SELECT, INSERT, UPDATE, and DELETE
- Applying server behaviors to custom-built forms
- Populating a drop-down menu with dynamic data
- Transforming data with MySQL functions and aliases
- Enforcing referential integrity with PHP logic
- Using LEFT JOIN to find an incomplete match

If you look closely at some of the names in the quotations table in the previous chapter, you'll notice that some of them are inconsistent. Shakespeare is sometimes referred to by his full name, sometimes by his family name alone, and on one occasion his first name is reduced to an initial. Similarly, Mark Twain appears both with his full name, and just an initial. This sort of inconsistency isn't terribly important with a list of quotations, but it could have a major impact in other circumstances. Let's say you're creating a product catalog or a contact list—you might spell a company name in different ways. For instance, friends of ED might sometimes be entered as foED, freinds of ED, or—heaven forbid—fiends of ED. To a human being, all four versions are likely to be recognized as meaning the same thing, but to a computer, they're completely different. Run a search for friends of ED, and anything spelled a different way will not turn up in the results. Consequently, vital data could be lost forever.

Even if you never make a spelling mistake, it's highly inefficient to type out the same information over and over again. The solution is to store frequently repeated data in a separate table, and link the tables together using the primary keys of each record. So, in this chapter, I'll show you how to convert the random quotation generator to a more logical structure by splitting the quotations table into two. Then I'll show you how to redesign the content management system by applying Insert Record, Update Record, and Delete Record server behaviors to custom-built forms. Dreamweaver automates much of the process for you, but there are quite a lot of steps involved, and it means the occasional dive into Code view. Once you have mastered the steps in this chapter, you will be equipped with the basic tools to build the content management system for a wide variety of multiple-table databases.

Storing related information in separate tables

In the previous chapter, I explained that an important principle of working with a relational database was the need to break larger units, such as addresses or names, into their component elements, and store them in separate columns. Another equally important principle is to get rid of columns that contain repetitive data, and move them to a separate table. As long as each record has a primary key to identify it, records in separate tables can be linked by storing the primary key from one table as a reference in the other. This is known as creating a **foreign key**.

> Although the default MyISAM table type doesn't yet have support for foreign key constraints, all MySQL tables can use foreign keys. I'll explain the difference after describing how foreign keys work.

Using foreign keys to link records

At the moment, each record in the quotations table stores the name of the person being quoted, along with the quotation itself. As you can see from Figure 9-1, the five records that contain quotations from Shakespeare list him in three different ways. In records 25 and 34, he's called William Shakespeare; in record 33 he's W Shakespeare; and in records 31 and 32, he's just plain Shakespeare.

quote_id	quotation	first_name	family_name
25	Sweet lovers love the spring.	William	Shakespeare
26	O, Wind, If Winter comes, can Spring be far behin...	Percy Bysshe	Shelley
27	In the spring a young man's fancy lightly turns to...	Alfred, Lord	Tennyson
28	It is not spring until you can plant your foot on ...		Proverb
29	The way to ensure summer in England is to have it ...	Horace	Walpole
30	’Tis the last rose of summer Left blooming ...	Thomas	Moore
31	Shall I compare thee to a summer's day? Thou art ...		Shakespeare
32	Now is the winter of our discontent Made glorious...		Shakespeare
33	Blow, blow, thou winter wind, Thou art not so unk...	W	Shakespeare
34	My age is as a lusty winter, frosty, but kindly.	William	Shakespeare

Figure 9-1. The original quotations table has multiple entries for Shakespeare presented in three ways.

To overcome this sort of problem, it's more logical to create a separate table for names—I've called it authors—and store each person's name just once. So, instead of storing the name with each quotation, you can store the appropriate primary key from the authors table. Figure 9-2 shows how the relationship works.

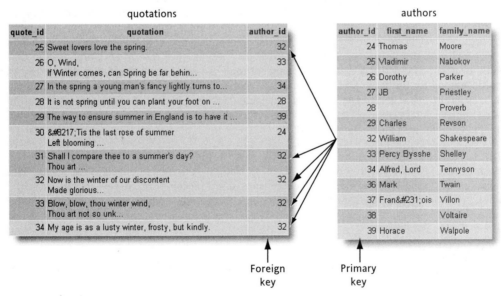

Figure 9-2. The primary key from the authors table (author_id) is used as a foreign key in the quotations table, making it possible to link multiple records with the same name.

- The primary key of the authors table is author_id. Because primary keys must be unique, each number is used only once.

- The author_id for William Shakespeare is 32.

- All quotations attributed to William Shakespeare are identified by the same author_id (32) in the quotations table. Because author_id is being used as a foreign key in this table, there can be multiple references to the same number.

287

> *As long as* author_id *remains unique in the* authors *table—where it's the primary key—you know that it always refers to the same person.*

I've only drawn arrows linking Shakespeare with his quotations, but you can see that quote_id 26 comes from the poet Shelley (author_id 33), and that quote_id 27 comes from Tennyson (author_id 34). Before any sense of panic sets in about how you are going to remember all these numbers, relax. MySQL generates the primary key numbers automatically when you create new records, and when you communicate with the database using SQL, you tell it to find the appropriate number for you. In other words, if you want to conduct a search for all quotations by Shakespeare, you issue a command that tells the database to do something like this (in pseudocode):

```
SELECT everything in the quotation column FROM quotations
WHERE the author_id in quotations is the same as
the author_id in authors for "William Shakespeare"
```

What foreign key constraints do

If you look at Figure 9-2, you'll see that if William Shakespeare is deleted from the authors table, author_id 32 will no longer have a value attached to it. Consequently, there will be no way of knowing who author_id 32 is, and the five quotations from Shakespeare will be orphaned. Foreign key constraints are designed to prevent this from happening. When creating InnoDB tables, you can establish a foreign key relationship in the table definition. Depending on how the relationship is defined, MySQL will prevent you from deleting records if they would leave foreign keys orphaned in other tables, or it will automatically delete all dependent records—known as a **cascading delete**. You can also do **cascading updates**, which automatically change the value of the foreign key in all related tables when its value is changed in the parent table. Making sure that the foreign key relationship always remains intact is known as maintaining **referential integrity**. In simple terms, it means that you don't end up with incomplete records.

Since the default MyISAM table type used by most hosting companies doesn't support foreign key constraints, I won't go into how to set them up. You can find the full details in the MySQL documentation at http://dev.mysql.com/doc/refman/5.0/en/innodb-foreign-key-constraints.html. Although it's hoped that MyISAM tables will support foreign key constraints in the not too distant future, you can reproduce the same effect with PHP. All that's required is a little conditional logic with if . . . else statements.

```
if (no dependent files) {
 delete;
 }
else {
 don't delete;
 }
```

It requires a little planning, but so too does the implementation of foreign key constraints. You'll put this strategy into action later in the chapter when building the delete form for records in the authors table.

Splitting the quotations table

Even if you discover that your database design is not optimal, all is not lost. Relational databases are very flexible, and you can redesign them. You *can*, but you shouldn't, unless it's really necessary. As the next few pages will demonstrate, it's a lot easier to design the database properly in the first place. So, why didn't I? The main reason is because working with a single table in the previous chapter gave me the opportunity to cover most of the basic steps of interacting with a database—selecting, inserting, updating, and deleting records—without the complication of handling multiple tables. It also means I can now show you how to add and drop columns from an existing table.

Creating the authors table

First of all, let's create the second table so that the names can be moved across from the existing one.

1. Launch phpMyAdmin, and select seasons from the Database drop-down menu in the navigation frame.

2. In the main frame, create a new table called authors with three columns (fields) by filling the Create new table form as shown. Click Go.

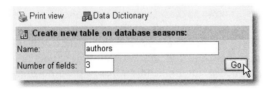

3. In the screen that opens, define the three table columns as shown in the following screenshot.

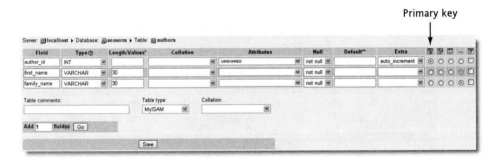

- author_id should have the values INT, UNSIGNED, not null, and auto_increment, and the primary key radio button should be selected.

- first_name should have the values VARCHAR, 30, and not null.

- family_name should have the values VARCHAR, 30, and not null.

Click Save when you have filled in all the definitions.

4. The table structure, as displayed in the next screen, should look like this:

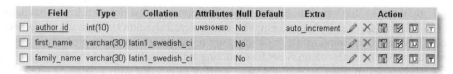

If necessary, use the pencil-like icons to edit any fields that are incorrect. Keep phpMyAdmin open, because you'll continue working with it in the next three sections.

Adding a new column to the quotations table

Although the quotations table will eventually have only three columns, you can't delete the first_name or family_name columns until you have created and populated the author_id column, which will hold the foreign key.

1. Click the link for the quotations table in the phpMyAdmin navigation frame. This will display the table's structure in the main frame.

2. Although Figure 9-2 shows author_id to the right of quotation, you should normally position foreign key columns immediately after the primary key column. As you can see in the following screenshot, there is a form beneath the table structure diagram that allows you to choose how many columns (fields) to add, and whether they should be at the beginning or end of the table, or after a particular column (chosen from a drop-down menu).

You want to add only one column, so the default value in the Add field(s) text box is fine. Select the After radio button, and make sure that quote_id is selected in the drop-down menu. Then click Go.

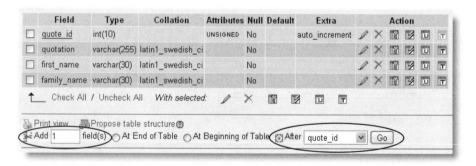

3. This will open the now familiar screen for you to define the column. Use the following settings:

- Field: author_id
- Type: INT
- Attributes: UNSIGNED
- Null: null

You should *not* select either auto_increment or the primary key radio button. Although author_id is the primary key in the authors table, a foreign key takes neither of these settings. The reason for choosing null is that you may not always be able to assign a foreign key—for instance, when inserting a new quotation for someone not yet registered in the authors table.

Click Save when you have made all the settings.

4. The revised table structure should now look like this:

	Field	Type	Collation	Attributes	Null	Default	Extra	Action					
☐	quote_id	int(10)		UNSIGNED	No		auto_increment	✎	✕	🔢	📝	🆄	🆃
☐	author_id	int(10)		UNSIGNED	Yes	*NULL*		✎	✕	🔢	📝	🆄	🆃
☐	quotation	varchar(255)	latin1_swedish_ci		No			✎	✕	🔢	📝	🆄	🆃
☐	first_name	varchar(30)	latin1_swedish_ci		No			✎	✕	🔢	📝	🆄	🆃
☐	family_name	varchar(30)	latin1_swedish_ci		No			✎	✕	🔢	📝	🆄	🆃

As you can see, author_id is not underlined, indicating that it's not a primary key. In fact, if you had attempted to select the primary key radio button, phpMyAdmin would have refused to make any changes to the table, because you cannot add another primary key to a table that already has one.

Transferring the names between the tables

You now need to move the names from the quotations table into the authors table, but without any duplicates. This involves creating a SQL command that will pick out just one instance of each name.

1. Click the SQL tab at the top of the main frame. This presents you with the following screen where you can run SQL queries and see the results.

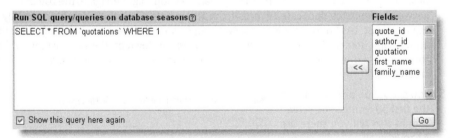

By default, the screen displays a SQL query for you to customize. If you click Go without making any changes, it will display the entire contents of the table. However, that's no different from clicking the Browse tab. The purpose of using this screen is to extract more refined results. The main text area is where you build the query, and the Fields list to the right shows you the names of all columns in the current table.

2. Click inside the main text area, and delete the asterisk to the right of SELECT. Type DISTINCT, followed by a space. Highlight first_name in the Fields list and click the button marked <<. This will insert `first_name` into the SQL query, which should now look like this:

SELECT **DISTINCT** `first_name` FROM `quotations` WHERE 1

291

The characters surrounding first_name *and* quotations *are not single quotes, but backticks. They are not strictly necessary around column names, but phpMyAdmin inserts them automatically to prevent your SQL from failing if you happen to choose a reserved word as the name for a table column. MySQL has nearly 500 reserved words, so it's easy to fall into the trap of using one unintentionally. You can find a full list of them at* http://dev.mysql.com/doc/refman/5.0/en/reserved-words.html. *Common ones to avoid are words connected with dates—such as week, year, day—and words like start and stop. If you find that SQL queries fail inexplicably, the reason could lie in your choice of column or table names. Either check the list and choose a safe alternative, or use backticks.*

In addition to avoiding reserved words, you should not use hyphens in table or column names. Although phpMyAdmin will handle such names without difficulty, Dreamweaver will report that no tables can be found in the database. To be safe, always begin column and table names with a letter, and use only alphanumeric characters (a–z and 0–9) and the underscore (_). Unlike phpMyAdmin, Dreamweaver doesn't surround all table and column names with backticks. However, it is clever enough to insert the backticks when it recognizes that you have used a reserved word.

3. Type a comma after `first_name`, and then insert family_name from the Fields list.

4. Delete WHERE 1 from the end of the SQL query, and replace it with ORDER BY `family_name`. The whole SQL query should now look like this:

```
SELECT DISTINCT `first_name`, `family_name` FROM `quotations`
ORDER BY `family_name`
```

This will select just the first_name and family_name columns from the quotations table, and order the results alphabetically by family_name. As you might imagine, the use of the DISTINCT keyword eliminates duplicate records from the results. Click the Go button directly beneath the Fields list. (As I noted earlier, phpMyAdmin frequently offers a number of different options on the same screen. There is another Go button lower down on the same screen, which is used for running a query from a text file. If you choose the wrong one, the query that you have just created won't run.)

5. You should be presented with the first 30 results. The screen should also tell you there are 42 rows in all.

To display all results on the same screen, change the values in both text fields shown in the screenshot from 30, so that it reads as follows:

Show: **42** row(s) starting from record #**0**

Click Show.

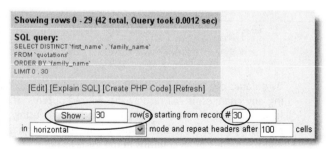

Showing rows 0 - 29 (42 total, Query took 0.0012 sec)

SQL query:
SELECT DISTINCT `first_name`, `family_name`
FROM `quotations`
ORDER BY `family_name`
LIMIT 0, 30

[Edit] [Explain SQL] [Create PHP Code] [Refresh]

Show : 30 row(s) starting from record # 30

in horizontal mode and repeat headers after 100 cells

6. Scroll down to the bottom of the results, and you will see there are still three instances of Shakespeare and two of Twain. This is because W Shakespeare is different from William Shakespeare, but at least you now have only one instance of each. Still, this is just a set of results; the names haven't been transferred.

7. Highlight the SQL query (just the first three lines shown in the screenshot in step 5, omitting the LIMIT 0, 30), and copy it to your clipboard (*CTRL*+*C*/⌘ +*C*). Then click the SQL tab at the top of the screen.

8. Now that you know you're getting the right results, you can convert the query into one that will copy the results into the authors table. Delete the default query; then paste (*CTRL*+*V*/⌘ +*V*) the query you copied to the clipboard in the previous step, and add a new first line so that the entire query looks like this:

```
INSERT INTO authors (`first_name`, `family_name`)
SELECT DISTINCT `first_name`, `family_name`
FROM `quotations`
ORDER BY `family_name`
```

What this query does is to insert the results of the existing query into the first_name and family_name columns of the authors table. The target columns are listed inside the parentheses, and they must be in the same order as the results. Click Go.

9. phpMyAdmin should report that the query has been successfully executed. Select the authors link from the navigation frame, and when the authors table structure appears in the main frame, click Browse.

10. Change the values in the text fields as you did in step 5 to display all 42 records on the same screen, and click Show.

11. Scroll down, and put check marks in the duplicate entries for Shakespeare and Twain as shown alongside. In this particular case, you know that these entries relate to the same person, but in a real-world scenario you would need to make sure that the initial in M Twain doesn't belong to someone else— for instance, Mark Twain's hitherto unknown sister, Margaret.

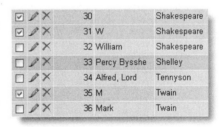

12. Delete the duplicates by clicking the large red X icon at the bottom of the screen. Alternatively, delete them individually by clicking the same icon in each record.

13. phpMyAdmin will ask you to confirm the deletion. Click Yes.

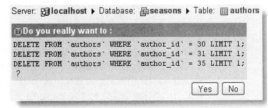

You now have an authors table with 39 unique entries. There are some gaps in the primary key sequence, but that doesn't matter. What's important is that each entry has its own unique identifier.

You now need to assign the correct author_id to each record in the quotations table. The way you do this is by identifying one or more fields that each table has in common. Since all the records in the family_name column are different, you can use that on its own. Otherwise, you would need to match both family_name and first_name.

1. Click the SQL tab at the top of the screen. The phpMyAdmin SQL query builder isn't designed to work with more than one table, so you need to type in the entire query by hand. Clear the text area by deleting the default SELECT query.

2. Since you need to add new information to existing records in the quotations table, the SQL command is UPDATE (INSERT is used only when creating a new record). Start building the query by typing the following in the Run SQL query text area:

UPDATE quotations, authors

Although only the quotations table will be updated, you need to specify the authors table, too, because you will be using information from the authors table to perform the update. The table names don't use reserved words, so to save typing, I have not surrounded them with backticks.

3. The SET keyword tells the database what new values to insert in each record, so add a new line to the SQL query like this:

UPDATE quotations, authors
SET quotations.author_id = authors.author_id

Both tables have a column called author_id, so you need to create an unambiguous reference to each one. You do this by specifying the table name and the column name joined together with a period (.). If you have ever worked with JavaScript or ActionScript, this dot notation will be immediately familiar.

> *When working with multiple tables, column references must always be unambiguous. If a column name exists in only one table, there is no need to qualify it with the table name. For instance, the* quotation *column exists only in the* quotations *table, so a SQL query could refer to it simply as* quotation *without any danger of confusion. Dreamweaver, however, always creates fully qualified names (such as* quotations.quotation*). This is safer, and a good practice to emulate. If you need to use backticks with a fully qualified name, they must be placed separately around both the table and the column names:*
>
> ```
> `quotations`.`quotation`  /* RIGHT */
> `quotations.quotation`    /* WRONG */
> ```

4. The SQL query so far tells the database to copy the values from the author_id column in the authors table to the author_id column in the quotations table, but you still need to specify which values belong to each record. You do this with the WHERE keyword. Add the following line (shown in bold) to the existing SQL:

UPDATE quotations, authors
SET quotations.author_id = authors.author_id
WHERE quotations.family_name = authors.family_name

This will now match the correct family_name with its corresponding author_id. If you had a situation where you also needed to match the first_name, you could add the following line at the end of the SQL query:

AND quotations.first_name = authors.first_name

If you add this extra line, however, the records that use M Twain, W Shakespeare, and Shakespeare on its own will not be updated. Run just the three-line query by clicking Go.

5. As long as you typed everything correctly, you should see a message saying: Affected rows: 50, and reporting how long the query took. Select the quotations table by clicking its link in the navigation frame, and when it loads into the main frame, click the Browse tab at the top of the screen. You should now see that the author_id column has been populated with the numbers drawn from the authors table. As the following screenshot shows, the quotations from Mark Twain all have the same author_id (36), even though there are variations of his name in the table.

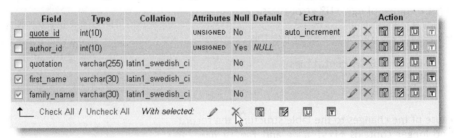

6. All that remains to do now is to delete the first_name and family_name columns from the quotations table. Click the Structure tab at the top of the screen.

7. Select the check boxes next to first_name and family_name, and click the large red X icon beneath the structure grid as shown.

Field	Type	Collation	Attributes	Null	Default	Extra	Action
quote_id	int(10)		UNSIGNED	No		auto_increment	
author_id	int(10)		UNSIGNED	Yes	NULL		
quotation	varchar(255)	latin1_swedish_ci		No			
first_name	varchar(30)	latin1_swedish_ci		No			
family_name	varchar(30)	latin1_swedish_ci		No			

Check All / Uncheck All   With selected:

8. phpMyAdmin will ask you to confirm that you want to drop the columns. (DROP is the SQL command for deleting a column, table, or database. DELETE refers only to individual records.) Click Yes. The conversion is now complete.

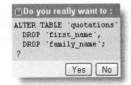

Although this conversion process has been relatively painless, it's not always so easy, particularly if you have a database with hundreds or thousands of records. Let's say I had misspelled some of the family names. It would have taken many more steps to clean everything up and make sure that the quotations were still identified with the correct names.

Deciding on the best structure

It's far better to design your database table structure before any live data is stored. Unfortunately, there is no "right" way to design a database. Each one is different. However, a process known as **normalization** lays down the basic principles of good database design. The main rules can be summarized as follows:

- Give each data record a unique means of identification, known as a primary key.

- Put each group of associated data in a table of its own.

- When columns contain data that is repeated, create a separate table and cross-reference with a unique identifier known as a foreign key.

- Store only one item of information in each field.

As long as you store the appropriate foreign keys, you can link tables with SQL queries. You also save a lot of duplicated effort, and reduce the likelihood of losing vital data.

People who work regularly with databases say they often spend far more time on planning the structure of a database than on building it and the associated content management system. It's a vast subject that I don't have room to go into here, but you can find more detailed advice in *Beginning MySQL Database Design and Optimization: From Novice to Professional* by Jon Stephens and Chad Russell (Apress, ISBN 1-59059-332-4).

Selecting records from more than one table

Now that you have split the data from the original quotations table into two separate ones, the recordset in index.php will still work, but it will no longer contain values for either first_name or family_name. Figure 9-3 shows what happens if you preview index.php in a browser. Instead of the name of the person being quoted, you get a couple of ugly PHP error messages.

The SQL query in index.php looks like this:

```
SELECT * FROM quotations
ORDER BY RAND()
LIMIT 1
```

Because of the changes to the table structure, the recordset no longer contains first_name and family_name. To get them, you need to find the matching record in the authors table using author_id. Fortunately, Dreamweaver doesn't have the same limitations as phpMyAdmin when it comes to building multiple-table SQL queries.

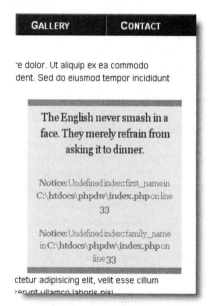

Figure 9-3. The dynamic data for the pull quote needs to be changed to work with the new table structure.

Updating the recordset in index.php

Continue working with index.php from the previous chapter, or use index_01.php from site_check/ch09.

1. Open index.php. To edit the SQL query, open the Server Behaviors panel, highlight Recordset (getQuote), and double-click to open the Recordset dialog box.

2. Highlight the last section of the existing SQL query (ORDER BY RAND() LIMIT 1), as shown alongside, and cut (*CTRL+X*/⌘ +X) it to your clipboard. Delete everything else in the SQL field.

3. In the Database items area at the bottom of the Recordset dialog box, expand Tables. You should now see both the authors and quotations tables listed. Expand quotations, highlight quotation, and click the SELECT button.

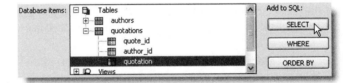

This starts building the SQL query. If you look at the SQL field at the top of the dialog box, you should now see the following code:

```
SELECT quotations.quotation
FROM quotations
```

4. Expand authors in the Database items area, and highlight first_name. Click SELECT.

5. Highlight family_name, and click SELECT. The SQL query should now look like this:

```
SELECT quotations.quotation, authors.first_name, authors.family_name
FROM quotations, authors
```

6. If you click Test now, you will see every quotation attributed first to Woody Allen, and then every quotation attributed to Matsuo Basho. The Dreamweaver test shows only the first 100 results, but if you run the same query in phpMyAdmin, you'll see there are 1,950 results altogether—every record in the quotations table has been matched with every record in the authors table. In other words, it produces every possible combination.

7. To get the result that you want, you need to add a WHERE clause that matches the foreign key in the quotations table to the primary key in the authors table. Highlight author_id in the quotations tree in Database items, and click the WHERE button. This adds WHERE quotations.author_id to the end of the SQL.

297

8. Expand the authors tree in Database items, and highlight the other author_id. Click WHERE again. Each time you click WHERE, it always adds whichever column is highlighted using AND, so the final line of the SQL query will now look like this:

```
WHERE quotations.author_id AND authors.author_id
```

Although AND is often what you want in a WHERE expression, it's not always the right choice, so you have to replace it manually. Click inside the SQL field, and replace AND with =. The SQL should now look the same as in the screenshot.

> SQL: SELECT quotations.quotation, authors.first_name, authors.family_name
> FROM quotations, authors
> WHERE quotations.author_id = authors.author_id

9. Click the Test button now, and you'll see that each quotation has now been correctly matched with the right name. It's important to use the Test button whenever you build a recordset. Even though Dreamweaver takes a lot of the hard work out of coding, it will only do what you tell it to do. Give it instructions that are nonsense, and it will happily produce a recordset that's equal nonsense. Click OK to close the test panel.

10. Click inside the SQL field, add a new line at the end of the code, and paste back (*CTRL*+*V*/⌘+*V*) the snippet that you cut to the clipboard in step 2. The entire SQL query should now look like this:

```
SELECT quotations.quotation, authors.first_name, authors.family_name
FROM quotations, authors
WHERE quotations.author_id = authors.author_id
ORDER BY RAND() LIMIT 1
```

11. Use the test panel several times to make sure that you're getting just one random quotation and the associated names. Once you're happy that everything is as expected, click OK to close the Recordset dialog box.

12. Use Live Data view or preview index.php in a browser. The error messages should have gone, and the name associated with the quotation should be correctly displayed again. Check your code against site_check/ch09/index_02.php, if necessary.

Injustice anywhere is a threat
to justice everywhere.

Martin Luther King

The four essential SQL commands

As you have just seen, the advanced Recordset dialog box helps build SQL queries that work with multiple tables. Using the SELECT, WHERE, and ORDER BY buttons in conjunction with the table trees in the Database items field helps avoid spelling mistakes, and always creates unambiguous references to columns. However, it cannot do everything. Not only do you need to hand-code some parts of SQL queries, you also need to have a reasonable understanding of the basic syntax. Fortunately, you don't need to be a SQL genius. You can achieve a great number of useful things with just four essential commands: SELECT, INSERT, UPDATE, and DELETE.

The following sections provide a brief overview of how each command is structured. Read through them to get a basic understanding of how SQL works, and use them later as a reference. This is not an exhaustive listing of every available option, but concentrates on the most important ones. I have used the same typographic conventions as the MySQL online manual at http://dev.mysql.com/doc/refman/5.0/en (which you may also want to consult):

- Anything in uppercase is a SQL command.
- Expressions in square brackets are optional.
- Lowercase italics represent variable input.
- A vertical pipe (|) separates alternatives.

When working with SQL, you should follow these simple rules:

- SQL commands are case-insensitive. Although the convention is to use uppercase, SELECT, select, and SeLeCt are all acceptable.
- White space is ignored. This means you can split queries over several lines for increased readability.
- The one exception where white space is not ignored concerns MySQL functions, such as CONCAT(). There must be *no* white space between the function name and the opening parenthesis.
- Each section of a query *must* be in the same order as presented here. For instance, in a SELECT query, LIMIT cannot come before ORDER BY.
- Pay particular attention to punctuation. A missing or superfluous comma will cause a query to fail. So will missing quotes around a string used in a WHERE expression.

SELECT

SELECT is used for retrieving records from one or more tables in a database. Its basic syntax is as follows:

```
SELECT [DISTINCT] select_list
FROM table_list
[WHERE where_expression]
[ORDER BY col_name | formula] [ASC | DESC]
[LIMIT [skip_count,] show_count]
```

The DISTINCT option tells the database you want to eliminate duplicate rows from the results. You used this earlier in the chapter to copy just one instance of each name to the authors table.

The *select_list* is a comma-separated list of columns that you want included in the result. To retrieve all columns, use an asterisk (*). If the same column name is used in more than one table, you must use unambiguous references by using the syntax *table_name.column_name*.

The *table_list* is a comma-separated list of tables from which the results are to be drawn. All tables that you want to be included in the results *must* be listed here, even if you use table names to avoid ambiguous references in the *select_list*.

The WHERE clause specifies any particular criteria you are looking for. You have already seen two examples in this chapter:

```
WHERE quotations.family_name = authors.family_name
WHERE quotations.author_id = authors.author_id
```

In both cases, the comparison is being made with the values in another column. However, you can also test for specific values, such as this:

```
WHERE quotations.family_name = 'Shakespeare'
WHERE quotations.author_id = 32
```

> You may have noticed a crucial difference between the PHP and MySQL equality operators. Whereas PHP uses two equal signs (==) to test for equality, MySQL uses only one (=). Don't get the two mixed up. Text or string values in a WHERE expression must be enclosed in quotes (single or double), but numbers are left unquoted.

Frequently, values used in WHERE expressions need to come from PHP variables. Dreamweaver doesn't allow you to use PHP variables directly in the Recordset dialog box. I'll show you later in the chapter how to create the temporary variables used by Dreamweaver.

WHERE expressions can use comparison, arithmetic, logical, and pattern-matching operators. Many of them are the same as in PHP, but MySQL has many more. The main ones are listed in Table 9-1.

Table 9-1. The main operators used in MySQL WHERE expressions

Comparison		Arithmetic	
<	Less than	+	Addition
<=	Less than or equal to	-	Subtraction
=	Equal to	*	Multiplication
!=	Not equal to	/	Division
>	Greater than	DIV	Integer division
>=	Greater than or equal to	%	Modulo
IN()	Included in list		
BETWEEN *min* AND *max*	Between (and including) two values		
Logical		**Pattern matching**	
AND	Logical and	LIKE	Case-insensitive match
&&	Logical and	NOT LIKE	Case-insensitive nonmatch
OR	Logical or	LIKE BINARY	Case-sensitive match
||	Logical or (best avoided)	NOT LIKE BINARY	Case-sensitive nonmatch

DIV is the counterpart of the modulo operator. It produces the result of division as an integer with no fractional part, whereas modulo produces only the remainder.

```
5 / 2     /* result 2.5 */
5 DIV 2   /* result 2   */
5 % 2     /* result 1   */
```

The reason I suggest you avoid using || is because it has a completely different meaning in standard SQL. By not using it with MySQL, you avoid confusion if you ever work with a different relational database.

IN() evaluates a comma-separated list of values inside the parentheses, and returns true if one or more of the values is found. Although BETWEEN is normally used with numbers, it also applies to strings. For instance, BETWEEN 'a' AND 'd' would return true for *a*, *b*, *c*, and *d* (but not their uppercase equivalents). Both IN() and BETWEEN can be preceded by NOT to perform the opposite comparison.

Conditions are evaluated from left to right, but can be grouped in parentheses if you want a particular set of conditions to be considered together.

> *Although the syntax of WHERE expressions is relatively simple, it's not always easy to craft an expression with the right criteria to select the records that you want, as you'll see later in the chapter.*

ORDER BY specifies the sort order of the results. As you saw in the previous chapter, this can be specified as a single column, a comma-separated list of columns, or an expression such as RAND(). The default sort order is ascending (a–z, 0–9), but you can specify DESC (descending) to reverse the order.

LIMIT stipulates the maximum number of records to return. If two numbers are given separated by a comma, the first tells the database how many rows to skip. For instance, LIMIT 10, 10 produces results 11 to 20. If fewer results exist than the limit specified, you get, however, many fall within the specified range. (You don't get a series of empty or undefined results to make up the number.) This can be useful for navigation through long lists of results.

For more details on SELECT, see http://dev.mysql.com/doc/refman/5.0/en/SELECT.html.

INSERT

The INSERT command is used to add new records to a database. The general syntax is as follows:

```
INSERT [INTO] table_name (column_names)
VALUES (values)
```

The word INTO is optional; it simply makes the command read a little more like human language. The column names and values are comma-delimited lists, and both must be in the same order.

The reason for this rather strange syntax is to allow you to insert more than one record at a time. Each subsequent record is in a separate set of parentheses, with each set separated by a comma:

```
INSERT numbers (x,y)
VALUES (10,20),(20,30),(30,40),(40,50)
```

As you saw earlier in the chapter, you can also copy values from one table to another by using a SELECT query. The results of the SELECT query must contain exactly the same number of columns—and in the same order—as are to be inserted. Although the following example uses the same column names in both parts of the query, it's the number and order that matter, not the names:

```
INSERT INTO authors (`first_name`, `family_name`)
SELECT DISTINCT `first_name`, `family_name`
FROM `quotations`
```

Any columns omitted from an INSERT query are set to their default value. *Never set an explicit value for the primary key where the column is set to auto_increment*; leave the column name out of the INSERT statement. For more details, see http://dev.mysql.com/doc/refman/5.0/en/INSERT.html.

UPDATE

This command is used to change existing records. The basic syntax looks like this:

```
UPDATE [IGNORE] table_name
SET col_name = value [, col_name = value]
[WHERE where_expression]
```

UPDATE generates an error and terminates the operation if you attempt to insert a duplicate value in a primary key column. The IGNORE option instructs MySQL to abandon such attempts silently. While this sounds useful, you should never design a system where this is likely to happen. Primary keys must always be unique.

The WHERE expression tells MySQL which record or records you want to update (or perhaps in the case of the following example, dream about).

```
UPDATE sales SET q1_2006 = 25000
WHERE title = 'Foundation PHP for Dreamweaver 8'
```

For more details on UPDATE, see http://dev.mysql.com/doc/refman/5.0/en/UPDATE.html.

DELETE

DELETE can be used to delete single records, multiple records, or the entire contents of a table, and it can even work on several tables at once. The general syntax for deleting from a single table is as follows:

```
DELETE FROM table_name [WHERE where_expression]
```

Although phpMyAdmin will prompt you for confirmation before deleting a record, you should be aware that MySQL itself takes you at your word, and performs the deletion immediately. DELETE is totally unforgiving—once the data is deleted, it is gone *forever*. The following query will delete all records from a table called subscribers where the date in expiry_date has already passed (as you can probably guess, NOW() is a MySQL function that returns the current date and time):

```
DELETE FROM subscribers WHERE expiry_date < NOW()
```

If you are using MySQL 4.0 or higher, you can also delete records simultaneously from multiple tables. The syntax is similar, and it comes in two alternative forms. The first, which can be used in any version of MySQL 4.0 or higher, is a little strange. The basic pattern is as follows:

```
DELETE table_name [, table_name] FROM table_name [, table_name]
WHERE condition
```

Although this looks as though it's an instruction to delete the entire table, it's not. The first list of tables indicates the tables from which the records are to be deleted, while the second list indicates the tables used in the condition. So this, for example,

```
DELETE table1, table2 FROM table1, table2, table3
WHERE table1.id = table2.id AND table2.id = table3.id
```

uses all three tables in determining which records to delete, but the deletions are done only from table1 and table2. A more intuitive syntax was introduced in MySQL 4.0.2. The pattern looks like this:

```
DELETE FROM table_name [, table_name] USING table_name [, table_name]
WHERE condition
```

So, the previous example can be rewritten in the following way:

```
DELETE FROM table1, table2 USING table1, table2, table3
WHERE table1.id = table2.id AND table2.id = table3.id
```

For more details, see http://dev.mysql.com/doc/refman/5.0/en/DELETE.html.

> *Although the* WHERE *clause is optional in both* UPDATE *and* DELETE, *you should be aware that if you leave* WHERE *out, the entire table is affected. This means that a careless slip with either of these commands could result in every single record being identical—or wiped out.*

Managing content with multiple tables

The decision to redesign the tables that store the data for the random quotation generator means the files that you created in the last chapter to insert, update, and delete records no longer work. Although the wizards that you used offer a quick way to create the forms, they have two serious limitations: once the form has been built, it's very difficult to change; and they don't work with multiple tables. Still, the related server behaviors make light work of building a more flexible system.

Inserting new quotations

Now that you have two tables—quotations and authors—you need to devise a strategy for managing the content. In the original setup, the insert form had three fields: first_name, family_name, and quotation, all of which were stored in the quotations table. However, the new setup stores the names separately, so instead of storing the name this time, you need to store the primary key from the authors table as a foreign key. Figure 9-4 shows how this is done.

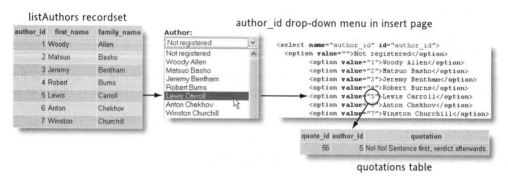

Figure 9-4. A diagrammatic representation of how the author_id primary key from the authors table is inserted as a foreign key in the quotations table

The process is quite simple. You query the database to create a recordset (listAuthors) containing the author_id, first_name, and family_name of every record in the authors table. The values in the recordset are used to create a drop-down menu, which stores the author_id as the value of each <option> tag. When you finally insert the record, the author_id of the selected name is inserted into the quotations table as the foreign key.

Creating the quotation insert form

The existing insert form cannot be adapted, so you need to build this page from scratch, although you can also follow the construction process by referring to the files in site_check/ch09. From now on, I will assume that you are familiar with all the basics of building web pages and forms in Dreamweaver, and will concentrate my instructions mainly on the server behaviors that interact with the database.

1. Create a new PHP page, save it in the admin folder as quote_insert_2tab.php, and attach the admin.css stylesheet from the styles folder. Give the page a suitable title and heading, and lay it out using the following illustration and instructions as a guide:

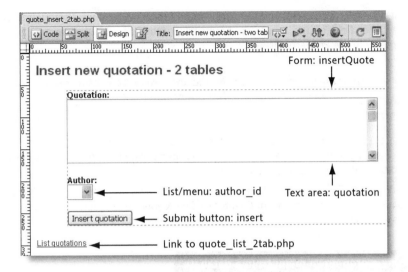

2. Insert a form, and in the Property inspector, name it insertQuote. Leave the Action field empty, and leave the Method field on the default POST.

> *If you're in Code view when the form is inserted, you will be presented with the more powerful, but less intuitive, Tag editor. One of the strange inconsistencies in Dreamweaver is that the default setting for Method in the Tag editor is GET, whereas it's POST in the Property inspector. All the forms that you use with server behaviors should be set to POST.*

3. Lay out the form input elements in the same way as you did with the feedback form in Chapter 6. First, insert a text area inside the form. When the Input Tag Accessibility Attributes dialog box opens, type Quotation: in the Label field, and select the radio button labeled Attach label tag using 'for' attribute. Click OK.

4. Open Split view, and change the value of the for attribute from textarea to quotation. Then select the text area in Design view, and change its name in the Property inspector to quotation. The size of the text area will be controlled automatically by a style rule in admin.css, but you should also set some default dimensions in the Property inspector by setting Char width to 80 and Num lines to 6.

5. Click between the text area and its label in Design view, and press *SHIFT+ENTER/SHIFT+RETURN* to insert a line break. If you check in Split view, the underlying code should now look like this:

```
<p>
  <label for="quotation">Quotation:</label>
  <br />
  <textarea name="quotation" id="quotation"></textarea>
</p>
```

6. Insert a list/menu object, and follow the same process as in steps 3 through 5. Use Author: for the Label field of the Input Tag Accessibility Attributes dialog box, and author_id for the name/ID in the Property inspector.

> *Note that the names I've chosen for the text area and the list/menu are the same as the column names in the database. This is very important.*

7. Insert a submit button. As in Chapter 6, select the No label tag option in the Input Tag Accessibility Attributes dialog box. In the Property inspector, set the button's name to insert and the Value field to Insert quotation.

8. Add a link to the page that will list all quotations, quote_list_2tab.php (you'll create this later by adapting quote_list.php from Chapter 8). Check your code against quote_insert_2tab_01.php in site_check/ch09.

Populating a drop-down menu from a database

When building drop-down menus in a static web page, you have to go through the tedious process of typing in all the values and labels manually. With a dynamic site, all this is done automatically. First, you create a recordset containing the details you want displayed in the menu. Dreamweaver then does the rest by creating a PHP loop that runs through the recordset filling in the details for you.

1. Continue working in the same page, or use quote_insert_2tab_01.php from site_check/ch09. Open the Server Behaviors panel, click the plus button, and select Recordset.

2. Make sure the advanced Recordset dialog box is open (click the Advanced button if the simple Recordset dialog box is open). In the Name field, type listAuthors, and select seasonAdmin from the Connection drop-down menu.

3. Build the SQL query by expanding Tables and then authors in the Database items area at the bottom of the dialog box. Highlight authors in the Tables tree, and click the SELECT button. This will enter SELECT * FROM authors in the SQL field.

4. Highlight family_name and click ORDER BY. Do the same with first_name. The top half of the Recordset dialog box should now look like the screenshot alongside:

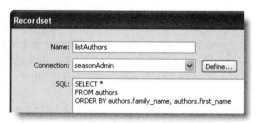

5. This will select all columns from the authors table, and order them first by family_name, and then by first_name. Click Test to make sure you get the right results. You will probably notice that the record numbers are the same as the author_id for the first 29 results. This is because you ordered the names alphabetically when splitting the tables earlier. Even though the names are currently in alphabetical order, they almost certainly won't be once you start adding new names, so it's necessary to specify the order now. Close the test panel, and click OK to save the recordset.

6. To populate the author_id drop-down menu with the recordset results, you need to open the Dynamic List/Menu dialog box. There are at least four ways to do this: from the Application Insert bar, from the Insert menu (choose Application Objects ➤ Dynamic Data ➤ Dynamic Select List), and from the plus button on the Server Behaviors panel (choose Dynamic Form Elements ➤ Dynamic List/Menu). The quickest way, though, is to highlight the author_id menu in Design view, and click the Dynamic button in the Property inspector, as shown in the screenshot.

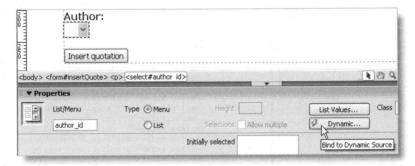

7. Whichever method you use, the Dynamic List/Menu dialog box will open and automatically select the author_id menu because it's the only one on the page.

8. In addition to using the results from the database, you need a default option for the drop-down menu. Click the plus button alongside Static options. Make sure the Value field is blank, and insert Not registered in the Label field. Since it has no value, the foreign key will be set to NULL if Not registered is selected when inserting a new record.

9. Activate the Options from recordset drop-down menu and select listAuthors. This will automatically populate the Values and Labels drop-down menus with the names of the available columns in your recordset. Set Values to author_id and Labels to family_name. Leave the final field (Select value equal to) blank. This is used when you want a dynamic value to be displayed automatically. You'll use it later when building the update form. The settings in the Dynamic List/Menu dialog box should be the same as shown alongside. Click OK.

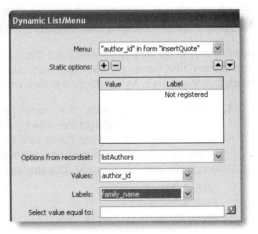

10. Save `quote_insert_2tab.php` and press *F12/OPT+F12* to view it in a browser. Activate the drop-down menu, and you will see that it has been populated with all family names from the authors table. If you view the underlying code in your browser, you will also see that the author_id has been used as the value of each option, as shown alongside. If necessary, check your code against `quote_insert_2tab_02.php`.

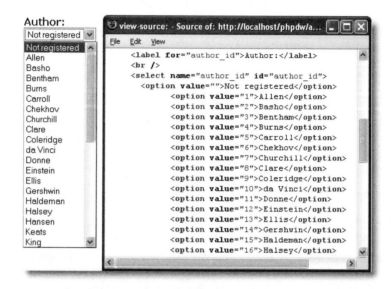

Combining the contents of two columns in a single field

Building a dynamic drop-down menu like this is pretty impressive, but there's one thing wrong with it: The authors' first names are not listed. You could fix this by diving into the PHP code, but there's a much better way—get MySQL to do the hard work.

1. Continue working with the same page, or use `quote_insert_2tab_02.php` from `site_check/ch09`. Highlight Recordset (listAuthors) in the Server Behaviors panel, and double-click to open the Recordset dialog box. Expand Tables and authors in the Database items area at the bottom of the dialog box. Highlight author_id, and click SELECT. Do the same for first_name and family_name. This changes the existing query:

```
SELECT *
FROM authors
ORDER BY authors.family_name, authors.first_name
```

to this:

```
SELECT authors.author_id, authors.first_name, authors.family_name
FROM authors
ORDER BY authors.family_name, authors.first_name
```

Both do exactly the same thing, but there is a method in my madness . . .

2. Click inside the SQL field, and amend the SQL query like this (new code in bold):

```
SELECT authors.author_id,
CONCAT(authors.first_name,' ', authors.family_name) AS author
FROM authors
ORDER BY authors.family_name, authors.first_name
```

CONCAT() is a MySQL function that is used to concatenate (join together) strings passed to it as a comma-separated list. The values of authors.first_name and authors.family_name are concatenated with a single space in between. Because the space is something that you are adding (as opposed to being drawn from a table column), it has to be enclosed in quotes. To handle the result, you assign it to an **alias**, using the keyword AS. In effect, this creates a temporary column called author containing the author's full name. If you click Test, the first few results should look like the screenshot alongside.

Make sure there is no space between CONCAT and the opening parenthesis. Also make sure that you don't have NULL values in any of the first_name or family_name fields. CONCAT() will not work if any of the arguments passed to it are NULL.

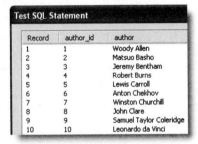

This demonstrates one of the most powerful aspects of a relational database. The SQL query enables you to manipulate the data and present results in an infinite variety of ways—without changing what's actually stored. Many beginners use SQL to extract raw data, and then rely on PHP or another server-side language to reformat it, whereas SQL is actually capable of doing most of the transformation itself.

3. Close the test panel, and click OK to save the revised record-set. If you look at the Server Behaviors panel, you'll notice there's a red exclamation mark next to Dynamic List/Menu (author_id). This is because the recordset no longer produces a result called family_name.

4. Highlight Dynamic List/Menu (author_id) in the Server Behaviors panel, and double-click to edit it. You will be presented with a warning that the column "family_name" was not found. Click OK, and select author as the value for the Labels field. Click OK to close the Dynamic List/Menu dialog box.

5. Save the page and preview it in a browser again. This time, the authors' names should be correctly displayed. Check your code against quote_insert_2tab_03.php.

Applying the Insert Record server behavior

When you used the Record Insertion Form Wizard in the previous chapter, Dreamweaver automatically applied the Insert Record server behavior behind the scenes. This time, you have to apply it yourself, but it's a simple operation, and it also has the great advantage that you can easily update it if you make any changes to your insert form.

1. Continue working with the same page, or use `quote_insert_2tab_03.php` from site_check/ch09. In the Server Behaviors panel, click the plus button, and choose Insert Record. Alternatively, choose Insert Record from the Application Insert bar.

2. The Insert Record dialog box will open. Since there's only one form on the page, Dreamweaver will automatically select `insertQuote` to fill in the first field (Submit values from). If you use this server behavior on a page that has more than one form, select the appropriate one from the drop-down menu for this field.

3. The Connection field currently displays None. Select seasonAdmin from the drop-down menu. Dreamweaver will connect to your database and populate the rest of the form with details from whichever table is first in alphabetical order, so Insert table should display authors. However, you want this page to insert new records into the quotations table, so select quotations from the drop-down menu. Dreamweaver will connect to the database again, and the dialog box should now look like this:

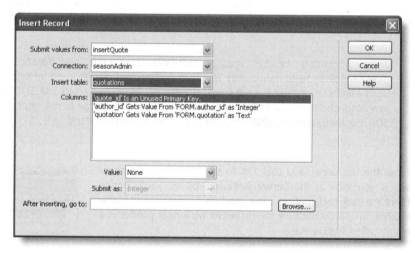

4. Take a close look at the details displayed in Columns. The first entry says: 'quote_id' Is an Unused Primary Key. Although this looks alarming, it's exactly what you want. When you defined the quotations table, you set quote_id to auto_increment. As a result, MySQL automatically generates the next number, and nothing is required from the insert form.

The two other entries in Columns show that author_id and quotation will both get their values from form fields of the same names. This is why I told you earlier to choose those names for the form's fields. If you use other names, or if you misspell them, you will see something like 'author_id' Does Not Get a Value. If that happens, select the correct form field from the Value drop-down menu. The value of Submit as is determined automatically from the column type in MySQL, so you should never need to change it.

The final field lets you choose which page to display after the record has been inserted. For the moment, leave this blank.

5. Click OK and save the page—that's all there is to it. Check your code, if necessary, against `quote_insert_2tab_04.php` from site_check/ch09. You can use the form to insert new quotations, but you won't be able to select authors not yet registered in the database. You will need to update the quotation once a record has been created for the author, but before you can do that, you need to build the content management system for authors.

Inserting new authors

Now that you have made your database more efficient by moving the authors' names into a separate table, it's vital to ensure that you don't undo all your good work by inserting the same name twice in the authors table. This means that you need to check whether an author has already been registered before proceeding. Although there's nothing stopping you from inserting duplicate quotations, it won't really matter unless you decide at some future point to use quote_id as a foreign key in another table. You will be able to delete duplicate quotations later without destroying the referential integrity of your database. The same cannot be said for authors.

Creating the author insert form

The form for inserting new authors requires just two text fields and a submit button.

1. Create a new PHP page, save it in the admin folder as author_insert.php, and attach the admin.css stylesheet.

2. Give the page a suitable title and heading, and lay out the form as shown in the screenshot. Name each of the form elements as indicated. Refer back to the section titled "Creating the quotation insert form" for details of how to apply the labels and IDs for each form element.

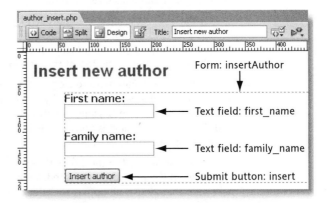

3. Apply an Insert Record server behavior as described in the previous section. The settings in the Insert Record dialog box should be the same as shown alongside. Compare your code, if necessary, with author_insert_01.php in site_check/ch09.

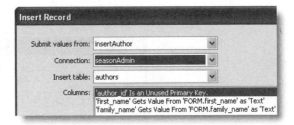

Preventing duplicate entries

This is where you need to roll up your sleeves and dive into the code generated for you by Dreamweaver. It's also where your knowledge of conditional statements will come in useful. There's nothing difficult about this next part of the process, but you do need to be careful that you select the right section of code and move it to the right place.

1. Continue working with the same page, or use author_insert_01.php from site_check/ch09.

2. To find out whether an author has already been registered, you need to create a recordset, so open the advanced Recordset dialog box from the Server Behaviors panel or the Application Insert bar. Name the recordset checkAuthor, and select the seasonAdmin connection.

3. Expand Tables in the Database items area, highlight the authors table, and click SELECT. Expand authors, highlight first_name, and click WHERE. Then do the same with family_name. You should now have a SQL query that looks like this:

```
SELECT *
FROM authors
WHERE authors.first_name AND authors.family_name
```

4. The WHERE expression needs to search for the names entered in the first_name and family_name fields. Although you don't know what the names will be, they will be stored in the POST array when the Insert author button is clicked. If you were hand-coding PHP, you would use the $_POST variables directly in the SQL query.

   Dreamweaver takes a different approach by creating temporary variables and using them in the query instead. Although this may sound a bit long-winded, it's designed to overcome the problem of escaping quotes, which can turn into an impenetrable maze if you're not careful. Click the plus button at the top of the Variables area.

5. This opens the Add Parameter dialog box for you to define your temporary variables. The first field, Name, is what you want to call your temporary variable. It's not a PHP variable, so don't use a dollar sign at the beginning. I chose var1. The next field, Default value, is what will be used if the dynamic value is unavailable, or if you want to check the SQL with the Test button. Anything will do, so I chose Dream.

   The important field is the third one, Runtime value. This is the actual value that Dreamweaver will use when the recordset is created. Type in $_POST['first_name']. (PHP is case-sensitive, so make sure that POST is all uppercase.) Click OK.

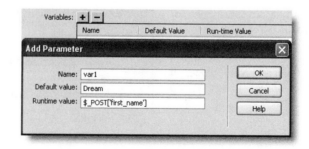

6. Click the Variables plus button again and create a second variable. The values I entered were as follows:

- Name: var2
- Default value: Weaver
- Runtime value: $_POST['family_name']

7. Click inside the SQL area and amend the WHERE expression like this:

WHERE authors.first_name = **'var1'** AND authors.family_name = **'var2'**

When the SQL query runs, var1 will be replaced by $_POST['first_name'] and var2 by $_POST['family_name']. Because first_name and family_name are text columns, you must enclose var1 and var2 in quotes (either single or double). Check that your settings are the same as shown below, and click OK.

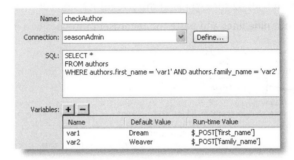

Save author_insert.php *before you go any further. From this point on, you need to dive into Code view to change the location of the recordset code. Dreamweaver has a handy feature for those dreadful occasions when you realize that you have made a mess. If things do go wrong, select* File ➤ Revert. *Dreamweaver will prompt you for confirmation, and then discard any changes since you last saved the file.*

---

8. Open Code view. Locate the section of code highlighted in the following screenshot.

```
41
42  $var1_checkAuthor = "Dream";
43  if (isset($_POST['first_name'])) {
44    $var1_checkAuthor = (get_magic_quotes_gpc()) ? $_POST['first_name'] : addslashes($_POST['first_name'
]);
45  }
46  $var2_checkAuthor = "Weaver";
47  if (isset($_POST['family_name'])) {
48    $var2_checkAuthor = (get_magic_quotes_gpc()) ? $_POST['family_name'] : addslashes($_POST[
'family_name']);
49  }
50  mysql_select_db($database_seasonAdmin, $seasonAdmin);
51  $query_checkAuthor = sprintf("SELECT * FROM authors WHERE authors.first_name = '%s' AND
authors.family_name = '%s'", $var1_checkAuthor,$var2_checkAuthor);
52  $checkAuthor = mysql_query($query_checkAuthor, $seasonAdmin) or die(mysql_error());
53  $row_checkAuthor = mysql_fetch_assoc($checkAuthor);
54  $totalRows_checkAuthor = mysql_num_rows($checkAuthor);
55  ?><!DOCTYPE html PUBLIC "-//W3C//DTD XHTML 1.0 Transitional//EN"
```

This is the code for the checkAuthor recordset. You can easily identify it because the first line begins with $var1_checkAuthor, which is the way Dreamweaver defines var1, which you created in step 5. The part of the code that interacts with the database begins with mysql_select_db on line 50 and continues to the end of the line that reads as follows:

$totalRows_checkAuthor = mysql_num_rows($checkAuthor);

As you can probably guess, $totalRows_checkAuthor contains the total number of records in the checkAuthor recordset. You can use this information to determine whether a record already exists for the same author. If the number of rows is zero, there are no matching records, so you can safely insert the new author. But if any matching records are found, you know it's a duplicate, so you need to skip the insert operation and display a warning.

Unfortunately, Dreamweaver places the recordset *after* the Insert Record server behavior, so you need to move it. (I know what you're thinking, but it doesn't matter which order you enter them. Dreamweaver always puts recordsets beneath other server behaviors.) Highlight the code shown on lines 42 through 54 in the screenshot, and cut them to the clipboard.

9. Scroll up about nine lines and paste the recordset in the position indicated here:

```
28  $editFormAction = $_SERVER['PHP_SELF'];
29  if (isset($_SERVER['QUERY_STRING'])) {
30      $editFormAction .= "?" . htmlentities($_SERVER['QUERY_STRING']);
31  }
32          [ Paste recordset here ]
33  if ((isset($_POST["MM_insert"])) && ($_POST["MM_insert"] == "insertAuthor")) {
34      $insertSQL = sprintf("INSERT INTO authors (first_name, family_name) VALUES (%s, %s)",
35                      GetSQLValueString($_POST['first_name'], "text"),
36                      GetSQLValueString($_POST['family_name'], "text"));
```

10. Make sure your cursor is at the end of the code you have just pasted, and press ENTER/RETURN a couple of times to create space. Then insert the following code:

```
// assume that no match has been found
$alreadyRegistered = false;

// check whether recordset found any matches
if ($totalRows_checkAuthor > 0) {
  // if found, reset $alreadyRegistered
  $alreadyRegistered = true;
  }
else {
  // go ahead with Insert Record server behavior
```

> Note that false *and* true *in this code block are keywords. They must not be enclosed in quotes.*

11. Position your cursor right at the end of the code shown on line 33 in the previous screenshot (it should now be around line 55). This is the beginning of the Insert Record server behavior. Click the Balance Braces button on the Coding toolbar (or press CTRL+'/⌘+') to find the end of the server behavior, and insert a closing brace (}) to match the one at the end of the code in step 10.

What you have done, in fact, is wrap the Insert Record server behavior in an else clause to prevent it from running if a matching record is found in the authors table.

12. All that remains now is to display a warning message if the insert is abandoned. Scroll down until you find the following code (around line 74):

```
<h1>Insert new author</h1>
```

13. Add the following code immediately after it:

```php
<?php
if ($_POST && $alreadyRegistered) {
  echo '<p class="warning">'.$_POST['first_name'].' '.
➥ $_POST['family_name'].' is already registered</p>';
  }
?>
```

This section of code will run only if the POST array has been populated (in other words, the insert form has been submitted), and if $alreadyRegistered has been set to true.

14. Save the page and preview it in a browser. Try inserting a name that you know already exists in the table, such as William Shakespeare. Then try a name you know hasn't been registered. If you reload quote_insert_2tab.php, you should now see the new name listed in the drop-down menu of authors' names. Check your code against author_insert_02.php from site_check/ch09, if you have any problems.

Insert new author

William Shakespeare is already registered

First name:
[   ]

Family name:
[   ]

[Insert author]

Although this is an adequate safeguard for a basic content management system, it won't prevent you from entering similar names or misspelled ones.

Updating authors

Because the authors table doesn't contain any foreign keys, you could make life simple by using the Record Update Form Wizard. However, that would leave you open to the danger of duplicate entries. There's little point in building in a safeguard at the record insertion stage only to have it sidestepped at the update stage. All it requires is some adaptation to the page you have just built. Essentially, this involves removing the Insert Record server behavior and replacing it with an Update Record server behavior. You also need to store the record's primary key in a hidden form field so that the Update Record server behavior can apply the changes to the appropriate record.

Because Dreamweaver accomplishes so much through the use of dialog boxes, I find that it helps to have a clear idea of what is going on in the background. Figure 9-5 shows how the primary key is used to keep track of the record through the update process. Initially it's passed through the URL query string and is used to create a recordset that populates the form in the update page. The form stores the primary key, ready to be passed back to the database in the WHERE expression of the SQL UPDATE query.

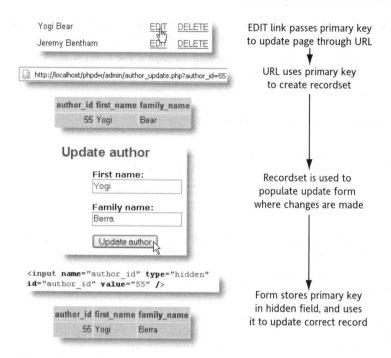

Yogi Bear   EDIT   DELETE

Jeremy Bentham   EDIT   DELETE

EDIT link passes primary key
to update page through URL

↓

http://localhost/phpdw/admin/author_update.php?author_id=55

URL uses primary key
to create recordset

author_id	first_name	family_name
55	Yogi	Bear

Update author

First name:

Yogi

Family name:

Berra

[Update author]

↓

Recordset is used to
populate update form
where changes are made

```
<input name="author_id" type="hidden"
id="author_id" value="55" />
```

↓

Form stores primary key
in hidden field, and uses
it to update correct record

author_id	first_name	family_name
55	Yogi	Berra

Figure 9-5. How the primary key is passed through the update process

Adapting the author insert form for updates

Continue working with the same file as in the previous section, or use `author_insert_02.php` from `site_check/ch09`.

1. Choose File ➤ Save As (*CTRL+SHIFT+S/SHIFT+*⌘*+S*) and save the file as `author_update.php`.

2. You now have an exact copy of `author_insert.php`. Change the title and heading to Update author. Also use the Property inspector to rename the form updateAuthor, and change the Button name and Value of the submit button to update and Update author, respectively.

3. In the Server Behaviors panel, highlight Insert Record, and click the minus button to delete it. Make sure you delete only the Insert Record server behavior, as you still need the checkAuthor recordset. (Use Edit ➤ Undo Remove Server Behavior or *CTRL+Z/*⌘*+Z* if you make a mistake.) If you're unsure whether you've made the right changes, check your code against `author_update_01.php` in `site_check/ch09`.

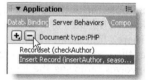

Dreamweaver server behaviors normally disappear from the Server Behaviors panel or cease to be editable with Dreamweaver dialog boxes if you alter them in any way. However, in the previous section I simply moved the recordset code and wrapped the Insert Record server behavior in an else *clause, without altering any of the actual code. Consequently, they still remain fully accessible through the Server Behaviors panel. When you remove them through the Server Behaviors panel in this way, the additional coding added in steps 10 and 11 in the previous section remains intact, ready for reuse in this page.*

4. In the same way as when you used the Record Update Form Wizard, you need to create a recordset for the Update Record server behavior to work with. Click the plus button in the Server Behaviors panel and select Recordset.

5. If the advanced Recordset dialog box opens, click the Simple button, and use the settings shown alongside. Click OK to create the getAuthor recordset. This will select just one author identified by author_id passed in a URL query string.

6. Open the Bindings panel. You should now have two recordsets listed there: checkAuthor and getAuthor. The second one will be used to set the initial values for the text fields in the updateAuthor form. Expand the getAuthor recordset in the Bindings panel, and then highlight the first_name text field in the form, followed by first_name in the recordset. The label on the Insert button at the bottom of the Bindings panel changes to Bind, and the dropdown menu alongside should display input.value. Click Bind, and a dynamic placeholder will appear inside the first_name text field. The Bind button changes to Unbind. Click this if you ever want to remove dynamic text bound in this way.

7. Repeat step 6 with the family_name text field and family_name in the recordset.

8. The Update Record server behavior also needs to know the author_id, which should be stored in a hidden field. Click any blank space inside the form, and choose Insert ➤ Form ➤ Hidden Field. In the Property inspector, change the name of the hidden field to author_id, and click the lightning bolt icon alongside the Value field, as shown.

9. In the Dynamic Data dialog box that opens, select author_id from Recordset (getAuthor) and click OK.

10. You're now ready to apply the Update Record server behavior. Click the plus button in the Server Behaviors panel, and select Update Record. If you have followed all the steps correctly, the Update Record dialog box will automatically apply the correct values as soon as you select seasonAdmin in the Connection field. Set the final field to go to author_insert.php after updating. Check your settings against those shown here, and click OK.

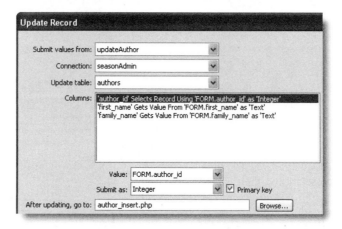

11. Switch to Code view and locate the following section of code:

```
33  if ((isset($_POST["MM_update"])) && ($_POST["MM_update"] == "updateAuthor")) {
34    $updateSQL = sprintf("UPDATE authors SET first_name=%s, family_name=%s WHERE author_id=%s",
35                  GetSQLValueString($_POST['first_name'], "text"),
36                  GetSQLValueString($_POST['family_name'], "text"),
37                  GetSQLValueString($_POST['author_id'], "int"));
38
39    mysql_select_db($database_seasonAdmin, $seasonAdmin);
40    $Result1 = mysql_query($updateSQL, $seasonAdmin) or die(mysql_error());
41
42    $updateGoTo = "author_insert.php";
43    if (isset($_SERVER['QUERY_STRING'])) {
44      $updateGoTo .= (strpos($updateGoTo, '?')) ? "&" : "?";
45      $updateGoTo .= $_SERVER['QUERY_STRING'];
46    }
47    header(sprintf("Location: %s", $updateGoTo));
48  }
```

This is the code for the Update Record server behavior. Highlight it, making sure you don't miss the closing curly brace shown on line 48 in the screenshot, and cut it to your clipboard.

12. Scroll down until you find the empty else clause just above the DOCTYPE declaration, and paste the Update Record server behavior between the braces.

13. Switch back to Design view. Click to the right of the form, and press *ENTER/RETURN* to insert a new paragraph. Type Insert/List Authors, and create a link to author_insert.php. Check your code against author_update_02.php in site_check/ch09 if necessary.

Listing authors

Before you can test the update page, you need to display a list of authors. Instead of creating a separate page, it's probably more convenient to show them on the same page as for inserting a new record. Many of the steps in this section are identical or very similar to the way you built quote_list.php in Chapter 8, so I will keep the description to the minimum.

1. Open author_insert.php or use author_insert_02.php from site_check/ch09. Make sure you're working in the right page. This is the one for inserting new records, not the one you have just been working in.

2. Highlight the insertAuthor form in the Tag selector and press the right arrow key to move the cursor outside the form. Insert a table with 2 rows and 3 columns. The settings I used are shown alongside.

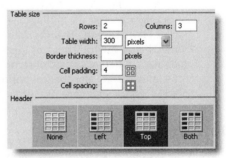

3. Type Name in the first cell of the top row, and EDIT and DELETE in the second and third cells of the second row.

4. Create a recordset called listAuthors using the seasonAdmin connection. Use the advanced Recordset dialog box to build the following SQL query:

```
SELECT *
FROM authors
ORDER BY authors.family_name, authors.first_name
```

You should have done it often enough by now to know how to build a simple query like this.

319

5. Use the Bindings panel to insert dynamic text placeholders for first_name and family_name in the first cell of the second row. Make sure you use the right recordset (listAuthors).

6. You now need to create the dynamic links for EDIT and DELETE. The update page already exists, but you need to create a blank PHP page in the admin folder called author_delete.php.

7. Highlight EDIT and click the Browse for File button to the right of the Link field in the Property inspector. Select author_update.php, and then click the Parameters button. Set the Name field to author_id, and then click the lightning bolt icon in the Value field. Select author_id from the listAuthors recordset, and click OK to close all of the open dialog boxes. (Refer back to steps 8 through 11 of the section titled "Creating a list of all records" in Chapter 8 if you have any difficulty.)

8. Do the same for DELETE, this time selecting author_delete.php.

9. Highlight the second row of the table, click the plus button on the Server Behaviors panel, and choose Repeat Region. You now have two recordsets on the page, so you must take care to choose the right one. Because it comes first in alphabetical order, Dreamweaver automatically selects checkAuthor. Change this to listAuthors, and change the number of records shown at a time to 25. Click OK.

10. Click to the right of the table, and insert a Recordset Navigation Bar from the Application Insert bar (or Insert ➤ Application Objects ➤ Recordset Paging ➤ Recordset Navigation Bar). This time, Dreamweaver should be smart enough to realize you want to navigate through listAuthors. Choose Text or Images, and click OK.

11. Save author_insert.php and preview it in a browser. You can now test your update page, navigate through your records, and add new ones. If you encounter problems, check your file against author_insert_03.php in site_check/ch09.

12. There's just one minor drawback: if you insert a new record, it doesn't appear immediately in the list. Rectify this by selecting Insert Record in the Server Behaviors panel, and double-clicking it to edit the settings. Set the After inserting go to field to author_insert.php, and click OK to save the changes. Although this is the same page, it forces the browser to reload it, thereby refreshing the list of existing records. If you have used the record navigation links to display a different section of records, the same section will be displayed, and the new entry will be in its correct alphabetical position, so you may have to navigate backwards or forwards to see it. Check your code against author_insert_04.php.

Deleting authors

As in the previous chapter, the easiest way to build the page to delete a record is by adapting the update page. This time, however, you need to build into the logic of the page the equivalent of a foreign key constraint. You do this by checking whether the author_id is still in use as a foreign key in the quotations table. Figure 9-6 shows a simplified diagram of how this is achieved. Clicking the DELETE link runs a query that determines whether to display the delete form. If matching records exist, the delete form is never displayed, but if there are no dependent records, the form is displayed, ready for the deletion to be confirmed.

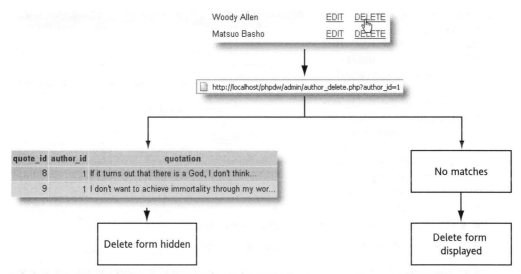

Figure 9-6. How referential integrity is maintained without foreign key constraints

Adapting the author update page to handle deletes

Use the version of author_update.php that you created earlier in this chapter, or work with author_update_02.php from site_check/ch09.

1. Open author_update.php and save it as author_delete.php. When Dreamweaver asks if you want to replace the existing file, click Yes (or Replace on the Mac).

2. Change the title and heading to Delete author. Use the Property inspector to change the name of the form to deleteAuthor. Also change the Button name and Value of the submit button to delete and Confirm deletion respectively.

3. In the Server Behaviors panel, highlight Recordset (checkAuthor) and delete it by clicking the minus button.

4. Do the same with Update Record.

5. Click the plus button in the Server Behaviors panel, and select Delete Record. As in the previous chapter, you will get the value of the record to be deleted from a hidden field, so make sure you choose Form Variable for Primary key value. Check that your settings are the same as shown in the screenshot, and click OK.

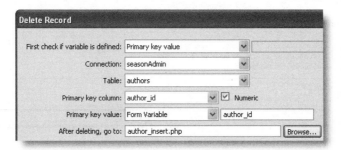

6. Before deleting a record from the authors table, you must check whether its primary key is still in use in the quotations table. Create a new recordset called checkForeign. Use the advanced Recordset dialog box with the settings shown alongside. This time I want to use the value of author_id passed through a query string, so I have set the Run-time value of my temporary variable var1 to $_GET['author_id'].

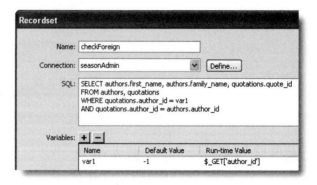

- $_GET is used for form variables passed through a URL.

- $_POST is used for form variables sent using the post method.

Since the value of author_id is a number, var1 is *not* enclosed in quotes in the SQL query. I have set Default Value to -1 because I don't want the variable ever to default to a genuine value by mistake.

7. Now it's time to take a deep breath and dive into Code view. (You may want to save your page at this stage and compare it with author_delete_01.php in site_check/ch09.) First of all, you need to move the Delete Record server behavior code inside the else clause of the custom code you created to handle duplicates. In the following screenshot, I have used Dreamweaver 8's new Code Collapse feature to hide the two recordsets on lines 43 through 61. Cut the code shown on lines 28 through 41 (don't miss the closing curly brace) and paste it to the position indicated inside the braces of the else clause.

```
28  if ((isset($_POST['author_id'])) && ($_POST['author_id'] != "")) {
29      $deleteSQL = sprintf("DELETE FROM authors WHERE author_id=%s",
30                          GetSQLValueString($_POST['author_id'], "int"));
31
32      mysql_select_db($database_seasonAdmin, $seasonAdmin);
33      $Result1 = mysql_query($deleteSQL, $seasonAdmin) or die(mysql_error());
34
35      $deleteGoTo = "author_insert.php";
36      if (isset($_SERVER['QUERY_STRING'])) {
37        $deleteGoTo .= (strpos($deleteGoTo, '?')) ? "&" : "?";
38        $deleteGoTo .= $_SERVER['QUERY_STRING'];
39      }
40      header(sprintf("Location: %s", $deleteGoTo));
41  }
42
43  $colnam...
62
63  // assume that no match has been found
64  $alreadyRegistered = false;
65
66  // check whether recordset found any matches
67  if ($totalRows_checkAuthor > 0) {
68      $alreadyRegistered  = true;
69      }
70  else {
71      // go ahead with Update Record server behavior
72
73  }
```

8. Next, amend the code shown on lines 63 through 71 of the preceding screenshot to match the name of the checkForeign recordset like this:

```
// assume that no match has been found
$recordsExist = false;

//check whether recordset found any matches
if ($totalRows_checkForeign > 0) {
  $recordsExist = true;
  }
else {
  // go ahead with the Delete Record server behavior
```

9. Scroll down until you find this line (it should be around line 84):

```
if ($_POST && $alreadyRegistered) {
```

The check for $_POST is not needed this time, because the checkForeign recordset will be created as soon as the page loads. You also need to change the variable to $recordsExist. Change the line to look like this:

```
if ($recordsExist) {
```

10. In the next line, $_POST['first_name'] and $_POST['family_name'] need to be replaced with dynamic data from the checkForeign recordset. Highlight $_POST['first_name'] and open the Bindings panel. Expand Recordset (checkForeign), select first_name, and click the Insert button. This will replace $_POST['first_name'] with $row_checkForeign['first_name']. Do the same with $_POST['family_name'], selecting family_name from the Bindings panel.

11. Change the remaining text in the warning paragraph, and add the opening part of an else clause so that the entire PHP code block now looks like this:

```
<?php
if ($recordsExist) {
  echo '<p class="warning">'.$row_checkForeign['first_name'].' '.
➥ $row_checkForeign['family_name'].' has dependent records.
➥ Can\'t be deleted.</p>';
  }
else {
?>
```

12. Scroll all the way down to the closing </form> tag (around line 108), and insert a closing curly brace inside a pair of PHP tags like this:

```
<?php } ?>
```

What you have done is enclose the entire form in an else clause, so it will be displayed only if there are no dependent records in the quotations table.

13. Switch back to Design view, click immediately to the right of the first PHP shield, and press *ENTER/RETURN* to create a new paragraph. Type a warning that the delete operation cannot be undone, and apply the warning class to the paragraph.

14. Save author_delete.php, and load author_insert.php into your browser. Select an author that you know has dependent records in the quotations table, and click DELETE. You should see a message like the one alongside.

> **Delete author**
>
> Woody Allen has dependent records. Can't be deleted.
>
> Insert/List authors

15. Now insert a new author. When the name appears in the list, click DELETE. This time you should see the delete form, as shown here. Click Confirm deletion. You will be taken back to the list of authors, and the new entry will have disappeared without a trace. Check your code against author_delete_02.php in site_check/ch09.

> **Delete author**
>
> Please confirm that you want to delete the following record. This operation cannot be undone.
>
> **First name:**
> Invisible
>
> **Family name:**
> Man
>
> [Confirm deletion]
>
> Insert/List authors

Updating quotations

Now that you can add new names to the authors table, it means that you can update any quotations where you needed to use Not registered. Instead of adding the list of quotations to the bottom of quote_insert_2tab.php, let's adapt the existing quote_list.php from the previous chapter.

Displaying a list of quotations

You can either use quote_list.php from the previous chapter or quote_list_01.php from site_check/ch09.

1. Open quote_list.php, and save it in the admin folder as quote_list_2tab.php.

2. The layout of the page is fine. All you need to do is update the SQL query in the recordset. Open the Server Behaviors panel and double-click Recordset (quoteList).

3. Inside the Recordset dialog box, delete the existing SQL query, and build a new query as shown in the following screenshot:

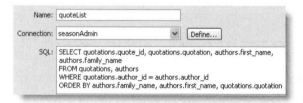

4. Save quote_list_2tab.php and view it in a browser. It should look exactly the same as in the previous chapter. If it doesn't, check your code against quote_list_2tab_01.php in site_check/ch09.

That was easy, wasn't it? Unfortunately, it was too easy, because there's a hidden flaw in the SQL.

The mystery of missing records

If you have entered any new quotations from people not already registered in the authors table, look carefully at all the entries in the list. Your new records are nowhere to be found. The reason for this lies in the WHERE expression:

```
WHERE quotations.author_id = authors.author_id
```

This works fine when there are matching records in both tables, but if the author_id foreign key hasn't been set in the quotations table, there will be nothing to match it in the authors table. You need a way to find all records, even if there isn't a corresponding match for the foreign key. This is achieved in SQL by what is known as a **left join**.

The SQL queries generated by Dreamweaver are known as full joins—there must be a complete match in both tables of all conditions in a WHERE expression. The difference with a left join is that when there's no match for a record in the table(s) to the "left" of the join, the result is still included in the recordset, but all the columns in the table to the "right" of the join are set to NULL. "Left" and "right" are used in the sense of which side of the keywords LEFT JOIN they appear in the SQL query. The syntax looks like this:

```
SELECT column_name(s) FROM first_table
LEFT JOIN second_table ON condition
```

If the condition is matching two columns of the same name (such as author_id), an alternative syntax can be used:

```
SELECT column_name(s) FROM first_table
LEFT JOIN second_table USING (column_name)
```

Using a left join to find incomplete records

Continue using quote_list_2tab.php, or use quote_list_2tab_01.php from site_check/ch09.

1. Highlight Recordset (quoteList) in the Server Behaviors panel, and double-click it to open the Recordset dialog box.

2. Edit the SQL query by hand like this:

```
SELECT quotations.quote_id, quotations.quotation, authors.first_name,
authors.family_name
FROM quotations LEFT JOIN authors USING (author_id)
ORDER BY authors.family_name, authors.first_name, quotations.quotation
```

3. Click the Test button to make sure you haven't made any mistakes in the query. I find that I frequently forget to remove the comma after the first table name when replacing a full join with a left join.

4. Click OK to save the recordset. Save the page and refresh your browser. Any quotations without an author_id will now appear at the top of the list with the name column blank.

Contents of quotations table

Name		Quotation		
		It is only with the heart that one can see rightly; what is essential is invisible to the eye.	EDIT	DELETE
Woody Allen		I don't want to achieve immortality through my work... I want to achieve it by not dying.	EDIT	DELETE

5. The EDIT and DELETE links still point to the old update and delete pages, so create two blank PHP pages in the admin folder, and call them quote_update_2tab.php and quote_delete_2tab.php. Update the links to the new pages. If you click the Browse for File button to the right of the Link field in the Property inspector, and navigate to the files, Dreamweaver will preserve intact the PHP parameter that adds the appropriate quote_id to the query string. Save the page and compare your code, if necessary, with quote_list_2tab_02.php in site_check/ch09.

Adapting the insert page for updates

Continue working with quote_insert_2tab.php from earlier in the chapter, or use quote_insert_2tab_04.php from site_check/ch09.

1. Open quote_insert_2tab.php. Edit the Insert Record server behavior by double-clicking its entry in the Server Behaviors panel. Click the Browse button alongside the After inserting, go to field, and select quote_list_2tab.php. Click OK to close the Insert Record dialog box. Users will now be taken automatically to the full list of quotations after inserting a new one. This change is also needed for the update and delete pages that will be adapted from quote_insert_2tab.php.

2. Save the page, and then save it again as quote_update_2tab.php. Click Yes/Replace when Dreamweaver prompts you. You will now adapt the renamed copy.

3. Change the title and heading to Update quotation. Also change the form name to updateQuote, and the Button name and Value of the submit button to update and Update quotation, respectively.

4. When the EDIT link in `quote_list_2tab.php` is clicked, you need to display the details of the record. So create a new recordset called getQuote, which will use the value of quote_id passed through the URL query string. Use the simple Recordset dialog box with the settings shown alongside.

5. Expand Recordset (getQuote) in the Bindings panel. Select the quotation text area in the form, and then select quotation in the recordset. Click Bind.

6. You also need the author_id drop-down menu to display the correct value. Select the menu object in the form, and click the Dynamic button in the Property inspector. All the existing values are fine, but to display the selected value dynamically, click the lightning bolt icon to the right of the Select value equal to field at the bottom of the Dynamic List/Menu dialog box.

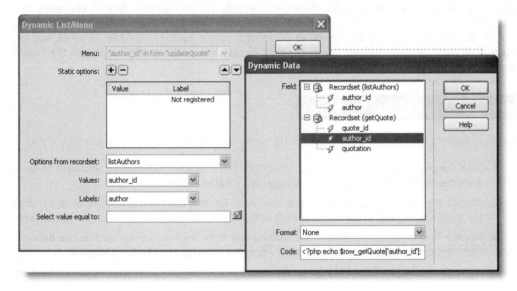

In the Dynamic Data dialog box, select author_id from Recordset (getQuote). Make sure you choose the correct recordset—both of them include author_id. The other recordset contains *all* author_id numbers; you want only the specific one associated with the quotation identified by the URL query string.

Click OK twice to close both dialog boxes. What you have just done will create the code to dynamically insert selected="selected" in the appropriate <option> tag to display the correct name from the authors table.

327

7. Select the Insert Record server behavior in the Server Behaviors panel, and click the minus button to remove it.

8. Before adding the Update Record server behavior, you need to create a hidden form field to store the correct quote_id. Click in a blank area of the form, and insert a hidden field. In the Property inspector, name the hidden field quote_id, and click the lightning bolt icon to insert dynamic data in the Value field. Choose quote_id from Recordset (getQuote), and click OK.

9. Click the plus button on the Server Behaviors panel, and choose Update Record. Use the following settings:

   - Submit values from: updateQuote
   - Connection: seasonAdmin
   - Update table: quotations
   - After updating, go to: quote_list_2tab.php

10. Save the page and test it. Compare your code, if necessary, with quote_update_2tab.php in site_check/ch09.

Deleting quotations

Nearly there! Just one more page to go. The page for deleting quotations is relatively simple to make, because there's no need to check for dependent records. It's only when a foreign key refers to a deleted record that you have a problem. Delete Shakespeare from the authors table, and you have no way of identifying author_id 32. Delete all his records in the quotations table, however, and the integrity of your database remains intact. The only loss is some of the greatest sayings in the English language.

Adapting the update page for deletes

Continue working with the previous page, or use quote_update_2tab.php from site_check/ch09.

1. Save the page as quote_delete_2tab.php. Click Yes/Replace when asked if you want to overwrite the existing file. It's only a blank page you created earlier.

2. Change the title and heading to Delete quotation. Rename the form deleteQuote, and change the Button name and Value of the submit button to delete, and Confirm deletion, respectively.

3. Insert a new paragraph between the heading and form asking users to confirm the deletion, and warning them that it's not undoable. Apply the warning class to the paragraph.

4. Highlight Update Record in the Server Behaviors panel, and click the minus button to delete it.

5. Click the plus button in the Server Behaviors panel, and select Delete Record. Use the settings shown in the screenshot, and click OK.

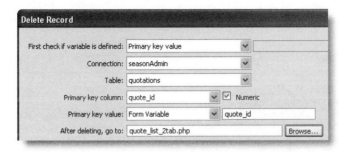

6. Save the page and compare your code, if necessary, against quote_delete_2tab.php in site_check/ch09.

You now have a complete management system for the two-table version of the random quotation generator. To improve its usability, create a menu page, and add some normal text links to navigate between the various pages.

Chapter review

What began as a single-table database with a simple content management system has been converted into a two-table one, which required a much more complex back end. You may be wondering whether it's really worth the effort. The answer is: *yes*. Creating a database and its related content management system is a time-consuming process, but the time spent on building a solid foundation for your database will be well rewarded. The original single-table quotations database contained just three columns of data (apart from the primary key), but was already showing signs of inconsistency and redundancy with only 50 records. Just imagine what a 10-column single table might be like with 1,000 records.

Although this chapter has involved a lot of steps, and you've needed to dive into Code view from time to time, it's important to realize that the Dreamweaver server behaviors have taken an enormous coding burden off your shoulders. Remembering how to fill in the different dialog boxes takes time and practice, but this chapter has covered the main aspects of database interaction.

Now that you have learned how to manage your database records, you need to protect them. That's the subject of the next chapter.

Chapter 10

USING SESSIONS TO TRACK VISITORS AND RESTRICT ACCESS

What this chapter covers:

- Understanding how sessions work
- Preserving information related to an individual visitor
- Registering users and administrators
- Preventing the creation of duplicate usernames
- Building your own custom server behaviors
- Restricting access to your pages
- Using a commercial extension to automate validation

Now that part of your site is database-driven, you need to make sure that only authorized people have access to your content management pages. One way of doing that is by password protecting the admin folder. While this is a perfectly good way of restricting access, the dialog box that browsers pop up asking for username and password doesn't look very elegant. PHP sessions offer a way of integrating login procedures with the overall look of your site. Sessions also offer a way to preserve information from page to page, keeping track of visitors. In an e-commerce environment, this means you can store details of purchases in a shopping cart. Although I don't intend to go into the details of shopping carts, you will learn the basics of how sessions work so that you can apply them to a wide variety of purposes.

After learning the fundamentals of sessions, you'll use Dreamweaver server behaviors to build a user registration system and restrict access to certain parts of the East-West Seasons website. Although the standard Dreamweaver server behaviors create all the basic PHP and SQL for you, the need to validate user input means a lot of hand-coding, too. So, at the end of the chapter, I'll take a brief look at MX Kollection 3, a commercial suite of Dreamweaver extensions, which automates the whole process.

What sessions are and how they work

The Web is a brilliant illusion. When you visit a well-designed website, you get a great feeling of continuity, as though flipping through the pages of a book or a magazine. Everything fits together as a coherent entity. The reality is quite different. Each part of an individual page is stored and handled separately by the web server. Apart from needing to know where to send the relevant files, the server has no interest in who you are, and, as I explained in Chapter 6, PHP variables are normally discarded as soon as the script finishes. Even variables in the POST and GET arrays persist only while being passed from one page to the next. To pass information to a further page, it has to be stored in a hidden form field, and it persists only if the form is submitted.

To get around these problems, PHP (in common with other server-side languages) uses **sessions**. A session ensures continuity by storing a random identifier on the web server and on the visitor's computer (as a cookie). Because the identifier is unique to each visitor, all the information stored in session variables is directly related to that visitor, and cannot be seen by anyone else.

> *The security offered by sessions is adequate for most user authentication, but it is not 100 percent foolproof. For credit card and other financial transactions, you should use an SSL connection verified by a digital certificate. To learn more about this and other aspects of building security into your PHP sites, Pro PHP Security by Chris Snyder and Michael Southwell (Apress, ISBN 1-59059-508-4) is essential reading. Although aimed principally at readers with an intermediate to advanced knowledge of PHP, it contains a lot of practical advice of value to all skill levels.*

Creating PHP sessions

Creating a session is easy. Just put the following command in every PHP page that you want to use in a session:

```
session_start();
```

This command should be called only once in each page, and it must be called before the PHP script generates any output, so the ideal position is immediately after the opening PHP tag. If any output is generated before the call to session_start(), the command fails and the session won't be activated for that page. (See "The 'Headers already sent' error" section for an explanation.)

Creating and destroying session variables

You create a session variable by adding it to the SESSION superglobal array in the same way you would assign an ordinary variable. Say you want to store a visitor's name and display a greeting. If the name is submitted in a login form as $_POST['name'], you assign it like this:

```
$_SESSION['name'] = $_POST['name'];
```

$_SESSION['name'] can now be used in any page that begins with session_start(). Because session variables are stored on the server, you should get rid of them as soon as are no longer required by your script or application. Unset a session variable like this:

```
unset($_SESSION['name']);
```

To unset *all* session variables—for instance, when you're logging someone out—set the SESSION superglobal array to an empty array, like this:

```
$_SESSION = array();
```

> *Do not be tempted to try* unset($_SESSION). *It works all right—but it's a little too effective. It not only clears the current session, but also prevents any further sessions from being stored.*

Destroying a session

By itself, unsetting all the session variables effectively prevents any of the information from being reused, but you should also destroy the session with the following command:

```
session_destroy();
```

That way, the link between the two computers is broken, and there is no risk of an unauthorized person gaining access either to a restricted part of the site or to any information exchanged during the session. If you fail to destroy the session, the variables remain on the web server even after the visitor's browser is closed. Although this represents a theoretical security risk, it's not always possible to guarantee that a visitor will trigger the session_destroy() command. For instance, the visitor may forget to log out, or the session may be expired by a time limit built into your script. For that reason, you should never store sensitive information such as credit card numbers in a session variable.

> *You may find* session_register() *and* session_unregister() *in old scripts. These functions are now deprecated and will almost certainly fail in PHP 5. Replace them with* $_SESSION['*variable_name*'] *and* unset($_SESSION['*variable_name*']).

The "Headers already sent" error

Although using PHP sessions is very easy, there's one problem that causes beginners a great deal of head banging. Instead of everything working the way you expect, you see the following message:

Warning: Cannot add header information - headers already sent

The session_start() command must come before any output is sent to the browser—even before any white space or blank lines. What normally catches people out is the presence of white space after the closing tag of a PHP include file that precedes the call to session_start(). Fortunately, Dreamweaver makes it easy to eliminate this problem. Open in Code view all PHP files that are included above the DOCTYPE declaration in the problem page. Make sure that the opening PHP tag of the include file is at the beginning of line 1, and that there are no line numbers below the closing PHP tag. Also make sure that there is no white space on the same line after the closing tag.

You may also encounter this problem with header() to redirect the visitor to another page. The solution is the same—remove any white space or new lines outside PHP tags that precede the call to header().

A simple session example

The following exercise is not part of the East-West Seasons case study, but the pages are very simple, and should take only a few minutes to build. You can also find the complete code in examples/ch10.

1. Create a new PHP page, and call it session1.php. Insert a simple form with a text field called name and a submit button. In the Property inspector, set the form's Method to POST and Action to submit2.php.

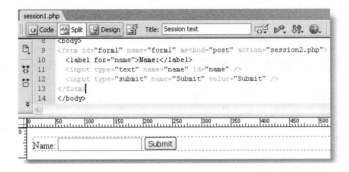

2. Create a new PHP page and call it `session2.php`. Open Code view and insert the following code above the DOCTYPE declaration:

```php
<?php
// initiate session
session_start();
// check that form has been submitted and that name is not empty
if ($_POST && !empty($_POST['name'])) {
  // set session variable
  $_SESSION['name'] = $_POST['name'];
  }
?>
```

The inline comments explain what's going on. The session is started, and as long as $_POST['name'] isn't empty, its value is assigned to $_SESSION['name']. Because $_SESSION is a superglobal array, press *ENTER/RETURN* after typing $_S, and Dreamweaver will automatically insert $_SESSION[into your code.

3. Insert the following code between the <body> tags in `session2.php`:

```php
<?php
// check session variable is set
if (isset($_SESSION['name'])) {
  // if set, greet by name
  echo 'Hello, '.$_SESSION['name'].'. <a href="session3.php">Next</a>';
  }
else {
  // if not set, send back to login
  echo 'Who are you? <a href="session1.php">Login</a>';
  }
?>
```

If $_SESSION['name'] has been set, a welcome message is displayed along with a link to session3.php. Otherwise, the page tells the visitor that it doesn't recognize who's trying to gain access, and provides a link back to the first page.

> *Take care when typing line 5. The first two periods (surrounding $_SESSION['name'])*
> *are the PHP concatenation operator. The third period (immediately after a single quote)*
> *is an ordinary period that will be displayed as part of the string.*

4. Create `session3.php`. Type the following above the DOCTYPE to initiate the session:

```php
<?php session_start(); ?>
```

5. Insert the following code between the `<body>` tags of `session3.php`:

```php
<?php
// check whether session variable is set
if (isset($_SESSION['name'])) {
  // if set, greet by name
  echo 'Hi, '.$_SESSION['name'].'. See, I remembered your name!<br />';
  // unset session variable
  unset($_SESSION['name']);
  // end session
  session_destroy();
  echo '<a href="session2.php">Page 2</a>';
  }
else {
  // display if not recognized
  echo 'Sorry, I don\'t know you.<br />';
  echo '<a href="session1.php">Login</a>';
  }
?>
```

The inline comments should be self-explanatory. If `$_SESSION['name']` has been set, the page displays it, then unsets it and destroys the current session. By placing `session_destroy()` at the end of the first code block, the session and its associated variables will cease to be available.

6. Load `session1.php` into a browser, and enter your name in the text field. Click Submit.

7. You should see something like the screenshot alongside. At this stage there is no apparent difference between what happens here and in an ordinary form.

Hello, Chris. Next

8. When you click Next, the power of sessions begins to show. As you can see, the page remembered your name, even though the POST array is no longer available to it.

Hi, Chris. See, I remembered your name!
Page 2

9. Click the link to Page 2. The session has been destroyed, so this time `session2.php` has no idea who you are.

Who are you? Login

10. Type the address of `session3.php` in the browser address bar and load it. It, too, has no recollection of the session, and displays an appropriate message.

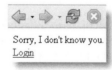

Sorry, I don't know you. Login

If it didn't work, check that your browser allows cookies. Also, Windows users should make sure that they have assigned a valid folder for temporary files to session.save_path in php.ini, and that there is no semicolon at the beginning of the line. The normal setting for Windows is as follows:

```
session.save_path = "C:\WINDOWS\Temp"
```

Registering and authenticating users

That brief exercise showed you just about all there is to know about PHP sessions, which lie at the heart of Dreamweaver's User Authentication server behaviors. As you have just seen, session variables enable you to keep track of a visitor. If you can identify visitors, you can also determine whether they have the right to view certain pages. There are four User Authentication server behaviors, as follows:

- **Log In User:** This queries a database to check whether a user is registered and has provided the correct password. You can also check whether a user belongs to a particular group to distinguish between, say, administrators and ordinary users.

- **Restrict Access to Page:** This prevents visitors from viewing a page unless they have logged in and (optionally) have the correct group privileges. Anyone not logged in is sent to the login page, but can be automatically redirected to the originally selected page after login.

- **Log Out User:** This brings the current session to an end, and prevents the user from returning to any restricted page without first logging back in again.

- **Check New Username:** This checks whether a particular username is already in use. It's rather badly designed, but can be easily adapted, and saves some hand-coding.

These server behaviors were missing from Dreamweaver MX, and the versions included in MX 2004 had quite a few bugs. All the bugs have been ironed out in Dreamweaver 8.

Creating a user registration system

To register users for your site, you need the following elements:

- A database table to store user details, such as username and password
- A registration form
- A page to display a list of registered users
- A form to update user details
- A form to delete users

Much of this involves building forms and applying the Insert Record, Update Record, and Delete Record server behaviors in exactly the same way as in the last chapter, so I will keep the description down to the minimum, concentrating mainly on new points.

Creating the users table in the database

I plan to use the same table for both site administrators and ordinary visitors. So the table will also have columns to store an email address and the level of user privileges.

1. Launch phpMyAdmin and select the seasons database. Create a new table called users. It requires seven columns, so enter 7 in Number of fields, and click Go.

2. Define the seven columns using the settings shown in the screenshot.

Primary key

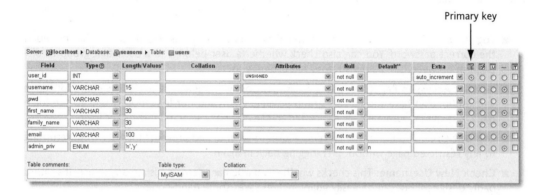

The table's primary key is user_id. The next five columns—username, pwd, first_name, family_name, and email—are all VARCHAR. I have set the length of username to 15, and pwd to 40. The password column must be 40 characters, because the function used to encrypt the passwords always produces a hexadecimal string exactly 40 characters long.

As in previous tables, I've used 30 characters for both first_name and family_name, and I have chosen a generous 100 characters for the email address. It's better to be over-generous than to end up with truncated data.

The final column, admin_priv, uses the ENUM column type. As I explained in Chapter 8, this is typically used for "choose one of the following" situations. In this case, it's whether a user has administrative privileges. Type the permitted values in the Length/Values field as comma-separated strings like this:

'n', 'y'

In the Default column for admin_priv, enter n without any quotes.

Note that all columns have been set to not null. This is because I want all of them to be required fields. Click Save.

3. Check that the table structure displayed in phpMyAdmin looks like this:

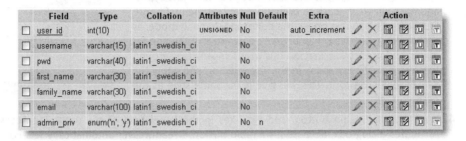

	Field	Type	Collation	Attributes	Null	Default	Extra	Action
☐	user_id	int(10)		UNSIGNED	No		auto_increment	✎ ✕ 🔡 🔣 🔟 🔠
☐	username	varchar(15)	latin1_swedish_ci		No			✎ ✕ 🔡 🔣 🔟 🔠
☐	pwd	varchar(40)	latin1_swedish_ci		No			✎ ✕ 🔡 🔣 🔟 🔠
☐	first_name	varchar(30)	latin1_swedish_ci		No			✎ ✕ 🔡 🔣 🔟 🔠
☐	family_name	varchar(30)	latin1_swedish_ci		No			✎ ✕ 🔡 🔣 🔟 🔠
☐	email	varchar(100)	latin1_swedish_ci		No			✎ ✕ 🔡 🔣 🔟 🔠
☐	admin_priv	enum('n', 'y')	latin1_swedish_ci		No	n		✎ ✕ 🔡 🔣 🔟 🔠

Creating the user registration form

This registration form will be for the use of administrators only, so it will be inside the admin folder.

1. Create a new PHP page, and save it in the admin folder as newuser.php. Attach the admin.css stylesheet.

2. Insert a form called newUser into the page, and lay it out as shown here. As before, I have used the column names of the users table for the input elements in the form. If you don't want to build the form yourself, use newuser_01.php from site_check/ch10.

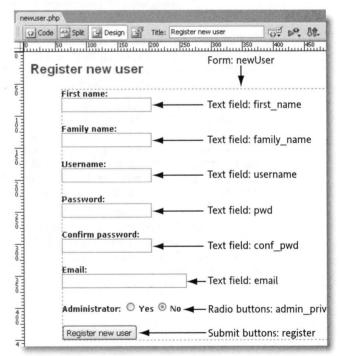

Set the Type of the pwd and conf_pwd text fields in the Property inspector to Password. This will ensure that any input into the field is displayed as a series of stars or bullets. It doesn't encrypt the passwords, but it prevents others from seeing the password in plain text if they happen to be looking over your shoulder.

The email text field needs to be a little wider than the default, so apply the mediumbox class, which is defined in the admin.css stylesheet, and makes it 200 pixels wide.

I built the form the same way as in previous chapters, using the Input Tag Accessibility Attributes dialog box to create <label> tags for the text fields. The radio buttons need to be handled slightly differently. I'll describe them in the following steps.

3. Insert a new paragraph after the email text field, and type Administrator:. Highlight the text that you have just typed, and right-click/*CTRL*-click to bring up a context menu. Choose Quick Tag Editor. This opens the editor in Wrap tag mode, as shown alongside. Type span or scroll down to it in the pop-up menu, and press *ENTER/RETURN*. This wraps <span> tags around the text. Select the <span> in the Tag selector, and apply the radioLabel style to it. This will give it the same style as the <label> tags.

4. Insert the first radio button, and type Yes in the Label field of the Input Tag Accessibility Attributes dialog box. Because it's a radio button, Dreamweaver automatically sets Position to After form item.

5. Insert another radio button alongside, and label it No.

6. Select the Yes radio button. In the Property inspector, name it admin_priv, and set the Checked value to y. Leave Initial state at the default Unchecked.

7. So that the Insert Record server behavior knows which radio button has been selected, all radio buttons in the same group must have the same name, so highlight the No button, and set its name in the Property inspector to the same as the Yes button: admin_priv. Set the Checked value to n, and Initial state to Checked.

8. When you set the name of other form elements in the Property inspector, Dreamweaver automatically sets the ID to the same value. This doesn't happen with radio buttons because, as I've just explained, all buttons in the same group have the same name, but you cannot have the same ID more than once on a page. Consequently, you need to dive into Code view to set the values manually of the for attribute and ID of each radio button. Use "administrator" for the Yes button, and "not_admin" for the No button. When you have finished, the entire radio button section should look like this in Code view:

```
<p><span class="radioLabel">Administrator: </span>
  <input name="admin_priv" type="radio" value="y" id="administrator" />
  <label for="administrator">Yes</label>
  <input name="admin_priv" type="radio" id="not_admin" value="n"
➡ checked="checked" />
  <label for="not_admin">No</label>
</p>
```

Many web developers ignore the rule that an ID must be unique on a page. Although it often makes no difference, it's an extremely bad habit and is one of the most frequent causes of problems with CSS and JavaScript. You can have as many instances of the same class on a page as you like, and you can use the same ID on different pages, but within a single page an ID must be used only once.

9. In the Property inspector, name the submit button register, and change the Value to Register new user. You can check your code against newuser_01.php in site_check/ch10.

Applying the server behaviors to the registration form

In theory, all you need to do is apply an Insert Record server behavior, and your registration form will work straight away. As always, though, you should conduct a series of checks to make sure that your database doesn't end up with incorrect or duplicate data. Dreamweaver does provide a server behavior to make sure that two people don't choose the same username. It's easy to use, but it is very user-unfriendly. That may sound like a paradox, but you'll soon see why. To get the registration form working efficiently involves a mixture of Dreamweaver automation and diving into Code view.

1. Continue working with newuser.php or use newuser_01.php from site_check/ch10. Apply an Insert Record server behavior. In the dialog box, select seasonAdmin for Connection, and users for Insert table. Check that each column except user_id gets a value from the form. Leave After inserting, go to blank. Click OK.

2. In the Server Behaviors panel, you'll see a red exclamation mark next to the Insert Record listing. Normally this indicates that you have edited the page in such a way as to cause the server behavior to break. In this case, it's a Dreamweaver bug triggered by the use of IDs on the radio button group. You can safely ignore it.

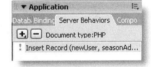

3. In the Server Behaviors panel, click the plus button and select User Authentication ➤ Check New Username.

4. The dialog box that opens is simplicity itself. As shown here, it consists of just two fields, and if you have used "username" as the column name in the database table, Dreamweaver is smart enough to select it automatically.

What's not smart about this server behavior is the second field. Nothing could be more guaranteed to annoy a user than to be taken to a different page if the registration process fails. Unlike other server behaviors, Check New Username won't let you leave the redirect field blank. So enter newuser.php in If already exists, go to, and click OK.

5. Open Code view. The Check New User server behavior is the code on lines 3 through 22 of the following screenshot. As you can see, it consists of two blocks. The first checks whether the username is already in use, while the second handles the redirect. The second block (on lines 14 through 21) begins with a conditional statement, so the code inside the curly braces will be executed only if a duplicate is found. You can use this to make the page much more user-friendly.

```
3    // *** Redirect if username exists
4    $MM_flag="MM_insert";
5    if (isset($_POST[$MM_flag])) {
6      $MM_dupKeyRedirect="newuser.php";
7      $loginUsername = $_POST['username'];
8      $LoginRS__query = "SELECT username FROM users WHERE username='" . $loginUsername . "'";
9      mysql_select_db($database_seasonAdmin, $seasonAdmin);
10     $LoginRS=mysql_query($LoginRS__query, $seasonAdmin) or die(mysql_error());
11     $loginFoundUser = mysql_num_rows($LoginRS);
12
13     //if there is a row in the database, the username was found - can not add the requested username
14     if($loginFoundUser){
15       $MM_qsChar = "?";
16       //append the username to the redirect page
17       if (substr_count($MM_dupKeyRedirect,"?") >=1) $MM_qsChar = "&";
18       $MM_dupKeyRedirect = $MM_dupKeyRedirect . $MM_qsChar ."requsername=".$loginUsername;
19       header ("Location: $MM_dupKeyRedirect");
20       exit;
21     }
22   }
```

6. Delete the code shown on lines 15 through 20 of the screenshot, and replace it with the code shown here in bold type:

```
    if($loginFoundUser) {
      $error['username'] = "$loginUsername is already in use. Please
➥ choose a different username.";
    }
}
```

This stores an error message in $error['username']. It uses $loginUsername, a variable created by the server behavior in line 7, to store the username submitted from the registration form. Note that I have used double quotes so that the value of $loginUsername will be displayed.

> Check New Username *will disappear from the listing in the Server Behaviors panel, indicating that it is no longer recognized by Dreamweaver, and is henceforth editable only in Code view.*

7. That's a good start, but you need to carry out a lot more checks. Start by amending lines 3 through 7 of the preceding screenshot like this (new code is shown in bold):

```
$error = array();
// Validate form input
$MM_flag="MM_insert";
if (isset($_POST[$MM_flag])) {
  // Check name
  if (empty($_POST['first_name']) || empty($_POST['family_name'])) {
    $error['name'] = 'Please enter both first name and family name';
    }
  // remaining checks go here
  // check username
  $_POST['username'] = trim($_POST['username']);
  $loginUsername = $_POST['username'];
```

This initializes $error as an empty array. If you cast your mind back to Chapter 5, you may remember that PHP treats an array with zero elements as false, so this can be used later to test whether any errors have been found.

Line 6 in the screenshot has been removed, because you no longer need to redirect the script to another page. It has been replaced by the first of a series of checks. It makes sure that neither the first name nor the family name has been left empty.

There follows a comment to indicate where all the remaining checks will go.

Finally, I have applied trim() to $_POST['username'] and reassigned the value back to the POST variable. I've done this for the very important reason that the Insert Record server behavior, which remains intact further down the page, requires the original POST variables, so you can't reassign them to shorter variables, as with the contact form in Chapter 6.

> You might think I'm contradicting myself because the next line assigns $_POST['username'] to $loginUsername. Actually, it's part of the original Check New Username server behavior. I've left it in to avoid the need for other changes to the existing code.

8. The next check makes sure that the password contains at least six characters, and that both versions are the same. If everything is OK, the password is encrypted ready for insertion in the database. Insert the following code at the point indicated by the "remaining checks go here" comment in the code from the previous step:

```
// set a flag that assumes the password is OK
$pwdOK = true;
// trim leading and trailing white space
$_POST['pwd'] = trim($_POST['pwd']);
// if less than 6 characters, create alert and set flag to false
if (strlen($_POST['pwd']) < 6) {
  $error['pwd_length'] = 'Your password must be at least 6 characters';
  $pwdOK = false;
  }
// if no match, create alert and set flag to false
if ($_POST['pwd'] != trim($_POST['conf_pwd'])) {
```

343

```
    $error['pwd'] = 'Your passwords don\'t match';
    $pwdOK = false;
    }
// if password OK, encrypt it
if ($pwdOK) {
    $_POST['pwd'] = sha1($_POST['pwd']);
    }
```

The code starts by setting a variable that assumes the password is OK. After trimming any white space, the password is then subjected to two tests. The first test uses the PHP function strlen(), which determines the number of characters in any string passed to it, and checks that the trimmed password contains at least six characters. The second test checks whether the passwords match.

If either test fails (or both of them do), a suitable message is added to the $error array, and $pwdOK is set to false. However, if $pwdOK is still true, the password is passed to the sha1() function, which converts any string passed to it into a 40-character hexadecimal number—in effect, encrypting the string.

9. Create a new line immediately below the code you inserted in the previous step, open the Snippets panel, and double-click the Email address check snippet in the PHP-DW8 folder that you installed in Chapter 6. The snippet positions your cursor in the right place for you to type $_POST['email'] between the parentheses.

```
// check for valid email address
$pattern = '/^[^@]+@[^\s\r\n\'";,@%]+$/';
if (!preg_match($pattern, trim($_POST['email']))) {
    $error['email'] = 'Please enter a valid email address';
    }
```

10. The final check uses strlen() again to make sure that the username consists of a minimum number of characters. I have chosen 6, but you can use whatever number you like. This code should go after the final line of code in step 7. I have included the existing lines above and below the new code so you can see exactly where it goes.

```
$loginUsername = $_POST['username'];
if (strlen($loginUsername) < 6) {
    $error['length'] = 'Please select a username that contains at least
➥ 6 characters';
    }
$LoginRS__query = "SELECT username FROM users WHERE username='" .
➥ $loginUsername . "'";
```

11. Now that the checks are complete, you need to build the logic that determines whether the Insert Record server behavior is executed. All it requires is to wrap the server behavior in a conditional statement. Scroll down until you find the following block of code—it should be immediately above the DOCTYPE declaration:

```
82   if ((isset($_POST["MM_insert"])) && ($_POST["MM_insert"] == "newUser")) {
83     $insertSQL = sprintf("INSERT INTO users (username, pwd, first_name, family_name, email,
     admin_priv) VALUES (%s, %s, %s, %s, %s, %s)",
84                          GetSQLValueString($_POST['username'], "text"),
85                          GetSQLValueString($_POST['pwd'], "text"),
86                          GetSQLValueString($_POST['first_name'], "text"),
87                          GetSQLValueString($_POST['family_name'], "text"),
88                          GetSQLValueString($_POST['email'], "text"),
89                          GetSQLValueString($_POST['admin_priv'], "text"));
90
91     mysql_select_db($database_seasonAdmin, $seasonAdmin);
92     $Result1 = mysql_query($insertSQL, $seasonAdmin) or die(mysql_error());
93   }
```

12. Wrap the entire block of code in the following `if` statement:

```
if (!$error) {
  // existing code on lines 82 through 93 in screenshot
}
```

If no errors have been found, the $error array will contain zero elements, which, as you know, PHP treats as `false`. By placing the negation operator (an exclamation mark) in front of it, you get the reverse meaning. So, if $error contains no elements, this test equates to true, and the Insert Record server behavior will be executed. If errors are found, the test will equate to false, and the server behavior will be ignored.

13. The final change is within the main body of the document. Scroll down to the page heading (around line 104) just below the `<body>` tag, and insert the following code block between the heading and the opening `<form>` tag:

```
<h1>Register new user </h1>
<?php
if ($error) {
  echo '<ul>';
  foreach ($error as $alert) {
    echo "<li class='warning'>$alert</li>\n";
    }
  echo '</ul>';
  }
?>
<form action="<?php echo $editFormAction; ?>" id="newUser" name="newUser"
➥ method="POST">
```

This uses the opposite test to the one in step 12. If the $error array contains any elements, a foreach loop iterates through the array and assigns each element to the temporary variable $alert, which is used to display the error messages as a bulleted list. Refer back to Chapter 6 if you need to refresh your memory about foreach loops.

Because $error is an empty array when the page first loads, the PHP script will ignore this block of code unless the form has been submitted and contains errors.

14. Save `newuser.php` and load it into a browser. Click the Register new user button without filling in any fields. The page should reload and display the following warnings:

If you have any problems, check your code against `newuser_02.php` in `site_check/ch10`.

15. Now fill in several fields, but leave one blank and submit the form again. You should see the appropriate error message, but all the fields are empty. Imagine the frustration of being forced to fill in all the details again because of a mistake in just one field. What you really need is a server behavior to provide the same solution you used in the contact form in Chapter 6. There isn't one, but you can make it yourself.

Building custom server behaviors

One reason for the great success of Dreamweaver is that, even though the core program has a massive range of features, it's also extendible. You have already installed two simple extensions that I have created: Lorem and More, and the collection of PHP code snippets. But there are many more extensions available for Dreamweaver. Some are free; others are sold on a commercial basis. However, you don't have to rely on others to build extensions—you can build simple ones yourself to take the tedium out of repetitive tasks.

As you may remember from Chapter 6, the way to redisplay the input of a text field is to insert a PHP conditional statement between the quotes of the value attribute like this:

```
value="<?php if (isset($_POST['field'])) {echo $_POST['field'];} ?>"
```

Apart from *field*, the code never changes, and it is always assigned to the value attribute of a text field. This consistency makes it ideal for creating a new server behavior, which involves the following steps:

- Creating a unique name for each block of code that the server behavior will insert into your page. The Server Behavior Builder generates this automatically for you.

- Typing the code into the Server Behavior Builder, and replacing any changeable values with Dreamweaver parameters. The parameters act as placeholders until you insert the actual value through a dialog box when the server behavior is applied.

- Telling Dreamweaver where to insert the code.

- Designing the server behavior dialog box.

Creating a Sticky Text Field server behavior

Because Dreamweaver is context sensitive, you must have a PHP page open in the Document window to be able to create a new server behavior.

1. In the Server Behaviors panel, click the plus button, and select New Server Behavior. In the dialog box that opens, make sure that Document type is set to PHP MySQL. Type Sticky Text Field in the Name field, and click OK.

2. This opens the Server Behavior Builder. Click the plus button next to Code blocks to insert, and accept the default name Dreamweaver 8 suggests by clicking OK. Dreamweaver fills in the remaining fields of the Server Behavior Builder like this:

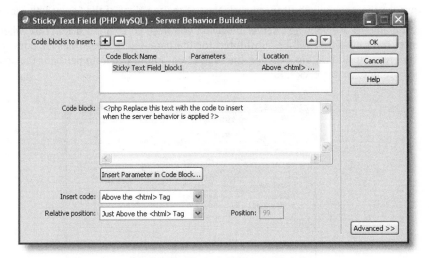

3. The Code block area in the center is where you insert the PHP code that you want to appear on the page. The value of *field* will change every time, so you need to replace it with a parameter. Parameter names must not contain any spaces, but they are used to label the server behavior dialog box, so it's a good idea to choose a descriptive name, such as FieldName. To insert a parameter, click the Insert Parameter in Code Block button at the appropriate point in the code, type the name in the dialog box, and click OK. Dreamweaver places it in the code with two @ characters on either side. You can also type the parameters in the code block directly yourself. Whichever method you use, delete the dummy text in the Code block area, and replace it with the following:

```php
<?php if (isset($_POST['@@FieldName@@'])) {
echo $_POST['@@FieldName@@'];} ?>
```

4. As soon as you add any parameters in the Code block area, the label on the OK button changes to Next, but first you need to tell Dreamweaver where you want the code to appear in the page. It needs to be applied to the value attribute of <input> tags, so select Relative to a Specific Tag from the Insert code drop-down menu.

5. This reveals two more drop-down menus. Select input/text for Tag, and As the Value of an Attribute for Relative position.

6. This triggers the appearance of another drop-down menu labeled Attribute. Select value. The bottom section of the Server Behavior Builder should now look like this:

This tells the Server Behavior Builder that the code you entered in step 3 should be applied as the value attribute of a text field. There is no need to change any of the settings accessed through the Advanced button, so click Next at the top right of the Server Behavior Builder.

7. To be able to use your new server behavior, you need to create a dialog box, where you can enter the values that will be substituted for the parameters. Dreamweaver does most of the work for you, and on this occasion the suggestions in the Generate Behavior Dialog Box dialog box are fine, so just click OK.

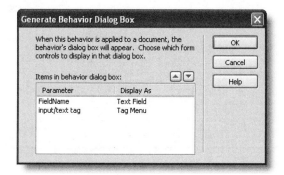

Creating a server behavior for Sticky Text Areas

The server behavior that you have just built works only with text fields, so before showing it to you in action, I think it's worth building a second server behavior to handle text areas. Unlike text fields, text areas don't have a value attribute, so they need slightly different treatment.

1. Repeat steps 1 and 2 of the previous section, only this time call the new server behavior Sticky Text Area.

2. In step 3 of the previous section, enter the following code in the Code block area:

```php
<?php if (isset($_POST['@@TextArea@@'])) {echo
➥ $_POST['@@TextArea@@'];} ?>
```

3. Fill in the bottom section of the Server Behavior Builder as shown here. This places the content of the POST variable between the opening and closing <textarea> tags.

4. Click Next, and accept the defaults suggested for the server behavior dialog box.

You now have two server behaviors that will be available in all your PHP sites from the menu in the Server Behaviors panel.

Completing the user registration form

You can now complete newuser.php by applying the Sticky Text Field server behavior to each text field. This will ensure that data already inserted won't be lost through the failure of any validation test.

Preserving user input when errors are generated

Continue working with newuser.php, or use newuser_02.php from site_check/ch10.

1. Switch newuser.php to Design view, and click the plus button in the Server Behaviors panel. The new server behaviors are now listed. Select Sticky Text Field.

2. The Sticky Text Field dialog box will appear. The input/text tag field is a drop-down menu that Dreamweaver automatically populates with all text fields on the page. Type the name of the field that you want to make "sticky" in FieldName, and select the appropriate field from the drop-down menu, as shown below. You need to make all text fields sticky, so start with first_name. Click OK.

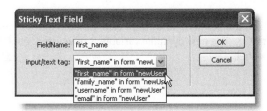

3. Dreamweaver inserts a dynamic content placeholder inside the text field in Design view. If you highlight the text field and open Split view, you will see that the conditional statement you created in the Code block area of the Server Behavior Builder has been inserted, but @@FieldName@@ has been replaced by the actual name of the field.

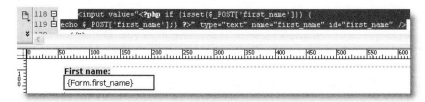

4. Apply the Sticky Text Field server behavior to family_name, username, and email. If you select the text field in Design view beforehand, it will be automatically selected in the input/text tag list. Dreamweaver doesn't include the password fields in the drop-down menu, so you can't apply the server behavior to them.

5. Look in the Server Behaviors panel. All instances of Sticky Text Field are now listed. If you ever need to edit one, highlight it and double-click; or use the minus button to remove it cleanly from your code.

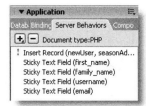

6. Save newuser.php and load it into a browser. Test it by entering an incomplete set of details. This time, the content of text fields will be preserved. However, there's still one part of the form that doesn't respond to changes: the Administrator radio buttons.

7. Switch back to newuser.php in Dreamweaver, and select the No radio button in Design view. In the Property inspector, change Initial state from Checked to Unchecked. This removes the code that automatically selects the No button.

8. When any errors are detected, you need checked="checked" to be inserted in the appropriate radio button tag. Since the radio group is called admin_priv, the value you want is contained in $_POST['admin_priv']. Although you can type the POST variable directly into the Dynamic Radio Group dialog box, Dreamweaver provides another way for you to create POST, GET, and other superglobal variables for use in your pages.

Open the Bindings panel, and click the plus button. Select Form Variable.

9. Type admin_priv in the Name field of the Form Variable dialog box, and click OK. The new dynamic variable is now listed in the Bindings panel.

10. Make sure that the No radio button is still selected, and click the Dynamic button in the Property inspector.

11. The admin_priv radio group will be automatically selected in the Dynamic Radio Group dialog box. Click the lightning bolt icon to the right of the Select value equal to field. Then choose admin_priv from the Dynamic Data panel. Click OK. The Dynamic Radio Group dialog box should now look like this. Click OK.

12. Save newuser.php and load the page into a browser. If you set error reporting in php.ini to the level I recommended in Chapter 3, you'll see there's a major problem, as shown here:

> **Administrator:**
> **Notice**: Undefined index: admin_priv in C:\htdocs\phpdw\admin\newuser.php on line **151**
> name="admin_priv" type="radio" value="y" id="administrator" /> **Yes**
> **Notice**: Undefined index: admin_priv in C:\htdocs\phpdw\admin\newuser.php on line **153**
> name="admin_priv" type="radio" id="not_admin" value="n" /> **No**

This is because the new code should only be executed *after* the form has been submitted. $_POST['admin_priv'] hasn't been defined when the page first loads. Hence the reference to an "undefined index." Not only does this look bad, it prevents the browser from displaying the radio buttons, and turns them into text fields instead.

> *The default setting for php.ini turns off the display of error notices, so the radio buttons would display correctly on most standard PHP servers. However, it's important to eliminate all errors, because you never know when they may trip you up or lay you open to security exploits.*

13. Switch back to Dreamweaver, highlight one of the radio buttons so that you can easily locate the relevant code, and switch to Code view.

Dreamweaver uses a rather unusual PHP function called strcmp() to check whether $_POST['admin_priv'] is y or n. The function takes two arguments, and returns 0 if they're exactly the same. Since 0 equates to false, the negation operator (!) converts it to true. If you find the logic difficult to follow, just take my word for it—it works.

The radio button section of code is shown on the next page.

```
149        <p><span class="radioLabel">Administrator:
150        </span>
151        <input <?php if (!(strcmp($_POST['admin_priv'],"y"))) {echo "checked=\"checked\"";} ?> name=
        "admin_priv" type="radio" value="y" id="administrator" />
152        <label for="administrator">Yes</label>
153        <input <?php if (!(strcmp($_POST['admin_priv'],"n"))) {echo "checked=\"checked\"";} ?> name=
        "admin_priv" type="radio" id="not_admin" value="n" />
154        <label for="not_admin">No</label>
```

14. You need to check whether the form has been submitted. Although the POST array is always set, it will be empty if the form hasn't been submitted. And as you should know by now, an empty array equates to false. Amend the beginning of both sections of radio button code (shown on lines 151 and 153 in the preceding screenshot) like this:

```
<input <?php if ($_POST && !(strcmp($_POST['admin_priv'],
```

15. Save the page and load it into your browser. The radio buttons should now be back to normal. The only problem is that you don't have a default checked value when the page first loads. In one respect, it shouldn't be a problem because you set a default value when defining the users table earlier. Unfortunately, as I explained in Chapter 8, Dreamweaver server behaviors treat unset values as NULL, causing your form to fail because admin_priv was defined as "not null." You can't even get round this by changing the column definition, because you would then end up with NULL as the default. Although NULL might be an acceptable alternative to "no," it won't work where you have a choice of more than two radio buttons.

16. Change the code shown on line 153 in the preceding screenshot like this (the change made in step 14 is also shown in bold type):

```
<input <?php if (($_POST && !(strcmp($_POST['admin_priv'],"n")))
➥ || !$_POST) {echo "checked=\"checked\"";} ?> name="admin_priv"
➥ type="radio" id="not_admin" value="n" />
```

I have enclosed the original test (as adapted in step 14) in an extra pair of parentheses to ensure that it's treated as a single unit. Then I added a second test:

```
|| !$_POST
```

This tests whether the POST array is empty. The result is this (in pseudocode):

if ((the form has been sent AND admin_priv is "n")
OR the form has not been sent) {mark the button "checked"}

17. Save newuser.php. You now have a user registration form that performs all the necessary checks before entering a new record into your database. Try it out. If all goes well, you should get no errors, but all the input fields will still be populated with the data you just input. Fortunately, that's easy to correct.

18. Scroll up to the last section of PHP code just above the DOCTYPE declaration, which looks like this:

```
91        mysql_select_db($database_seasonAdmin, $seasonAdmin);
92        $Result1 = mysql_query($insertSQL, $seasonAdmin) or die(mysql_error());
93        }
94        }
95        ?><!DOCTYPE html PUBLIC "-//W3C//DTD XHTML 1.0 Transitional//EN"
```

Lines 91 through 93 in the screenshot are the last few lines of the Insert Record server behavior, followed (on line 94) by the closing brace that you inserted in step 12 of the section titled "Applying the server behaviors to the registration form."

19. Insert a new line between the braces shown on lines 93 and 94, and add this code:

```
// if the record has been inserted, clear the POST array
$_POST = array();
```

After the record has been inserted, you no longer need the contents of the POST array, so this simply turns it into an empty array.

20. There's just one last thing. If your PHP configuration has magic_quotes_gpc turned on (and most hosting companies seem to use this setting), your Sticky Text Fields will end up with backslashes escaping apostrophes in users' names, like the figure alongside:

21. Scroll down to the section of code that displays the error messages (shown in the screenshot alongside), and insert a new line after the code shown on line 113. Open the Snippets panel, and insert the POST stripslashes snippet that you installed in the PHP folder in Chapter 6.

22. Save newuser.php and check your code against newuser_03.php in site_check/ch10.

Building an apparently simple user registration form has taken a lot of steps. You could have used it almost straight away, after applying the Insert Record server behavior, but before long, you would almost certainly have ended up with a lot of unusable data in your database, not to mention the frustration of users when an input error results in all their data being wiped from the screen. The more time you spend refining the forms that interact with your database, the more time you will save in the long run.

Updating and deleting user records

The way you update and delete user records follows the same pattern as before. First, you create a page to display a list of registered users, complete with links to the update and delete forms. You build it exactly the same way as the authors and quotations tables in the last chapter, so I won't give any instructions. Take a look at listusers.php in site_check/ch10 if you have any problems.

The next step is to adapt newuser.php to work as the update form. Again, this is almost identical to the way you converted the insert pages in the last chapter. However, the value attributes of each text field currently have the Sticky Text Field server behavior applied to them. This makes it impossible to bind the values from the record that you want to update, unless you remove the Sticky Text Field server behavior. You could trust that no errors will occur when the update form is submitted, but that's trusting a great deal to fate. A better idea is to create a new server behavior that can then be reused on any update page.

Adapting the Sticky Text Field server behavior

As you have already seen, it's only when the form has been submitted—and errors detected—that the Sticky Text Field code executes. So if the POST variables haven't been set, you know the form hasn't been submitted, and that you need to display the values stored in the database instead.

Dreamweaver always uses the following naming convention to refer to the results of a recordset: $row_*RecordsetName*['*FieldName*']. So, all that's needed is to add an else clause to the existing code:

```
<?php if (isset($_POST['field'])) {echo $_POST['field'];} else {
echo $row_RecordsetName['FieldName']; } ?>
```

Creating the Sticky Edit Field server behavior

Most of the settings are identical to the Sticky Text Field server behavior that you built earlier, so you can use the existing server behavior to create the new one.

1. Make sure that you have a PHP page open, and click the plus button in the Server Behaviors panel. Select New Server Behavior.

2. Name the new server behavior Sticky Edit Field, and place a check mark in the box labeled Copy existing server behavior. This will populate a drop-down menu with the names of server behaviors you have already built (unfortunately, you can't base a new server behavior on one of Dreamweaver's). Select Sticky Text Field and click OK.

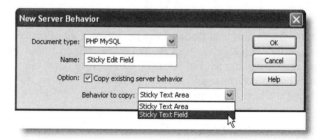

3. Edit the contents of the Code block area like this:

```
<?php if (isset($_POST['@@FieldName@@'])) {echo
$_POST['@@FieldName@@'];} else {
echo $row_@@RecordsetName@@['@@FieldName@@'];} ?>
```

Dreamweaver will use the new parameter—@@RecordsetName@@—in combination with @@FieldName@@ to build a variable like $row_getUser['family_name'].

> *There's a bug in the Mac version of Dreamweaver 8 that prevents you from using the same parameter name in more than one server behavior. So, if you're using a Mac, change both instances of @@FieldName@@ to @@Field@@, and all will be well with the world (well, at least in the world of sticky server behaviors).*

4. Click Next. Dreamweaver presents you with the warning shown here. This is because it assumes that you want to use the same dialog box as before. However, the old dialog box is no longer any use, so click Yes to overwrite the existing file.

5. Use the arrows at the top right of the area labeled Items in behavior dialog box to reorder them as shown below. Also, reset the Display as value for RecordsetName and FieldName by clicking to the right of the existing value and activating the pop-up menu. Set RecordsetName to Recordset Menu and FieldName to Recordset Field Menu. (If you're using a Mac, FieldName should be listed as Field.) Click OK.

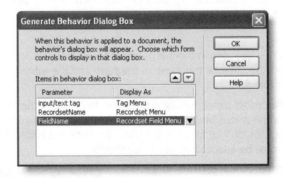

To create a similar server behavior for text areas, name it Sticky Edit Area, and select Sticky Text Area in step 2. All the other steps are identical, including the code block used in step 3.

Just before sending this book to the printers, I discovered what appears to be a bug in the way that Dreamweaver 8 detects code inserted by some server behaviors. When building the Sticky Edit Area server behavior, I removed all new line characters from the code block in step 3. This resulted in Dreamweaver 8 being unable to distinguish between a Sticky Text Area and a Sticky Edit Area, even if I used completely different parameters. However, as long as you format the code with new lines, as shown in step 3, everything will work fine. This problem appears to be new to Dreamweaver 8, and will hopefully be resolved in an updated release.

Building the update and delete pages

Although the update page can be adapted from the insert page in much the same way as in the previous chapter, there are three issues that might catch you out:

- The pwd and conf_pwd text fields use the password type, so you can't display the value retrieved from the database. Even if you could, the password is stored in a format that can't be decrypted.

- The current validation code will actually prevent you from updating a user's details because the same username already exists in the database—and belongs to none other than the user you're trying to update!

- Changes made to the Dynamic Radio Group code for the admin_priv field mean that the code is no longer editable through the Server Behaviors panel.

Adapting newuser.php to update existing user details

In these instructions, I have concentrated mainly on issues that require special attention. Refer back to the previous chapter if you need to refresh your memory about applying server behaviors and creating hidden fields.

1. Save a copy of newuser.php in the admin folder as updateuser.php. Adjust the title and heading of the page. Also, change the name of the form and the submit button's details to indicate the page's new function.

2. In the Server Behaviors panel, highlight the Insert Record and the four Sticky Text Field server behaviors. Click the minus button to remove them from the page. The Check New Username server behavior shouldn't be listed in the panel because you edited it in newuser.php. You still need it, but it must be adapted, as you'll see shortly.

3. Create a recordset called getUser to get the details of the record to be updated in the users table. The user_id will be passed through a query string from listusers.php, so use that to filter the results. The correct settings are shown alongside.

4. Add a hidden field called user_id to the form, and use the lightning bolt icon in the Property inspector to set its value to user_id from the getUser recordset.

5. Apply an Update Record server behavior. Use the seasonAdmin connection to update the users table, and select listusers.php as the page to display after the update has been executed.

6. Open Code view. Just above the DOCTYPE declaration, you will find an empty conditional statement, which was left behind when you removed the Insert Record server behavior in step 2. You now need to move the Update Record server behavior code (shown on lines 33 through 52 of the following screenshot) to inside the braces shown on lines 113 and 117. I have used Dreamweaver 8's Code Collapse feature to hide the recordset code and all the validation checks, so take careful note of the actual code.

```
33  if ((isset($_POST["MM_update"])) && ($_POST["MM_update"] == "updateUser")) {
34    $updateSQL = sprintf("UPDATE users SET username=%s, pwd=%s, first_name=%s, family_name=%s,
      email=%s, admin_priv=%s WHERE user_id=%s",
35                         GetSQLValueString($_POST['username'], "text"),
36                         GetSQLValueString($_POST['pwd'], "text"),
37                         GetSQLValueString($_POST['first_name'], "text"),
38                         GetSQLValueString($_POST['family_name'], "text"),
39                         GetSQLValueString($_POST['email'], "text"),
40                         GetSQLValueString($_POST['admin_priv'], "text"),
41                         GetSQLValueString($_POST['user_id'], "int"));
42
43    mysql_select_db($database_seasonAdmin, $seasonAdmin);
44    $Result1 = mysql_query($updateSQL, $seasonAdmin) or die(mysql_error());
45
46    $updateGoTo = "listusers.php";
47    if (isset($_SERVER['QUERY_STRING'])) {
48      $updateGoTo .= (strpos($updateGoTo, '?')) ? "&" : "?";
49      $updateGoTo .= $_SERVER['QUERY_STRING'];
50    }
51    header(sprintf("Location: %s", $updateGoTo));
52  }
53
54 ⊞ $colnam...
112
113  if (!$error) {
114
115  // if the record has been inserted, clear the POST array
116  $_POST = array();
117  }
118  ?><!DOCTYPE html PUBLIC "-//W3C//DTD XHTML 1.0 Transitional//EN"
```

7. Although it won't do any harm if it's left in, the line of code that clears the POST array (shown on line 116 of the preceding screenshot) is no longer necessary. You can remove it and its accompanying comment.

8. If you used Code Collapse while moving the Update Record server behavior in the previous step, expand the collapsed section and scroll up to the following line of code (it should now be around line 45):

```
$MM_flag = "MM_insert";
```

Change it to

```
$MM_flag = "MM_update";
```

This is the name of a hidden field that Dreamweaver uses to check whether to execute the Update Record server behavior code. It will now ensure that the form validation checks are run before updating the database.

9. About half a dozen lines further down is the code that checks the password. When a user's record is being updated, you either want to preserve the same password or to set a new one. There are several ways to handle this, but the simplest is to decide that if pwd is left blank, the existing password will be maintained. Otherwise the password needs to be checked and encrypted as before.

Amend the password validation code as follows (new code shown in bold type):

```
$_POST['pwd'] = trim($_POST['pwd']);
// if password field is empty, use existing password
if (empty($_POST['pwd'])) {
  $_POST['pwd'] = $row_getUser['pwd'];
  }
// otherwise, conduct normal checks
else {
  // if less than 6 characters, create alert and set flag to false
  if (strlen($_POST['pwd']) < 6) {
    $error['pwd_length'] = 'Your password must be at least 6
➥ characters';
    $pwdOK = false;
    }
  // if no match, create alert and set flag to false
  if ($_POST['pwd'] != trim($_POST['conf_pwd'])) {
    $error['pwd'] = 'Your passwords don\'t match';
    $pwdOK = false;
    }
  // if new password OK, encrypt it
  if ($pwdOK) {
    $_POST['pwd'] = sha1($_POST['pwd']);
    }
  }
```

This checks whether $_POST['pwd'] is empty. If it is, the value of the existing password as retrieved by the getUser recordset is assigned to $_POST['pwd']. Because the existing password is already encrypted, there is no need to pass it to sha1(). If $_POST['pwd'] isn't empty, the else clause executes the checks inherited from newuser.php.

> If you discover that your password fields are blank after updating, make sure that the getUser recordset code is above the validation check. You can recognize it easily. It is nine lines long, and nearly every line includes getUser. If in doubt, check the download files.

10. The final validation check that needs to be amended is the one that tests whether the username is already in use in the database. Because you're updating an existing user, it should be obvious that this test will always return true: the username already belongs to the record that you're updating.

What's needed this time is to check whether the username is being used by anyone except the current user. The New Username server behavior is no longer editable through the Server Behaviors panel. What's more, it doesn't have the option that you need. So there's nothing else for it, but to edit the SQL query manually. Scroll down until you find the following section of code:

```
88   $LoginRS__query = "SELECT username FROM users WHERE username='" . $loginUsername . "'";
89   mysql_select_db($database_seasonAdmin, $seasonAdmin);
90   $LoginRS=mysql_query($LoginRS__query, $seasonAdmin) or die(mysql_error());
91   $loginFoundUser = mysql_num_rows($LoginRS);
```

11. Amend the final section of the code shown on line 88 in the screenshot like this:

```
WHERE username='" . $loginUsername . "' AND user_id !=" .
➥ $_POST['user_id'];
```

The user_id is stored in the form's hidden field, so it can be retrieved from the POST array and used to exclude the current user's record from the results.

12. Save updateuser.php and check your code, if necessary, against updateuser_01.php in site_check/ch10.

13. Apply the Sticky Edit Field server behavior to the first_name, family_name, user-name, and email fields. This time you can select the appropriate field name from a drop-down menu, which is populated by the getUser recordset. Since getUser is the only recordset on this page, it's selected automatically, but make sure you choose the right one if you use this server behavior on a page that has two or more recordsets.

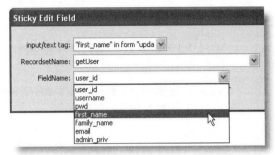

14. The radio buttons present an interesting challenge. When the page first loads, you want the value stored in the database for admin_priv to be selected; but if the form is submitted with errors, and you have changed the value of admin_priv, you want the new value to be shown. You could build another server behavior to handle this, but it's actually quite easy to hand-code. Because you edited the Dynamic Radio Group server behavior in newuser.php, Dreamweaver no longer recognizes it, so it lets you apply the server behavior again.

Select one of the radio buttons in Design view, and click the Dynamic button in the Property inspector. In the Dynamic Radio Group dialog box, click the lightning bolt icon, and select admin_priv from the getUser recordset. Click OK in both dialog boxes.

15. Switch to Code view. The code for the radio group should now look like this:

```
187    <p><span class="radioLabel">Administrator: </span>
188      <input <?php if (!(strcmp($row_getUser['admin_priv'],"y"))) {echo "checked=\"checked\"";} ?>
<?php if ($_POST && !(strcmp($_POST['admin_priv'],"y"))) {echo "checked=\"checked\"";} ?> name=
"admin_priv" type="radio" value="y" id="administrator" />
189      <label for="administrator">Yes</label>
190      <input <?php if (!(strcmp($row_getUser['admin_priv'],"n"))) {echo "checked=\"checked\"";} ?>
<?php if (($_POST && !(strcmp($_POST['admin_priv'],"n"))) || !$_POST) {echo "checked=\"checked\"";}
?> name="admin_priv" type="radio" id="not_admin" value="n" />
191      <label for="not_admin">No</label>
192    </p>
```

If the sight of all this code strikes terror into your heart, don't worry; the changes you need to make are very simple. Before diving into the code, though, you should also take this as a warning. Because Dreamweaver no longer recognized the original server behavior, it has let you insert the same one again. On this occasion, it happens to be exactly what you want, but that may not always be the case. The code here is perfectly valid, but it will produce unpredictable results in its current form. Even if you don't become an expert PHP programmer, you should always be aware of what is happening in the underlying code.

16. The extra code that Dreamweaver has inserted consists of the first block of PHP on both line 188 and line 190. Basically, all that you need do is ensure that this new section of code runs when the page is first loaded, and that the original code runs only after the form has been submitted. Since that was the way it was designed to run, the original code doesn't need changing. You know that the POST array will have zero elements (and therefore equate to false) when the page first loads, so the necessary check can be performed by inserting !$_POST into the conditional statements of the new code. You also need to change the if in each radio button's original code to elseif. To make the changes easier to follow, you may find it helpful to indent the code as I have done here. The changes are shown in bold type.

```php
<input
<?php
if (!$_POST && !(strcmp($row_getUser['admin_priv'],"y"))) {
  echo "checked=\"checked\"";
  }
elseif ($_POST && !(strcmp($_POST['admin_priv'],"y"))) {
  echo "checked=\"checked\"";
  }
?>
name="admin_priv" type="radio" value="y" id="administrator" />
<label for="administrator">Yes</label>
<input
<?php
if (!$_POST && !(strcmp($row_getUser['admin_priv'],"n"))) {
  echo "checked=\"checked\"";
  }
elseif ($_POST && !(strcmp($_POST['admin_priv'],"n"))) {
  echo "checked=\"checked\"";
  }
?>
name="admin_priv" type="radio" id="not_admin" value="n" />
```

There are two other important points to note about the preceding code. First, I have removed the closing and opening PHP tags (?> <?php) immediately preceding elseif. Dreamweaver's automatic code generation normally surrounds each new block of PHP code with opening and closing tags, even when there is no XHTML code in-between. In the vast majority of cases, this makes no difference. However, in this particular case, leaving the redundant tags in the code causes a syntax error. The second point to note is that some code has been removed from the final elseif clause, as shown here:

```php
elseif ((($_POST && !(strcmp($_POST['admin_priv'],"n"))) || !$_POST)
```

The code is no longer appropriate, because the !$_POST situation is now covered by the if part of the conditional statement.

17. That completes the changes to the code. Switch back to Design view, and add some text to the Password label, indicating that the field should be left blank if the same password is being kept. Save updateuser.php and compare your code with updateuser_02.php in site_check/ch10 if you have any problems.

Creating the delete user page

Up to now, I have always suggested adapting the update page for deleting records. On this occasion, however, all the validation required by the update page is unnecessary. You simply need to display the basic details of the record about to be deleted, and get confirmation that the operation should go ahead.

1. Create a new PHP page and save it in the admin folder as deleteuser.php.

2. Open updateuser.php or switch to it if it's still open.

3. In the Server Behaviors panel, highlight Recordset (getUser), and right-click/*CTRL*-click. Select Copy from the context menu.

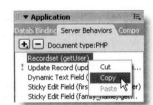

4. Switch back to deleteuser.php, right-click/*CTRL*-click inside the Server Behaviors panel, and select Paste. Bingo, one quick, easy recordset—something I thought you'd appreciate after all that digging around inside Code view.

5. Give the page a heading and title, and insert a form called deleteUser. Use the Bindings panel to insert some details that will identify the user, and add a submit button named delete with a suitable label. The screenshot shows a suggested layout.

6. Insert a hidden field into the form. Name it user_id, and click the lightning bolt icon in the Property inspector to set the field's Value to user_id from the getUser recordset. The Delete Record server behavior needs this to know which record to delete.

7. Apply a Delete Record server behavior. As in all previous cases, Primary key value should be set to Form Variable. Set the After deleting, go to field to listusers.php. The screenshot below shows the correct settings.

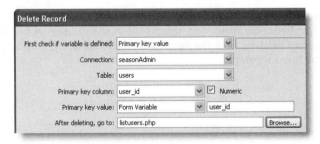

8. That's all there is to it. You can check your code against deleteuser.php in site_check/ch10.

Creating a login system

Now that you have a way of registering users, you need to create a way for them to log in to restricted areas of your site. Building the login system is a lot simpler than the registration system.

Creating the login page

Before starting, make sure you have at least one user registered as an administrator in your database.

1. Create a PHP page in the `admin` folder, and save it as `login.php`. Attach the `admin.css` stylesheet, and lay out the page with a form, two text fields, and a submit button as shown here.

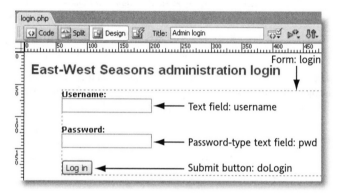

Since you will be applying a server behavior to the form, there is no need to specify a value in the Property inspector for Action, and Method should be left at the default POST. Set the Type for the pwd text field to Password.

2. The Log In User server behavior expects you to designate two pages: one that the user will be taken to if the login is successful, and another if it fails. If you didn't create an admin menu at the end of the last chapter, create a page called `menu.php` in the `admin` folder. This should contain a list of text links to all the insert pages that you have built so far, as well as to the pages that list your database records. You don't need links to the update and delete pages, because they should always be accessed from an up-to-date list of records. Also, create a page in the `admin` folder called `loginfail.php`. Insert a message telling the user that the login failed, and a link back to `login.php`. If you don't want to code the pages yourself, use `menu_01.php` and `loginfail.php` from `site_check/ch10`.

3. Make sure `login.php` is the active page in the Dreamweaver workspace. Click the plus button on the Server Behaviors panel, and select User Authentication ➤ Log In User. (You can also apply the server behavior from the Application Insert bar or from the Application Objects submenu of the Insert menu.)

4. The Log In User dialog box has a lot of options, but their meaning should be fairly obvious, at least for the first two sections. Make sure you select the seasonAdmin connection, the users table, and the appropriate username and password columns, using the settings shown alongside.

The third section asks you to specify which pages to send the user to, depending on whether the login succeeds or fails. Between the text fields for the filenames is a check box labeled Go to previous URL (if it exists). This works in conjunction with the Restrict Access to Page server behavior that you will use shortly. If someone tries to access a restricted page without first logging in, the user is redirected to the login page. If you select this option, after a successful login, the user will be taken directly to the page that originally refused access. Unless you always want users to view a specific page when first logging in, this is quite a user-friendly option. What makes it even user-friendlier is the fact that it now works—the version in MX 2004 didn't.

The final section of the dialog box allows you to specify whether access should be restricted simply on the basis of username and password (the default), or whether you also want to specify an access level. The access level must be stored in one of your database columns. For this login page, set Get level from to admin_priv. Click OK to apply the server behavior.

5. A drawback with the Dreamweaver Log In User server behavior is that it has no option for handling encrypted passwords, so you need to make a minor adjustment by hand. Open Code view, and place your cursor immediately to the right of the opening PHP tag on line 2. Press *ENTER/RETURN* to insert a new line, and type the following code:

```
if (isset($_POST['pwd'])) { $_POST['pwd'] = sha1($_POST['pwd']); }
```

This checks whether the form has been submitted, and it uses sha1() to encrypt the password. As before, I have reassigned the value back to $_POST['pwd'] so that Dreamweaver continues to recognize the server behavior, so you can still edit it through the Server Behaviors panel. Although Dreamweaver doesn't object to you placing the line of code here, it will automatically remove it if you ever decide to remove the server behavior.

> It's important to realize that you're not decrypting the version of the password stored in the database. You can't—all the encryption functions are one-way. The way you verify the user's password is by encrypting it again, and comparing the two encrypted versions. This prompts a lot of people to ask what to do when a user forgets his or her password. The answer is that you have to generate a new password. Once users have been issued a new password, you can provide an online form that enables them to log in and then change the password to one of their own choice—in other words, a form that uses an Update Record server behavior.

6. Save login.php and check your code, if necessary, against login.php in site_check/ch10.

Restricting access to individual pages

Now that you have a means of logging in administrators, you can protect sensitive pages in your admin folder. When working with PHP sessions, there is no way of protecting an entire folder, as you might have done with an .htaccess file. Sessions work on a page-by-page basis, so you need to protect each page individually.

Applying the Restrict Access to Page server behavior

I will show you how to apply the server behavior to just one page. Unfortunately, you cannot copy and paste this server behavior in the same way as a recordset. You need to repeat the process for every page that you want to protect. Still, as you'll see, it's very simple.

1. Open menu.php. Click the plus button on the Server Behaviors panel, and select User Authentication ➤ Restrict Access to Page.

2. In the Restrict Access to Page dialog box, select the radio button to restrict access based on Username, password, and access level. Then click the Define button, as shown.

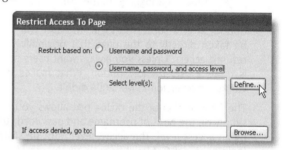

3. The Define Access Levels dialog box that opens lets you specify acceptable values. What may come as a bit of a surprise is that it's not the column name that Dreamweaver is interested in, but the value retrieved from the column. Consequently, it's not admin_priv that you enter here, but y. Enter y in the Name field, click the plus button to register it in the Access levels area, and click OK.

4. Either browse to login.php or type the filename directly in the field labeled If access denied, go to, and click OK.

5. Save menu.php and press *F12/OPT+F12* to view the page in a browser. Instead of menu.php loading in your browser, you should see login.php. You have been denied access, and taken to the login page instead.

6. Enter the username and password that you registered earlier as an administrator, and click Log in. You should now be taken to menu.php. Check your code, if necessary, against menu_02.php in site_check/ch10.

You should apply this server behavior to all pages in the admin folder, *except* loginfail.php and login.php. If you apply it to login.php, nobody will ever be able to log in!

When developing pages that will be part of a restricted area, I find it best to leave the application of this server behavior to the very last. Testing pages becomes an exercise in frustration if you need to be constantly logging in and out.

Logging out users

By default, PHP sessions stay alive until they are actively destroyed or the browser window is closed, whichever comes first. Relying on the second method to end a session is inherently insecure, because you have no way of knowing whether another user has access to the same computer as an authorized person. The Dreamweaver Log Out User server behavior is quick and easy to apply.

Applying the Log Out User server behavior

You can apply the Log Out User server behavior to every page if you like, but the most important one is menu.php.

1. Continue working with menu.php or use menu_02.php from site_check/ch10.
2. The Log Out User server behavior will automatically insert a logout link in your page, so you need to position your cursor at the point you want the link to be created. Place it to the immediate right of the final link on the menu page, and press ENTER/RETURN to create a new paragraph.
3. Click the plus button in the Server Behaviors panel, and select User Authentication ➤ Log Out User.
4. The Log Out User dialog box gives you the option to log out when a link is clicked or when the page loads. In this case, you want the default option, which is to log out when a link is clicked, and to create a new logout link. Browse to login.php or type the filename directly into the field labeled When done, go to. Click OK.
5. Save menu.php and load the page into a browser. Click the Log out link, and you will be taken back to the login page. Type the name of any protected page in the browser address bar, and you will be taken back to the login page until you log in again. You can check your code against menu_03.php in site_check/ch10.

Automating the validation process with MX Kollection 3

After all that hard work, you are probably beginning to wonder if there isn't an easier way of doing it. There is—and it comes in the form of a commercial suite of Dreamweaver extensions called MX Kollection 3. In spite of the MX in the name, version 3 was designed with Dreamweaver 8 in mind, although it's also backwards compatible with both Dreamweaver MX and MX 2004. MX Kollection 3 comes from an enterprising software company called InterAKT (www.interaktonline.com). At the time of this writing, the suite costs $299, so it's almost as expensive as Dreamweaver itself, but if you plan to develop a lot of database-driven sites, it's certainly worth considering. Whereas many extensions offer just one or two enhancements to Dreamweaver, MX Kollection 3 could be said to transform it into a new program. Figure 10-1 shows the dedicated tab that MX Kollection adds to your Insert bar. If you're not using the tabbed interface, MX Kollection appears at the bottom of the Insert bar's category menu.

Figure 10-1. MX Kollection 3 adds an impressive collection of enhanced server behaviors to Dreamweaver.

What distinguishes the MX Kollection server behaviors from the standard Dreamweaver server behaviors is the level of automation and validation that they provide. In addition to enhanced versions of the Dreamweaver Insert Record, Update Record, and Delete Record server behaviors, and User Authentication, the rather oddly named NeXTensio enables you to design a sophisticated content management and website search system. It's impossible for me to describe everything here: the fact that there are nearly 18.5MB of help files should give you an indication of the vast range covered by MX Kollection 3, which supports not only PHP/MySQL, but also PHP/ADODB (a universal database connection method), ASP (VBScript), and ColdFusion. (The help files are in the Windows CHM format only, so clicking the Help button on a Mac takes you to the relevant page of the online help.)

In the next few pages, I will show you how MX Kollection 3 automates the creation of a user registration form and login system, and in the next chapter, you'll use the Looper wizard to display images in a repeated region that goes both across and down the page.

> *There is no obligation to buy MX Kollection 3 to finish the rest of the book. You can download a 30-day trial version from InterAKT at www.interaktonline.com. You can also buy most of the modules separately, although many of them rely on a core module called ImpAKT. At the time this book was being written, ImpAKT was being offered free to anyone buying Dreamweaver 8 through the InterAKT website (check directly with InterAKT for current offers). If you already own ImpAKT, it contains everything you need for the rest of this chapter.*

Installing MX Kollection 3

The trial version of MX Kollection 3 doesn't include the help files, so it's a 4.2MB download, which you can get from www.interaktonline.com/Products/Bundles/MXKollection/Try-Download/. Unzip the files to a folder on your hard disk, and read Readme.txt, as it may contain important information that was not available at the time of writing this book. You should also read License.txt, which stipulates the terms of use for the trial version. You can install the trial on a single workstation, and use it for 30 days for noncommercial purposes. If you want to continue using it after that period, you need to purchase a license code. Although the help files are missing, you can read them online at the InterAKT site.

To install MX Kollection, either double-click on MXKol3-x_x_x.mxp, or open the Extension Manager from Dreamweaver and choose File ➤ Install. Because of the size of the extension suite, it may take some time for the installation to complete. Before you can access the extensions, you need to close Dreamweaver and restart the program. When Dreamweaver restarts, you are greeted by a dialog box listing the trial products you have installed. Unless you have already purchased a license, click the Continue button. This will appear every time you start Dreamweaver.

When the 30-day trial period is up, the Continue button will change to Cancel. If you click Cancel, it doesn't just cancel loading MX Kollection; Dreamweaver itself will close immediately. So if you decide not to buy a license, you need to open the Extension Manager from the Windows Start button (Finder on the Mac), and uninstall MX Kollection. Otherwise, you won't be able to get into Dreamweaver.

If you decide to buy a license, activation is quick and—in my experience, at least—trouble-free. Once activation has been completed, MX Kollection loads just like any other Dreamweaver extension, and the "nag" dialog box goes away.

Defining your MX Kollection site preferences

Some of the more sophisticated features in MX Kollection rely on a common code library, which needs to be created in a folder called includes. This code library also stores site-specific information, so the first step when using MX Kollection on a new site is to define your preferences. All site settings and other administration of the MX Kollection are done through the InterAKT Control Panel. Many of the settings are optional, so I'll just run through the most important ones required for user authentication.

Setting up for user authentication

To keep everything separate from the forms you have already built, I suggest you create a new folder called mxkollection, and save all your files there.

1. Create two PHP pages in the mxkollection folder, and save them as login.php and registeruser.php. Leave both pages blank.

2. Create a subfolder called restricted inside the mxkollection folder. Create two PHP pages called admin.php and member.php, and save them in the restricted folder. Type some text in each page to indicate successful login as an administrator and regular member, respectively.

3. Open the InterAKT Control Panel by selecting the MX Kollection category of the Insert bar, and clicking the InterAKT Control Panel icon (it's on the far right, but the actual position depends on whether you have the full version or the trial one), or by clicking the plus button in the Server Behaviors panel and choosing MX Kollection ➤ Control Panel.

4. The control panel is split into two sections: settings specific to the current site, and global settings for all sites. The icon for each one is accompanied by a brief description, and clicking the Help button in each dialog box takes you directly to the relevant page in the MX Kollection help files or online help.

   If you are building a site in a language other than English, click the Language settings icon. This controls the default warning messages and validation hints that appear in the forms created by MX Kollection. You can currently choose from 10 other Western European languages, including French, German, and Spanish.

5. Click the Login settings icon. This opens a dialog box with a tabbed interface, where you define settings that will apply to all login-related activities on the current site.

6. The first tab, Options, has three settings:

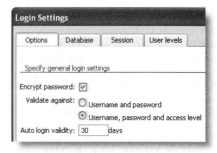

- Encrypt password: Select this to use encrypted passwords, a feature sorely missing in Dreamweaver. This is deselected by default.

- Validate against: This offers the same choices as Dreamweaver—username and password only (default), or username, password, and access level.

- Auto login validity: This allows you to specify how many days a user's login remains valid without the need to log back in. This is done by setting a cookie that records the date and time of the most recent login. So, if you accept the default setting of 30 days, visitors who come at least once a month are automatically logged in each time. Confusingly, 0 is *not* accepted as a valid setting, giving the impression that you can't impose a requirement to log in each time. In fact, automatic login is enabled only if you select it as an option when building the login page later.

Since this is for an administrative area, select Encrypt password, and Username, password and access level. Leave Auto login validity at its default setting. Then click the Database tab.

7. The Database tab contains many settings familiar from the Dreamweaver dialog boxes. After selecting a connection and table, select the appropriate column name for each setting. Most are self-explanatory, but the following require special explanation:

- Active: This allows you to specify a table column in your database that indicates whether a user's account has been activated. Account activation is often a legal requirement if people registering will be added to a mailing list. Since the users table set up in this chapter doesn't have such a column, leave the drop-down menu on the default None.

- Random key: This is for login systems that assign a random string as an extra level of security to identify users. The Login Settings leaves this option grayed out, as it cannot detect a suitable column in the users table.

8. After selecting the appropriate columns in the Database tab, click the Session tab. This displays the session variables that MX Kollection will automatically generate, together with the name of the column from which the value will be drawn. You can add or delete the selection by using the plus and minus buttons. However, the defaults created by MX Kollection are fine. Click the User levels tab.

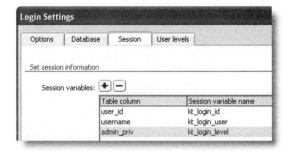

9. The User levels tab is divided into two sections. The top section is where you define global redirect pages. Use the Browse buttons to select the login page, and where users should be redirected after a successful or failed login attempt. Even though you're working in the mxkollection folder, the dialog box requires the full site path to each file because these are settings that will be used globally. So, if you prefer to fill in each field manually, you must include the folder name.

The first two settings, Login page and Default redirect on success, need no explanation. Not all users will have administrative privileges, so I have set Default redirect on success to mxkollection/member.php.

However, Default redirect on fail is used in a slightly different sense from the Dreamweaver server behaviors. This *isn't* where users will be redirected if their login fails, but where they will be sent if they try to access a restricted page without first logging in. So this field also needs to be set to the login page, as shown here.

10. The lower half of the User levels tab is where you define the criteria on which access is granted according to levels stored in the database. There is no need to fill in this section if access is determined solely on the basis of username and password, but in the case of the registration system designed earlier in this chapter, access is also determined according to the value of admin_priv.

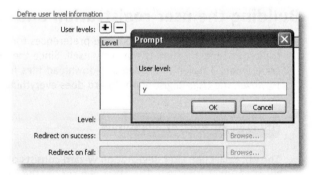

The way you define user levels follows the familiar Dreamweaver pattern of clicking the plus button to add each new definition. Enter y into the User level field, and click OK. This activates the Redirect on success and Redirect on fail fields. Use the Browse buttons to select admin.php and login.php, respectively.

11. Create a user level definition for n, selecting `member.php` and `login.php` for the two redirect fields. The lower half of the User levels tab should look like this:

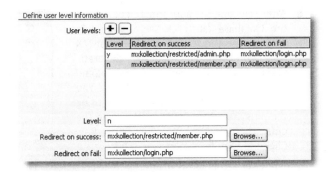

12. Click OK to save the login settings. If you haven't defined a remote server for the site, you will see a warning that you need to do so before you can use the feature, and asking if you want to define one now. Click No. MX Kollection creates the common code library in a folder called `includes` in your site root. When you eventually deploy your site on a remote server, you need to upload the `includes` folder and all its subfolders. Otherwise, your pages won't work.

13. You will be returned to the InterAKT Control Panel. Click on the Update includes folder icon immediately above Login settings. This opens a very useful dialog box that lists the various modules included in MX Kollection, together with the version number on your local computer, and the version on your site. The dialog box also informs you if any includes files haven't been uploaded, and enables you to upload any missing or outdated files in a single operation. Click Cancel to return to the control panel.

14. Click the CSS skins icon, and select the style that you want applied to the online forms created by MX Kollection. You can select None, and attach your own stylesheet later. There's also a tutorial in the help system on how to create your own custom skins. Click OK and then click Close to save your settings.

Building the user registration and login system

Now that you have defined your site preferences for MX Kollection, putting together the user registration and login system is simplicity itself. Since the server behaviors depend on the MX Kollection code library, I haven't included any download files for you to work with in this part of the chapter. However, the User Registration Wizard does everything for you, so you should have no problems.

Creating the registration form

The MX Kollection User Registration Wizard consists of four linked dialog boxes, two of which need little or no input from you. The other two specify the form layout and validation criteria, entirely taking the burden off your shoulders.

1. Open `registeruser.php`, and click the User Registration Wizard button in the MX Kollection category of the Insert bar.

2. Step 1 of the wizard loads the values defined in the previous section. All fields are grayed out, and are just shown for confirmation. Clicking Change Login Settings takes you back to the tabbed dialog box that you completed in the previous section. Since the settings are fine, go straight to Step 2 of the wizard by clicking the Next button.

3. Step 2 is where you define the fields for the registration form. It works in exactly the same way as the Dreamweaver Record Insertion Form Wizard that you used in Chapter 8. Use the arrow buttons on the top right of the Form fields area to rearrange the fields as shown here. The wizard uses the same names as the database columns, so edit each Label field to remove underscores, and rename pwd and admin_priv.

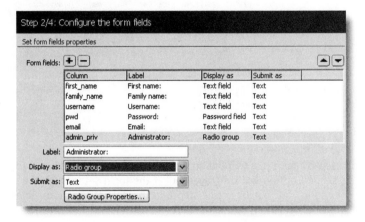

4. When you edit admin_priv, use the Display as drop-down menu to select Radio group. This triggers the display of the Radio Group Properties button.

5. Click Radio Group Properties. This brings up another dialog box that works almost identically to the Dreamweaver equivalent. However, you set the initial state of the radio group inside the dialog box, rather than in the Property inspector. Create the Yes and No radio buttons by using the values shown alongside, and type n in the field labeled Select value equal to. Click OK to save the values.

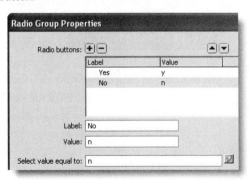

6. Click Next to move to the Step 3 dialog box. This is where the MX Kollection really scores over the standard Dreamweaver wizard by allowing you to set validation tests for each field. Choose each field, and stipulate whether it is a required value and what type of validation format you require.

The Validation format drop-down menu contains 20 options, including credit card types, zip codes, and so on. You can also use a regular expression to check the format of a particular field. Even if you select No validation, the field can still be checked for the minimum and maximum number of characters permitted (leave blank to specify no limit). You can also replace the standard error message with your own custom message for individual fields. Use the settings shown here. Also remember to set the minimum number of characters for username and password. Click Next.

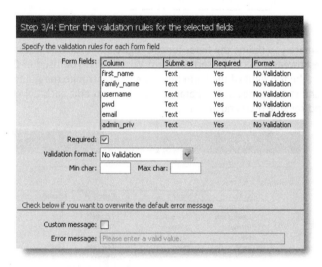

7. The final step contains just two options: to send a welcome email, and to use account activation. This second option will be grayed out if the login settings for the site don't specify an Active column in your database (see step 6 in the previous section). Since you don't need to send an email, deselect the option, and click Finish.

The User Registration Wizard generates all the code, and you have a ready-made user registration form with nothing more to worry about. Before testing it in your browser, you need to build the login page, because that's the page that will be loaded after a user is registered.

Creating the login page

This is a two-step process, but involves hardly any input at all.

1. Open login.php and click the Login Form Wizard button on the Insert bar.

2. The Step 1 dialog box is identical to the first step of the User Registration Wizard—it simply confirms the database connection and table being used. Click Next.

3. Step 2 consists of just two check boxes with the following options:

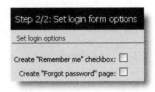

- Create "Remember me" checkbox: If you select this, visitors will be able to log in automatically as long as their most recent visit was within the number of days specified for Auto login validity in the Options tab of Login settings. Leave this unset for a secure site.

- Create "Forgot password" page: If you select this option, the wizard automatically creates a page called `forgot_password.php`, which builds a simple form for users to request a password reminder. Behind the deceptively simple form, however, is the code that automatically looks up the user's password and sends the reminder email. Obviously, this is of value only when passwords are not encrypted. However, you could adapt the form through other MX Kollection server behaviors to send the email to an administrator, who would then generate a new password.

You require neither of these options, so just click Finish. The login page is automatically created.

Logging out users

The MX Kollection Logout User server behavior is applied in the same way as the Dreamweaver one, but you cannot access it from the Insert bar. You need to use the Server Behaviors panel instead.

1. Open `admin.php`. Make sure that your cursor is at the end of any text in the page, and click the plus button in the Server Behaviors panel. Choose MX Kollection ➤ User Login ➤ Logout User.

2. The dialog box gives you the same options as Dreamweaver. Choose the options to create a logout link, and to send the user back to the login page. Click OK.

3. Apply steps 1 and 2 to `member.php`, and save both pages.

Restricting access to an entire folder

As I explained earlier in the chapter, PHP sessions cannot be used to restrict access to an entire folder: the Restrict Access to Page server behavior needs to be applied to each page individually. The MX Kollection not only has an equivalent server behavior (accessed from the Server Behaviors panel menu), but it also has a wonderful timesaver that applies the necessary code to every page in a folder in a single operation. The pages don't even need to be open for the server behavior to insert the code. In fact, if they are open, you will be prompted to close them first.

1. Click the Restrict Access to Folder button in the MX Kollection Insert bar.

2. The dialog box that opens has two tabs. In the Basic tab, click the Browse button to select the folder you want to protect, and navigate to the restricted subfolder. When you click Select, a list of all the files in the selected folder appears in the bottom half of the Basic tab. You cannot deselect any files: This is an all-or-nothing operation.

3. Click the Levels tab and select the Username, password and access level radio button. In the Select level(s) list, hold down the *SHIFT* key to select both y and n. Even though admin.php needs to be restricted to the y level only, you can change the levels for individual pages later.

4. Click OK to apply the code to all the pages in the restricted folder.

5. Open admin.php and double-click Restrict Access to Page (Level) in the Server Behaviors panel. This opens a very similar dialog box to the one in step 3, but which controls only the access level. Confusingly, the tab is labeled Basic, instead of Level. Click in the Select level(s) list to highlight just y, and click OK. The page will now be accessible only to administrators, whereas both administrators and ordinary members will be able to view member.php.

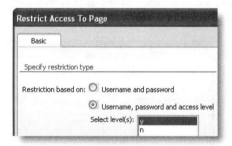

Assessing the pros and cons of MX Kollection

Load registeruser.php into a browser and give the MX Kollection-generated code a test run. Apart from the fact that registering a user automatically takes you to the login page, it works in an identical way to the similar setup you created earlier in the chapter. There's a massive difference, though, in the amount of coding involved. Dreamweaver's basic server behaviors leave validation of user input entirely up to you. MX Kollection speeds up the process exponentially without you ever needing to dive into Code view—a major productivity boost to anyone who doesn't want to learn the mechanics of PHP.

For it to work well, however, you need to plan your project carefully. Using a wizard to build the forms makes it more difficult to change things. Most of the time, you need to start again from scratch, but you can rebuild a complex form in minutes, so it's not such a great burden. This brief demonstration has barely scratched the surface of what MX Kollection is capable of doing. At its core is Transaction Engine 3, which forms the major part of the common library in the `includes` folder. Advanced users can use the PHP classes in the Transaction Engine to build sophisticated applications suited to their own needs.

To my mind, MX Kollection's great strength is also potentially its greatest weakness. By hiding much of the coding in the vast common library, MX Kollection puts great power at your disposal. At the same time, it can make customization difficult. I wanted to change the message that is displayed when a new user is registered. Although I had no difficulty identifying the PHP code that displays the message, I was unable to find where the text of the message is stored. There are nearly 30 folders in the code library, and some pages contain more than 1,500 lines of code. Of course, the whole idea is that you shouldn't need to hunt around in the code library, any more than Dreamweaver expects you to do the same with the even vaster number of files in its `Configuration` folder. MX Kollection is designed to save you the need to handle PHP code directly, and it does it very well. InterAKT has also got a very good reputation for the speed with which it responds to queries. Another advantage is that MX Kollection supports not only PHP, but ASP and ColdFusion. So, if you don't want to get your hands dirty with code, MX Kollection is probably a good investment. The Transaction Engine puts a lot of sophisticated code at your disposal, so it has attractions for advanced users, too. The only way to find out if MX Kollection suits your needs is to give it a good workout during the 30-day trial.

Two approaches to PHP

This chapter has shown you two very different approaches you can take to working with PHP in Dreamweaver: adapting the standard server behaviors and building simple ones of your own, or relying on a sophisticated commercial suite of extensions to handle everything for you automatically. Both approaches involve learning curves of a different sort. It takes time to learn how to code your own PHP, but it also takes time to learn how to get the best out of MX Kollection. And both have different rewards. I enjoy immensely writing my own code, but I know that many others don't.

By this stage, however, you can pride yourself on having learned a lot. In the next chapter, I'll show you how to create a simple blog, which incorporates the fundamental principle of linking from a master page to another containing more detailed information, as well as demonstrating other important aspects of working with a database, such as handling dates and extracting the first couple of sentences from a longer record. You'll also build a simple online photo gallery that uses another part of the MX Kollection, the MX Looper, which is much more versatile than the Dreamweaver Repeated Region server behavior.

Chapter 11

DISPLAYING A BLOG AND PHOTO GALLERY

What this chapter covers:

- Storing and formatting dates in MySQL
- Handling image details in a database
- Displaying a message when no records are found
- Alternating the colors of table rows
- Displaying an extract of a long text item
- Using Live Data view with a URL parameter
- Dynamically generating the code for the dimensions of an image
- Using a commercial extension to loop horizontally

Now that you know how to store, update, and delete records, it's time to turn to the display and formatting of material stored in a database. I've chosen a blog because it helps illustrate such things as working with dates. It also gives me an opportunity to show you how to display a short extract from a longer item and link to the full version on a different page, a technique that can also be used in online catalogs and a wide variety of other applications.

The other main focus of this chapter is how you work with images in a database-driven site. A lot of beginners try to store images in their database, and are then distressed to discover that, instead of a beautiful image, they get a stream of incomprehensible text. You *can* store images in a database, but I'll explain why it's not a good idea, and what to do instead.

Creating the blog back-end

As always, the first step in building a database-driven site is deciding what information needs to be stored in the database. You then need to build four pages for each table:

- An insert form for new records
- A page to list all records, with links to update and delete forms
- An update form
- A delete form

Planning and building the required components

In the interest of keeping things simple, the blog won't have such features as being sortable by categories, a calendar, or a facility for others to post comments. Each record will simply have a title, an article, the date and time it was originally created, the date and time it was most recently updated, and the option to include an image. The images will be kept outside the database in an ordinary folder, so all that needs to be stored in the database is the filename. Each image will need some alternative text, which can also double up as a caption. This means that a single database table with seven columns, plus one set of administration pages, will be sufficient.

Creating the blog table in the database

1. Open phpMyAdmin and select the seasons database. Create a new table called blog with seven columns (fields).

2. Define the columns as follows (see also screenshot at the top of the next page):
   - article_id is the table's primary key.
   - title has been given the maximum length (255) permitted for VARCHAR column types prior to MySQL 5.0. This should be more than enough for a headline.
   - article is where you will write your blogging masterpieces, so it has been given a column type of TEXT.

- updated and created will store the date and time of changes to each article, along with the date and time of its original creation. Although it may seem more logical to put created first, the columns *must* be in this order. I'll explain why shortly. When you select the TIME-STAMP column type, phpMyAdmin adds a check box labeled CURRENT_TIMESTAMP. Leave this unchecked for both columns.

- image will store the name of any image associated with the article. I've used a VARCHAR column type with a length of 50, which should be more than adequate. Because not every article will be associated with an image, the Null drop-down has been set to null.

- caption will store the alt text for the image. Captions and alt text are best kept short on the Web, so I've used a VARCHAR column with a length of 50, and set the Null drop-down to null.

Primary key

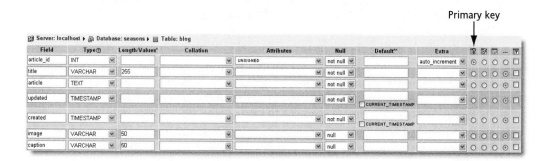

3. Click Save when you have finished. The table structure should look like this:

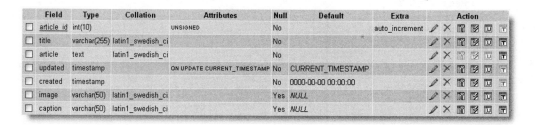

Note the Attributes and Default values for the updated field. (If you are using an old version of phpMyAdmin or MySQL prior to the 4.1 series, the values will be empty. However, the behavior of the updated column will be the same.) These indicate a useful feature of MySQL TIMESTAMP columns. The first TIMESTAMP column in a table is automatically updated to the current date and time whenever changes are made to a record. However, subsequent TIMESTAMP columns have to be set specifically.

What this means is that you can set the value of created when you first insert a record into the table, and it will never change. The updated column, on the other hand, will always change whenever the record is updated. What's more, because they're TIMESTAMP columns, MySQL automatically inserts the date and time in the correct format without any need for user input.

Creating an insert form for new blog entries

Because of the emphasis on simplicity, the insert and update forms won't include any validation. The quickest way to build the forms is with the Dreamweaver wizards.

1. Create a new PHP page in the admin folder. Save it as blog_insert.php, and attach the admin.css stylesheet. Give the page a suitable title and heading.

2. Make sure that your cursor is outside the closing </h1> tag, and click the Record Insertion Form Wizard icon on the Application Insert bar. Set the Connection field to seasonAdmin, and the Table field to blog.

3. Use the minus button to remove article_id and updated from the Form fields area.

4. Set the Display as setting for article to Text area.

5. Set the Display as setting for created to Hidden field, and type NOW() in the Default value field. Use the down arrow button to move created to the bottom of the list. NOW() is a MySQL function that generates a current date and time. Dreamweaver doesn't have a method of passing MySQL functions like this, so you need to tweak the server behavior code later.

6. Set the Display as setting for image to Menu. This reveals a button labeled Menu Properties. Click the button, and enter Select image in the Label field. Leave the other fields blank, and click OK.

7. Leave the settings for caption unchanged, check that the Record Insertion Form dialog box settings are like those in the screenshot, and click OK.

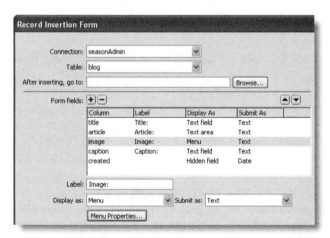

8. After Dreamweaver has built the insert form, select the title text field, and choose widebox from the Class drop-down menu in the Property inspector. This is a style in admin.css that makes the text field the same width as the text area beneath it. Set Max Chars to 255 to avoid entering text that exceeds the maximum length for the title column.

9. Select the caption text field and apply the widebox class. Set Max Chars to 50.

10. Highlight the form in the Tag selector, and press your right arrow key once to move the cursor outside the form. Add two text links: one to the admin menu (menu.php), and the other to list_blog.php. This second page will display a list of all blog entries. If necessary, create list_blog.php as a blank page. Your page should now look like this.

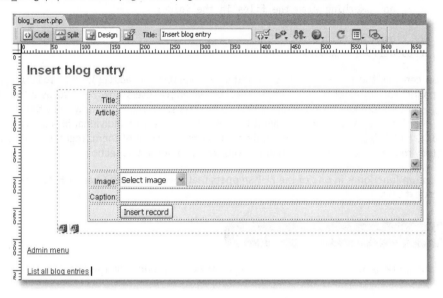

11. The page still needs the code for the image drop-down menu, which will be added in the next section. Check your code so far against blog_insert_01.php in site_check/ch11.

Building a list of images in a folder

One of the main reasons for using a server-side language like PHP is to reduce the amount of effort it takes to create a website. In Chapter 9, you learned how to populate a drop-down menu from a database. It's not only a time-saver; a dynamically populated menu is always up to date. However, you don't always need to store information in a database for PHP to be able to interact with it. PHP has an extensive suite of built-in functions that allow you to work directly with your computer's file system (www.php.net/manual/en/ref.filesystem.php).

I have written a custom function that makes use of several of these built-in functions to open an images folder, build an array of all image files, close the folder, and then use the array to populate a drop-down menu. Although I don't intend to explain all the details of this rather complex function, the basic way most PHP file system functions work is that you create a variable known as a file handler to open the file or folder, and then pass the file handler as the argument to the functions that interact directly with the file or folder. To traverse the contents of a folder called images_blog, for instance, this is the sequence of events:

```
// create a file handler
$fileHandler = opendir('path_to_folder/images_blog/');
// use a while loop to go through the folder
while (readdir($fileHandler)) {
  // do something with the files in the folder
  }
// close the folder
closedir($fileHandler);
```

As you can see, the function names are intuitive: opendir(), readdir(), and closedir(), with dir being short for "directory," which most Mac and Windows users now refer to as a "folder." (Such changes in terminology are aimed at making computers seem more "friendly," but they often end up simply confusing people.) The equivalent functions that work with individual files are called fopen(), fread(), and fclose(). You will find links to descriptions of all of them, together with examples of how they're used in the PHP manual at the URL given earlier in this section.

The custom function is in one of the PHP snippets that you installed in Chapter 6, so most of the work in this next section is done for you.

Dynamically populating the image menu

Continue working with the same file as in the previous section, or use blog_insert_01.php from site_check/ch11.

1. Select the menu object in Design view to locate the underlying code, and switch to Code view. Insert a call to the custom function like this (new code is shown in bold):

```
<td><select name="image">
  <option value="">Select picture</option>
  <?php buildImageList('../images_blog/'); ?>
</select></td>
```

The buildImageList() function can take up to two arguments, but only the first one is required—the path to the folder from which you want to build the list. I have given you the correct relative path to images_blog, but if you're ever in doubt about the path to a folder, right-click/CTRL-click in Code view and select Code Hint Tools ➤ URL Browser from the context

menu. Click Browse and navigate to the target folder. The correct relative path appears in the URL field of the Select File dialog box. Highlight the contents of the field, and copy (CTRL+C/⌘+C) it to your clipboard. Click Cancel to close the dialog box, and then paste (CTRL+V/⌘+V) the URL into your script.

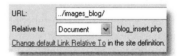

2. Unless you put it in an external file, it doesn't matter where you define a PHP function, so scroll down to the bottom of the page, create a pair of PHP tags after the closing </html> tag, and place your cursor between them. Open the Snippets panel, and double-click Build image list in the PHP-DW8 folder. (Alternatively, you can right-click/*CTRL*-click the snippet name, and select Insert from the context menu.) It will insert the following code:

```php
function buildImageList($imageFolder, $recordset=NULL) {
// Check whether image folder has trailing slash, add if needed
$imageFolder = strrpos($imageFolder,'/') == strlen($imageFolder-1)
➥ ? $imageFolder : "$imageFolder/";
// Execute code if images folder can be opened, or fail silently
if ($theFolder = @opendir($imageFolder)) {
  // Create an array of image types
  $imageTypes = array('jpg','jpeg','gif','png');
  // Traverse images folder, and add filename to $img array if an image
  while (($imageFile = readdir($theFolder)) !== false) {
    $fileInfo = pathinfo($imageFile);
    if (in_array($fileInfo['extension'],$imageTypes)) {
      $img[] = $imageFile;
      }
    }
  // Close the stream from the images folder
  closedir($theFolder);
  // Check the $img array is not empty
  if ($img) {
    // Sort in natural, case-insensitive order, and populate menu
    natcasesort($img);
    foreach ($img as $image) {
      echo "<option value='$image'";
      // Set selected image if recordset details supplied
      if ($recordset != NULL && $recordset == $image) {
        echo  ' selected="selected"';
        }
      echo ">$image</option>\n";
      }
    }
  }
}
```

The inline comments explain what each stage of the function does, but I don't expect most readers to delve into the details. If you *are* interested, visit the PHP online documentation at www.php.net/manual/en and type the names of the functions I've used into the search field at the top of the page.

The second (optional) argument is needed only when you want one of the images to be selected when the menu is displayed. I'll explain how to set the second argument when building the update page.

383

> *If you decide to put the definition in an external file, the include command must come before you call the function.*

3. Finally, you need to tweak the server behavior code to pass the MySQL NOW() function to the SQL query. Scroll up until you find this section of code:

```
33  if ((isset($_POST["MM_insert"])) && ($_POST["MM_insert"] == "form1")) {
34    $insertSQL = sprintf("INSERT INTO blog (title, article, image, caption, created) VALUES (%s,
    %s, %s, %s, %s)",
35                        GetSQLValueString($_POST['title'], "text"),
36                        GetSQLValueString($_POST['article'], "text"),
37                        GetSQLValueString($_POST['image'], "text"),
38                        GetSQLValueString($_POST['caption'], "text"),
39                        GetSQLValueString($_POST['created'], "date"));
```

4. GetSQLValueString() is a Dreamweaver custom function that prepares user input for insertion into a SQL query with all quotes properly escaped. It's not capable of handling the NOW() function. Amend the final line (shown on line 39 of the preceding screenshot) so that just the POST variable, the closing parenthesis, and the semicolon are left remaining. It should look like this:

```
$_POST['created']);
```

This change may cause Dreamweaver to display a warning message about a JavaScript error. Just click OK. Both the page and Dreamweaver remain fully functional. Check your code against blog_insert_02.php in site_check/ch11.

> *Dreamweaver frequently runs JavaScript in the background to populate the various panels and the Property inspector, and a missing piece of code usually triggers an error. If you close and reopen blog_insert.php, you will see a detailed message telling you where the error occurred. This page is now complete, so you can close it to avoid being disturbed by error messages.*

Displaying a message when no records are found

Before you test the insert record page, let's build list_blog.php, as this presents an opportunity to use the Show Region server behavior. As the name suggests, this server behavior selectively shows a section of your page, depending on the results of a recordset. If the recordset produces no results, you can hide the section where the results would normally be displayed and show an alternative message instead. The process involves two stages:

1. Apply a Show Region server behavior to the section of the page where the results are normally displayed.

2. Create alternative content that you want to display if the recordset is empty, and apply the opposite Show Region server behavior to the alternative content.

Before you can do that, you need to build the table to display the recordset results in the normal way.

Displaying a list of blog entries

1. If you haven't already created a blank page for list_blog.php, do so now. Also create two blank pages for blog_update.php and blog_delete.php. Save all three pages in the admin folder.

2. Give list_blog.php a suitable title and heading, and attach the admin.css stylesheet.

3. Make sure the cursor is outside the closing </h1> tag of the heading, and insert a table. In the Table dialog box, set Rows to 2, Columns to 6, and Table width to 750 pixels. Leave Border thickness, Cell padding, and Cell spacing blank, and select Top for the Header setting. Click OK.

4. Select the entire table, and set Table Id in the Property inspector to striped. This will enable it to pick up the style rules in admin.css that set padding on the table cells. Using CSS instead of the cellpadding attribute enables you to set different amounts of padding on each side of a table cell, rather than a single value all round.

5. Create a recordset. You should know how to do this by now, so I'll just give the basic details. Use the simple Recordset dialog box with the following settings:

- Name: getArticles
- Connection: seasonAdmin
- Table: blog
- Columns: Selected (highlight article_id, title, created, image, and caption)
- Filter: None
- Sort: created Descending

> *If you installed MX Kollection in the previous chapter, you will notice a new button labeled* QuB3 *in the Recordset dialog box. This is for the MX Kollection advanced SQL query builder. Since it's not a standard part of Dreamweaver, it's not covered in this book. Read the MX Kollection help files for an explanation of how to use it.*

6. Expand Recordset (getArticles) in the Bindings panel, and drag dynamic text placeholders for created, title, image, and caption into the first four cells of the table's second row. Create EDIT and DELETE links in the final two cells in exactly the same way as you have done since Chapter 8 (refer to the "Creating a list of all records" section in that chapter if you need to refresh your memory). The EDIT link should point to blog_update.php, and the DELETE link to blog_delete.php. Both links should use a parameter named article_id, which draws its value from article_id in the getArticles recordset. Insert appropriate column headings in the first four cells of the top row. Your page should now look like this:

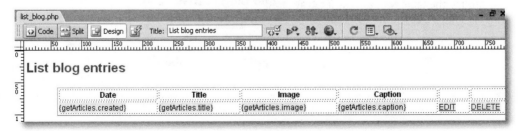

385

7. Highlight the second table row, and apply a Repeat Region server behavior (this was covered in the same section of Chapter 8). Select the option to show all records.

8. Save `list_blog.php`, and press *F12/Oᴘᴛ+F12* to view the page in a browser. As long as you have no records in the blog table, you should see something like this:

If you hover your mouse pointer over either of the links, you will see that the query string contains no value for the `article_id` parameter. For an administration page that the public will never see, this is perhaps acceptable, but it would give a very bad impression in the front-end of a dynamic website. The answer lies in using the Show Region server behavior, which I'll show you how to apply in the next section. If you want to check your code so far, compare it with `list_blog_01.php` in `site_check/ch11`.

Applying the Show Region server behavior

Continue working with the same file as in the previous section, or use `list_blog_01.php` from `site_check/ch11`.

1. Position your cursor anywhere inside the table, and click the <table#striped> tag in the Tag selector to select the whole table.

2. Click the plus button in the Server Behaviors panel, and select Show Region ➤ Show If Recordset Is Not Empty. Alternatively, you can select the same options by clicking the Show Region icon on the Application Insert bar, or from the Application Objects submenu of the Insert menu.

3. The dialog box that opens couldn't be simpler. All you need to do is select the correct recordset. Since getArticles is the only recordset on the page, just click OK.

4. Dreamweaver puts a gray border around the table with a Show If tab at the top left, as shown alongside.

5. Save the page, and view it in a browser. All you should see is the page heading.

6. Since you want to display a message indicating that no records have been found, it doesn't matter whether you place it above or below the table. Either the table will be shown and the message hidden, or the other way round. Click in a blank area of the Document window to make sure nothing is selected, and then insert a new paragraph containing the words "No records found." To make the message stand out, apply the warning class to the paragraph.

7. Highlight the paragraph by clicking the <p.warning> tag in the Tag selector. Then apply a Show Region server behavior. This time choose Show If Recordset Is Empty. Again, the dialog box simply requires you to select the recordset. Since there is only one on the page, just click OK. Your page should now look like this:

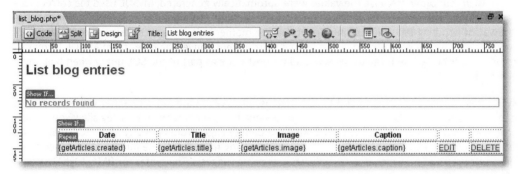

8. Save list_blog.php, and view it in a browser. You should now see the No records found message. You can check your code against list_blog_02.php in site_check/ch11.

As soon as you insert the first record in the blog table, list_blog.php will hide the No records found message and start displaying the date and time of creation, the title, and the name of any image linked with a blog entry.

A quick way to load some blog entries To save you the effort of typing out genuine masterpieces of blog literature, open a temporary page in Dreamweaver and use the Lorem and More extension to create about 15 paragraphs of corporate mumbo-jumbo, which you can cut and paste into the Article field of blog_insert.php to insert three or four records. Display the list of blog entries by clicking the link at the bottom of blog_insert.php. You should see something like Figure 11-1.

http://localhost/phpdw/admin/list_blog.php

List blog entries

Date	Title	Image	Caption		
2005-09-29 17:04:44	More corporate baloney...			EDIT	DELETE
2005-09-27 17:13:46	Shocked faces outside Oxford theatre	sheldonian.jpg	Sculpture outside Sheldonian Theatre, Oxford	EDIT	DELETE
2005-09-27 17:11:46	Never mind Big Brother... Eye keeps watch on parliament	eye.jpg	Big Ben seen through London Eye	EDIT	DELETE
2005-09-27 17:10:29	Straight from the horse's mouth	horse.jpg	Horse's head	EDIT	DELETE

Figure 11-1. The value of the MySQL TIMESTAMP column isn't in a very friendly format.

387

Although the page is reasonably usable, the format of the date and time is rather inelegant. In fact, if your hosting company is still using MySQL 3.23 or 4.0, the date and time in the first line would look like this: 20050929170444. The numbers are the same, but with no punctuation the date and time becomes extremely difficult to read. Definitely a case for treatment . . .

Formatting dates and time in MySQL

Figure 11-1 shows the TIMESTAMP format used by MySQL since the release of the 4.1 series. The date portion at the beginning follows the only pattern that MySQL accepts for dates—year, month, and day of month *in that order*. Because the values were automatically generated, MySQL used the correct format. I'll come back at the end of the chapter, in the section "Storing dates in MySQL," to discuss the best way of handling dates in user input, but, for the moment, your main concern is how to display a date that has already been stored in this format. Fortunately, converting dates from MySQL format to a more user-friendly one is relatively easy, and it's best done as part of the SQL query when building a recordset.

MySQL has a wide range of date and time functions, all of which are listed together with examples at http://dev.mysql.com/doc/refman/5.0/en/date-and-time-functions.html. They allow you to perform many useful calculations, such as working out people's ages from their birthdates, calculating the difference between two dates, and adding to or subtracting from dates. The function that concerns us here is DATE_FORMAT(), which does exactly what its name suggests. The syntax for DATE_FORMAT() is as follows:

    DATE_FORMAT(*date, format*)

Normally, *date* is the name of the table column that you want to format, and *format* is either a string or another function that tells MySQL which format to use. The DATE_FORMAT() function works in a very similar way to the PHP date() function, in that you build the format string from specifiers. Table 11-1 lists those most commonly used.

Table 11-1. Frequently used MySQL date format specifiers

Period	Specifier	Description	Example
Year	%Y	Four-digit format	2005
	%y	Two-digit format	05
Month	%M	Full name	January, September
	%b	Abbreviated name, 3 letters	Jan, Sep
	%m	Number, with leading zero	01, 09
	%c	Number, no leading zero	1, 9
Day of month	%d	With leading zero	01, 25
	%e	No leading zero	1, 25

Period	Specifier	Description	Example
	%D	With English text suffix	1st, 25th
Weekday name	%W	Full text	Monday, Thursday
	%a	Abbreviated name, 3 letters	Mon, Thu
Hour	%H	24-hour clock, with leading zero	01, 23
	%k	24-hour clock, no leading zero	1, 23
	%h	12-hour clock, with leading zero	01, 11
	%l (lowercase L)	12-hour clock, no leading zero	1, 11
Minute	%i	With leading zero	05, 25
Second	%S	With leading zero	08, 45
AM/PM	%p		

The specifiers can be combined with ordinary text or punctuation in the format string. As always, when using a function in a SQL query, assign the result to an alias using the AS keyword, in the same way as you did with CONCAT() in Chapter 9. Referring to Table 11-1, you can now format the date in the created column in a variety of ways. To present the date in a common U.S. style and retain the name of the original column, use the following:

```
DATE_FORMAT(created, '%c/%e/%Y') AS created
```

To format the same date in European style, reverse the first two specifiers like this:

```
DATE_FORMAT(created, '%e/%c/%Y') AS created
```

Keeping all these specifiers in your head is a problem, so MySQL 4.1 introduced a new function that creates some standard formats using easy-to-remember strings. It's called GET_FORMAT(), and it takes two arguments: the type of date output that you want and the format. The first argument can be one of three values, DATE, TIME, or DATETIME, which produce the date or time on its own, or both together. The two most useful formats are 'USA' and 'EUR'. You use GET_FORMAT() like this:

```
DATE_FORMAT(date, GET_FORMAT(type, format))
```

Table 11-2 shows how different combinations of GET_FORMAT() render the TIMESTAMP value in the first blog entry in Figure 11-1 (2005-09-29 17:04:44).

Table 11-2. The same date and time value rendered in different ways by GET_FORMAT()

Arguments	Output
GET_FORMAT(DATE, 'USA')	09.29.2005
GET_FORMAT(DATE, 'EUR')	29.09.2005
GET_FORMAT(TIME, 'USA')	05:04:44 PM
GET_FORMAT(TIME, 'EUR')	17:04:44
GET_FORMAT(DATETIME, 'USA')	2005-09-29 17.04.44
GET_FORMAT(DATETIME, 'EUR')	2005-09-29 17.04.44

These formats are fixed, so if you don't like periods instead of slashes, you need to build your own formats with the specifiers listed in Table 11-1, as you'll also need to do if your server uses a version of MySQL earlier than 4.1.

You can now format the TIMESTAMP value in list_blog.php in a way that's easier to read.

Formatting the date in the blog entry list

Continue working with the same file as in the "Applying the Show Region server behavior" section, or use list_blog_02.php from site_check/ch11.

1. In the Server Behaviors panel, double-click Recordset (getArticles). When the Recordset dialog box opens, click the Advanced button.

2. The first line of the SQL query looks like this:

   ```
   SELECT article_id, title, created, image, caption
   ```

3. For a U.S.-style date, amend it like this:

   ```
   SELECT article_id, title, DATE_FORMAT(created, '%b %e, %Y') AS created,
   ➥ image, caption
   ```

   Reverse the order of the first two specifiers for a European-style date.

4. Click the Test button to make sure that everything is working correctly. You should still have a column called created, but the dates will now be formatted as shown here:

If Dreamweaver displays a MySQL error message instead, check that you have not left any space between DATE_FORMAT and the opening parenthesis of the function. Although some computer languages allow you to leave a space, MySQL doesn't. Also make sure that the format string is enclosed in matching quotes. Although I have used single quotes, double quotes are equally acceptable.

5. Assuming that the test is successful, click OK to close the test panel and then to close the Recordset dialog box.

6. Save list_blog.php, and view it in a browser. The dates should now be formatted in a more user-friendly way. You can check your code against list_blog_03.php in site_check/ch11.

Creating striped table rows

Viewing a long list of similar items on a computer screen can be tiring on the eyes, so it's often useful to give alternate rows a subtle background color. This is very easy to do with a CSS style rule, but it can be a nightmare to maintain on a static site. You need to apply the CSS class to every alternate row, and if you add another row in the middle of the table at a later date, everything has to be restyled. With a dynamically generated table, that's no problem.

The way that you do it relies on a little bit of simple math and the way that PHP treats 1 and 0. In Chapter 5, I introduced you to the modulo operator (%), which produces the remainder of a division. If you divide any number by 2, the remainder will always be either 1 or 0. I also explained in Chapter 5 that PHP treats 0 as false, but 1 is treated as true. So, if you create a variable as a counter, and increment it by 1 each time a new table row is added, you can use modulo to divide the variable by 2. This will produce a result of 1 (true) or 0 (false) every alternate row, which can be used as the test of an if statement that inserts the CSS class for the different background. Let's try it out on list_blog.php.

Using modulo to create stripes in alternate rows

Continue working with the same file, or use list_blog_03.php from site_check/ch11.

1. Switch to Code view, and locate the following section of code:

```
30    </tr>
31    <?php do { ?>
32      <tr>
33        <td><?php echo $row_getArticles['created']; ?></td>
```

The code shown on line 31 is the start of the do . . . while loop that iterates through the getArticles recordset to display the list of blog entries. (The do . . . while loop was explained in the "Using loops to handle repetitive tasks" section of Chapter 6.)

2. Amend the code like this (new code is shown in bold type):

```
</tr>
<?php $counter = 0; // initialize counter outside loop ?>
<?php do { ?>
  <tr <?php if ($counter++ % 2) {echo 'class="hilite"';} ?>>
    <td><?php echo $row_getArticles['created']; ?></td>
```

391

It involves just two short blocks of PHP code to perform the following tasks:

- Initialize the counter outside the loop

- Increment the counter by 1 inside the loop, and use modulo to create a Boolean (true/false) test to insert the hilite class in every alternate row

As you may remember from Chapter 5, the increment operator (++) performs the current calculation and then adds 1 to the variable. So, the first time through the loop $counter will be 0. When divided by 2, the remainder will be 0. Since this equates to false, the hilite class won't be inserted into the <tr> tag. However, $counter is incremented by 1, so the next time through the loop, the calculation will attempt to divide 1 by 2, producing a remainder of 1, which equates to true. The third time through the loop, $counter will be 2, producing a remainder of 0, and so on until the loop comes to an end.

When hand-coding, I would normally combine the initialization of the counter with the do PHP block. However, I have used separate blocks here to avoid breaking Dreamweaver's Repeat Region server behavior code.

3. Save list_blog.php, and view it in a browser. Voilà, stripes. You can check your code against list_blog_04.php in site_check/ch11.

The code inserted in step 2 creates a class that affects only even-numbered rows. Some developers use slightly more complex code to insert a different class in odd-numbered rows, too. This isn't necessary. By utilizing the cascade in your CSS, you can set a default background color for the table, and override it with the hilite class like this:

```
#striped tr {background-color: #EEE;}
#striped tr.hilite {background-color: #E8F2F8;}
```

These rules will produce alternate pale gray and pale blue stripes in a table with an ID called striped. If you want to use the same effect in more than one table, change striped from an ID to a class.

Finishing the back-end

All that remains for the back-end of the blog is to build the update and delete forms. These will be very simple to build, again using the Dreamweaver wizards. The only point that requires special attention is in the update form. The drop-down menu that lists the images will need to display the correct filename. That's easily handled with the buildImageList() function.

Creating the update page

1. Open `blog_update.php`, the blank page that you created earlier in the chapter. Attach the `admin.css` stylesheet, and give the page a suitable title and heading.

2. You need a recordset called getArticle to retrieve the details of the blog entry that you are going to update. Use the simple Recordset dialog box with the settings shown in the screenshot alongside. Click OK to create the recordset.

3. Make sure that your cursor is to the right of the closing `</h1>` tag of the heading, and select Record Update Form Wizard from the Application Insert bar.

4. In the Record Update Form dialog box, set Connection to seasonAdmin and Table to update to blog. Dreamweaver should automatically set the correct values for Select record from and Unique key column.

5. Set the value of the After updating go to field to list_blog.php.

6. In the Form fields area, use the minus button to remove article_id, updated, and created. MySQL will automatically insert a new date and time value in the updated column, and you don't want to change the value of the created column.

7. Change the value of Display as for article to Text area.

8. Change the value of Display as for image to Menu. Click the Menu Properties button, and set the value of Label to No picture. Leave the other fields as they are, and click OK.

9. Check that the settings in the Record Update Form dialog box look like this, and click OK to create the form.

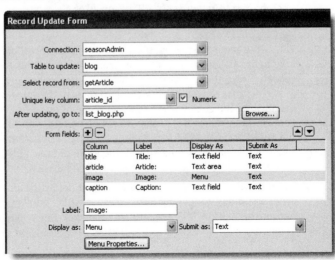

393

10. Highlight the title text field, and select widebox from the Class drop-down menu in the Property inspector. Set Max Chars to 255. Apply the same class to the caption text field, and set Max Chars to 50. These are the same values as in the insert form.

11. Select the entire form, and press your right arrow key once to move your cursor outside the closing </form> tag. Create two new paragraphs containing text links back to menu.php and list_blog.php. Your page should now look like this:

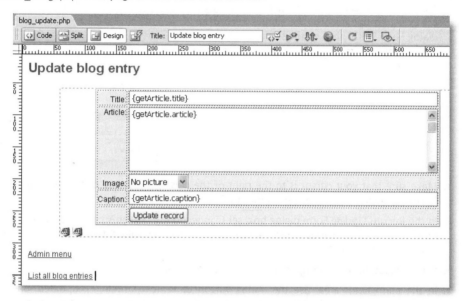

12. Select the image menu object to highlight the underlying code, and switch to Code view. Amend the menu code like this:

```
<td><select name="image'>
  <option value="">No picture</option>
  <?php buildImageList('../images_blog/', $row_getArticle['image']); ?>
</select></td>
```

This is the same function you used in the insert form, but this time I have passed it a second argument. As you may remember from the "Adapting the Sticky Text Field server behavior" section in the previous chapter, Dreamweaver uses the naming convention $row_*RecordsetName*['*FieldName*'] to refer to the value of each column or field in a recordset result. Since the getArticle recordset contains only one result, $row_getArticle['image'] will contain the name of the image (if any) associated with the record you are about to update. As the buildImageList() function loops through the names of all the images in the images_blog folder, it compares each name with the value of $row_getArticle['image']. If there is a match, it inserts selected="selected" into the <option> tag.

13. Scroll down to the bottom of the page. Just below the closing </html> tag, you will see a short PHP code block containing mysql_free_result($getArticle);. Insert one or two blank lines before the closing PHP tag, and double-click Build image list in the PHP-DW8 folder of the Snippets panel to insert the buildImageList() function definition.

14. Save `blog_update.php`, and test it by loading `list_blog.php` into a browser and selecting one of the UPDATE links. You can check your code against `blog_update.php` in `site_check/ch11`. Keep the page open in the Document window, as you will need it again during the next section.

Creating the delete page

1. Open `blog_delete.php`, the blank page that you created earlier in the chapter. Attach the `admin.css` stylesheet, and give the page a suitable title and heading.

2. Switch to `blog_update.php`, and highlight Recordset (getArticle) in the Server Behaviors panel. Right-click/*CTRL*-click and select Copy from the context menu.

3. Switch back to `blog_delete.php`, right-click/*CTRL*-click in the Server Behaviors panel, and select Paste to transfer a copy of the recordset into the page. (Alternatively, choose Edit ➤ Paste.) The date in the created column won't be formatted, but it probably doesn't matter since this page is just to confirm the deletion of a record.

However, if you want the date in a more readable format, double-click the recordset listing in the Server Behaviors panel, and edit the SQL query. Use the advanced Recordset dialog box. The first line of the query will look like this:

```
SELECT *
```

Change it to this:

```
SELECT article_id, title, DATE_FORMAT(created, '%b %e, %Y') AS created
```

4. Insert a paragraph warning that the deletion cannot be undone, and then insert a form named delRecord.

5. Inside the form, drag dynamic content placeholders for created and title from the Bindings panel. Insert a hidden field called article_id, and click the lightning bolt icon alongside the Value field in the Property inspector to bind it to `article_id` from the getArticle recordset. Make sure that Method is set to POST. You have done this several times before, so refer back to the previous chapter to refresh your memory if you have forgotten how.

6. Insert a submit button into the form, name it delete in the Property inspector, and set its Value to Confirm deletion.

7. Add text links at the foot of the page to `menu.php` and `list_blog.php`. Your page should now look similar to this:

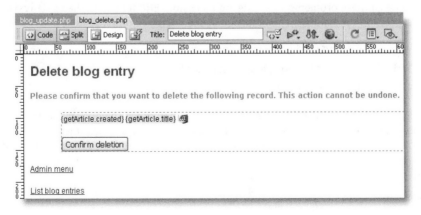

8. Apply a Delete Record server behavior using the settings shown here:

9. Save the page and test it by using one of the DELETE links in list_blog.php. You can check your code against blog_delete.php in site_check/ch11.

Displaying the blog

Some blogs are of the "let it all hang out" type, where anything and everything gets put into one page. Others are more selective, giving you just a taste of each item, and inviting you to click a link to read individual entries in full. I'm going to take the second approach, because it gives me the opportunity to show you some nice little techniques, such as automatically extracting a specified number of sentences from a longer item, and returning the visitor to the correct page after reading the full article. These techniques would work equally well in a number of other situations, so they are worth getting to know.

Extracting the first section of a long item

One of PHP's great strengths is its ability to manipulate text. The PHP online documentation lists nearly a hundred string manipulation functions (www.php.net/manual/en/ref.strings.php). As impressive as this is, PHP has no concept of what constitutes a word or a sentence. It's very easy to look for the hundredth space or the third period to try to extract the first hundred words or three sentences. However, this isn't really very satisfactory. Simply counting the number of words means you will almost always break off mid-sentence; and counting periods means you ignore all sentences that end with an exclamation mark or question mark. You also run the risk of breaking a sentence on a decimal point, or of cutting off a closing quote after a period.

To overcome all these problems, I have devised a custom PHP function called getFirst() that uses a regular expression to identify the punctuation at the end of a normal sentence:

- A period, question mark, or exclamation mark
- Optionally followed by a single or double quote
- Followed by one or more spaces

The getFirst() function takes two arguments: the text from which you want to extract the first section, and the number of sentences you want to extract. The second argument is optional, and if it's not supplied, the function extracts the first two sentences. The function definition is in a snippet called

Extract first sentences, which you installed in the PHP-DW8 folder of the Snippets panel in Chapter 6. The code looks like this:

```php
function getFirst($text, $number=2) {
    // regular expression to find typical sentence endings
    $pattern = '/([.?!]["\']?)\s/';
    // use regex to insert break indicator
    $text = preg_replace($pattern, '$1bRE@kH3re', $text);
    // use break indicator to create array of sentences
    $sentences = explode('bRE@kH3re', $text);
    // check relative length of array and requested number
    $howMany = count($sentences);
    $number = $howMany >= $number ? $number : $howMany;
    // rebuild extract and return as single string
    $remainder = array_splice($sentences, $number);
    $result = array();
    $result[0] = implode(' ', $sentences);
    $result[1] = empty($remainder) ? false : true;
    return $result;
}
```

The inline comments explain how the function works. You don't need to understand the fine detail, but the fifth line uses preg_replace() to insert bRE@kH3re at the end of each sentence. I chose this as a combination of characters so unlikely to occur in normal text that it can be used to break the text into an array. What you do need to know is that the function returns an array containing two elements: the extracted sentences, and a Boolean variable indicating whether there's anything more following the extract. You can use the second element to create a link to a page containing the full text. Let's put it into action.

Building the main blog page

Use the version of blog.php that you created in Chapters 4 and 5. Alternatively, use blog_01.php from site_check/ch11.

1. Save a copy of blog.php as blog_detail.php. Close blog_detail.php for the time being, and work with blog.php.

2. Create a recordset using the advanced Recordset dialog box. Enter getArticles in the Name field.

3. This is a public page, so set Connection to seasonQuery, rather than seasonAdmin. For public pages, always use the account with the minimum privileges necessary for the page to work correctly.

4. Build the following query in the SQL field:

```sql
SELECT blog.article_id, blog.title, blog.article,
DATE_FORMAT(blog.created, '%b %e, %Y') AS theDate
FROM blog
ORDER BY blog.created DESC
```

This time, I have used theDate as the alias for the created column. This is because I plan to use this as the basis for another recordset later, when I'll need the unformatted value of created in addition to the formatted one. Test the query, and then click OK to save the recordset.

5. Click inside the placeholder text for the maincontent <div> in Design view, and select Heading 2 from the Format drop-down menu in the Property inspector. Highlight the placeholder text, and drag title from the recordset in the Bindings panel to replace it.

6. Click your cursor to the right of the dynamic content placeholder, and press ENTER/RETURN to insert a new paragraph. Drag theDate from the recordset in the Bindings panel into the new paragraph. Press your right arrow key once to move the cursor to the right of the dynamic content placeholder for theDate. Insert a colon and a space. Then drag article from the Bindings panel, and place it alongside theDate.

7. Create a space after the dynamic content placeholder for article, and type More.

8. Select the dynamic content placeholder for theDate, together with the colon, and click the Bold button in the Property inspector. The maincontent <div> should now look like this in Design view.

9. You need to turn More into a link, so double-click to select it, and click the Browse for File icon to the right of the Link field in the Property inspector. Select blog_detail.php in the Select File dialog box, and click the Parameters button. In the Parameters dialog box, set the Name and Value fields to article_id, drawing the setting for Value from the recordset in the same way as you have done many times before when creating EDIT and DELETE links in the administration pages. Close all the dialog boxes to return to Design view.

10. Open Split view, and select the content of the maincontent <div> from the opening <h2> tag to the closing </p> tag, as shown in the following screenshot:

```
29    <h2><?php echo $row_getArticles['title']; ?></h2>
30    <p><strong><?php echo $row_getArticles['theDate']; ?>:</strong> <?php echo $row_getArticles[
      'article']; ?> <a href="blog_detail.php?article_id=<?php echo $row_getArticles['article_id']; ?>"
      >More</a> </p>
```

Make sure the correct section is highlighted, because it will be turned into a repeated region. Missing part of the opening or closing tag will turn your page into a mess.

11. Apply a Repeat Region server behavior. Normally, you would want to show at least ten records, but for the moment, choose a small number such as 2, and then click OK.

12. Click the Live Data view button to make sure that your repeat region is working correctly. Retrace your steps if you encounter any problems. Switch off Live Data view. Check your code if necessary against blog_02.php in site_check/ch11.

13. Select the repeat region by clicking the gray tab labeled Repeat in Design view, or by selecting Repeat Region (getArticles) in the Server Behaviors panel. Open Split view, and position your cursor between the closing PHP tag and the closing </div> tag, as indicated by the arrow in the following screenshot:

```
47    <?php } while ($row_getArticles = mysql_fetch_assoc($getArticles)); ?></div>
48    <div id="footer"><?php include('copyright.php'); ?></div>
49    </div>                                          Position cursor here
50    </body>
```

14. Insert a new line in Code view at that point, and then insert a recordset navigation bar, either from the Application Insert bar or from the Application Objects ➤ Recordset Paging submenu of the Insert menu.

15. Now it's time to dive into Code view to apply the getFirst() function. To make it easy to locate the correct code, select the dynamic content placeholder for article in Design view before switching to Code view. The following code should be highlighted:

```
64    <p><strong><?php echo $row_getArticles['theDate']; ?>:</strong> <?php echo $row_getArticles
      ['article']; ?> <a href="blog_detail.php?article_id=<?php echo $row_getArticles['article_id']; ?>
      ">More</a> </p>
```

16. Amend the code shown on line 64 of the preceding screenshot like this (new code is shown in bold, and the code has been spread over several lines for ease of reading):

```
<p><strong><?php echo $row_getArticles['theDate']; ?>:</strong>
<?php $extract = getFirst($row_getArticles['article']);
echo $extract[0];
if ($extract[1]) { ?>
<a href="blog_detail.php?article_id=<?php echo
➥ $row_getArticles['article_id']; ?>">More</a> <?php } ?></p>
```

Instead of using echo to display $row_getArticles['article'], the second line passes the variable containing the article to getFirst(), and assigns the result to $extract. The getFirst() function returns an array of two elements. Array elements are numbered from 0, so the first element ($extract[0]) is displayed using echo, while the second element ($extract[1]) is used as a Boolean test. If the article is longer than the extract, the value is true, so the <a> tag is displayed. If $extract[1] is false, the PHP braces around the <a> tag prevent it from being sent to the browser.

17. Before you can test the page, you need to insert the getFirst() function declaration. Scroll right to the bottom of the page, where you should find the following code:

```
<?php
mysql_free_result($getArticles);
?>
```

18. Insert one or two new lines just before the closing PHP tag, and insert the Extract first sentences snippet from the PHP-DW8 folder in the Snippets panel.

19. Save blog.php, and view it in a browser. You should see something similar to Figure 11-2. Just the first two sentences of each article have been extracted for display, and there are links to the full articles. You can check your code against blog_03.php in site_check/ch11.

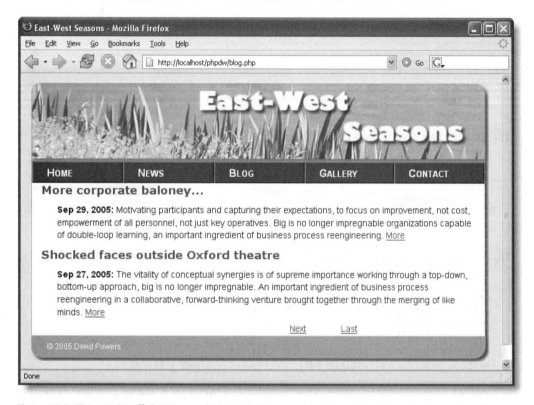

Figure 11-2. The getFirst() function enables you to display a selected number of sentences extracted from longer articles, together with a link to the full article.

Experiment with different settings for getFirst(). Supply a number as the second argument like this:

```
$extract = getFirst($row_getArticles['article'], 4);
```

This will extract the first four sentences, but the value of $extract[1] will be true only if there is more material to display. If the article is shorter than the number of sentences requested, getFirst() returns the full article in $extract[0], and sets $extract[1] to false, preventing the More link from displaying.

Using Live Data view with a URL parameter

Up to now, when testing a dynamic page that relies on a URL parameter, you have always used a browser to access a link to the page, rather than using Live Data view. This is the best way of testing that all your links work correctly, but it's also useful to know how to supply a URL parameter to Live Data view, so that's the technique you'll use to test blog_detail.php. This next section also shows you what happens when you create a recordset based on an existing one, but with a different name.

Displaying the full article

1. Open blog.php if it's not open, and select Recordset (getArticles) in the Server Behaviors panel. Right-click/*CTRL*-click and select Copy from the context menu.

2. Open the blog_detail.php file that you made in step 1 of the previous section. Right-click/*CTRL*-click in the Server Behaviors panel, and paste the recordset from blog.php.

3. With blog_detail.php in the Document window, double-click Recordset (getArticles) in the Server Behaviors panel to edit it.

4. Change the value of Name to getArticle, because this recordset will be used to retrieve just one article.

5. Edit the SQL query like this (new code is shown in bold):

   SELECT blog.article_id, blog.title, blog.article,
   DATE_FORMAT(blog.created, '%b %e, %Y') AS theDate,
   DATE_FORMAT(blog.updated, '%l.%i %p on %b %e, %Y') AS latest,
   blog.updated, blog.created, blog.image, blog.caption
   FROM blog
   WHERE blog.article_id = var1

   Make sure you don't omit the comma at the end of the second line. The third line uses more date format specifiers from Table 11-1 to include the time as well as the date. The fourth line adds updated and created in their original forms, along with the value of image. The final line creates a WHERE clause to select the correct article, using var1.

6. Click the plus button at the top left of the Variables area to define var1. In the Add Parameter dialog box, set Name to var1, Default value to -1, and Runtime value to $_GET['article_id']. Click OK.

7. The top half of the advanced Recordset dialog box should now have the settings shown alongside. I have removed the line breaks in the SQL query so that it all fits inside the visible area, but it doesn't matter if you leave them in. Click OK.

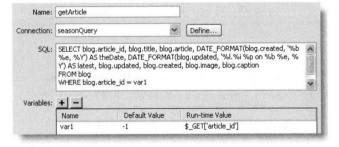

8. Dreamweaver displays the following alert, because you renamed the recordset:

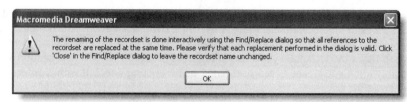

9. Click OK. Dreamweaver now displays the Find and Replace dialog box correctly filled out to replace getArticles with getArticle in the source code. Because getArticles is used only in the recordset name, you can safely click the Replace All button to make the change. However, if you want to be doubly sure, click Find Next. Dreamweaver should report that it found 0 instances. However, you still need to click Replace All to finish the operation. If you click Close, the recordset name will revert to the original getArticles.

10. The Results panel will open. Normally, this shows all the changes made by Find and Replace, but this time it will be empty. Press *F7* to close the panel (in the Mac version, this just collapses the Results panel, so click the close button in the panel's title bar).

11. Open the Bindings panel, and lay out the maincontent <div> as shown alongside, using a mixture of ordinary text and dynamic content placeholders.

12. One way to test this page would be to load blog.php into a browser, and then click one of the More links. However, you can also use Live Data view as long as you know the article_id of one of the records in your blog table. Choose View ➤ Live Data Settings. By default, the dialog box that opens sets Method to GET, so all you need to do is create a name/value pair for URL request. Click the plus button, set the Name value to article_id, insert the primary key of one of the articles in the Value field, and click OK. When you click the Live Data view button, the article should be displayed, and the last two lines should look like the screenshot shown alongside.

When Live Data view is switched on, an address bar similar to the one in a browser appears at the top of the Document window, as shown here. The section that contains the URL query string is editable. If you want to view a different article in Live Data view, insert another value for article_id, and click the circular arrow to reload the page.

13. You now need to add the code that will display the "Last updated" details only if there has been a change since the item was originally created. Open Code view, and locate the following line of code (around line 35):

```
<p>Last updated: <?php echo $row_getArticle['latest']; ?></p>
```

14. Surround it with a conditional statement like this:

```
<?php if ($row_getArticle['updated'] != $row_getArticle['created']) {
  <p>Last updated: <?php echo $row_getArticle['latest']; ?></p>
<?php } ?>
```

In this section of code, updated and created can be directly compared using their original values, whereas in other parts of the script they are displayed in a user-friendly format using latest and theDate as aliases. The "last updated" date and time will now appear only if the record has been updated since its original creation.

15. You may have noticed when testing the page in Live Data view that the article appeared as a continuous block. This is because browsers ignore new lines in text. The code that displays the article is on the line immediately above the section you amended in step 14. To restore the new lines, apply the nl2br() function like this:

```
<?php echo nl2br($row_getArticle['article']); ?>
```

16. You can check your code against blog_detail_01.php in site_check/ch11.

> Although Live Data view is a useful tool, it's not 100 percent perfect. Dreamweaver 8 seems to have difficulty parsing some pages, particularly if they include custom functions. If Live Data view reports an error, always check the page in a browser before tearing your hair out trying to locate the problem. As with CSS, the only true test is in a browser on a live server.

Creating an intelligent link

Visitors to your site need a way of getting back to the main blog page. The most obvious way of doing this is to create an ordinary link to blog.php. But that would always take them back to the page showing the most recent entry. It would be very frustrating if they have used the recordset navigation bar to go back several pages, and clicking the link lost the place they had got to. Of course, savvy visitors will probably use their browser's back button, but there is a very easy way to build an intelligent link using the SERVER superglobal array. The PHP variable $_SERVER['HTTP_REFERER'] contains the URL of the page that the visitor has just come from. Since this also contains any query string attached to the end of the URL, you can use this to send a visitor back to exactly the same place in a dynamic page.

"Aha," I can hear some of you say, "what about someone who's come from outside the site?" That's not a problem, because you can use a PHP function called parse_url() to find the name of the domain that the visitor has come from. All that's necessary is to compare the referring domain name with the domain name of your own site, and if they're different, use a different link. It just requires a few lines of code.

Using the SERVER superglobal array to create a link

1. Continue working with the same page as in the previous section, or use blog_detail_01.php from site_check/ch11.

2. In Design view, highlight the text Back to the blog, and create a link to blog.php.

3. Switch to Code view, and locate the link you have just created. It should be around line 38 and look like this:

```
<p><a href="blog.php">Back to the blog</a></p>
```

4. Amend it like this (the new code is shown in bold):

```
<p><a href="<?php
// find if visitor was referred from a different domain
$url = parse_url($_SERVER['HTTP_REFERER']);
if ($url['host'] == $_SERVER['HTTP_HOST']) {
  // if same domain, use referring URL
  echo $_SERVER['HTTP_REFERER'];
  }
else {
  // otherwise, send to main page
  echo 'blog.php';
  } ?>">Back to the blog</a></p>
```

The parse_url() function creates an associative array containing various elements of a URL. The fourth line of code compares the value of the host element of the referring URL with the value of $_SERVER['HTTP_HOST'], which contains the name of your own domain. When testing on your local computer, the value of $_SERVER['HTTP_HOST'] will be localhost, but when you upload it to your remote server, it will automatically reflect the correct domain name.

If the domains match, that means the visitor has come from your own site, and a dynamic link is created using $_SERVER['HTTP_REFERER'].

If the domains don't match, the else clause creates a hard link back to blog.php.

5. To see the advantage of this dynamic link, save blog_detail.php, and load blog.php into your browser. Click one of the More links. You will be taken to blog_detail.php, where the full article will be displayed. When you click the Back to the blog link, you will be returned to the beginning of the blog page.

6. Now click one of the recordset navigation bar links at the bottom of blog.php. (If the recordset navigation bar isn't visible, add some more dummy blog entries, or reduce the number of records displayed by the Repeat Region server behavior.) Click one of the More links, and then click the Back to the blog link. This time, you will be taken back to the same place in the recordset. However, anybody referred from a different domain will be taken to the beginning of the list.

7. You can check your code against blog_detail_02.php in site_check/ch11.

Although this is a rather neat little trick to use with a blog, it really comes into its own when used with a product catalog. Visitors are often likely to find a detail page through a search engine. This technique ensures that you provide a direct link to the main page of your catalog for such visitors, while customers from your own site are returned to the same place they were previously.

The only thing that remains to be done with the blog is to insert the code to display images in blog_detail.php for those records that contain the name of an image and a caption. Displaying images in a dynamic site is not difficult, but it does involve a little planning.

Displaying images in a dynamic site

The question of how to deal with images in a database-driven website causes a lot of confusion. If you're storing information in a database, the natural assumption is that that's where everything should go. However, it's not quite as simple as that.

Weighing the pros and cons of storing images in a database

The idea of keeping everything in the same location is attractive, but several important factors usually make storing images in a database more trouble than it's worth. The main problems are as follows:

- Images are binary data that cannot be indexed or searched without storing textual information separately.
- Images are usually large, bloating the size of tables.
- Table fragmentation affects performance if images are deleted frequently.
- Inserting images into a database is a two-stage process that involves uploading to a temporary folder and storing details of the correct MIME type.
- Retrieving images from a database is also a two-stage process that involves passing the image to a separate script before it can be displayed in a web page.
- This two-stage process usually slows down the display of images.
- Dreamweaver doesn't have server behaviors to automate either side of the process.

Since I've painted a pretty bleak picture of storing images in a database, it will come as no surprise that my advice is: *don't do it*. However, there are two scenarios where database storage does make sense:

- When the same images are required on multiple hosts, storing them centrally in a database can avoid the need for duplication.
- If there's a requirement to delete images at the same time as the related record is deleted, only a single operation is needed to keep the images and database in synch.

Nevertheless, I believe the disadvantages of storing images in a database far outweigh any small advantages. Consequently, I suggest you take my advice, and store images that you want to display dynamically in exactly the same way as all other images—in an ordinary folder on your website. To handle images dynamically, you need to store just two pieces of information—the filename of the image and a caption that can also be used as alt text. There is *no* need to store the image's height and width. You can generate that information dynamically with PHP as long as the GD extension has been installed. If you followed the instructions in Chapter 3, GD will be enabled on your system. It's also fairly standard on hosting company servers (run phpinfo() if you're not sure).

Positioning dynamically inserted images

A major difference between inserting an image into your web page in the normal way and dynamically is that you have less freedom of choice over where the image is placed. If you think back to the example of Amazon.com in Chapter 1, every book page has the same layout: The book cover is always in the same place, it's cropped to a standard size, and when there's no image, it's replaced by a placeholder. This solution works very well for Amazon, but you may not want such a rigid layout. As long as your images don't break out of the design, it's possible to use a range of sizes. You can also use a conditional statement to skip inserting the `<img>` tag when no image is available. However, the location of the image will remain constant.

Dynamically inserting an image at the top of a blog entry

Continue working with `blog_detail.php` or use `blog_detail_02.php` from `site_check/ch11`.

1. In Design view, select the dynamic content placeholder for theDate, and then click the `<strong>` tag in the Tag selector at the bottom of the Document window. Press your left arrow key once. This positions the cursor in the correct place between the opening `<p>` and `<strong>` tags to insert the image. Open Split view to confirm that your cursor is in the correct position. Alternatively, if you're comfortable moving around in code, you can just open Split view and position your cursor manually.

2. Inserting an image from a recordset is very similar to inserting an ordinary image. Open the Select Image Source dialog box by one of the following methods:

   - Click the Image icon on the Common Insert bar.
   - Select Image from the Insert menu.
   - Press *CTRL+ALT+I/OPT+⌘+I*.

3. In Windows, select the Data sources radio button at the top of the dialog box. In the Mac version, click the Data sources button at the bottom of the dialog box. This displays any recordsets available to the page. The data sources are displayed in a separate dialog box in the Mac version, but everything works the same.

4. If necessary, expand Recordset (getArticle), and select image. This inserts the following code in the URL field of the Select Image Source dialog box:

   `<?php echo $row_getArticle['image']; ?>`

   This variable contains only the name of the image file, and not the path. You need to add that manually by clicking inside the URL field just before the opening PHP tag, and typing images_blog/. Don't forget the trailing slash. Check that your settings look like those shown in the screenshot, and click OK.

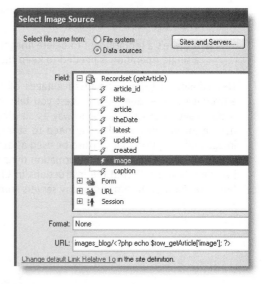

5. Unless you have turned off the accessibility preferences, you will be presented with the Image Tag Accessibility Attributes dialog box. Select <empty> from the Alternate text drop-down menu, and click OK.

6. Your page should now look like this in Split view:

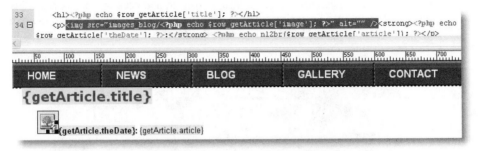

Dreamweaver has inserted a dynamic image placeholder in Design view; and in Code view, there's an <img> tag with a block of PHP code inside the src attribute. As you can see, the name of the images_blog folder, followed by a trailing slash, is also included in the src attribute ahead of the PHP code block. If the value of $row_getArticle['image'] is "horse.jpg", the highlighted section of code shown on line 34 of the preceding screenshot will resolve to the following:

```
<img src="images_blog/horse.jpg" alt="" />
```

7. Add the following style rule at the bottom of styles/bluebells.css, and save the page:

```css
/*style for blog*/
.floatRight {
  float: right;
  padding: 10px;
  }
```

8. Select the dynamic image placeholder in Design view, and choose floatRight from the Class drop-down menu in the Property inspector. Dreamweaver adds the class to the underlying code, and floats the dynamic placeholder to the right of Design view.

9. The alt attribute in the <img> tag still has no value. The way to apply a dynamic value to an attribute is by highlighting the target element and then selecting the attribute from a drop-down menu in the Bindings panel. (You did this with the value attribute of text fields in Chapter 9.) Check that the dynamic image placeholder is selected, open the Bindings panel, and highlight caption in the getArticle recordset. You will notice that the Insert button at the bottom of the Bindings panel has been relabeled Bind, and there's a drop-down menu to the left of it labeled Bind to. Open the drop-down menu, and select img.alt as shown alongside. Then click the Bind button.

10. If you have Split view open, you will see that a PHP code block has been inserted in the empty alt attribute. The label on the Bind button also changes to Unbind. If you ever want to remove the dynamically generated value of a tag attribute, such as alt, use the Unbind button to remove the code cleanly.

11. Save blog_detail.php. Load blog.php into a browser, and click one of the More links. If the blog entry has an image associated with it, you should see it displayed at the top right of the page, as shown in Figure 11-3. Check your code, if necessary, against blog_detail_03.php in site_check/ch11.

Figure 11-3. The src attribute of the <img> tag is generated dynamically to insert the appropriate image.

Dynamically inserting an image in the middle of a blog entry

A problem with combining images with text drawn from a database is that you can't display an image in the middle of the text unless you can find a way of splitting the text in two. The "secret" behind doing this is a simple adaptation of the getFirst() function that was used to extract the first few sentences from a blog entry. Instead of the second array element containing a Boolean value, the remainder of the text is reconstituted as a string and returned.

1. Continue working with the file from the previous section, or use blog_detail_03.php from site_check/ch11.

2. In Design view, select the dynamic content placeholder for article to highlight the underlying code, as shown alongside. This is the section of code that needs to be amended to split the text into two.

3. Alter the code highlighted in the previous screenshot so that it looks like this:

```php
<?php $text = splitText($row_getArticle['article']);
echo nl2br($text[0]); ?>
<!-- image code goes here -->
<?php echo nl2br($text[1]); ?>
```

Instead of using echo to display $row_getArticle['article'], you pass the variable to splitText() and assign the result to $text. You'll insert the function definition for splitText() a little later, but it takes the same arguments as getFirst(). The second argument is optional. It sets the number of sentences in the first half. If you don't set the second argument, it defaults to 4.

The amended code then uses echo to display the two array elements, passing them both to nl2br() to preserve any line breaks in the text.

4. Select the dynamic image placeholder in Design view, and press *CTRL+X*/⌘ +X to cut it to your clipboard.

5. You need to paste the code for the image at the point indicated by the HTML comment in the code that you inserted in step 3. However, if you click inside Code view and press *CTRL+V*/⌘ +V, nothing will happen. This is because of Dreamweaver's context sensitivity. Anything cut or copied in Design view must be pasted back in Design view. Use your mouse pointer to click between the two PHP shields, as shown in the following screenshot. Then press *CTRL+V*/⌘ +V to paste the code in the right place.

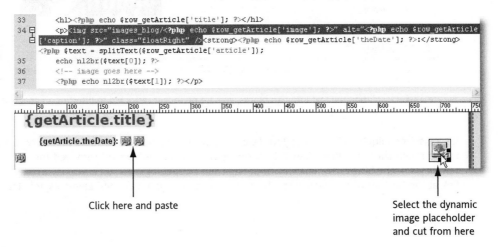

Click here and paste

Select the dynamic image placeholder and cut from here

409

6. When you paste the dynamic image placeholder between the two PHP shields, it won't be displayed there, but it will reappear in its original position on the right of the page because of the CSS class still applied to it. However, if you look in Code view, you should see the `<img>` tag immediately beneath the HTML comment.

7. In Code view, scroll right to the bottom of the page. Insert a new line or two after `mysql_free_result($getArticle)`, and then insert the splitText() function definition by double-clicking Split long text in the `PHP-DW8` folder of the Snippets panel.

8. Save `blog_detail.php`, and test some of your blog entries. As you can see in Figure 11-4, the image is now floated to the right after the first four sentences.

Figure 11-4. By splitting the text into two blocks, you are no longer restricted to inserting an image at the top.

It's a nice technique, but one that you should use with care, because it would look very strange with a much shorter article. Figure 11-5 shows what happened when I removed the last four sentences of the blog entry. The way to prevent this happening is to add a new style rule to the link at the bottom of the `maincontent` `<div>` to ensure that any floated elements are cleared.

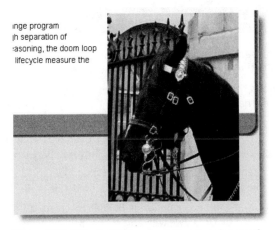

Figure 11-5. If the text is too short, there's a danger of the image spilling out of the maincontent `<div>`.

9. Add the following style rule to the bottom of bluebells.css:

#backlink {clear: both;}

10. In blog_detail.php, insert your cursor anywhere inside the Back to the blog link, select the `<p>` tag in the Tag selector, right-click/*CTRL*-click, and select Set ID ➤ backlink. This will prevent the overspill seen in Figure 11-5, but will still leave a lot of blank space at the bottom of the page. Consequently, this technique is only suitable for situations where there will always be sufficient text to produce a balanced layout. You can check your code against blog_detail_04.php in site_check/ch11.

Getting an image's dimensions dynamically

PHP has an impressive range of functions for working with images. As I mentioned earlier, they rely on the GD extension being installed, but they're so popular, it's unusual to find a PHP server that doesn't have it installed. The image functions not only enable you to manipulate images, you can also generate images and text on the fly. You can find details of all the PHP image functions at www.php.net/manual/en/ref.image.php.

I'm going to use just one of them: getimagesize(), which returns an array of four elements containing the following information about an image in this order:

- Width
- Height
- A number indicating image type (GIF, JPEG, etc.)
- A string with the correct width and height ready for inserting in an `<img>` tag

It's the fourth element that we're interested in. I have created a custom function called getDims(), which takes two arguments: the name of the image, and the path to the image folder. It checks that the image exists, and then returns the string containing the correct dimensions for the `<img>` tag. The code for getDims() is in the Get image dimensions snippet in the PHP-DW8 folder, but it's so useful, I suggest you turn it into a custom server behavior.

Making a server behavior to generate image dimensions

1. Open the Snippets panel, highlight Get image dimensions in the PHP-DW8 folder, and click the Edit Snippet icon in the bottom-right corner of the panel.

2. Select all the code in the Insert code area, and press *CTRL+C/⌘ +C* to copy it to your clipboard. Make sure you get the opening and closing PHP tags. Click Cancel to close the Snippet edit window without changing the code.

3. Make sure that you have a PHP page open in the Document window, and then click the plus button on the Server Behaviors panel. Select New Server Behavior.

4. In the New Server Behavior dialog box, make sure that Document type is set to PHP MySQL, and type Generate Image Dimensions in the Name field. Click OK.

5. Click the plus button in the Server Behavior Builder to create a new code block. Accept the default name suggested by Dreamweaver, and click OK.

6. Type the following code in the Code block area:

```php
<?php echo getDims($row_@@RecordsetName@@['@@FieldName@@'],
➥ '@@ImageFolder@@'); ?>
```

As in the server behaviors that you built in the last chapter, parameters are used as placeholders—this time for the recordset and field containing the name of the image, and for the path to the images folder.

7. You now need to specify where the code block should be inserted. Set the Insert code drop-down menu to Relative to a Specific Tag. Select img from the Tag drop-down menu, and set Relative position to Inside the Opening Tag.

8. Although this will insert the correct code in the <img> tag, you also need to insert the getDims() function declaration somewhere. Click the plus button alongside Code blocks to insert, accept the default name that Dreamweaver suggests for the second code block, and click OK.

9. This clears the Server Behavior Builder dialog box so it is ready for you to enter details of the second code block. Delete all the placeholder text in the Code block area, including the opening and closing PHP tags. Then press *CTRL+V/⌘ +V* to paste the code from the Get image dimensions snippet.

10. Since this is just a function definition, it can go at the bottom of the PHP page, so select Below the </html> Tag as the setting for Insert code, and Before the End of the File for Relative position. Click Next.

11. Reorder the items and change the Display As settings in the Generate Behavior Dialog Box dialog box, as shown in the screenshot alongside. Click OK when you have made the changes. You now have a server behavior that can be used to generate the width and height attributes for all dynamically inserted images.

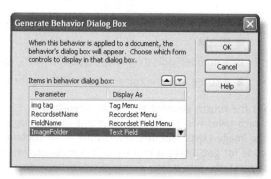

Applying the Generate Image Dimensions server behavior

Continue working with blog_detail.php from before, or use blog_detail_04.php from site_check/ch11.

1. To make sure that you apply the server behavior to the correct <img> tag, it's helpful to give the image an ID. Select the dynamic image placeholder in Design view, and name the image blogImage in the Property inspector.

2. Click the plus button in the Server Behaviors panel, and select Generate Image Dimensions. If the dynamic image placeholder is still selected, the Generate Image Dimensions dialog box will automatically select blogImage in the img tag drop-down menu. Check that you have the settings shown alongside, and click OK.

> *You should use a relative path in the* ImageFolder *field. Normally, the path should end with a trailing slash, but the* getDims() *function will add one if you forget. Leave the* ImageFolder *field blank if the image is in the same folder as the current file.*

3. If you open Code view, you will see that the server behavior has inserted code both in the <img> tag and in the PHP code block below the closing </html> tag. Save the page, and test the blog in a browser. You won't necessarily see any difference onscreen, but if you view the source code, you'll see that the width and height attributes have been added to the <img> tag. Check your code, if necessary, against blog_detail_05.php in site_check/ch11.

There's just one final thing you need to do to blog_detail.php. To prevent the <img> tag for the dynamically inserted image from being processed if no image is associated with a blog entry, you should surround it with a conditional statement like this (I've omitted the detailed code in the <img> tag):

```php
<?php if (!empty($row_getArticle['image'])) { ?>
  <img . . . >
<?php } ?>
```

Displaying a photo gallery

Once you know how to store image details and use them to display images dynamically, it doesn't take much more to be able to display a photo gallery. I don't intend to show you how to build the database back-end, because it's almost identical to the blog table. The gallery table has just three columns: gallery_id, image, and caption. The gallery_id is the primary key, and the other two columns are both set to VARCHAR(50) and not null. However, there is no need for you to build the table. I have created a SQL file that will create the gallery table in your database and populate it with all the necessary data. All the images are in the images_gallery folder of the download files, so it's just a question of building the page to display the photos. Figure 11-6 shows what the finished gallery looks like.

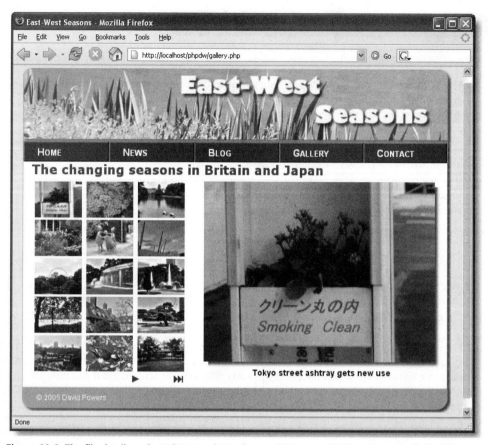

Figure 11-6. The file details and captions are drawn from a database and laid out dynamically by PHP.

The design is clean and simple. On the left of the page are 15 thumbnail images, each 80×60 pixels, with the main photo (400×300 pixels) on the right. When you click one of the thumbnails, a JavaScript function uses DOM (Document Object Model) manipulation to replace the main image and caption without the need to reload the page. This means that you avoid the heavy overhead of preloading a large number of images, as only those photos that the visitor selects are ever downloaded. The script has been designed to degrade gracefully in browsers that either don't understand DOM manipulation or have JavaScript disabled. Instead of the image loading on the right, it will replace the current page, and visitors will need to click their browser's back button to return to the gallery—not as elegant, but certainly much better than denying access to people using older browsers.

> *Using JavaScript to manipulate the DOM has at long last become a practical reality, now that the market share of older browsers, such as Netscape 4, has dwindled to an insignificant level. To learn more, read* DOM Scripting: Web Design with JavaScript and the Document Object Model *by Jeremy Keith (friends of ED, ISBN 1-59059-533-5).*

The really cool feature about this photo gallery is that all the coding for the images is done with just two dynamic image placeholders: one for the thumbnails, and the other for the main image. The hard work is done by the MX Looper server behavior, which builds the table on the left side of the page to house the thumbnails. Unfortunately, this server behavior isn't part of Dreamweaver 8's standard features; it's a commercial extension created by InterAKT, the company that created the MX Kollection, which was demonstrated in Chapter 10. If you installed MX Kollection in the last chapter, MX Looper is included. It's also available separately, as a trial version and for purchase (currently $30). You can find more at www.interaktonline.com/Products/Dreamweaver-Extensions/MXLooper/Overview/.

This, by the way, is the only section of the book where I don't provide a hand-coded alternative. Since a trial version of MX Looper is available, you can test it to see if it meets your needs. Using MX Looper is incredibly easy. What I particularly like about it is that you can combine it with Dreamweaver's Recordset Navigation Bar server behavior to create a limitless photo gallery with just one page.

How the photo gallery is structured

Since this is a CSS-based design, the basic structure involves wrapping the main photo and its accompanying caption in a wrapper <div>, and floating it to the right of another <div> that houses the thumbnails. As you can see from Figure 11-7, the design also includes two tables, but unlike traditional table layout, the tables aren't nested inside others. This makes the underlying code a lot easier to maintain. The first table accommodates the grid of thumbnail images, and the second is used for the recordset navigation bar. Figure 11-7 also shows the IDs of each element in the gallery. Most of them serve a dual purpose, controlling not only the CSS, but also allowing the JavaScript function to manipulate the DOM to replace the main image and caption. The only element that doesn't require an ID is the table that houses the thumbnails.

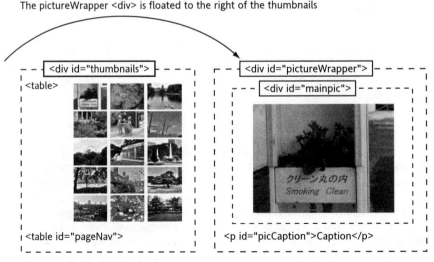

Figure 11-7. The structure of the photo gallery is controlled by wrapping both sides of the page in <div>s and floating the main picture to the right.

The following CSS style rules need to be added to bluebells.css for the photo gallery. You can either type them in directly or you can use bluebells_04.css from site_check/styles. The necessary styles are already in the original versions of tulips.css and maples.css.

```css
/*styles for photo gallery*/
#pictureWrapper {
  width: 408px;
  float: right;
  text-align: center;
  font-weight: bold;
  margin: 10px 20px 10px 0;
  }
#pictureWrapper p {
  margin: 0;
  padding: 0;
  }
#mainpic {
  float: right;
  background: url(../images_common/shadow.gif) bottom right no-repeat;
  }
#mainpic img{
  margin: -8px 8px 8px -8px;
  }
#thumbnails {
  min-height: 345px;
  }
#thumbnails img {
  margin: 0 2px;
  border: none;
  }
#thumbnails table {
  margin: 0 15px;
  }
#pageNav {
  width: 310px;
  }
```

Although the rule that floats the main photo area to the right is in the first style block (#pictureWrapper), you'll notice that the #mainpic rule also uses float: right. This is because I have used a background image on the mainpic <div> to create a drop shadow behind the main photo. The second float rule is to keep the photo snug up against the background image. The negative top and left margins on the #mainpic img rule move the main photo and background slightly apart to create the illusion of the drop shadow. You may be surprised to see the use of min-height, even though Internet Explorer 6 doesn't support it. It's to prevent the main photo spilling out of the maincontent <div> in Firefox and Safari. For some reason, IE6 and Opera 8.5 don't need it. Let us be thankful for small mercies.

To keep the coding as simple as possible, the thumbnail images have the same name as the equivalent full-size photo. The only difference is that they're kept in a subfolder of images_gallery called thumbs.

Putting the photo gallery together

Before you can start building the gallery page, you need to create the gallery table in the seasons database and populate it with data.

Populating the gallery table in the database

There are three versions of the necessary SQL file in site_check/ch11: gallery.sql, gallery323.sql, and gallery40.sql. Use gallery.sql if your version of MySQL is 4.1 or higher. If you are using MySQL 3.23 or 4.0, use the appropriately numbered version.

1. Launch phpMyAdmin and select the seasons database. Click the SQL tab at the top of the main frame, and then use the Browse button to navigate to the appropriate version of gallery.sql in the field labeled Location of the text file. Click the bottom Go button. This is the same technique as you used in Chapter 8 to load the contents of quotations.sql into your database. If the file loads successfully, skip to step 3.

2. The SQL file is designed to prevent overwriting an existing table called gallery. If you need to use a different table name, right-click/CTRL-click the appropriate version of gallery.sql in the Dreamweaver Files panel, and choose Open With ➤ Dreamweaver. (The file won't open if you double-click it, because Dreamweaver doesn't recognize SQL files.) Scroll down to line 19, which should look like this:

   CREATE TABLE `gallery` {

   Change gallery to a name that doesn't conflict with an existing table, save the file, and go back to step 1.

3. Click the Browse tab at the top of the main frame in phpMyAdmin. You should see the contents of the new table displayed like this (only the first five rows are shown):

←T→	gallery_id	image	caption
□ ✎ ✕	1	ashtray.jpg	Tokyo street ashtray gets new use
□ ✎ ✕	2	azaleas.jpg	A blaze of color at Capel Manor in North London
□ ✎ ✕	3	buck_palace.jpg	Pelicans on the lake in St James's Park, London
□ ✎ ✕	4	countrygarden.jpg	A typical English country garden in Oxford
□ ✎ ✕	5	daisydance.jpg	Dancing round the daisies at Capel Manor

Building the main image area

Because the <div> that houses the main photo is floated to the right of the thumbnails, it needs to come first in the underlying code, so that's the first part of the page that you'll build. Use gallery.php from Chapters 4 and 5. Alternatively, use gallery_01.php from site_check/ch11.

1. This page will be used to display the photos listed in the gallery table, so let's begin by creating a recordset. Use the simple Recordset dialog box with the following settings:

   - Name: getPictures
   - Connection: seasonQuery
   - Table: gallery
   - Columns: All
   - Filter: None
   - Sort: None

2. In Design view, highlight the placeholder text for the maincontent <div>, replace it with "The changing seasons in Britain and Japan", and select Heading 1 from the Format drop-down menu in the Property inspector.

3. Click the <h1> tag in the Tag selector at the bottom of the Document window, and press your right arrow key once to move the cursor outside the closing </h1> tag. Open Split view to make sure that the cursor is to the right of the tag, but still inside the maincontent <div>. (The closing </div> tag is on the next line.)

4. Click the Insert Div Tag icon on the Common Insert bar. Set the Insert field to At insertion point, and type pictureWrapper in the ID field. Click OK.

5. Press *DELETE* to remove the placeholder text in the new <div>, and click the Insert Div Tag icon again.

6. Set the Insert field to At insertion point, type mainpic in the ID field, and click OK.

7. This is where the main photo will be displayed, so press *DELETE* to remove the placeholder text. The procedure for inserting the image is the same as in blog_detail.php. Open the Select Image Source dialog box by using any of the methods to insert a new image. When the dialog box opens, chose Data sources as the setting for Select file name from.

8. Expand Recordset (getPictures), and select image. The main images are in the images_gallery folder, so click inside the URL field, and add images_gallery/ before the PHP code block, as shown here.

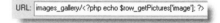

9. Click OK, and select <empty> as the value for Alternate text if the Image Tag Accessibility Attributes dialog box has not been turned off.

10. With the dynamic image placeholder still highlighted, open the Bindings panel, select caption from Recordset (getPictures), and set the Bind to drop-down menu to img.alt. Click Bind to apply the dynamic value to the alt attribute of the main image.

11. To complete the code for the main photo, switch to the Server Behaviors panel, click the plus button, and select Generate Image Dimensions. Although the main photo is inside a `<div>` that has an ID, the `<img>` tag itself has no specific identification. However, as long as the dynamic image placeholder was selected when you selected the server behavior, the correct image will be selected in the img tag field. It will be identified simply as img[1]. Set FieldName to image, and type images_gallery/ in the ImageFolder field. Click OK.

12. You now need to move the cursor outside the mainpic `<div>` to create the paragraph that will hold the caption. The most accurate way of doing this is to click `<div#mainpic>` in the Tag selector at the bottom of the Document window. Then press the right arrow key once to move the cursor outside the closing `</div>` tag, and press *ENTER/RETURN* to insert a new paragraph.

13. Open the Bindings panel, select caption, and click Insert.

14. Click the `<p>` tag in the Tag selector, right-click/*CTRL*-click, choose Quick Tag Editor from the context menu, and press *SPACE*. A pop-up menu should appear, showing you the available attributes for the `<p>` tag. Select id, and give the ID a value of picCaption. Press *ENTER/RETURN* to close the Quick Tag Editor.

15. After all that effort, you will have very little to see in either Design view or Code view, as the following screenshot shows.

However, this is one of the main features of PHP—a little code goes a long way. The four lines of code in the preceding screenshot get the image, its dimensions, alternate text, and caption—all generated dynamically. Use Live Data view to check.

16. The footer `<div>` may now look as though it has been sliced in two, but this is nothing to worry about. Switch off Live Data view, and check your code, if necessary, against gallery_02.php in site_check/ch11.

Building the thumbnails area

Continue working with the same file, or use `gallery_02.php` from `site_check/ch11`.

1. The thumbnails `<div>` needs to be inserted after pictureWrapper, but getting the right position is easy with the Insert Div Tag dialog box. On the Common Insert bar, click the Insert Div Tag button, and choose the settings shown alongside. Then click OK.

2. Press *DELETE* to remove the placeholder text, and replace it with a dynamic image placeholder for one of the thumbnails. Do this by repeating steps 7 through 11 of the previous section. However, this time use `images_gallery/thumbs/` as the path to the images in steps 8 and 11. The code inserted should look like this:

3. With the dynamic image placeholder for the thumbnail still highlighted, click the Looper Wizard button on the MX Kollection category of the Insert bar. (You can also access the Looper Wizard by clicking the plus button in the Server Behaviors panel, and then choosing MX Kollection ➤ Dynamic Lists ➤ Looper Wizard.)

4. Unlike the Dreamweaver Repeat Region, which just repeats the same section over and over again, the MX Looper has a sense of direction. It creates all the PHP code necessary to build a table, with each repeated region in a cell of its own.

   The dialog box that opens is very simple. The Looper type drop-down menu offers two options—Horizontal and Vertical. Horizontal repeats across each table row and then down. Vertical builds the table in columns, repeating down each column before moving across to the next one. With photos, the direction is unimportant, but the ability to present data in columns is extremely useful.

   The two other settings are the recordset that you want to loop through, and whether to show a specified number of rows and columns or to show all records. As Figures 11-6 and 11-7 show, the thumbnails in the gallery are laid out in five rows and three columns. Check that your settings are the same as shown alongside, and click Finish.

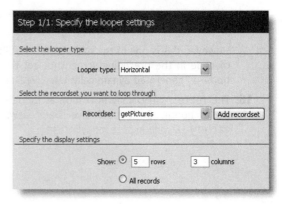

5. By default, the MX Looper puts a 1-pixel border around table cells. I think that spoils the look, so click in any blank part of the document window to remove the focus from the current selection. A gray border with a tab labeled Horiz Looper now surrounds the dynamic placeholder for the thumbnail. Click the placeholder. You should now be able to select the <table> tag in the Tag selector at the bottom of the Document window. This brings up the details of the horizontal looper table in the Property inspector. Click inside the Border field, delete the number, and press *Enter/Return*. This removes the border attribute from the <table> tag in the underlying code.

> *Although the MX Looper isn't one of Dreamweaver's standard server behaviors, instances of the horizontal and vertical looper applied to a page are listed in the Server Behaviors panel in the normal way. To remove a looper, highlight it in the Server Behaviors panel and click the minus button. This removes all the PHP code, but leaves behind the <table>, <tr>, and <td> tags. It's important to go into Code view to remove them manually. Otherwise, it could have unpredictable consequences for your layout.*

6. There are more than 15 photos listed in the gallery table, so you need to add a recordset navigation bar to display the others. Click immediately to the right of the horizontal looper in Design view. It's important to get your cursor in the correct position, so check in Split view that it's immediately to the right of the closing </table> tag, as shown in the following screenshot:

7. Insert a recordset navigation bar, either by clicking the Recordset Paging button on the Application Insert bar, or by choosing Insert ➤ Application Objects ➤ Recordset Paging ➤ Recordset Navigation Bar. In the dialog box that opens, select the radio button labeled Images and click OK. Dreamweaver will probably then display the following warning:

421

This is because Dreamweaver can't detect that the horizontal looper is, in fact, a repeat region server behavior. It's not a problem. Just click OK, and the recordset navigation bar will be inserted into your page.

8. As I mentioned in Chapter 8, Dreamweaver automatically inserts old-style <table> attributes to control the look of the navigation bar. This will make a mess of the design, so you need to remove most of them to let the CSS take control.

    Click inside the first cell of the recordset navigation bar. This displays the cell's settings in the Property inspector. Change the setting in the Horz field at the bottom left from Center to Default to remove the align attribute from the <td> tag. Do the same with the three remaining cells in the recordset navigation bar.

9. Click the <table> tag in the Tag selector at the bottom of the Document window to display the table's settings in the Property inspector. Type pageNav in the Table Id field, remove the values in the W and Border fields, and reset Align to Default. The settings in the Property inspector should now look like this:

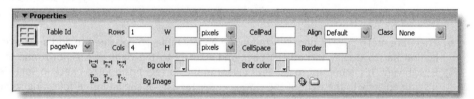

10. Save gallery.php, and view it in a browser. It should now look like Figure 11-6. Test the navigation buttons at the bottom of the thumbnail display. The final page has only one thumbnail, but the CSS keeps everything together in all modern browsers. The only minor difference is that in some browsers the navigation buttons sit directly below the thumbnail at the top of the page, while in other browsers they remain at the bottom. This variation doesn't affect the functionality or overall look of the page. Don't forget: Visitors to your site will normally only ever use one browser. They don't make the minute comparisons that obsess many web designers unnecessarily.

    All that remains to be done is to create the links for the thumbnails and activate the DOM manipulation script. Check your code so far against gallery_03.php in site_check/ch11.

> *If you attempt to view the page in Live Data view, the thumbnails table will not render correctly, and Dreamweaver will display a tag highlighted in yellow, which normally indicates incorrect code. This is a limitation of Live Data view and not a problem with the code.*

Activating the thumbnails

Continue working with the same page, or use `gallery_03.php` from `site_check/ch11`.

1. For the benefit of people using older browsers or who browse with JavaScript turned off, the thumbnails need to link directly to the equivalent full-size image. Select the thumbnail dynamic image placeholder in Design view, and click the Browse for File icon to the right of the Link field in the Property inspector.

2. In the Select File dialog box, choose Data sources for the Select file name from setting. Expand the getPictures recordset, and select image. Amend the content of the URL field to add the path to the `images_gallery` folder in front of the PHP code block. Don't forget the trailing slash on the folder name. Refer to the screenshot in step 8 of the "Building the main image area" section if you're unsure. Click OK.

3. With the thumbnail still selected so that you can identify the correct section of code, switch to Code view. You need to add an onclick event to the opening `<a>` tag. Amend the tag like this (new code is shown in bold):

```
<a href="images_gallery/<?php echo $row_getPictures['image']; ?>"
➥ onclick="showImage(this);return false;">
```

The `showImage()` JavaScript function, which you'll add in the next step, takes just one argument, a reference to the current element using the keyword this. By adding `return false;`, browsers capable of DOM manipulation ignore the link and use the onclick event instead.

4. The code for the `showImage()` function is in `gallery.js` in `site_check/ch11`. Copy the file to the site root or put it in a separate `scripts` folder. Alternatively, if you're feeling ultra-enthusiastic, type it out yourself, as it's only a few lines long.

```
function showImage(elem) {
  if(!document.getElementById) {
    return false;
  } else {
    var bigPic = elem.getAttribute('href');
    var newCaption = elem.firstChild.getAttribute('alt');
    document.getElementById('mainpic').firstChild.setAttribute('src',bigPic);
    var theCaption = document.getElementById('picCaption');
    theCaption.firstChild.nodeValue = newCaption;
  }
}
```

I won't go into all the detail of how it works. Jeremy Keith's book *DOM Scripting* (friends of ED, ISBN 1-59059-533-5) does a far better job of explaining the intricacies of the DOM than I can. The important thing to know about this script is that it works in all modern browsers, including Internet Explorer 6, and current versions of Firefox, Opera, and Safari; and the beauty of DOM scripting is that it doesn't require any browser "sniffing" that made writing JavaScript a nightmare only a few years ago. Although this script was designed for this book, you can adapt it for use in any website. The key points are in lines 7 and 8: mainpic and picCaption are the IDs for the main image <div> and the <p> tag that contains the caption. Either use the same IDs in your site, or change the values in this script to match your IDs.

5. Dreamweaver 8 finally has a way of attaching an external JavaScript file, although it was added as something of an afterthought, so it's not quite as slick as attaching an external stylesheet. The code that links to the external file is inserted wherever your cursor happens to be at the time, so you need to get in the right position beforehand.

   In gallery.php, scroll up in Code view until you find the closing </head> tag (it should be around line 47). Position your cursor immediately to the left of the tag, and choose Insert ➤ HTML ➤ Script Objects ➤ Script. Alternatively, click the Script button on the HTML Insert bar. In the dialog box that opens, click the little folder icon to the right of the Source field, and navigate to gallery.js. Select it, and then click OK to close the Script dialog box.

6. That's it. The photo gallery is complete. If you have any problems, check your code against gallery_04.php in site_check/ch11.

Improving the blog and photo gallery

There are many ways in which you could improve both the blog and the photo gallery. For instance, you could adapt the user registration system from the previous chapter to allow visitors to register on your site—giving them non-administrative privileges, of course—so they can post comments. Store the comments in a separate table. As long as you include the article_id and user_id along with each record in the comments table, you can link all three tables to display a blog item together with comments and the names of the people who contributed them.

> If you want to delve deeper into the delights of blogging, take a look at Blog Design Solutions by Phil Sherry and others—including yours truly (friends of ED, ISBN 1-59059-581-5).

Another idea for the photo gallery would be to add an ENUM column with the values uk and jp to distinguish between photos of Britain and Japan. You could also add another table with categories of different subjects: birds, trees, plants, urban landscapes, and so on. By building different SQL queries, you could then display different aspects of the photo gallery. The possibilities are endless. Now that you know how to use all the database-related server behaviors in Dreamweaver 8, it's just a question of planning and experimentation.

Storing dates in MySQL

The blog and photo gallery are now complete, but you may have noticed that there's one outstanding issue—the problem of converting user-supplied dates to the format expected by MySQL. People have many different ways of writing dates, but MySQL accepts only one format: YYYY-MM-DD. Using TIME-STAMP columns to get MySQL to format the dates automatically was very convenient, but it's not an approach that is appropriate to all situations. So this final part of the chapter will be devoted to dealing with human-generated dates.

> *Actually, MySQL accepts other separators in addition to hyphens, and it's intelligent enough to accept months and days of the month without a leading zero. However, for safety's sake, it's better to adhere to the standard format. If, for technical reasons, you have a pressing need to use different separators, consult* http://dev.mysql.com/doc/refman/5.0/en/datetime.html.

Although MySQL is very fussy about the format of the date, it will blithely accept a date such as September 31 or February 30. The solution to this problem, as always, is to validate user input before storing it in your database. The simplest way to ensure accurate date input is to provide separate fields for month, day of the month, and year, and then to use PHP to verify and format the input.

Validating and formatting dates for database input

In the examples/ch11 folder of the download files, you will find a page called date_converter.php. When you load it into a browser, it displays a drop-down menu preset to the current month, together with two text fields for the date and year, as shown in the screenshot. The Max Chars setting for the text fields has been set to 2 and 4, respectively, to limit the range of mistakes that can be made.

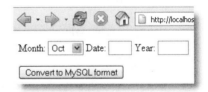

Experiment with the page, inserting a variety of valid and invalid input. When you click the Convert to MySQL format button, either the correctly formatted date or an error message is displayed at the top of the page. You can incorporate the construction and validation techniques used in this example page in any of your PHP forms.

The drop-down menu for the month is created in two parts. The first section of code goes in a PHP block above the DOCTYPE declaration, and consists of an array of the names of the months, plus the PHP getdate() function. This is how it looks:

```
$months = array('Jan','Feb','Mar','Apr','May','Jun','Jul','Aug','Sep',
➥ 'Oct','Nov','Dec');
$now = getdate();
```

The getdate() function produces an associative array that contains a number of useful date parts, such as the year, weekday name, and so on. When used without an argument like this, getdate() returns information about the current date, so we can find the number of the current month in $now['mon'], and use it to preset the drop-down menu. There's a full list of the array elements returned by getdate() at www.php.net/manual/en/function.getdate.php.

The code for the form looks like this (the section that builds the drop-down menu is highlighted in bold):

```
<form id="convert" name="convert" method="post" action="<?php
➥ $_SERVER['PHP_SELF']; ?>">
  <p>
    <label for="month">Month:</label>
    <select name="month" id="month">
      <?php for ($i=1;$i<=12;$i++) { ?>
      <option value="<?php echo $i < 10 ? '0'.$i : $i; ?>"
      <?php if ($i == $now['mon']) {
        echo ' selected="selected"'; } ?>><?php echo $months[$i-1]; ?>
      </option>
      <?php } ?>
    </select>
    <label for="day">Date:</label>
    <input name="day" type="text" id="day" size="2" maxlength="2" />
    <label for="year">Year:</label>
    <input name="year" type="text" id="year" size="4" maxlength="4" />
  </p>
  <p>
    <input type="submit" name="Submit" value="Convert to MySQL format" />
  </p>
</form>
```

The PHP code uses a for loop to populate the menu's <option> tags. Although counters normally begin at 0, I have set the initial value of $i to 1, because I want to use it for the value of the month. The second line highlighted in bold uses a piece of computing shorthand known as the **ternary operator** to test whether $i is less than 10. If it is, a leading zero is added to the number; otherwise, it is left alone.

The ternary (or conditional) operator is a rather strange beast. It consists of a question mark and a colon. The condition being tested goes to the left of the question mark. If the condition evaluates to true, the value to the right of the question mark is used. If it evaluates to false, the value to the right of the colon is used instead. So, this line,

```
echo $i < 10 ? '0'.$i : $i;
```

is the equivalent of writing this:

```
if ($i < 10) {
  echo '0'.$i;
  }
else {
  echo $i;
  }
```

As you can see, the first version is a lot shorter, but it's not so easy to follow. You don't need to worry about this operator, but it's useful to know its meaning when you come across it in someone else's code.

The third line of PHP checks whether the value of $i is the same as $now['mon']. If it is, the following line inserts selected="selected" into the opening <option> tag. The final part of the script displays the name of the month by drawing it from the $months array. Because indexed arrays begin at 0, you need to subtract 1 from the value of $i to get the right month.

> *I have not created similar drop-down menus for the day and year because PHP is a server-side language. Although you could create a script to display the correct number of days for the month, you would have to reload the page every time the month was changed. You could create an intelligent date input system with JavaScript, but that makes the dangerous assumption that all users will have JavaScript enabled. I demonstrate an alternative solution using Flash in* Foundation PHP 5 for Flash *(friends of ED, ISBN 1-59059-466-5).*

The code that validates the input and formats the date for MySQL also goes above the DOCTYPE declaration. It's a straightforward chain of if . . . else statements, which looks like this:

```php
if ($_POST) {
  $m = $_POST['month'];
  $d = trim($_POST['day']);
  $y = trim($_POST['year']);
  if (empty($d) || empty($y)) {
    $error = 'Please fill in all fields';
    }
  elseif (!is_numeric($d) || !is_numeric($y)) {
    $error = 'Please use numbers only';
    }
  elseif (($d <1 || $d > 31) || ($y < 1000 || $y > 9999)) {
    $error = 'Please use numbers within the correct range';
    }
  elseif (!checkdate($m,$d,$y)) {
    $error = 'You have used an invalid date';
    }
  else {
    $d = $d < 10 ? '0'.$d : $d;
    $mysqlFormat = "$y-$m-$d";
    }
}
```

You don't need to perform any checks on the value of the month, because the drop-down menu has generated it. So, after trimming any white space from around the day and year, they are subjected to the first three checks: to see if they are empty, not numeric, or out of range. You have met the empty() function before. The second check uses is_numeric(), which is basically self-explanatory. It takes advantage of PHP's loose typing. In strict terms of data types, the content of a text field is always a string, but is_numeric() also returns true if a string contains a number, such as '5'. (No, it's not clever enough to recognize 'five' as a number.) The third test looks for numbers within acceptable ranges. The values set for the day are immediately understandable (even though they don't apply to every month), but the range for years is dictated by the legal range for MySQL. In the unlikely event that you need a year out of that range, you must choose a different column type to store the data.

By using a series of elseif clauses, this code stops testing as soon as it meets the first mistake. If the input has survived the first three tests, it's then subjected to the PHP function checkdate(), which really puts a date through the mill. It's smart enough to know the difference between February 29 in a leap year and an ordinary year.

Finally, if the input has passed all these tests, it's rebuilt in the correct format for insertion into MySQL. The first line of the final else clause uses the ternary operator, as described earlier, to add a leading zero to the day of the month if necessary.

The way to integrate this routine into your own pages is by testing whether the POST array has any values, and whether the $error or $mysqlFormat variables have been set. The following code shows the way that it's done in date_converter.php:

```php
if ($_POST) {
  echo '<p>';
  if (isset($error)) {
    echo $error;
    }
  elseif (isset($mysqlFormat)) {
    echo $mysqlFormat;
    }
  echo '</p>';
  }
```

In the case of the example file, the tests are used to display the result. When adapting it for an insert form, for example, you would use the tests like this:

```php
if (isset($error)) {
  // abandon insertion of data and display error messages
  }
elseif (isset($mysqlFormat)) {
  // go ahead with insertion of data
  }
```

Mission almost accomplished

You have now worked with all the database-related server behaviors in Dreamweaver 8. At times, it has involved quite a lot of diving into Code view, but don't let that fool you. Dreamweaver has taken a huge amount of coding off your back and has reduced considerably the learning curve involved in working with a server-side language such as PHP.

As the photo gallery demonstrated, the total amount of PHP code that ends up in a complex page can actually be quite small. What takes the time—and expertise—is planning everything from the start. When working with a static website, you move around page elements that are immediately visible. With dynamic pages, you need to be able to step back and visualize the elements of a page in a more abstract way. As I mentioned in Chapter 4, there are two ways of approaching dynamic design: You can either create the code to generate totally unstyled pages and then use CSS to manipulate the page content, or you can design a static page and then work out how to generate the same code dynamically. Whichever approach you take, it requires a different mindset from standard web design.

Talking of which . . . Manipulating XML really does require a completely different approach, as you'll see in the next—and final—chapter.

Chapter 12

USING XSLT TO DISPLAY LIVE NEWS FEEDS AND XML

What this chapter covers:

- Understanding what XSLT does
- Examining the difference between client-side and server-side XSLT
- Determining whether your host supports XSLT
- Introducing Dreamweaver 8's XSL Transformation server behavior
- Drawing data from a live news feed into your site
- Creating an XSLT Fragment in Dreamweaver 8
- Embedding an XSLT Fragment into a PHP page
- Experimenting with the XPath Expression Builder

And now for something completely different . . .

No, it's not Monty Python, but XSLT (Extensible Stylesheet Language Transformations), which is very different from everything in the preceding 11 chapters. XSLT is a web technology that, among other things, can take the content of an XML file, such as a news feed, and transform it into an ordinary web page.

Support for XSLT is an important new feature of Dreamweaver 8, and the development team has put considerable effort into making XSLT as easy to work with as XHTML and PHP. However, it does require a slightly different mindset, which is why I've left the XSL Transformation server behavior right to the end of the book. The other reason I've left it to the end is because not all hosting companies support XSLT in PHP. Even if that's the case, you'll still be able to experiment with everything in this chapter as long as you created a local testing environment as described in Chapter 3.

In this chapter, you'll incorporate a live news feed from the BBC News website into the East-West Seasons site—a process that will take you only a few minutes. Then I'll show you how to do some more advanced things with an XML document using the XPath Expression Builder.

A quick guide to XML and XSLT

XSLT became a W3C (World Wide Web Consortium) standard in November 1999. Because of the "stylesheet" in its name, its role is often described as being to format XML (Extensible Markup Language) documents in a similar way to CSS. However, it's not really the *S* of XSLT—its stylesheet aspect—that's impressive (in my mind, that's still best handled with CSS), but the *T*—its ability to transform a document. XSLT can be used to traverse an XML document, selecting, sorting, and generally reorganizing the content in much the same way as you have been doing with PHP and MySQL. For example, if the elements in an XML document have an attribute called price, XSLT can present the elements in ascending or descending price order, or it can select items only above, below, or between specified amounts. You can't do that with CSS.

What an XML document looks like

XML is closely related to (X)HTML, so it looks reassuringly familiar, but there are two fundamental differences between them:

- (X)HTML has a fixed range of tags and attributes. In XML, you create your own.

- (X)HTML tags are concerned with the structure of a page (<head>, <body>, <p>, <table>, and so on), whereas XML tags normally describe the data they contain (for instance, the following example uses <Book> to store details of individual books.

An XML document can be regarded as a logical way of storing data, rather like in a database. The following is a simple example of an XML document:

```
<?xml version="1.0" ?>
<BookList>
  <Book ISBN="1590595696">
    <Title>Foundation PHP for Dreamweaver 8</Title>
    <Authors>
      <Author>David Powers</Author>
```

```
      </Authors>
      <Publisher>friends of ED</Publisher>
      <ListPrice>34.99</ListPrice>
    </Book>
    <Book ISBN="1590595688">
      <Title>Foundation ASP for Dreamweaver 8</Title>
      <Authors>
        <Author>Omar Elbaga</Author>
        <Author>Rob Turnbull</Author>
      </Authors>
      <Publisher>friends of ED</Publisher>
      <ListPrice>34.99</ListPrice>
    </Book>
  </BookList>
```

The first line is the **XML declaration**, often also referred to as the **XML prolog**, which tells browsers and processors that it's an XML document. The XML declaration is recommended, but not required. However, if you do include it, the XML declaration *must* be the first thing in the document. The W3C recommends using XML 1.0 unless you need the highly specialized features of XML 1.1 (www.w3.org/TR/2004/REC-xml11-20040204/#sec-xml11). The XML declaration can also contain an encoding attribute. If this attribute is omitted, as in the previous example, XML parsers automatically use Unicode (UTF-8 or UTF-16). Unaccented English uses ASCII, which is a subset of UTF-8, so there is usually no need to specify an encoding. However, UTF-8 encodes accented characters differently from region-specific encodings, such as ISO-8859-1 for Spanish, French, and most Western European languages. Consequently, if you're working with languages other than English, you should specify the appropriate encoding in the XML declaration, like this:

```
<?xml version="1.0" encoding="ISO-8859-1" ?>
```

Alternatively, save your document in UTF-8. In either case, you should use accented characters in the same way as in ordinary text. Don't use HTML entities.

- Teléfono is fine in XML

- Teléfono is not

If your XML source contains many HTML entities, you can get round this restriction by defining the entities yourself. How to do this is explained later in the chapter, in the section "Understanding how XSLT is structured."

As you can see from the previous example document, the tags give no indication as to how the document is intended to look. In fact, it's normally recommended that they shouldn't, because XML is intended primarily to store data in a hierarchical structure according to meaning, and without any reference to presentation. Unless you are working in a large collaborative project, which needs to use a standardized vocabulary, you can make up your own tags, as I have done here. They can be made up not only of alphanumeric characters, but can also include accented characters, Greek, Cyrillic, Chinese, and Japanese—in fact, any valid Unicode character. However, they cannot include any white space or punctuation other than the hyphen (-), underscore (_), and period (.). Nor can they begin with xml in any combination of uppercase or lowercase letters.

The goals of XML include being human-legible, and terseness is considered of minimal importance. So, instead of using <pub>, which could mean publisher, publication date, or somewhere to get a drink, I have been specific and used <Publisher>. The most important thing about an XML document is that it must be what is known as **well-formed**. The main rules of what constitutes a well-formed document are as follows:

- There can be only one root element.
- Every start tag must have a matching closing tag.
- Empty elements must have a forward slash before the closing angle bracket (/>).
- Elements must be properly nested.
- Attribute values must be in quotes.
- In the content of an element or attribute value, < and & must be replaced by < and & respectively.

If you look at the previous example, you will see that it's well-formed. It has only one root element: <BookList>. All other elements are nested inside the root element, and the nesting follows an orderly pattern. Even when a book has only one author, the <Author> tag is still nested inside <Authors>, and the value of the ISBN attribute is always in quotes. While these strict rules make XML more time-consuming to write, the predictability of a well-formed document makes it a lot easier to process. As you will see shortly, when you define an XML source, Dreamweaver 8 instantly builds a diagrammatic representation of the document structure that enables you to manipulate its content with XSLT.

> *A good starting place to learn more about XML is the XML FAQ, edited by Peter Flynn, at* http://xml.silmaril.ie.

Using client-side and server-side transformations

There are two ways of using XSLT: client-side and server-side. With client-side XSLT, you create an XSL page, and link it to the XML document just like linking a CSS stylesheet to an ordinary web page. The job of interpreting the XSLT instructions is then left up to the visitor's browser. Figures 12-1 and 12-2 show how two modern browsers handle the BBC news feed that you will use later in the chapter.

Figure 12-1. Viewed in a compatible browser, client-side XSLT renders an XML document like an ordinary web page.

In Figure 12-1, the Mac version of Firefox 1.0.7 has correctly interpreted the XSLT, and the feed looks like an ordinary web page. At the time of this writing, the minimum version of popular browsers that support XSLT is as follows: Internet Explorer 6, Firefox 1.0.2, Netscape 8, Mozilla 1.8, and Safari 1.3.

Opera 8.5, on the other hand, does *not* support client-side XSLT, so it simply presents the news feed as a jumble of continuous text, as shown in Figure 12-2. This lack of universal support for client-side XSLT means that you can only use it in controlled environments, such as an intranet, where you know that everyone is using a compatible browser.

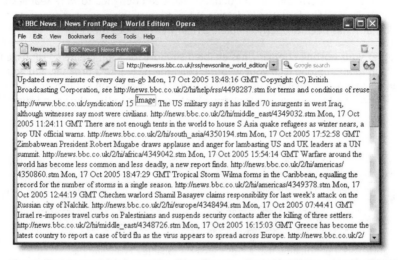

Figure 12-2. Opera 8.5 is incapable of handling the client-side XSLT used by the BBC RSS feed.

Another drawback of client-side XSLT is that the XSLT and XML documents must both reside in the same folder on the web server. So if you want to display the contents of a news feed from another site, you must first download the XML feed and store it locally.

To get round these problems, you can use XSLT to transform the XML document on the server and send the resultant (X)HTML output to the user. Because the server does everything, your visitors see exactly the same page regardless of which browser they're using. Moreover, with server-side transformation, you can pull the XML feed from any publicly available source on the Internet. There's only one fly in the ointment—your server must be capable of handling XSL transformations. I'll show you how to tell whether it does in the next section.

> I don't plan to say any more about client-side XSLT, but I suggest that you try the excellent tutorial that comes with Dreamweaver 8. You can find it by opening Help ➤ Getting Started with Dreamweaver ➤ Tutorial: Displaying XML Data. Even if you don't use client-side XSLT, the tutorial gives you a good feeling for how XML and XSLT fit together.
>
> Although the Dreamweaver server behavior outputs only (X)HTML, XSLT can be used to format XML documents in many ways. It's a massive subject, but a good starting point is the W3C FAQ, which can be found at www.w3.org/Style/XSL/WhatIsXSL.html. If you want to go into more detail, Jeni Tennison has written a very clear (but long) tutorial-style book called Beginning XSLT 2.0: From Novice to Professional (Apress, ISBN 1-59059-324-3).

Checking your server's capability

PHP has supported XSLT since version 4.0.3, but it's not enabled by default, and the implementation in PHP 4 isn't very easy to use. As a result, most hosting companies running PHP 4 don't support it. PHP 5 handles XSLT in a completely different way, and all the old functions have been deprecated. It's still not enabled by default, but it uses a standard external library (libxslt), so it is much easier to implement than before.

Dreamweaver 8's XSL Transformation server behavior has been designed to work seamlessly with both PHP 4 and PHP 5. The code automatically detects the version running on your server, so all you need to do is check that it has been properly enabled. Dreamweaver does the rest.

To check whether your hosting company has enabled support for XSLT, create a PHP page with <?php phpinfo(); ?> in it, and upload it to your website. Load the page into a browser, and you will see the same PHP configuration page that you used to test your local installation in Chapter 3. Scroll almost all the way to the bottom of the page, and look for a section similar to that shown in Figure 12-3.

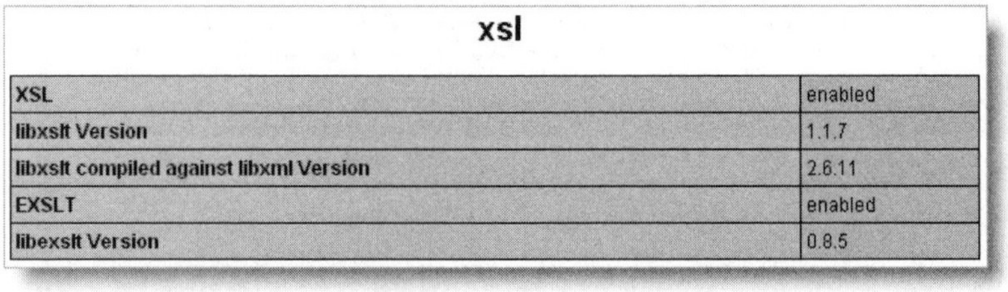

xsl	
XSL	enabled
libxslt Version	1.1.7
libxslt compiled against libxml Version	2.6.11
EXSLT	enabled
libexslt Version	0.8.5

Figure 12-3. Confirmation that a PHP 5 server is capable of handling the XSL Transformation server behavior

The figure shows what you are likely to see on a server running PHP 5 if it has been configured to handle XSLT. The configuration details will look slightly different on a PHP 4 installation. Instead of xsl, it should say xslt, but it should be in the same position just above the Additional Modules section, close to the bottom of the page. The difference in name simply reflects the functions they use. If you can't find either xsl or xslt, contact your host, and ask for the server to be upgraded. If hosts realize there is a genuine demand for new features, they are likely to respond, or risk losing business. If your host doesn't support XSLT, you can build the pages in the rest of this chapter and test them on your local computer, but you won't be able to upload them to your website.

> *Before continuing with the rest of the chapter, check that your local PHP installation supports the XSL extension by running* phpinfo(). *If you followed the setup instructions for Windows in Chapter 3 or used one of Marc Liyanage's PHP packages for the Mac, you should see the configuration section shown in Figure 12-3. If you can't see it and are running Windows, amend* php.ini *to enable* php_xsl.dll, *as described in step 10 of the "Downloading and installing PHP on Windows" section of Chapter 3. Save* php.ini *and restart Apache or IIS for the change to take effect. This won't work on a Mac. Support for all extensions must be enabled either through a precompiled package or by compiling PHP from source.*

Pulling in an RSS news feed

Figure 12-4 shows how news.php will look when it's finished. Obviously, the actual content will depend on the day's news, because it displays the latest international headlines from BBC Online (http://news.bbc.co.uk). Each headline is accompanied by a brief description of the news story, and a link back to the main BBC site, where visitors can read the story in detail. The page works in a very similar way to all those that you have created so far with a database. The difference this time is that the database you're drawing results from is not your own, but the BBC is accessed through an RSS feed.

Figure 12-4. What news.php looks like after the XSL Transformation server behavior has imported an external news feed.

RSS is one of those sets of initials that no one can agree on what they really stand for. Some say it means Really Simple Syndication. Others say it's Rich Site Summary. Yet others insist that it stands for RDF Site Summary, and that RDF is the Resource Description Framework. They're all equally valid; the fact is that RSS feeds are now a very common way of disseminating snatches of information over the Internet. Some web browsers, such as Safari and Firefox, let you bookmark RSS feeds and alert you when new articles appear on selected feeds. The important thing as far as you're concerned is that RSS feeds all conform to the rules of XML, so they're ideal for handling with the Dreamweaver XSL Transformation server behavior.

How Dreamweaver handles server-side XSLT

When a visitor requests news.php on the East-West Seasons website, the page that is served up looks and works in exactly the same way as any other web page. However, what goes on in the background is considerably more complex. Figure 12-5 shows a simplified outline of what happens.

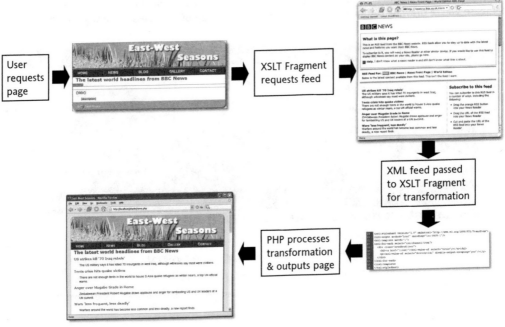

Figure 12-5. How a live XML feed is incorporated into news.php

Using the XSL Transformation server behavior involves a two-stage process:

1. Create a Dreamweaver XSLT Fragment that communicates directly with the XML document, which can be stored locally or pulled from a live Internet source.

2. Embed the XSLT Fragment in a PHP page.

All communication with the XML source is conducted by the XSLT Fragment, which Dreamweaver creates using the same drag-and-drop interface as for all dynamic data. Instead of PHP code, everything in the XSLT Fragment uses XSLT syntax. Where PHP comes into the picture is in processing the XSLT instructions. Most of the code is contained in an include file that Dreamweaver creates in a separate folder. The great thing from the developer's point of view is that you don't need to know any XSLT syntax for it to work. Of course, if you *do* know XSLT syntax, you can get the XSL Transformation server behavior to do a great deal more.

Choosing a suitable news feed

I've chosen to use one of the news feeds from BBC Online for several reasons, but primarily because it offers very good news coverage. The feed is also very easy to work with, and the BBC welcomes its use on websites, subject to certain simple terms and conditions. You can find the full details at http://news.bbc.co.uk/2/hi/help/rss/4498287.stm, but the main conditions are as follows:

- You cannot use the BBC logo on your site.
- You must provide a link back to the original story on the BBC website.
- You must attribute the source, using a specified formula, such as "From BBC News."
- You are not allowed to edit or alter the content in any way.
- You cannot use the content on sites that promote pornography, hatred, terrorism, or any illegal activity.

Of course, another reason for choosing the BBC is sentimental. I worked in BBC News for nearly 30 years, both as a correspondent and as an editor. I remember sitting in a basement in Marylebone High Street more than a decade ago talking to Mike Smartt about the Internet's potential for news. In spite of skepticism all around, he was convinced it was the way of the future. I knew he was right, but without Mike's vision and drive as first editor of BBC Online, it wouldn't have become the force that it is today.

To see all RSS feeds available from BBC News, go to http://news.bbc.co.uk/2/hi/help/3223484.stm. There are nearly 20 specialist news feeds, ranging from world news, health, science, and business to British news and entertainment. If you prefer news with an American flavor, try the New York Times (www.nytimes.com/services/xml/rss/index.html) or CNN (www.cnn.com/services/rss). In fact, you can get RSS feeds wherever you see the orange RSS or XML logos shown alongside. Much RSS content is copyright protected, so always make sure that you study the terms of use carefully.

Creating the XSLT Fragment

Because you are working with a live feed, you will need to be connected to the Internet for several steps during the following section.

1. From the Dreamweaver File menu, choose New. In the New Document dialog box, select the General tab, and then Basic Page from the Category list on the left. There are two options for XSLT—Entire page and Fragment. Entire page is used only for client-side XSLT. So choose XSLT (Fragment) and click Create.

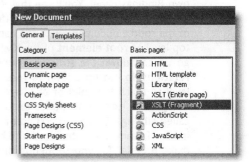

2. Dreamweaver immediately presents you with the dialog box shown here. It offers two options: to work with a local XML file or a remote one on the Internet. Select the radio button labeled Attach a remote file on the Internet, and insert the following URL: http://newsrss.bbc.co.uk/rss/newsonline_world_edition/front_page/rss.xml. Click OK.

Of course, you can use a different URL, if you prefer. The structure of all RSS feeds is very similar, so you should have no difficulty adapting the following instructions. However, you may find it easier to practice with the BBC feed first.

3. If you don't know the URL of the XML file, clicking Cancel doesn't stop Dreamweaver from creating an XSLT Fragment page. You can reopen the Locate XML Source dialog box by clicking either Source or XML in the Bindings panel, as shown.

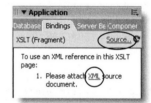

4. As long as you are connected to the Internet, Dreamweaver will contact the BBC Online site and populate the Bindings panel with a document tree like that shown in Figure 12-6. This shows you the structure (Dreamweaver uses the technical term, **schema**) of the XML document sent by the RSS feed.

5. Before working with the XML data, save the page as bbc_feed.xsl. On Windows, Dreamweaver will automatically add the .xsl on the end of the filename, even if you delete it in the Save As dialog box.

6. Take a good look at Figure 12-6 or the actual schema in your own Bindings panel. You'll see that it's like a family tree. The angle brackets (<>) represent the different elements or **nodes** of the source document, with the name shown alongside. The top level or **root element** of the XML document is rss. As you go up and down the structure, nodes share a **parent-child relationship**. Go up a level to reach the parent; go down a level to reach the child or children. This genealogical termi-nology also extends to nodes on the same level, which are called **siblings**. So item is a child of channel and a sibling to image. Dreamweaver builds this diagrammatic hierarchy to make it easier for you to identify the elements you want to manipulate, and XSLT uses it as a sort of road map to perform the transformation.

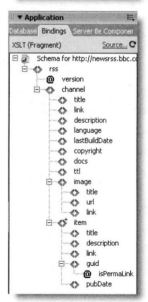

Figure 12-6. Dreamweaver builds a tree (or schema) of the XML source in the Bindings panel.

Attributes that appear within XML tags are designated by @. So at the top of Figure 12-6, you can see that rss has an attribute called version. The channel and image nodes contain child nodes that describe the feed. The news comes much further down: in the sixth node from the bottom labeled item.

The important thing to note about item is that it has a tiny plus sign to the upper-right of the angle brackets. This indicates that it's a repeating element.

Branching off item are five child nodes: title, description, link, guid (with an attribute isPermaLink), and pubDate. The ones we are interested in are title, which contains the headline, description, which contains a summary of the news story, and link, the URL to the full story.

7. Click anywhere inside Design view to make sure it has the focus, and then click the Insert Div Tag icon on the Common Insert bar. In the Insert Div Tag dialog box, select At insertion point for the Insert setting, and type newsHeadlines in the Class field. Click OK.

8. In the Property inspector, select Heading 2 from the Format drop-down menu, and then press *DELETE* to remove the Dreamweaver place-holder text. Select title from the item node in the Bindings panel. Drag title from the Bindings panel into the <div>.

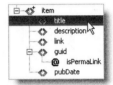

> It's very easy to go wrong when selecting nodes, because several share the same name. There are three nodes each called title and link, and two called description. All the nodes that you need to select in steps 8 through 12 are children of the item repeating node.

9. You should now see a dynamic placeholder inside the <div>. It will be displayed in a large font, because of the Heading 2 format. The placeholder indicates the path to title within the hierarchy of the XML document.

10. Click to the right of the dynamic placeholder, and press *ENTER/RETURN* to insert a new paragraph. Highlight description in the item node, and drag it into the paragraph that you have just created. You should now have a similar dynamic placeholder for {rss/channel/item/description}.

11. As part of the BBC conditions of use, you must provide a link back to the complete story, so let's turn the headline into a link. Highlight the title dynamic placeholder, and click the Browse for File icon to the right of the Link field in the Property inspector.

12. When the Select File dialog box opens, choose Data sources as the option for Select file from. (It's a radio button at the top of the dialog box in Windows, but an ordinary button at the bottom of the dialog box in the Mac version.) Scroll down inside the area labeled Select node to display and select link. This will insert rss/channel/item/link in the URL field. Leave the other options at their default settings, and click OK. You will see there's now a dynamic placeholder in the Link field of the Property inspector.

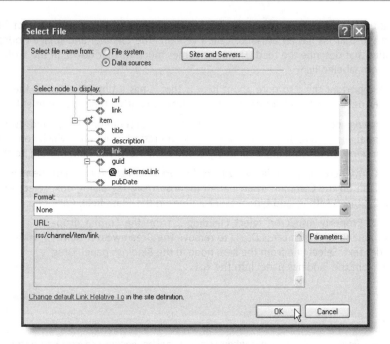

13. Because item is a repeating element, you need to tell XSLT to display the <div> as a repeated region. In the Tag selector at the bottom of the Document window, select <div.newsHeadlines> to highlight the whole <div>. Then select the XSLT category on the Insert bar. (If you're wondering why you have never noticed XSLT before, it's because it's displayed only when you're in an XSL file.) Click the Repeat Region icon.

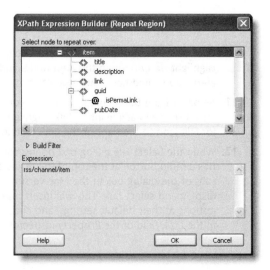

14. This brings up a completely different dialog box from the one you used with the PHP server behavior. It's the XPath Expression Builder. XPath is the W3C standard that describes how to identify parts of an XML document. In many ways, it's very similar to ordinary file paths and URLs, but it has many more options (www.w3.org/TR/xpath), including functions. The XPath Expression Builder incorporates a lot of these functions and builds an XPath with the correct syntax for you.

All you need to do is highlight the parent node of the elements that you want to repeat—in other words, item. In the XPath Expression Builder, scroll down to the bottom of the section labeled Select node to repeat over, and select item. Dreamweaver inserts rss/channel/item into the Expression field at the bottom. Click OK.

15. When the XPath Expression Builder closes, you will see a gray tabbed border around the <div>, and the dynamic placeholders will have changed to just the node names, as shown alongside. This is because the XPath expression created in the previous step tells the underlying XSLT code where to find them.

16. Save `bbc_feed.xsl` and press *F12/OPT+F12* to view the page in a browser. If all has gone well and you are connected to the Internet, you should see something like Figure 12-7, except with the very latest headlines, not something from all those months ago when I was writing this book. Look in the browser address bar, and you will see that Dreamweaver is using a temporary file, even if you have set your preferences not to use temporary files. You can't use an XSLT Fragment in a browser on its own, nor can you use Live Data view, but Dreamweaver processes it internally so you can check that everything is working as expected before embedding it into a PHP file. Test some of the links to make sure that your XSLT Fragment is linking correctly to the BBC site. You can check your code against `bbc_feed.xsl` in `site_check/ch12`.

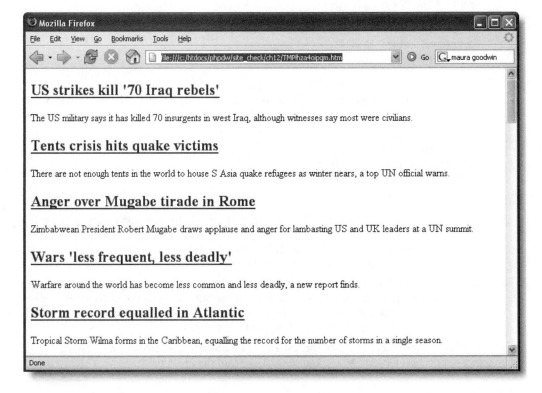

Figure 12-7. Dreamweaver uses a temporary file to confirm that the XSLT Fragment is working as expected.

You can't use the XSLT Fragment on its own; you need to serve it through a dynamic page so that the PHP server behavior can perform the necessary server-side transformation.

1. In the previous section, you created a class called newsHeadlines for the <div> that contains the XSLT placeholders. Let's start by adding the necessary style rules to the stylesheets. The styles for the links don't do anything that is likely to upset older browsers, so put these rules in basic.css:

```
/* styles for headlines in XSLT page */
.newsHeadlines a {
  text-decoration: none;
}
.newsHeadlines a:link {
  color: #524872;
}
.newsHeadlines a:visited {
  color: #A8B2A3;
}
.newsHeadlines a:hover, .newsHeadlines a:active {
  background-color: #A8B2A3;
  color: #fff;
}
```

2. There's one other rule to give the headlines a bit of padding. Put this at the bottom of bluebells.css:

```
/* style for XSLT */
.newsHeadlines h2 {
  padding: 3px 5px !important;
  font-size: 110% !important;
}
```

3. Open news.php, which you created in Chapters 4 and 5. (If you don't have a copy, use news_01.php from site_check/ch12.) Highlight the placeholder text in the maincontent <div>. Use the Format field in the Property inspector to style it as Heading 1, and replace the text with The latest world headlines from BBC News.

4. Select the <h1> in the Tag selector to highlight the heading, and press your right arrow key once so that the cursor is outside the closing </h1> tag but still inside the maincontent <div>. Use Split view to check the position of the cursor if you're not sure. You need to do this to prevent adding extra space when the XSLT Fragment is embedded.

5. In the Application Insert bar, click the XSL Transformation icon. Alternatively, select Application Objects ➤ XSL Transformation from the Insert menu.

6. In the XSL Transformation dialog box that opens, click the top Browse button and navigate to `bbc_feed.xsl`. When you click OK in the Select XSLT File dialog box, Dreamweaver will automatically populate the XML URI field. This is the address of the BBC RSS feed, which Dreamweaver gets from the XSLT Fragment. You don't need to bother with XSLT parameters, so just click OK.

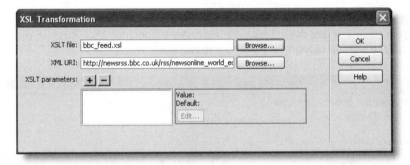

7. Your page should now look like Figure 12-8. Although it looks as though the XSLT Fragment has just been included in the page in the same way as the include files that you used in Chapters 5 and 6, the underlying code is completely different. You cannot make any changes to the XSLT Fragment in the PHP page—you need to return to `bbc_feed.xsl` if you want to make any adjustments. However, that shouldn't be necessary. Save `news.php` and press *F12/OPT+F12* to view it in a browser.

Figure 12-8. The XSLT Fragment looks the same when it's embedded in a PHP page, but the underlying code is very different.

445

8. Your page should now look like Figure 12-4. This time, instead of using a temporary file, the RSS feed is being transformed by PHP through your web server. When uploading this page to your remote server, you must remember to upload not only news.php and bbc_feed.xsl, but also the PHP class that does all the hard work. It's MM_XSLTransform.class.php, which is located in includes/MM_XSLTransform. Compare your code, if necessary, with news_02.php in site_check/ch12.

If instead of the latest news headlines, you get the message shown in Figure 12-9, it means that your remote server doesn't have the necessary support for XSLT. Pressure your hosting company to provide support, or move to one that does.

Figure 12-9. The message that nobody wants to see: The news feed can't be processed because XSLT hasn't been enabled on the server.

Being a bit more adventurous with XSLT

Up to now, I have deliberately not dived under the hood to show you what's going on in Code view. There's actually very little code, but it's very different from what you've been working with in previous chapters. In the last few pages of this book, I'd like to show you just a few of the things you can do if you decide to experiment with XSLT and XPath. Instead of using a live news feed as the XML source, I've prepared an XML document that contains details of the friends of ED and Apress catalog.

Setting up a local XML source

Getting XML data from a local source involves nothing more complicated than telling Dreamweaver where to find it. You will find a copy of booklist.xml in the site_check/ch12 folder of the download files, and you can access it directly from there. Open it and take a look at its structure. The root element is called BookList, and it contains ten elements each called Book, which look like this:

```
<Book ISBN="1590595696">
  <Title>Foundation PHP for Dreamweaver 8</Title>
  <Authors>
    <Author>David Powers</Author>
  </Authors>
  <Publisher>friends of ED</Publisher>
  <ListPrice>34.99</ListPrice>
</Book>
```

Each Book element or node has an attribute called ISBN and four child elements: Title, Authors, Publisher, and ListPrice. In turn, Authors can have one or more child elements called Author.

Displaying the node tree (schema) of booklist.xml

1. Choose File ➤ New ➤ Basic Page ➤ XSLT (Fragment).

2. In the Locate XML Source dialog box, choose the default option (Attach a local file on my computer or local area network) and click the Browse button to navigate to booklist.xml. Notice that the dialog box you use to locate the XML file is called "Locate Source XML for XSL Template." Although XSL templates are very different from Dreamweaver templates, the idea is the same: an XSL template defines the basic pattern that will be applied to all the data passed to it. After locating booklist.xml, click OK (or Choose on a Mac). Click OK to close the Locate XML Source dialog box.

3. This will attach booklist.xml to the XSLT Fragment and display the structure of the document in the Bindings panel, as shown in Figure 12-10. Although the document tree is much shorter than the BBC RSS feed, it contains two repeating nodes: Book and Author. Moreover, Author is a grandchild of Book. In other words, you have a repeating region within a repeating region. Each book can have more than one author, so this makes handling more complex than the BBC feed.

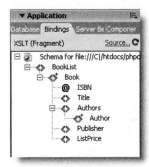

Figure 12-10. The node tree (schema) of booklist.xml

4. Save the XSLT Fragment page as books1.xsl in a new folder called xsl_tests. As you progress through the rest of this chapter, save all pages connected with the booklist in the same folder.

5. Even after naming the page, the Bindings panel continues to display the full path name. This makes no difference, but if you click the circular arrow alongside Source in the top-right of the Bindings panel, the local file path will replace the full path.

Displaying the book list in a table

Since the purpose is to show you a few of the things you can do with XSLT in Dreamweaver, I don't plan styling the content. The data in the book list is best displayed in a table, so that's what I'll use. Copies of all the files used in the rest of this chapter are in site_check/ch12.

1. Insert a table in books1.xsl. The table should have two rows and five columns. I also set Table width to 80 percent, and Cell padding to 4, leaving both Border thickness and Cell spacing blank.

2. Give the first row the following headings: Title, Author(s), Publisher, ISBN, and Price.

3. Drag the Title node from the Bindings panel and drop it in the second row, so that the dynamic placeholder sits beneath the Title heading in the first row. Do the same for Publisher, ISBN, and ListPrice, dropping them in the appropriate cells in the second row. What should you do about the Author(s) cell? You want to show the names of all the authors, so you probably think you should use the Author node. Illogical though it may seem, drag the parent node, Authors, *not* the child node.

4. Click anywhere in the second row, and then select <tr> in the Tag selector to highlight the entire table row.

5. In the XSLT Insert bar, click the Repeat Region icon, and select the Book node in the XPath Expression Builder (Repeat Region) dialog box. Click OK. Your page should now look like this:

6. Save books1.xsl and press *F12/OPT+F12* to view the XSLT Fragment in a browser. Surprise, surprise . . . all the authors' names are listed. To understand why, you need to dive into the mysteries of XSLT syntax.

Understanding how XSLT is structured

If you've not done so already, now is the time to look at an XSLT Fragment in Code view. In Dreamweaver, switch to Code view in books1.xsl. The first line looks like this:

```
<?xml version="1.0" encoding="ISO-8859-1"?>
➥ <!-- DWXMLSource="../site_check/ch12/booklist.xml" -->
```

You may recognize the first part as the XML declaration. By default, Dreamweaver inserts the encoding attribute using the same value as in your Dreamweaver preferences. If your XML source uses a different encoding (the default is UTF-8), you should change the setting for your XSLT Fragment and any dynamic page that you intend to embed it in. Do this by choosing Page Properties from the Modify menu. In the Page Properties dialog box, select the Title/Encoding category and set Encoding to the appropriate value.

The second part of the first line is an XML comment (the same format as HTML is used), where Dreamweaver stores the location of the XML source.

The next 12 lines define some common HTML entities. This is because only the following five entities are predefined in XML: < (<), & (&), > (>), " ("), and ' (').

Defining new entities If you discover that your XSLT Fragments are having problems with unrecognized entities, add a new definition on a new line within this section, using the same format. For example, if you want to add the entity for lowercase e acute (é), add this line:

```
<!ENTITY eacute    "&#233;">
```

In other words, remove the leading & and trailing semicolon from the HTML entity, and put the character entity equivalent in quotes. You can find a full list of HTML entities and their character entity equivalents at www.w3.org/TR/html4/sgml/entities.html.

Embedding XHTML in XSLT The rest of the code in the page is a mixture of XSLT and XHTML. The two fit together in a very similar way to PHP and XHTML. The XSLT processor handles anything in an XSLT tag (they all begin with <xsl:), and it treats anything outside as literal text. I have reproduced here the main XSLT code from books1.xsl, and highlighted some key points in bold:

```
<xsl:stylesheet version="1.0" xmlns:xsl="http://www.w3.org/1999/
➥ XSL/Transform">
<xsl:output method="html" encoding="ISO-8859-1"/>
<xsl:template match="/">
<table width="80%" cellpadding="4">
  <tr>
    <th scope="col">Title</th>
    <th scope="col">Author(s)</th>
    <th scope="col">Publisher</th>
    <th scope="col">ISBN</th>
    <th scope="col">Price</th>
  </tr>
  <xsl:for-each select="BookList/Book">
    <tr>
      <td><xsl:value-of select="Title"/></td>
      <td><xsl:value-of select="Authors"/></td>
      <td><xsl:value-of select="Publisher"/></td>
      <td><xsl:value-of select="@ISBN"/></td>
      <td><xsl:value-of select="ListPrice"/></td>
    </tr>
  </xsl:for-each>
</table>
</xsl:template>
</xsl:stylesheet>
```

The first line that I have highlighted creates an XSLT template. XSLT templates match a certain part of the XML source (hence the attribute match). The closing </xsl:template> tag is on the second line from the bottom, so all the code in between is part of the template. The value of match is /, which is the XPath way of indicating the document root. In other words, this set of XSLT instructions will be applied to the whole of the XML source, rather than just a specific part of it.

449

The next highlighted line uses <xsl:for-each>. As you can probably guess, this is the way that XSLT creates a loop. The value of select is BookList/Book, so the loop applies to every Book node or element in the XML document. As the loop goes through each Book node, the <xsl:value-of> instruction gets the selected value. When it gets to the Authors node, it also loops through the child nodes. That's why you see all the author's names displayed in the table, even though you haven't selected the Author node in your XSLT Fragment.

Accessing nested repeating elements

In some respects, the way that XSLT loops through the child nodes is quite useful, but there are no commas between the authors' names. You need a way of getting to the Author nodes and manipulating them. This is where things get interesting or fiendishly complicated, depending on your point of view. I'll try to keep things as simple as possible. Once you understand what's happening, it's a lot simpler than it may seem at your first attempt.

Accessing the Author elements directly

1. Save books1.xsl as books2.xsl. Select the {Authors} placeholder in the second row of the table, and press *DELETE*. Your page should look like this:

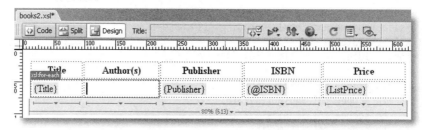

2. Select the Author repeating node in the Bindings panel, and drag and drop it into the empty cell. Instead of inserting an Author dynamic placeholder, as you might expect, Dreamweaver inserts an XSLT repeat region with a text placeholder, as shown here.

3. Highlight the words Content goes here, and press *DELETE*. Make sure you remove only the text, and not the gray tab labeled xsl:for-each. Don't click anywhere in the document, because the cursor *must* remain inside the repeat region.

4. From the Insert menu, choose XSLT Objects ➤ Dynamic Text. This opens the XPath Expression Builder. Select Author. It may appear as though Dreamweaver hasn't created anything in the Expression field, but look a bit closer. There's a single period (.) there, which is the XPath way of saying "current node." Click OK.

5. You should now have a current-node dynamic placeholder inside the repeat region.

6. Save `books2.xsl` and press *F12/OPT+F12* to view the output in a browser. The authors' names are there, but things have got worse—there's no space between them any more. Switch back to Dreamweaver, where you'll put it right.

7. Select the current-node dynamic placeholder that you created in step 5. Open Split view. You will see the following line highlighted in the underlying code:

```
<xsl:value-of select="."/>
```

8. Click inside Code view and add the following code on a new line underneath. I've shown the preceding and following lines to help you get the right location.

```
<xsl:value-of select="."/>
<xsl:text>, </xsl:text>
</xsl:for-each></td>
```

When you start typing, Dreamweaver code hints will display the available XSLT tags. To save typing, you can scroll down to xsl:text and press *ENTER/RETURN*. Automatic code completion will also insert the correct closing tag after you type </.

This inserts a comma followed by a space after the name of each author. You could just type the comma, but to get the space you need to wrap it in the `<xsl:text>` tags.

9. Save `books2.xsl` and view it in a browser. This is progress, but you don't want a comma after the last name. To deal with that, you need to use a conditional region.

Creating conditional regions

The XSLT Insert bar has two options for creating a conditional region—Conditional Region and Multiple Conditional Region. The first is the direct equivalent of a PHP `if` statement, and is quite easy to use. The second works the same way as an `if . . . else` statement but is a little more complex.

Inserting a simple conditional expression

1. Save `books2.xsl` as `books3.xsl`. Open Split view and highlight the line that you inserted in step 8 of the previous exercise. Alternatively, click the xsl:text tab in Design view. Click the Conditional Region icon in the XSLT Insert bar.

2. XSLT uses functions to determine the position of an element in a node. They are very intuitively named: position() determines the position, and last() determines whether an element is in the last position. You don't want the comma to be displayed if the author's name is the last one, so type position() != last() in the Test field of the Conditional Region dialog box.

3. Save `books3.xsl` and view it in a browser. The author's names are now nicely formatted.

Although there's a comma between each of the author's names when there are more than one, it would be more natural to replace the comma with "and" or "&" before the last name. The logic behind how you do this is simple. Instead of placing the comma *after* each author's name, create a conditional statement that decides whether to put a comma or "and" *before* the name. In pseudocode this becomes:

```
if (position is greater than 1 AND position is not last) {
  insert a comma before the name
  }
else if (position is greater than 1 AND position is last) {
  insert "and" before the name
  }
```

Inserting a multiple conditional region

1. Save `books3.xsl` as `books4.xsl`. Things are beginning to look rather crowded in the table cell that contains the dynamic placeholders for the authors' names. You need to click the xsl:if tab indicated by the arrow in the screenshot alongside.

   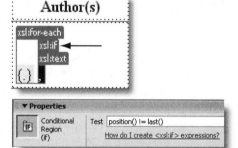

   You will know that you have selected it correctly if the Property inspector displays the test expression for the conditional region as shown here (this is also how you would edit it).

   > *If you have difficulty selecting the tab, use the Zoom tool in the Status bar at the bottom right of the Document window (it looks like a magnifying glass). When you select the Zoom tool, click on the area that you want to magnify until it's big enough to work with. Then choose the Select tool (an arrow) from the Status bar. To zoom out again, hold down ALT/OPT while clicking.*

2. Open Split view. You will see the following code highlighted:

```
<xsl:if test="position() != last()">
  <xsl:text>, </xsl:text>
</xsl:if>
```

   The syntax is very intuitive. However, XSLT uses completely different syntax for a multiple conditional region, so you cannot adapt a simple condition. Moreover, you need to move the comma. Press *DELETE* to remove the highlighted code.

3. In Code view, your cursor will be just below `<xsl:value-of select="."/>`. You need to insert the comma as `<xsl:text>` on a new line above, like this:

```
<td><xsl:for-each select="Authors/Author">
  <xsl:text>, </xsl:text>
  <xsl:value-of select="."/>
```

4. Highlight the line that you have just inserted, and click the Multiple Conditional Region icon on the XSLT Insert bar.

5. Type the following in the Test field of the Multiple Conditional Region dialog box:

position() > 1 and position != last()

This will show the comma and space if the element is neither first nor last. Click OK.

6. If you thought the table cell was crowded before, just look at it now! The XSLT syntax uses <xsl:choose> to wrap the whole of a multiple conditional, <xsl:when> equates to if, and <xsl:otherwise> equates to else. Dreamweaver inserts Content goes here as a placeholder inside <xsl:otherwise>. This is where you are expected to create a default value if all tests fail. However, you don't want a default for this conditional region, so highlight Content goes here and delete it. Keep Split view open to make sure you don't delete any XSLT tags.

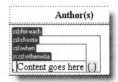

7. To create the second condition, you need to position your cursor inside Code view immediately before the opening <xsl:otherwise> tag. Then click the Conditional Region icon on the XSLT Insert bar. Make sure you click the one for a single condition (marked with IF), and *not* the icon for a multiple condition.

8. Type the following in the Test field of the Conditional Region dialog box, and then click OK:

position() > 1 and position() = last()

You'll use this test to insert "and" surrounded by a space on either side before the last author's name. It's necessary to check that the position is greater than 1 because you don't want "and" to appear before the names of single authors.

9. There's now a severe overcrowding problem in the table cell, as Dreamweaver inserts another Content goes here to indicate where to insert what will be displayed when the test evaluates to true. It's easier to work in Code view at this stage, so click inside Code view and replace Content goes here with **<xsl:text> and </xsl:text>**.

> *As you're typing, you'll notice that the greater-than sign you added in step 8 has been replaced by >. This is because > indicates the end of a tag, so XSLT conditional expressions use the HTML entity instead. XSLT also requires quotes in expressions. Dreamweaver handles all the necessary conversions automatically if you use the appropriate dialog boxes.*

10. Save books4.xsl and view it in a browser. You should see commas between names, with "and" separating the final two.

11. Change <xsl:text> and </xsl:text> to <xsl:text> & </xsl:text> and view the page again. It won't work. You get the following error:

SAXParseException: Expected entity name for reference (books4.xsl, line 34, column 25)

This is because & is used by XML-related languages, such as XSLT, to designate an entity. Replace & with &, and all will be well.

Sorting elements

So far all of the books in the table appear in the same order as in the original XML source. Dreamweaver doesn't provide an option for sorting, but it's very easy to do by coding manually.

Sorting the book list by title and publisher

1. Save `books4.xsl` as `books5.xsl`, and open the document in Code view.

2. Locate the following code (it should be around line 25):

   ```
   <xsl:for-each select="BookList/Book">
   ```

3. Insert a new line immediately below, and add the code shown in bold:

   ```
   <xsl:for-each select="BookList/Book">
   <xsl:sort select="Title"/>
   ```

4. Save the page and view it in a browser. The value of `select` determines which node is used to sort the document. The list is now sorted by the books' titles.

5. You can use multiple sort conditions by adding similar tags in the order of priority that you want to give each element. Since the titles are unique, that sort order will always prevail, so to sort by publisher and then by title, use the following:

   ```
   <xsl:for-each select="BookList/Book">
   <xsl:sort select="Publisher"/>
   <xsl:sort select="Title"/>
   ```

   All Apress books now appear first, with their titles sorted in correct alphabetical order, followed by all friends of ED books similarly sorted. Like PHP, *XSLT is case-sensitive*, so make sure you use the correct case for the node names.

Formatting elements

You may have noticed that there's a drop-down menu labeled Format in the middle of the XPath Expression Builder. This allows you to apply 22 preset formats to the content of a node. Most of them deal with formatting numbers or currency.

Formatting the book prices

1. Save `books5.xsl` as `books6.xsl`.

2. In Design view, double-click the ListPrice dynamic placeholder in the second row of the table. This opens the XPath Expression Builder.

3. Activate the Format drop-down menu, and select Currency – Leading 0, 2 Decimal Places. The Expression field displays the XPath function that will be inserted in the underlying code: format-number(ListPrice, '$#0.00'). Click OK.

4. Save `books6.xsl` and view it in a browser. Nothing is different—the prices don't have any currency symbol. This is because the parser used by Dreamweaver can't process all XSLT functions.

5. Create a PHP page called books.php. The only reason you need this page is to embed the XSLT Fragment, but it's best to insert some ordinary text. Otherwise, you won't be able to click inside the Document window after the fragment has been embedded. Type a heading, such as Book list. Move the cursor out of the heading, and select Insert ➤ Application Objects ➤ XSL Transformation.

6. In the XSL Transformation dialog box, click the top Browse button and select books6.xsl as the XSLT file. Click OK (or Choose on a Mac) to close both dialog boxes.

7. Save books.php and view it in a browser. The currency symbols now appear correctly.

At the bottom of the Format drop-down menu in the XPath Expression Builder is an option to edit the format list. Ideally, this should be the place to create a custom currency format for sterling or euro. Unfortunately, Dreamweaver converts both the £ and € symbols to their HTML equivalents, which not only prevents them being displayed in the final page, but also prevents you from using the XPath Expression Builder to edit any element to which you apply the format. The solution, fortunately, is very simple: apply one of the standard currency formats and edit it manually in Code view.

Change this:

```
format-number(ListPrice, '$#0.00')
```

to this (for pounds sterling):

```
format-number(ListPrice, '£#0.00')
```

or this (for euro):

```
format-number(ListPrice, '€#0.00')
```

You may wonder why the actual symbol is used instead of an entity. It's because the second argument to format-number() is a string literal. If you use an entity, it will be ignored.

Displaying output selectively

There are two ways of displaying output that meets certain criteria. One is to use an XPath filter. The other is to use a parameter. Let's take a quick look at both of them.

Using a filter to select books by price

1. Save books6.xsl as books7.xsl.

2. Select the repeat region for the second table row by clicking the xsl:for-each tab above the {Title} dynamic placeholder. You can tell that you have selected it correctly by checking the Property inspector, which should look like this:

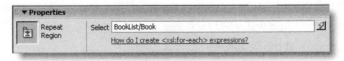

455

3. Click the lightning bolt icon to the right of the Select field in the Property inspector to open the XPath Expression Builder.

4. Click the triangle to the side of Build Filter in the middle of the XPath Expression Builder. This reveals an area where you can build filters to select nodes according to certain criteria. This is very similar to using a WHERE expression in a SQL query.

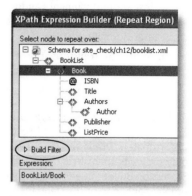

5. Click the plus button at the top of the Build Filter area. Click in the Where field to activate the drop-down menu that contains a list of all nodes. Select ListPrice.

6. Click in the Operator field and choose <= (less than or equal to).

7. Click in the Value field and type 45. Click anywhere inside the dialog box to remove the focus from the Value field. The Build Filter area should now look lke this:

8. Click OK. Save `books7.xsl` and view the page in a browser. Instead of the previous ten books, you should now see just eight—all priced $45 or less.

> If you are using the Windows version of Dreamweaver on a monitor with the minimum required resolution (1024X768), the OK, Cancel, and Help buttons will be hidden behind the Windows taskbar when the Build Filter area is open. Click and drag upwards the title bar of the XPath Expression Builder to reveal them. The development team is aware of this problem, but was unable to fix it in time for the release of Dreamweaver 8.

Using a multiple filter

1. Save `books7.xsl` as `books8.xsl`, and repeat steps 2 and 3 of the previous exercise to open the XPath Expression Builder. Expand the Build Filter area if it's not already open.

2. Click in the and/or field, and select and from the drop-down menu.

3. Click the plus button at the top left of the Build Filter area to add another filter.

4. Click the Where field and select Publisher.

5. Leave Operator at the default =.

6. Click the Value field and type 'Apress'—it *must* be in quotes (single or double: it doesn't matter). The Build Filter area should now look like this.

7. Click OK, save the page, and view it in a browser. You will now see just two titles listed.

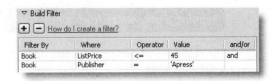

As you can see, using XPath filters is very similar to creating WHERE clauses in SQL. Look at the underlying code and you will see that Dreamweaver has converted quotes and the less-than operator to HTML entities, saving you a lot of effort with building XPath expressions. Remember to use the normal characters in the dialog boxes so that Dreamweaver can convert them correctly. It's also vital to remember that strings entered in the Value field must always be in quotes.

The other way of selecting output is by passing one or more parameters from the PHP page to the XSLT Fragment. This is much more interactive, because the decision about what to display is dynamically generated, unlike filters, which are hard-coded into the XSLT instructions.

Using an XSLT parameter to select the publisher

1. Save books8.xsl as books9.xsl.

2. Switch to Code view and locate the following code (around line 15):

```
<xsl:output method="html" encoding="ISO-8859-1"/>
<xsl:template match="/">
```

3. Insert an XSLT parameter like this:

```
<xsl:output method="html" encoding="ISO-8859-1"/>
<xsl:param name="pub" select="'friends of ED'"/>
<xsl:template match="/">
```

The <xsl:param> tag takes two attributes: name, which is self-explanatory, and select, which sets the default value for the parameter. Note that there are two sets of quotes around friends of ED. The double quotes surround the value of select, which is a string and must itself be enclosed in quotes. To avoid a clash, single quotes are used for the inner pair.

By declaring the parameter immediately after the <xsl:output> tag, you make it global in scope—in other words, available throughout the XSLT script.

4. Switch back to Design view, select the xsl:for-each tab that controls the repeat region for the entire table row, and click the lighting bolt icon in the Property inspector to open the XPath Expression Builder. You should see the same two filters as in step 6 of the last exercise.

5. Highlight the first filter (based on ListPrice) and click the minus button to remove it.

6. Click inside the Value field of the remaining filter to reveal a drop-down menu. You should now see your XSLT parameter listed with a dollar sign in front of it. Select $pub in place of 'Apress'. The Expression field should now read: BookList/Book[Publisher = $pub]. Click OK.

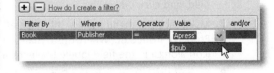

7. Save books9.xsl and view it in a browser. Only friends of ED books should be listed, because that was the default you set for the parameter in step 3.

457

Sending a parameter from a PHP page

The real value of using parameters doesn't become obvious until you embed the XSLT Fragment into a dynamic page. This simple exercise demonstrates how you can toggle between displaying books published by Apress and friends of ED, using a jump menu to send the parameter to the XSLT fragment through a URL query string.

1. Create a new PHP page called books_param.php.

2. From the Insert menu, select Form ➤ Jump Menu.

3. In the Insert Jump Menu dialog box, insert Apress in the Text field, and ?pub=Apress in the field labeled When selected, go to URL. This will add the name and value of the parameter to a query string that will be added to the URL when the page reloads.

4. Click the plus button to add a second menu item. Insert friends of ED in the Text field, and ?pub=friends of ED for When selected, go to URL. Leave the other options in the dialog box unchanged. When you have finished, it should look like this:

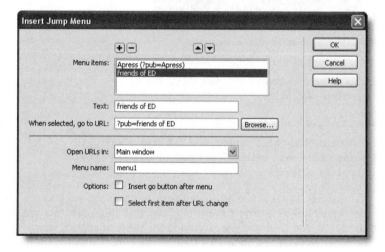

5. Click OK to insert the jump menu, and then select the menu object in Design view. In the Property inspector, change the name of the menu to pub. You also need the menu to display the currently selected value. Apart from the first time the page loads, this comes from the value of pub in the URL query string. Before clicking the Dynamic button in the Property inspector, you need to create a URL variable for Dreamweaver to use.

6. Open the Bindings panel, click the plus button, and select URL variable. Type pub in the Name field, and click OK.

7. Make sure the menu item is still selected in Design view, and click the Dynamic button in the Property inspector. When the Dynamic List/Menu dialog box opens, click the lightning bolt icon alongside the field labeled Select value equal to.

8. Expand the URL tree in the Dynamic Data dialog box, select pub, and click OK. Also click OK in the Dynamic List/Menu dialog box to close it.

9. Unfortunately, the code created by Dreamweaver needs tweaking slightly. Open Code view or Split view. The jump menu code should look like this:

```
17  <form name="form1" id="form1">
18    <select name="pub" id="pub" onchange="MM_jumpMenu('parent',this,0)">
19      <option value="?pub=Apress" <?php if (!(strcmp("?pub=Apress", $_GET['pub']))) {echo
    "selected=\"selected\"";} ?>>Apress</option>
20      <option value="?pub=friends of ED" <?php if (!(strcmp("?pub=friends of ED", $_GET['pub']))) {echo
    "selected=\"selected\"";} ?>>friends of ED</option>
21    </select>
22  </form>
```

Delete these two sections

10. Delete the two sections indicated in the preceding screenshot by removing ?pub= from the PHP code generated by Dreamweaver. This is necessary because $_GET['pub'] contains just the value of the pub variable, not the whole query string. Be careful to remove the correct sections—you still want the full query string in the value attribute of each <option> tag.

11. $_GET['pub'] won't be set when the page first loads, so add the following code immediately above the opening <form> tag:

`<?php if (!isset($_GET['pub'])) {$_GET['pub'] = 'Apress';} ?>`

This sets the default value of pub to Apress, and prevents any error from being generated if the query string is missing. I've deliberately chosen the opposite default from the one in the XSLT Fragment to show how passing a parameter from outside takes precedence over the value of select in <xsl:param>.

12. Position your cursor just after the closing </form> tag, and switch back to Design view.

13. Embed the XSLT Fragment by selecting Insert ➤ Application Objects ➤ XSL Transformation. In the XSL Transformation dialog box, click the top Browse button and select books9.xsl as the XSLT file. Then click the plus button alongside XSLT parameters. Type pub in the Name field of the Add Parameter dialog box, and click the lightning bolt icon to the right of the Value field. This opens the Dynamic Data dialog box, where you should select pub from the URL tree.

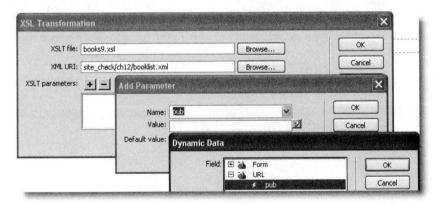

14. When you click OK to close the Dynamic Data dialog box, the Default value field is no longer grayed out in the Add Parameter dialog box. This is where you can insert a default value to be passed to the XSLT Fragment. However, it's not necessary because you created a default value in the <xsl:param> tag in the previous exercise.

459

15. When you click the OK button to close the Add Parameter dialog box, you will see the pub parameter listed, as shown below. An Edit button has been added in case you need to make any changes. You can add extra parameters by clicking the plus button, or remove existing ones with the minus button. Click OK to close the XSL Transformation dialog box.

16. Save books_param.php and press *F12/OPT+F12* to view it in a browser. It should look like Figure 12-11. Even though the default parameter in the XSLT Fragment was set to friends of ED, the parameter sent from the PHP page takes precedence.

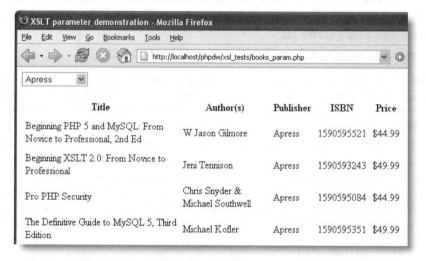

Figure 12-11. The contents of the XML document have been sorted, formatted, and displayed selectively through a combination of XSLT and PHP.

17. Select friends of ED from the jump menu, and the display will change, showing only foED books.

Going further

This has been only a brief introduction to working with XSLT. It's a massive and complex subject, but I think Dreamweaver has done a good job of making it more accessible to non-experts. Certainly, the ability to manipulate simple XML feeds without needing to touch the underlying code is likely to be welcomed by many independent web developers. It will be interesting to see how XSLT and XML capabilities are developed in future versions of Dreamweaver—and the development team was talking about the next one enthusiastically even as the final touches were being added to this one.

This excursion into the marriage of XSLT and PHP also brings us to the end of a long—and, I hope, enjoyable—journey through working with PHP and Dreamweaver 8. Although you have covered a lot of ground, there are many more aspects of PHP that I've not been able to touch on. For instance, PHP has now developed into a sophisticated programming language with extensive support for OOP (object-oriented programming). If you work with Flash, I suggest you take a look at my earlier book, *Foundation PHP 5 for Flash* (friends of ED, ISBN 1-59059-466-5). It concentrates entirely on hand-coding and will give you a solid understanding of the basics of both PHP and MySQL, as well as a first introduction to OOP in PHP. Other books that will help build upon your current knowledge are listed in Figure 12-11.

Even if you don't want to bury yourself in yet another book, I strongly recommend that you make a habit of using the PHP online documentation at www.php.net/manual/en. It's not suitable for reading from one end to the other, but it's packed with practical examples of how most functions work. Dip into it from time to time whenever someone suggests that a particular function might help solve a problem for you. Also, take a look at the MySQL online documentation at http://dev.mysql.com/doc/refman/5.0/en/index.html. It's vast, but well indexed and generally well written. One section that you should definitely bookmark is Problems and Common Errors at http://dev.mysql.com/doc/refman/5.0/en/problems.html. With the help of this book, you shouldn't need to visit that section often—if at all—but it may save you a lot of time if you do run into difficulties with MySQL.

Above all, have fun working with PHP, MySQL, and Dreamweaver.

Appendix A

USING LANGUAGES OTHER THAN ENGLISH IN MYSQL

MySQL is a truly international database. A standard installation has support for more than 20 different encoding systems, including UTF-8 (since version 4.1). This means that MySQL now supports just about every living language in the world—and some dead ones, too. If you want to store data in Hmong, Bugis, or Tamazight, you're out of luck: UTF-8 doesn't support them *yet*—but it will eventually.

How MySQL uses character sets and collation

It's important to realize that the default character set of a MySQL server has no bearing whatsoever on the range of languages in which data can be stored. The choice of character set affects just two things:

- The characters permitted in database, table, and column names
- The default sort order of query results

Collation also determines the sort order, but it offers a greater degree of control, and it is the setting that concerns you most in a multilingual or non-English environment. Until the introduction of collation in MySQL 4.1, the only way to change the sort order of results was to change the character set for the entire server. This was extremely inconvenient for storing data in more than one language because Spanish, English, and German, for instance, all follow different sorting rules.

MySQL's default collation is latin1_swedish_ci, which reflects the fact that MySQL AB is based in Sweden. Fortunately, the sort orders for Swedish and English are the same. So, unless you create databases in other languages, or need to use accented characters, you can forget about collation.

Table A-1 shows the available settings for Western European languages using the latin1 character set. Table A-2 shows the different ways some of the main ones sort the same items. As you can see, the default Swedish order sorts *ü* after *x*, so for English-based material that uses accents, latin1_general_ci is the preferred setting.

Table A-1. Collation settings in MySQL for the latin1 character set

Collation	Description
latin1_bin	Binary, follows the latin1 encoding order (all uppercase letters come before lowercase ones: *Z* comes before *a*)
latin1_danish_ci	Danish/Norwegian, case-insensitive
latin1_general_ci	Multilingual, case-insensitive
latin1_general_cs	Multilingual, case-sensitive
latin1_german1_ci	German DIN-1
latin1_german2_ci	German DIN-2
latin1_spanish_ci	Modern Spanish
latin1_swedish_ci	Swedish/Finnish

Table A-2. Comparison of sort order produced by different collations

latin1_swedish_ci (default)	latin1_bin	latin1_general_ci	latin1_german1_ci	latin1_german2_ci
muffin	MX Kollection	muffin	muffin	Müller
MX Kollection	MySQL	Müller	Müller	muffin
Müller	Müller	MX Kollection	MX Kollection	MX Kollection
MySQL	muffin	MySQL	MySQL	MySQL

Setting the right sort order

Collation (sort order) can be set at four different levels in MySQL:

- Server
- Database
- Table
- Column

The ability to set collation at these different levels means that it's perfectly acceptable to have a mixture of collations in the same database. So, for instance, if you work in both English and Spanish, you can set the default collation for a database to latin1_swedish_ci, but tables or columns that store data in Spanish can be set individually to latin1_spanish_ci. As a consequence, all database results will be sorted in the correct order for each language.

Normally, you have no control over changes at the server level unless you are the server administrator. Specifying the sort order for the other three categories—both at time of creation and subsequently—is very easy in phpMyAdmin.

Setting collation at the time of creation

1. Select the required setting from the appropriate Collation drop-down menu at the same time as defining other properties of the database, table, or column.

   If you leave the Collation setting blank, the database, table, or column will inherit the collation of its parent. So, a database on a latin1_swedish_ci server will automatically use latin1_swedish_ci as its collation, but if a table in the same database is set to latin1_spanish_ci, all columns within that table will use the Spanish sort order, unless specifically set to a different value.

Changing the collation of an existing database or table

1. Select the database or table in phpMyAdmin, and click the Operations tab at the top of the main frame.

2. When the next screen opens, select the required setting from the Collation drop-down menu, and click the Go button immediately to the right.

Changing the sort order of a column

1. Use the links in the phpMyAdmin navigation frame to select the table that contains the column or columns you want to change.

2. In the table-structure grid in the main frame, place a check mark in the check box to the left of the names of the columns that are to be given a different collation. Then click the pencil icon at the bottom of the grid, as shown here.

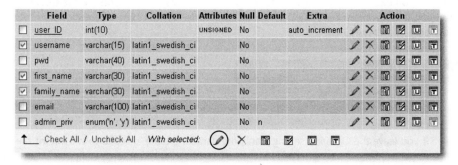

3. Change the value of the Collation field as required, and click Save.

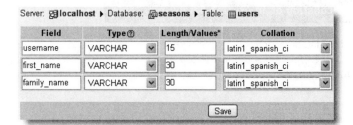

Appendix B

ESSENTIAL MYSQL MAINTENANCE

One of the joys of working with MySQL is that—in my experience, at least—it requires little or no maintenance. It runs unobtrusively in the background and does its job quietly and efficiently. However, that doesn't mean that you should forget about it entirely. There are some essential tasks that need to be done from time to time. The most important of these is backing up your data. Making a backup is also the way that you transfer your data to another server. This appendix covers the following subjects:

- Backing up your data
- Using a backup file to transfer data to another server
- Updating the privilege tables after upgrading to a later series
- What to do if you forget your root password
- Upgrading and uninstalling MySQL on Mac OS X

Backing up and transferring a database

Something that confuses a lot of people is that you can't just copy a MySQL database file from your hard drive and upload it to your website. Even if you find the right files (on Windows, they're located in C:\Program Files\MySQL\ MySQL Server x.x\data, where x.x represents the MySQL series number), you are likely to damage them unless the MySQL server is turned off. Anyway, most hosting companies won't permit you to upload the raw files, because it would also involve shutting down their server, causing a great deal of inconvenience for everyone.

Nevertheless, moving a database from one server to another is very easy. All it involves is creating a backup "dump" of the data, and loading it into the other database with phpMyAdmin. The dump is a text file that contains all the necessary SQL commands to populate an individual table, or even an entire database, elsewhere. phpMyAdmin can create backups of your entire MySQL server, individual databases, selected tables, or individual tables.

Creating a backup of a single table

1. Launch phpMyAdmin and select the database that contains the table you want to back up. Then click the link for the table in the navigation frame.

2. When the table details have loaded into the main frame, select Export from the tabs along the top of the screen.

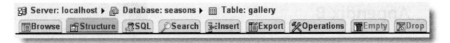

3. This opens the rather fearsome looking screen shown in Figure B-1. In spite of all the options, you need concern yourself with only a few.

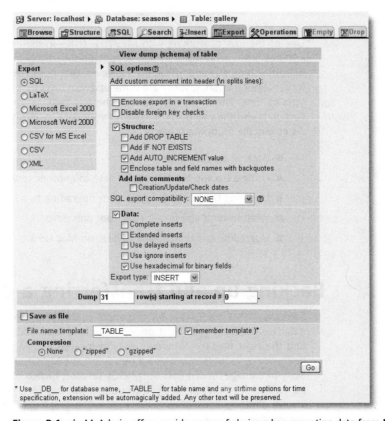

Figure B-1. phpMyAdmin offers a wide range of choice when exporting data from MySQL.

4. The Export section on the left of the screen lists the various export formats available. Unless you're exporting the data to a different program, leave the radio buttons on the default SQL.

5. The only section that needs your attention on the right side of the screen is the middle one labeled Structure. Figure B-1 shows the default settings.

- If a table of the same name doesn't exist in the database that you want to copy it to, leave the check boxes at their default settings.

- If the target database already has a table of the same name, select Add DROP TABLE. This will drop the existing table in the target database, and replace it with the data in the backup file.

- If you have already created the correct table structure on the target database, select Add IF NOT EXISTS. You should use this option only if the target table has exactly the same structure *and* has no existing data.

6. The other important setting in the Structure section is the drop-down menu labeled SQL export compatibility. The setting depends on the version of MySQL running on the other server (only the first two numbers, such as 3.23, 4.0, 4.1 or 5.0, are important):

- If the other server is running the same version of MySQL, choose NONE.

- If the other server is running MySQL 3.23, choose MYSQL323.

- If the other server is running MySQL 4.0, choose MYSQL40.

- If the transfer is between MySQL 5.0 and MySQL 4.1 (in either direction), choose NONE.

7. Put a check mark in the box alongside Save as file at the bottom of the screen. The default setting in File name template is __TABLE__. This will automatically give the backup file the same name as the table being exported. So, in the case of a table called gallery, it will become gallery.sql. If you add anything after the final double underscore, phpMyAdmin will add this to the name. For instance, you might want to indicate the date of the backup, so you could add 20060228 for a backup made on February 28, 2006. The file would then be named gallery20060228.sql.

8. Click Go to create the backup file. Options for where the file is saved will depend on your browser.

The export processes for multiple tables, a single database, and multiple databases are very similar. However, you should beware of creating very large backup files. Although there is no limit on the size of file that you can export, phpMyAdmin imposes a 2MB limit on loading data from a file.

If you need to transfer a very large database or a collection of databases, you should consult your server's system administrator. Someone with root access (and the requisite knowledge) can move large databases very quickly. If you're interested in learning how to do it yourself, read up on mysqldump at http://dev.mysql.com/doc/refman/5.0/en/mysqldump.html.

Backing up a single database or multiple tables from the same database

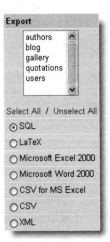

1. In phpMyAdmin, select the database that you want to export from the drop-down menu in the navigation frame.

2. When the database details have loaded into the main frame, click the Export tab at the top of the screen.

3. The screen that loads is identical to the one shown in Figure B-1, except that the Export section now contains a multiple choice list with the names of all the tables in the selected database, as shown alongside. To export the entire database, click Select All. Otherwise use your mouse pointer in combination with *SHIFT* or *CTRL*/⌘ to highlight the tables you require. Leave the radio button on the default SQL.

4. Choose the required options from the Structure section on the right side of the screen. (The meaning of the options is described in steps 5 and 6 of the previous set of instructions.)

5. Put a check mark in the box alongside Save as file at the bottom of the screen. The default setting in File name template is __DB__. This will automatically give the backup file the same name as the database being exported. Click Go to create the backup file.

Backing up multiple databases

These instructions are intended principally to help you transfer your local MySQL data to another local computer or to a new location on the same computer. On Mac OS X, it's essential to back up your data and reload it every time you upgrade MySQL. Otherwise, your data will be locked in a redundant folder. Windows users also need to transfer their data when upgrading from one series to another, such as from MySQL 4.1 to MySQL 5.0.

Although you can use these instructions for transferring multiple databases to a remote server, remember the 2MB limit on reloading through phpMyAdmin. Also, deselect the mysql database unless you're transferring the data to your own server and understand the consequences of replacing all user accounts on the target server.

1. Launch phpMyAdmin and click the Export link at the bottom of the left-hand column of the phpMyAdmin Welcome page.

2. The screen that opens is similar to the one shown in Figure B-1, but has one extra option, as highlighted in Figure B-2. Use the following settings:

   - Select All: Choose this to select all databases. If you are making a backup of MySQL 5.0 or higher, you must use your mouse pointer in combination with *CTRL*/⌘ to deselect information_schema. The information_schema database is new to MySQL 5.0. It's a virtual database that contains information about all the other databases on the server, which MySQL builds automatically. It's a read-only file, so any attempt to overwrite it on the target server will fail.

   - Add DROP DATABASE: This will force any database of the same name in the destination location to be dropped and replaced by your backup. If you don't do this, the default mysql and test databases in MySQL will prevent you from loading data from the backup file. By copying the mysql database, you can transfer all user accounts and passwords to another server. However, you should do this *before* any new accounts have been created on the server that you are moving to. The DROP DATABASE command completely replaces any existing database with the version from the backup file.

- Set SQL export compatibility: If you are upgrading, the default, NONE, is the correct setting. Otherwise, use the criteria laid out in step 6 of the instructions for backing up a single table.

- Save as file: phpMyAdmin automatically names the backup file after your server. Normally, this will produce a file called localhost.sql.

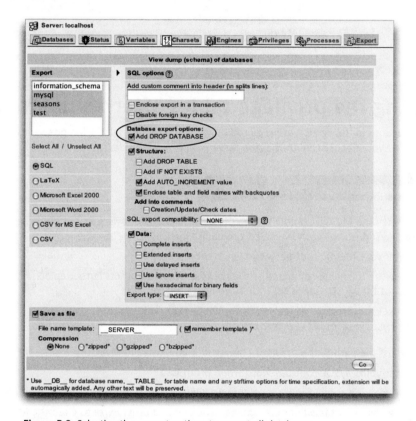

Figure B-2. Selecting the correct options to export all databases

Loading data from a backup file

1. Upload the SQL file to your remote server. (This is not necessary if you are upgrading a local computer or transferring to a new local computer.)

2. If you are transferring a single database, and a database of the same name doesn't already exist on the target server, create the database, but don't create any tables.

473

3. Launch the version of phpMyAdmin on your target server, and select the database that you plan to transfer the data to. If you are transferring multiple databases, choose any database on the target server. Click the SQL tab in the main frame. In phpMyAdmin 2.7.0 or later, click the Import tab instead.

4. Use the Browse button to locate the SQL file, and click Go. That's it!

Updating the privilege tables after an upgrade

The instructions in this section are required only if you have upgraded from one series to another and have copied your mysql table to the new server.

Updating the privilege tables on Windows

1. Launch the MySQL Command Line Client from the Windows Start button: Programs ➤ MySQL ➤ MySQL Server *x.x* ➤ MySQL Command Line Client.

2. Enter your MySQL root password when prompted.

3. Type the following command at the mysql prompt, and press *ENTER* (replace *x.x* with the number of the MySQL series that you have upgraded to):

   ```
   SOURCE C:/Program Files/MySQL/MySQL Server x.x/scripts/
   ➥ mysql_fix_privilege_tables.sql
   ```

   Adjust the path in the previous command if you installed MySQL in a different location.

4. Enter your MySQL root password when prompted.

5. You may see some duplicate column warnings as the script runs. These can be safely ignored.

6. When the script has finished running, type exit and press *ENTER* to close the MySQL Command Line Client.

7. Stop and restart MySQL for the changes to take effect. (See the "Starting and stopping MySQL manually on Windows" section in Chapter 7.)

Updating the privilege tables on Mac OS X

These instructions assume that you have added MySQL to your environment variables, as described in the "Adding MySQL to your PATH" section of Chapter 7.

1. Launch Terminal from the Utilities subfolder of Applications.

2. At the Terminal prompt, type the following command followed by *RETURN* (substitute your MySQL root password for *root_password*):

   mysql_fix_privilege_tables --password=*root_password*

3. You may see some duplicate column warnings as the script runs. These can be safely ignored.

4. When the script has stopped running, stop and restart MySQL using the MySQL pane in System Preferences.

What to do if you forget your root password

Fortunately, it's not as catastrophic as it sounds. You can find the instructions for resetting the root password at http://dev.mysql.com/doc/refman/5.0/en/Resetting_permissions.html. It's relatively straightforward on Windows.

Mac OS X users should open a Terminal window and follow the instructions for Linux, but you will need to invoke superuser privileges through sudo. Using sudo is simple. You simply precede each command with sudo followed by a space. To use sudo, you must be logged in as a Mac administrator, and you will be prompted for your Mac password the first time you use sudo, or if more than five minutes have elapsed since you last used it. Better still, don't forget your password!

Upgrading and uninstalling MySQL on Mac OS X

Installing MySQL on Mac OS X is incredibly easy, thanks to the PKG files created by MySQL AB, but you can get a very nasty shock (as I did) if you don't plan your upgrades correctly.

According to MySQL, the Mac OS X Installer "does not yet offer the functionality required to properly upgrade previously installed packages." What this means is that when you "upgrade" MySQL on Mac OS X, you are, in effect, installing a completely new version of MySQL that sits alongside the old version, and, like bad neighbors, they never talk to each other. Apart from the old version taking up unnecessary disk space, that might not be so bad. The problem is that *all your data is locked inside the old version*. Consequently, you should always back up your databases before installing a newer version of MySQL.

Backing up and upgrading on Mac OS X

1. Make a backup of all your databases with phpMyAdmin as described earlier. Make sure that you include the `mysql` database in your backup.

2. Stop MySQL in System Preferences.

3. Install the new version of MySQL. Follow the instructions onscreen.

4. When the installation has completed, restart MySQL.

5. Your new installation of MySQL won't have a root password, so you won't be able to run phpMyAdmin unless you alter `config.inc.php` or create a new root password. A much simpler solution is to load the backup data directly from the command line in a Terminal window.

   Copy the backup file to the top level of your home folder.

6. Launch Terminal from the `Utilities` subfolder of `Applications`, and restore your data by issuing the following command followed by *RETURN*:

   ```
   mysql -u root < backup_file
   ```

   Your upgraded version of MySQL should now be working with all previous data in place. If you have upgraded from one MySQL series to another, follow the instructions in the section titled "Updating the privilege tables after an upgrade."

Removing the older version of MySQL

After installing a new version of MySQL, you may want to remove the old one to save disk space. This section is completely optional, and should not be attempted unless you are comfortable working at the Terminal command line. An old installation of MySQL interferes in no way with the new one.

1. Once you have checked that everything is working correctly with your new installation, you can remove the old files to save disk space. Type the following commands in a Terminal window to change directory and list the files:

   ```
   cd /usr/local
   ls -l
   ```

2. You should see a list of files as in the following screenshot. There are three references to `mysql`. The first contains ->, which indicates that it's a symbolic link. The actual name of the folder is `mysql-standard-5.0.13-rc-osx10.4-powerpc` in this example, which is a bit much to expect you to type out every time you want to access `mysql`. So, the symbolic link acts as an alias.

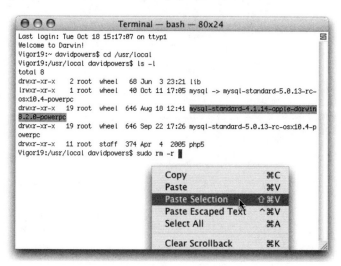

Immediately following are two more references to mysql. These contain the actual files. As you can see from the screenshot, the last one has the same number as the symbolic link. It was also created on September 22, so it is more recent than the middle one (which was created on August 18).

To remove the older files, type the following command followed by a space (but don't press *RETURN* yet):

```
sudo rm -r
```

3. Use your cursor to highlight the folder name of the older version, as shown in the following screenshot. Make sure you have the full name, particularly as it's likely to run over two lines. *CTRL*-click and select Paste Selection from the pop-up menu.

You should now have a line that looks like this (the actual folder name is likely to be slightly different, depending on when you installed your original version):

```
sudo rm -r mysql-standard-4.1.14-apple-darwin8.2.0-powerpc
```

4. Make sure the command is correct. If it isn't, use *Backspace* to remove anything that shouldn't be there. Equally, if you change your mind, use *Backspace* to remove the entire command.

5. Once you're sure the command is correct, press *Return*, and enter your Mac password when prompted. That's it—the old files are gone. And when I say "gone," I really mean it. You cannot restore them from the Trash if you make a mistake.

6. One final bit of housekeeping: You should remove the old version from the `Package Receipts` directory. Change directory and list the contents by typing the following commands:

```
cd /Library/Receipts
ls
```

7. The name of the package receipt you need to delete will be the same as in step 3, but with `.pkg` on the end. Remove it by typing this (substitute the correct name for the version on your computer):

```
sudo rm -r mysql-standard-4.1.14-apple-darwin8.2.0-powerpc.pkg
```

Press *Return*. If prompted, enter your Mac password.

Hopefully, by the time it comes for you to upgrade, the Mac OS X Installer will have overcome these problems. It's not a lot of work, but it's fiddly and very annoying if you forget to back up your databases first!

INDEX

Symbols

& predefined entity, 434
' predefined entity, 449
> predefined entity, 449, 453
< predefined entity, 434, 449
" predefined entity, 449
* (asterisk), as wildcard, 299
@ (at) character, with XML attributes, 441
@import statement
  attaching stylesheets, 111, 116
  HTML comments with, 116
` ` (backticks), in SQL queries, 292
\ (backslash) character
  in escape sequences, 145–146
  with PHP quotes, 62
, (commas)
  in arrays, 201
  in MySQL databases, 256
$ (dollar sign), in PHP code, 25, 135
$row array element, 266
$this variable, cautions, 136
$_POST superglobal array, 170–171
$_SERVER superglobal array
  creating intelligent links using, 403–405
  uses for, 203
  viewing options for, 25
$_SESSION superglobal array, 333, 335
== (double equal signs), in PHP syntax, 137
-- (double minus sign), as decrement operator, 149
|| (double pipes), as logical OR operator, 156
++ (double plus sign), as increment operator, 149
" " (double quotes)
  in PHP code, 124
  with text, 143–144
  with literals, 134
= (equal sign), as assignment operator, 136–137
=> (equal sign followed by angle bracket) operator
  creating arrays using, 201
! (exclamation point), as negation operator, 156
!= (exclamation point and equal sign), as inequality
  operator, 154

!== (exclamation point plus double equal signs), as
  identical operator, 154
/ (forward slash)
  in Apache configuration file, 66
  as division operator, 149
  in site-root–relative links, 49
/* */ (forward slash plus asterisk) pair, for PHP
  comments, 139
> (greater than) operator, in comparisons, 155
>= (greater than or equal to) operator, in
  comparisons, 155
< (less than) operator, in comparisons, 155
<= (less than or equal to) operator, in comparisons,
  155
<> (less than, greater than) symbols, as inequality
  operator, 154
- (minus) button, removing behaviors using, 40
() (parentheses), with echo and print commands,
  143
% (percent sign), modulo operator, 149
  creating striped table row displays, 391–392
. (period) character
  for linking table and column names (dot
    notation), 294
  joining strings (concatenation operator), 146
  represents current node (XPath), 450
+ (plus) button, 9
  adding behaviors using, 40
(pound or hash sign)
  for adding comments in PHP, 139
  in Apache configuration file, 67
<?php tag
  function, 134
  interpretation of, 132
; (semicolon), in PHP code, 61, 138
' '(single quotes)
  in PHP code, 124
  with text, 143–144
[ ] (square brackets), in code hints, 132
=== (triple equal signs), as identical operator, 154
_ (underscore) character, in variable names,
  135–136

A